Another Season Cookbook

*Recipes for Every Season
from the Chef/Owner of
Boston's Another Season Restaurant*

by Odette J. Bery

illustrations by Ippy Patterson

The
Globe
Pequot
Press   CHESTER, CONNECTICUT 06412

To my parents, Doris and Theodore Bery

Shown on front of jacket: Trout Piment (page 282) with asparagus added for garnish; salad with Hazelnut Dressing (page 168).
Shown on back of jacket: Italian Chocolate-Orange Torte (page 455).

Jacket photograph by Tom Hopkins
Jacket design by Barbara Marks
Book design by K. A. Lynch

Library of Congress Cataloging-in-Publication Data

Bery, Odette J.
    Another Season cookbook.

    Bibliography: p.
    Includes index.
    1. Cookery.   2. Entertaining.   3. Another Season
(Restaurant) I. Title.
TX652.B4756   1986   641.5'09744'61   86–25715
ISBN 0-87106-802-8

Manufactured in the United States of America
First Edition/First Printing

Contents

Acknowledgments

This book, along with many other projects, would never have happened without the wisdom and confidence of a very special friend, Ann Leibowitz.

I am so fortunate to have had Cary Hull as my editor for this book. Her fine work, never-ending patience, and good guidance made this all come together. Cary, with my thanks.

Steven Marsh, it is impossible for me to put into words how much I have appreciated all your diligent research, great instruction, hard work, and fine humor through this project. I am so fortunate and forever grateful that you worked with me on this book.

Running a restaurant and writing a book could not have been accomplished without the ongoing support and hard work from Philip Allen, Phyllis Briskin, and Gary Pfahl. Thank you all so much.

Hilary Nando took on the difficult task of putting my thoughts, my theory, and my ideas on paper. With humor and never-ending tolerance, she chased me down and kept me to my deadlines. To her, I am truly grateful.

For your sensitivity to the needs of cookery at home, and for your creative input while testing and tasting each recipe, Mimi Santini-Ritt, I offer you my sincerest thanks. In the final stages of this project, you have been invaluable for your careful work.

And to the rest of the testers: Debbie Costa, Harriet Davis, Sally Giuliani, Judith Samson, and Deborah Weiogard: Not an easy task, but you all came through.

Ippy Patterson, thank you for the beautiful illustrations in this book, and Kevin Lynch, thank you for the book's wonderful design. Susan McWilliams, thank you for your photographic work. Kate Bandos, my sincere appreciation for all your promotional work. Eric Newman, thank you for your fine guidance and good humor.

Jack Milan, thank you for your kind support, good guidance, and motivation. Your word processor made this project so much easier.

Typing the manuscript was not easy. Leah Jewitt, Steven Parkey, and Anne Samson, thank you for all your hard work.

Brian Pfeiffer and Rhoda Wienman, thank you for your never-ending support and encouragement through my many projects.

To my good friend Albert Gordon—thank you.

There are those who have been so supportive of my endeavors: Maggie

De Wolfe, Bob and Sally Gelardin, John Harlor, Lawrence Hartmann, Sy Kassman, Miranda Leonard, and Elinor and Charles Mikulka.

I will forever be indebted to my teachers, Muriel Downs, the late Rosemary Hume, Maurice Moore-Betty, and Mapie, the Comtess de Toulouse-Lautrec. You taught me so much and were so patient and encouraging.

Susan Alder, Barbara Beckham, Debby Davidson, Alexis Driscoll, Jennifer Esten, Harriet Goodman, Dr. Alexander Harrison, Bess Hopkins, Constance Hsia, Rebecca Karas, Lolly Mitchell, Barbara Morse, Jill Nathanson, Doris Sasser, Ruth Shea, Charlotte Thomson, Alvene Williams, Dura Winder, Josefina Yanguas: With your influence and good support, many projects, including this one, came to fruition.

No restaurant succeeds without creative business advisors. My thanks to: Stanley Charmoy, Richard Fisher, Robert Friedman, Michael Keating, Jack Polatin, Sandra Shapiro, and John Tyler.

Thank you, David Barry Floyd, for all your hard work and support over the years.

To produce fine dishes, one needs fine food and wines. Thank you: Susan Bates of Victorian Bouquet, Nick Bourke at Branded Wines, Mr. and Mrs. Leonard of Brigham Provisions, Charlie Crone and Chris O'Brien at J.A. Sanborn, John Dewar, Fred Ek at Classic Wines, Bill Friedberg of Boston Wine Company, Josh Hamilton at Diamond Hill Farms, Fred Hart of Hart Importing, Max J. Horvitz at Imported Foods, Julie Hyde, Nick and Ted Katsiroubas, Brian Keeping at Silenus Wines, Margaret Mansour at Syrian Grocery, Al Tammaro, Luigi Tonetti, and West Lynn Creamery.

To these fine chefs who inspired me throughout the years: Judy Bolton, Patricia Buckley, Edner Caymite, Shannon Doyle, Don Fields, Yaja Golabeck, Michael Ivas, Bonny Lane, Nancy Madden, Michele Mattingly, Peter Pastan, Clark Rothauser, Joyce Scardina, Jeffrey Starr, Cameron Watson, Betsy West, Scott Wiegman, and Nelda Zapprauskis. Your style and creations always give me something to look forward to.

With special thanks to: Gail Banks, Raj and Marjorie Bery, Andrea and David Bono, Lewis and Susan Cabot, Norma Jean and Stanford Calderwood, Richard Dannhauser, Nathanial Dexter, Lee Eisemann, Jordon Ferraro, Alfred Fiandaca, Nicki and Richard Gamble, Alex Gill, Morris and Ellen Gordon, Felice and Hugh Gordon, James Groves, Susan Hillis, Timothy Hollingworth, Gary Longtime, Anastasia Kucharski, John McLaren, Betty Anne and Steven Mead, Betsy and Walter McMeel, Jim Mitchell, Rajan Nanda, Vin O'Neil, Edward Pinkus, Dr. Mitchell Rabkin, Peter Redmayne, Ruth and Alan Ross, Mary Runkel, Roger Sametz, Terry Schaeffer, Susy and Garret Schenck, Brent Sikkema, Evelyn Smith, Ann and John Sullivan, Richard Teller, and Kevin and Katherine White.

And finally to a very important group of people, thank you for your care, hard work, and support throughout this project: Jane Barish, Anne Bentley, Jean Bonnet, Gifford Booth, Mary Boyne, Leah Carlsen, Liatte Charles, Gesner Cotin, Christina Cunningham, Rick Eger, Lori Frech, Elizabeth Gallagher, Ray Gillespie, Martha-Jean Charles, Brian Kydd, Gary Lammery, Ellen Leibowitz, Ginny Mazur, Mark Minder, David Moses, Kathy St. Hiliare, Tyrone Seldon, Gary Shelton, Mimi Shields, David Taylor, Lourdes Vincent, Kim Walter, Michael Welch, and Lisa Wildy.

Introduction

I love to cook and have for as long as I can remember. After nearly thirty years of creating a personal cuisine and collecting recipes from around the world, I am quite excited about being able to share them with you.

I was seven years old, living in Sussex, England, when I planted my first radish, and I still remember how thrilled I was to later be able to create sandwiches from those beautiful vegetables. Little did I know that twenty-five years later that radish would become the logo for my restaurant, and the basis for the philosophy behind my cooking. During those early years, I was encouraged by my mother to be her helpful companion in the kitchen, and never too young to be my father's companion at various restaurants.

Later, at boarding school, I was fortunate to have Miss Hall as my Home Economics teacher. She was slightly reserved and a staunch believer that knowledge of food theory should precede the practical applications. Her recipes were the best of English fare and the perfect preparation for my continued education.

At seventeen, I enrolled as a student at the Cordon Bleu in London. It was there, under the fine tutelage of Rosemary Hume, Muriel Downes, and Anne Willan, that I acquired the technical training that has stood me in good stead throughout my career. I learned the importance of preparing food in advance and with ease. Those lessons I hope to pass on to you in this book.

Four months later I moved to Paris, where I completed my studies under Mapie, the Comtess Toulouse-Lautrec, at Maxim's Academy. The experience was incredible, to say the least. Already secure in my technical expertise, I was exposed to the creation of innovative dishes, making combinations of ingredients and using food products that were totally new to me. Mapie taught with ease, elegance, and style.

Then at nineteen, I went to South Africa to cook for Hilary and Barbara Young at the British Embassy. At last, I was putting my culinary education into action. It was there that a whole new aspect of cooking opened up for me. I was asked to conduct a cooking demonstration for 100 people, as a major fund-raiser for African children. I was terrified by this project, but I found myself enjoying the role of teacher, happy to be able to dispel myths and give hints about fine food preparation. We raised a lot of money that day, and I was delighted to discover this new facet of my capabilities, which I was to develop over the next two years through private cooking lessons.

My years in Africa, then traveling back to Europe, up the east coast of the African continent, introduced me to an extraordinary array of cuisines. To this day, I have never eaten an Italian meal as exquisite as the one I had in Mombasa nor forgotten the delicious spicy shrimp dish I tasted in Egypt. The outstanding meals I ate on this trip were rivaled only by the people I met and the magnificent landscapes and architecture I saw.

After another year in England, it was time for me to travel again. I came to the United States in 1966 and was initiated immediately into the joys of high technology. When I walked into the private kitchen where I was to work, I was stunned to find two ovens, two refrigerators, two dishwashers, and a wonderful array of appliances. This was a family that loved to entertain, and, although their kitchen was not quite typical, it did stress the point that Americans have an appreciation of all those wonderful gadgets that are available to ease food preparation. All this was a little overwhelming. I floundered for a while. I catered, taught, and went to work in the antiques business.

Fortunately, and quite unexpectedly, I was hired by Polaroid Corporation to cook executive lunches. This was an excellent job, as it gave me not only the opportunity to cook fine foods in a compact, well-designed kitchen, but also an exposure to the corporate world. At that time, I was also becoming more involved in teaching, giving lessons part-time, presenting cooking demonstrations, and discovering my talent for importing practical techniques and the implementation of food theories. I particularly enjoyed my years at Garland Junior College, teaching under the first-rate supervision of Mercie Fogg and Doris Sasser; then, later, gaining enormously from my teaching of special-needs children at the Charles River Academy.

All this experience led, quite naturally, to opening my own restaurant, which I did, in partnership with Joyce Scardina, in 1970. Our start-up budget was laughably low, the facilities were far from ideal, and our experiments were sometimes overambitious, but the Turtle Café became known in Cambridge, Massachusetts, for its exciting fare and reasonable prices. Seven years later, I felt ready for a larger, more upscale restaurant, and I opened Another Season on Beacon Hill in Boston.

So there I was, cooking and managing a beautiful restaurant, in full creative control of my own kitchen, and deriving a tremendous amount of satisfaction from serving food to a discerning clientele.

But seven years later, I felt a need for a new challenge. I had amassed such a fine collection of creative recipes and been asked for recipes by so very many people that I felt it was time to share my knowledge with a wider public. You will notice that many of the recipes in this cookbook call for unusual combinations of ingredients, and those of you who have eaten my food in Another Season will recognize these dishes as my hallmark. Of course, in the restaurant, I cook for large numbers, so I have been careful to have all my recipes for this book tested in home kitchens. After testing and retesting, some of the recipes were adjusted and others rejected.

But, do not think for a moment that I have not had my share of disasters over the years. I have burnt many nuts; my beurre blancs and mayonnaises have, at times, not emulsified; and some of my cakes have refused to rise. At times, I have even overcooked vegetables. Still, for the most part these disasters have been part of my learning process. I am a believer that cooking is made much easier by a good understanding of food theory and practical techniques, and I want to pass along to you the ways in which you can make food preparation an easier process.

I should also like to pay my respects to two Eastern influences on my cooking: India and Boston. The former touched my life via my paternal grandfather, whose gift to me of an Indian heritage is echoed in my use of the spices of that subcontinent. I became familiar with the delectable tastes of Indian food when I met my cousin Raj Bery and his wife, Marjorie, in the United States and learned from Raj how to use and balance spices to superb effect. As for Boston, what a wonderful city! One has always been able to dine at restaurants of first-rate repute. In the past ten years, the number of establishments with fine and exciting fare has increased enormously. At the same time, it is encouraging for local restauranteurs to see a heightened appreciation from their guests for food imaginatively prepared and served.

I hope that Another Season Cookbook will have a culinary influence on you and that you will enjoy preparing my recipes as much as I do. The cooking teacher aspect of me says that you will find these recipes easier to prepare and guaranteed to succeed if you take the time to read the chapters and apply the techniques that I suggest. It is my philosophy that care in cooking, combined with the use of quality ingredients, will result in a well-prepared dish, a happy cook, and delighted diners. Just remember the key word: Enjoy!

Kitchen Strategies

Life magazine said it first: In its September 19, 1946, issue it highlighted the kitchen as an area of wasted space and effort with a one-word message to the cooks at home—organize! Forty years later, the message is still the same. Now, as then, the key to ease of food preparation lies in good working surfaces, well-chosen kitchen equipment, and easy access to tools and appliances.

I cannot stress enough the importance of organization. Before you crack your first egg, slice your first onion, or choose your first sprig of fresh basil, take a long, hard look at your kitchen. Is your work area compact enough to minimize time-wasting moving around? How easy is it to work at your kitchen counters? You will want to keep as much counter space as possible clear for preparation, but do not make the mistake of hiding your most-used gadgets and tools out of sight. Have your food processor out for constant use, hang cooking spoons and spatulas close at hand, and put out a jar for plastic spatulas, wooden spoons, and whisks.

The organized cook will find a few other kitchen aids essential:

1. If you are designing a kitchen from scratch, a heatproof surface next to the stove, on which to place hot pots, will be very beneficial. However, if this is not possible, place heat-resistant tiles on the counter next to the stove.
2. Have a good number of measuring cups so that you can pre-measure all your ingredients.
3. Have handy an accurate set of scales, preferably combining ounces with grams as metric measurements are used in European cookbooks.
4. Major appliances that are large enough to fill your cooking needs. Before purchasing an oven or refrigerator, consider your equipment needs, thinking in terms of major occasions such as holidays and entertaining.

Ease of Preparation

Once the work space has been organized to your satisfaction, cooking is a matter of strategy and planning. I am a strong believer in marshalling my forces well in advance of preparing a recipe. Some of these steps may seem strange to you, but, once mastered, they will save you an enormous amount of time and stress. Planning ahead for food preparation eliminates those frantic searches for equipment in the midst of preparation that are, at best, irritating, and, at worst, possibly ruinous to a recipe.

1. Place all the utensils you will be using on the counter.
2. Pre-measure all ingredients needed for the recipe, and place them on the counter.
3. Whenever a recipe calls for advance preparation, take the opportunity to make these items in quantity ahead of time and freeze them in suitably sized batches. This applies particularly to stocks, compound butters, and soup bases.
4. Look at the recipes in this book that have been coded to indicate some advance preparation.

Meal Planning and Shopping

You can save yourself valuable time and energy by investing a little effort in sketching out menus for a few days at a time, rather than on a daily basis. When you are planning advance menus, remember to consider the following elements:

1. The availability of ingredients;
2. Your budget;
3. The time you will be able to spend on each meal;
4. How much advance preparation you can do;
5. The creation of a balanced menu.

Until quite recently, the European housewife made such meal plans routinely, keeping records of her menus in a log book that was revised and referred to constantly. Buy yourself a three-ring binder so that you can keep a record of menus, the cost of ingredients for menus, notes on the ease of preparation, and family reactions to each meal. Of course, you could resort to your home computer for meal planning, but a floppy disk does not have the sentimental appeal of a well-worn menu book.

It is just as important to be an organized shopper as it is to be efficient in your kitchen. When you plan several days' menus in advance, you can exert greater control over your expenditures by building in provisions for use of leftovers and by balancing high-cost items with more economical buys. When you refer to earlier entries in your log book, you will get a clear picture of cost effectiveness and ease of preparation.

When you're making your shopping lists, bear in mind the type of time constraints that you might have. Remember that you can save yourself a lot of valuable time by cooking in large batches and freezing bases for dishes you may want to cook at later dates. Your freezer will be invaluable, too, for preserving foods that have a short season, as you will want to take advantage of foods when they are in their prime. It is always a good idea to keep seasonality in mind when you are shopping, and you can do particularly well by building a relationship with a store that can give you guidance as to what is the best current buy. If you hold off after a new commodity first enters the market, you will still be getting it at its peak, but you will often get it at a better price. This applies to such foods as asparagus, shad roe, and soft-shell crabs. If you are planning ahead for several days' menus, plan to use your more perishable items, such as fish, early in your menu schedule.

Balancing a Menu

In planning a menu, it is extremely important to provide a balance, weighing the elements of taste, aesthetic appeal, and food value. The simplest way to ensure a well-balanced meal is to vary color, texture, and ingredients when choosing recipes. This is best illustrated in an examination of contrasting menus:

Menu 1: Balanced
Autumn Chicken Casserole
Steamed Broccoli
Cucumber and Watercress Salad
  with Tomato-Yogurt Dressing
Lime Caramel

Menu 2: Unbalanced
Potage Longvielle
Chicken Breasts Clara
Cabbage with Prosciutto
White Chocolate Almond Torte with
  whipped cream

The balance in Menu 1 is achieved by the use of both raw and cooked vegetables in a variety of colors and textures. Menu 2 relies heavily on cooked vegetables with no change of pace in terms of texture. There is a significant difference, too, in the quantity of cream used in each menu. Menu 2 is far too rich and high in fats. Beware, too, of repetition in your meal pattern. The soup in Menu 2 uses a chicken base; then chicken is repeated in the entree. I find the appearance of nuts in more than one dish per meal to be excessive. We can adjust the second menu by substituting Sole Piedmontese for the Chicken Breasts Clara, thereby eliminating the nuts from one course and providing a fish contrast to the chicken base of the soup. Menu 2 is now balanced, but the dessert is still on the rich side. If desserts are a weakness of yours, you can decrease the richness of Menu

2 by serving a small portion of the torte with plenty of fresh fruit. Consider also the colors of the foods in the two menus. The color of the first menu and of the second menu with its substitutions can be a guideline for helping you learn to balance a menu.

The need to serve a balanced menu is particularly pertinent to children. Parents are often frustrated by a child's reluctance to try a variety of foods. I have found that children are responsive to the food experience when they become involved in actual preparation. From the age of five, they can be involved in such simple tasks as hulling strawberries, shelling fresh peas, and even baking bread. If children are offered a wide variety of foods at an early age, you may well avoid the problem of finicky eating habits.

Finally, take time to read through a new recipe well in advance of cooking, so that you can be sure you have all the ingredients on hand and understand how the recipe is prepared.

Entertaining Suggestions

Probably the most rewarding aspect of cooking is the sharing of your creations with friends. This section will help you to do just that, however simple or elaborate your presentation may be.

My first suggestion should prove to be fun. Buy an attractive book to use as a log whenever you entertain guests. Yes, use it as an entertaining diary. It will be a wonderful item to pass on to your children, as well as a valuable resource book for you.

In this diary you should document the date, the guests attending, the menus, those items that were easy or difficult to prepare, the cost, the allergies (if any) of guests attending, their acceptance of the menu, and the wine served. After ten events you will, on reviewing this diary, gain a great deal of knowledge of what will work best for you, and what you should not try again. And please, do not shy away from repeating dishes. Make a note of recipes you enjoy preparing: exciting hors d'oeuvres, soups, appetizers, main courses, salads, or desserts that your friends loved and will enjoy again on a future visit.

Success in entertaining is merely a matter of extending the laws or the strategy of the kitchen into the dining room. Once again, the secret lies in planning—knowing what you want to do and how to do it.

Let's say that you have decided to have a dinner party. Your decision as to whether to serve a sit-down or buffet meal will depend on (1) the number of guests you are inviting; (2) your furniture (if your dining room table seats eight and you are entertaining twelve, either you rent or borrow additional tables and chairs or you consider a buffet with seating in other areas of the house); (3) how casual or elegant a tone you want to set. You will have to make your final choice in conjunction with the menu you plan, because certain foods, such as soup, may be inappropriate for some settings. Think about how difficult it can be to cut a piece of roast beef when you're not sitting at a table.

After having selected the style of party, keep in mind the following guidelines:

1. *Who will be attending?* This will help you decide what to serve. Different people have different tastes. Some prefer seafood, others beef, and so on. Do any of the guests have allergies? If one of your friends is allergic to shellfish (a commonly overlooked allergy), you would not want to serve oysters on the half-shell. Are there any other restrictions? In today's

increasingly health-conscious society, many more people are becoming vegetarians and do not eat seafood or meat. Certain religions place restrictions on what their followers can and cannot eat. All of this should be considered when planning a menu, and if you have kept an up-to-date Entertaining Diary, it will be very helpful here.

2. *Do you have a budget?* If you are operating on a restricted budget, take that into account in your choice of menu. Finding out *after* the event that you have spent more than you can afford can spoil your enjoyment of entertaining.

3. *What foods are available and what is in season?* This I cannot stress enough. The success of your meal can weigh heavily on fresh, seasonal items. Nothing is better than salmon fresh off the boat or fennel straight from the garden.

4. *What are your time constraints?* There is no question that today's lifestyles are filled to the brim with schedules. If you get home from the office at six o'clock and have planned dinner at eight, you are going to run into problems, unless you have prepared ahead. You should design a menu that is not only practical but also fits into your schedule. Plan several dishes that can be prepared one or two days ahead of time to spread your workload, and for same-day cooking, consider some items that have a minimum of preparation. (The notations after my recipes will help you in your planning.) With thoughtful planning, your dinner can be a pleasure, and you will have more time with your guests; if not, it could be a disaster.

5. *What kitchen equipment do you have, and how will it affect the meal?* In planning a menu you should be aware of your resources. Balance your use of the range, broiler, oven, and cooking utensils; you will not, for instance, be able to prepare three dishes that must cook simultaneously in the oven at three different temperatures.

6. *Similarly, when planning your menu, make allowances for the serving pieces, flatware, china, and glasses that you have at your disposal.*

7. *Be sure that your menu is well balanced for color, texture, and ingredients.* (For more information, see page xv.)

8. *It is not advisable to try new dishes when entertaining.* If you must, choose a dish that can be prepared a couple of days in advance. This way, if it fails, you can easily substitute another dish.

9. *Avoid planning a menu that demands you spend too much time in the kitchen after your guests have arrived, unless you are comfortable with your guests' joining you or even helping you cook.*

Once you have determined your menu, you are ready to begin. Follow the advice in my Kitchen Strategies section to make your job easier and more enjoyable.

Sooner or later, the occasion will arise when you are faced with the tough task of giving a large party (more than 25 guests). This requires special planning:

1. Allow time to clear space in your refrigerator for incoming food.
2. Consult the section in this book on the packaging and cooling of foods (see page 539). It is particularly important to chill food quickly when handling large batches, and domestic refrigerators do not have the consistency or cooling capacity of their commercial counterparts.
3. Make as much food ahead of time as possible. Consider serving foods in non–egg-based dressings, and non-protein, acidic dishes, such as marinated mushrooms, that can be held in the refrigerator several days. Also think about recipes that you can make ahead and freeze.
4. Make protein foods, chicken salads, mayonnaises, fish dishes, and other perishable items as close to the event as possible.
5. Plan to put out buffet food in small batches, replenishing platters often. This will ensure the freshness and attractiveness of your dishes. (After the party, be wary of eating leftover food that was prepared in advance and left sitting out.)
6. Stock up on the basics, such as coffee, sugar, cream, and cleaning supplies.
7. Consider hiring outside help. If you do decide to use serving people, try to arrange a meeting with them prior to the day of the party. You can alleviate last-minute stress by going over details with them at your leisure.

If you are serving wine at your dinner party, note that the availability of low-cost to medium-priced wines is ever increasing. It would be impossible for me to enumerate in this book the wines that you might serve at a party, but I can recommend two highly readable books that give a clear and concise evaluation of available wines: *Michael Broadbent's Pocket Guide to Wine Tasting* (published by Simon & Schuster) and *Frank Schoonmaker's Encyclopedia of Wine* (published by Hastings House). In addition to these, many liquor store managers are helpful and informative and will suggest appropriate wines if you show them your menu. I prefer to serve dry wines with all foods but dessert, but my true recommendation is to drink what you enjoy.

And finally, enjoy yourself. Those of us who are concerned with details tend to forget that the real pleasure of a party lies in the company of friends.

About the Recipes

Recipe codes: To help you plan your time, my recipe testers and I developed a code to define the ease of preparation and the time needed for each recipe. (Although we believe this coding system to be reliable, it may differ from one cook to another.) For preparation they are: *Easy* (can be made easily and quickly); *Fairly easy* (a little more time-consuming); *Fairly difficult* (be cautious in areas of this recipe and allow time for preparation); *Difficult* (I hope, with the diligent help of my testers, to have alerted you to the potential difficulties. Allow plenty of time to master the techniques in these recipes, and even the novice cook will be excited by the results).

For time the codes are: *Quick* (several minutes up to about 45 minutes); *Fairly time consuming* (approximately 45 to 60 minutes); *Time consuming* (more than one hour). (Keep in mind, however, that a time-consuming recipe is likely to be quicker to make the second time around.) This line of information also states whether a recipe can be partially or completely prepared in advance or frozen. Within the recipe there will be indications to what point this advance preparation can be done.

Salt and pepper: As the amount of salt and pepper desired or needed in a dish is so subjective, I generally do not include them in the list of ingredients but rather suggest near the end of preparation of the recipe that you add salt and freshly ground black pepper to taste. I feel that salt should always be used carefully, because the right amount of salt intensifies or enhances the flavor of food, whereas too much salt can ruin a dish. Also, I believe that we all should try to decrease our salt intake, as the more salt added to our diets tends to increase the amount we feel we need. I recommend the use of freshly ground black pepper. Pre-ground pepper loses the aromatic qualities, leaving behind the spiciness without the scented flavor.

Herbs: I generally call for fresh herbs rather than dried herbs in my recipes. I feel that in many cases dried herbs give an astringent flavor to a dish, whereas fresh herbs have a milder, more appealing flavor. (Read more about herbs in the Appendix, on page 531). You will note that many of the measurements for fresh herbs call for loosely packed herbs. In putting together these recipes, both the recipe testers and I had a problem adjusting the measurements of fresh herbs to give the perfect balance of flavor. In certain cases, we found that a measurement for prechopped herbs would vary the flavor of a dish, because cooking and chopping techniques vary. At times this produced a problem. Two of my testers, Mimi Santini Ritt and Sally Guilliano, then devised the process of measuring loosely packed leaves or sprigs prior to chopping. We found this to be much more successful. Of course there are certain herbs, such as chives, that cannot be loosely packed. We have used the precut measurement in these cases. Above all, I must stress that, depending on your taste and the strength of the herbs, you should adjust the measurement to suit your taste.

Butter: All the recipes in this book specify unsalted butter when butter is used. This conforms to my policy of baking without salt, as it is far easier to control salt levels in food if the ingredients you are using do not contain salt.

Chopping or dicing thickness: Everyone's idea of what is fine, medium, or coarsely chopped or diced can differ. In these recipes we define them as follows: *very finely* (almost paper thin); *finely* (a little thicker than paper thin); *medium* (⅛-inch thick); *coarsely* (¼-inch thick).

The Basics

Stocks

It has always been my feeling that the finest quality soups and sauces are produced when one uses homemade stocks; the flavor is light, fresh, and not too salty. Stocks are also integral to the cooking of fish, seafood, and meats. I cannot emphasize enough their value in reduction sauces.

The finest stock is made with spring water; should this be unavailable, be sure to use water from the cold faucet only. The flavor of heated water is affected by the sediment that collects in hot water pipes.

Please note that in all of the following stocks, no salt is added. When a stock is reduced for a sauce, it will have a much richer flavor, so salt should not be added until the last minute. Once you are accustomed to home-made stocks, you will notice that canned broths have a high salt content. This is why I recommend only low-salt canned broth.

As a rule of thumb, I run all stocks through a cotton cloth or cheesecloth once they have been cooked and strained. This removes particles and imparts a far cleaner taste to the stock. Quite often I will then reduce the stock, a particularly good step for freezing, as reductions take up consid-erably less space in the freezer. (If you reduce the stock by 50 percent, it is referred to as a strong stock.) If you do reduce the stock at this point, then you will generally not reduce the stock again for a recipe.

Stocks may be refrigerated for several days. If you are careful to keep the fat seal on the top of the stock, it will prevent absorption of refrigerator odors and will keep the stock fresh an additional one to 3 days.

Keep in mind four important rules for freezing any stock: First, the container you use should be immaculately clean. Second, the container should have a very tight-fitting lid. Third, the container should be filled only three-quarters of the way, as a stock will often swell during the freezing process. Finally, only freeze a chilled rather than a warm stock. Once a warm stock is placed in the freezer, it will swell in the center and rise. To chill a warm stock, leave it in the refrigerator or add several ice cubes. On defrosting, reduce the stock to compensate for the ice cubes used earlier.

For a more efficient kitchen, make large batches of stocks and freeze them in small, well-sealed containers in order to have them readily avail-able for cooking. Mark and date the containers. If your freezer is running at a constant zero degrees, the stocks should keep up to 9 months in the freezer.

Chicken Stock

There are two methods of making a chicken stock: One uses a combination of giblets and bones, the other uses giblets only. If you want to make an all-giblet stock, use 7 pounds giblets in the following recipe and no chicken bones. This stock would then take just 3 to 4 hours to cook. It is essential to remove all chicken livers from the giblets, as they can impart bitterness to the stock. You should get in the habit of freezing giblets and uncooked chicken bones obtained from boning chicken breasts until you have enough on hand to make stock.

4 pounds chicken bones
3 pounds giblets, no livers
½ cup rendered chicken fat (or 6 chicken skins or ¼ cup
    unsalted butter)
2 large onions, unpeeled, washed, and sliced
4 stalks celery, sliced
2 small carrots, peeled and sliced
1 bay leaf
pinch of allspice

1. To render chicken fat, place chicken skins in a roasting pan. Place in a 350-degree oven for 30 to 45 minutes until light golden brown and ½ cup fat is rendered. Be careful that the chicken skins are only cooked to a light golden brown. If darker, they will impart a burnt flavor to the stock.
2. Heat rendered chicken fat or butter in a heavy 3- to 4-gallon stock pot. Add unpeeled onions (the onion skins add a rich color to the stock), carrots, and celery. (Do not add any more carrot as the stock will become too sweet when reduced.) Cover and gently saute on low heat for 10 to 15 minutes until vegetables are soft but not browned.
3. Add bay leaf, chicken bones, giblets, and allspice. (The tiny pinch of allspice helps bring out a good flavor.) Cover with enough cold water to come 2 inches above the bones, bring to a boil, and boil for 5 minutes. Skim off beige foam that comes to the top. This is an important step because it will clarify the stock. Turn down the heat and gently simmer,

uncovered, for 5 to 6 hours, skimming occasionally. If any liquid evaporates during cooking time, add some cold water.

4. Strain stock through a cotton cloth placed in a fine sieve until the stock is clear. Discard vegetables, giblets, and bones. Cool stock.

5. The stock may be refrigerated for 4 days as long as the fat seal is kept on top. It also may be frozen (see page 2).

6. For a strong stock, return it to the pan and boil until reduced by 50 percent.

Yield: 3 quarts   Preparation: Easy
Time: Time consuming; may be frozen

Chicken-Beef Consomme

Consommes are clarified stocks. Although a little time consuming, consommes are not difficult to prepare, have a much cleaner and richer flavor than a stock, and make an even better reduction sauce. For a reduction sauce I reduce consomme by 50 percent in a saucepan over high heat, which gives a very rich base to the sauce. You will find other cookbooks recommend vegetables and egg whites to clarify the stock to make a consomme, but I use ground beef, which also adds to the richness in flavor.

3 quarts strong chicken stock
2 medium tomatoes, finely chopped
1 carrot, finely chopped
1 stalk celery, finely chopped
1 medium onion, finely chopped
few sprigs parsley, finely chopped
½ pound lean ground beef
3 egg whites

1. Heat stock in a 3-quart stainless steel or enamel saucepan until warm. Do not use an aluminum pan; I have found that one out of ten consommes made in an aluminum pan has not cleared.
2. Place all vegetables, including parsley, in a bowl with the ground beef. Add egg whites and mix well. Form into a large, cohesive ball.
3. Float ball on top of the stock. Gently simmer, uncovered, for 30 minutes, then stir and continue to simmer an additional 30 minutes until stock is clear.
4. Soak a cotton cloth in warm water, squeeze out water, and place cloth in a sieve. Pour stock through. Save the meat in the freezer for adding to a chicken, beef, or veal stock; it will give more flavor.
5. Consomme may be kept in the refrigerator for 4 days or frozen. Defrosted, it may take on a cloudy appearance, but once heated the clarity is redefined.

Yield: 2 quarts   Preparation: Easy
Time: Fairly time consuming; may be frozen

Beef or Veal Stock

In many cookbooks you will find that veal or beef bones are roasted in the oven before making a stock. This procedure does give the stock a lovely golden brown color, but I have found that it also gives the stock a slightly bitter flavor. I prefer my veal or beef stock to be rich, yet clean in flavor.

5 to 6 pounds meaty beef or veal bones
4 tablespoons unsalted butter
1 large onion, unpeeled, washed, and thinly sliced
1 large or 2 small carrots, thinly sliced
3 celery stalks, thinly sliced
1 bay leaf
parsley stalks (optional)

1. Heat the butter in a 3-gallon saucepan and add the unpeeled onion, carrot, and celery. Saute on low heat until soft, being careful not to brown.
2. Add bones, bay leaf, and parsley sprigs; cover with enough cold water to come 2 inches above the bones. Bring to a boil and boil for 5 minutes, skimming off any foam that comes to the top. Turn down heat and gently simmer, uncovered, for 6 hours. Keep skimming occasionally; this step will give the stock more clarity. If any liquid evaporates during cooking time, add some cold water.
3. Strain stock through a fine sieve. Discard bones and vegetables. For a very clear stock, run stock through several layers of cheesecloth. Cool.
4. The stock may be refrigerated for 5 days as long as the fat seal is kept on top. It also may be frozen (see page 2).
5. For a strong stock, return it to the pan and boil until reduced by 50 percent.

Yield: 3 to 5 quarts   Preparation: Easy
Time: Time consuming; may be frozen

Fish Stock

Of all the stocks, fish stocks are the easiest to prepare. They take approximately 45 minutes to cook and do not improve with longer cooking. In fact, overcooking a fish stock is likely to make it quite bitter. The interesting thing about fish stocks is that, once strained, they are deceptively bland in taste; but when used in a fish soup or a fish sauce, they are the making of the recipe. A soup made with wine or water instead of fish stock generally has a less distinctive flavor. Again, as with any stock, be wary of store-bought fish stock because it will have a high salt content.

This basic stock is made with haddock, cod, or pollock bones. Thoroughly clean bones by rubbing a little salt into the bloody parts until the blood dissolves; then run bones under cold water. (If all blood is not completely removed, the stock will have a bitter taste.) Do not use fish heads, as they are difficult to clean. I do not use carrots in a fish stock because the carotene in carrots may give a white fish sauce a brownish tinge and a sweet flavor.

> 3 pounds of haddock, cod, or pollock bones, well washed
> 3 tablespoons unsalted butter
> 1 medium onion, thinly sliced
> 2 celery stalks, thinly sliced
> coarsely chopped parsley stalks (optional)
> ½ bay leaf
> pinch of ground mace (optional)

1. Heat the butter in a 2- to 3-gallon stainless steel or enamel pan. Do not use an aluminum pan. The minerals and iodine in fish can adversely affect the stock with a somewhat metallic flavor and coloring (an unappealing gray) when an aluminum pan is used.
2. Gently saute onion and celery in the butter over medium heat until soft, being careful not to brown. Add parsley, bay leaf, bones, and mace. Cover with enough cold water to come 2 inches above bones.

3. Bring to a rapid boil, then boil for 5 minutes, skimming off and discarding the foam that comes to the top. Turn down heat and gently simmer, uncovered, for 45 minutes.
4. Strain stock through a fine sieve. Discard vegetables and bones. Pour stock through several layers of cheesecloth. Return to pan and reduce on high heat by 50 percent.
5. The stock may be kept 3 to 4 days in the refrigerator. Keep fat seal on top of stock. It also may be frozen (see page 2).

Yield: 4 to 6 cups   **Preparation: Easy**
Time: Fairly time consuming; may be frozen

Quick Fish Stock

I have put together this recipe because I have found that it is not always easy to find fish bones, nor do all people like to deal with them. This recipe calls for fish fillets or scraps, and works well with both fresh and frozen fish. Although it might seem extravagant to use whole fish this way, it is so much quicker than cleaning bones. When defrosting frozen fish, save all the liquid to use in the stock. Because it lacks bones, this stock will not become gelatinous when cool; however, it works wonderfully in fish and seafood recipes.

1 pound haddock, cod, or pollock
2 tablespoons unsalted butter
1 small onion, thinly sliced
1 celery stalk, thinly sliced
½ bay leaf
pinch of mace (optional)
few sprigs parsley (optional)
1 cup white wine
4 cups cold water

1. Heat the butter in a 2- to 3-quart stainless steel or enamel pan. (Do not use an aluminum pan.) Add the onion and celery. Gently saute over medium heat until soft, being careful not to brown. Add fish, bay leaf, mace, parsley, wine, and water. Bring to a boil and boil for 5 minutes, then skim off and discard any foam.
2. Gently simmer, uncovered, for 45 minutes, then strain through a fine sieve. (If you have cats, the fish is a wonderful treat for them; otherwise, discard.)
3. If there are a lot of particles in the stock, run through a couple of layers of cheesecloth to remove particles. The stock may be refrigerated 3 to 4 days. Keep fat covering on top of stock. It also may be frozen (see page 2).

Yield: 1 quart   Preparation: Easy
Time: Fairly time consuming; may be frozen

Vegetable Stock

The growing interest in vegetarian cooking is helping promote vegetable stock to a position of increasing usefulness. In this book, this stock can be substituted for the chicken stock in the soup recipes. When tasting a strained vegetable stock, you might feel that, not unlike a strained fish stock, it does not have much pronounced flavor. Nevertheless, a vegetable stock is invaluable in lending a soup a richer flavor.

In the making of a vegetable stock, there are some vegetables to avoid. Root vegetables such as turnips and potatoes, and the vegetables high in sulphur, such as broccoli, green beans, cauliflower and cabbage, can impart a very strong and sometimes unpleasant flavor.

2 medium leeks
6 tablespoons unsalted butter
2 medium onions, thinly sliced
2 carrots, thinly sliced
2 celery stalks, thinly sliced
4 medium tomatoes, sliced
1 cup loosely packed fresh parsley, coarsely chopped
½ cup mushroom peelings or stalks (optional)
4 fresh thyme sprigs (or 2 teaspoons dried thyme leaves)

1. Remove and discard the coarse outside layer from the leeks. Slice up to the medium-green part, and place slices in cold water for 30 minutes. Drain, rinse, drain well and pat dry.
2. Heat the butter in a 2- to 3-gallon stainless steel or enamel pan. Do not use aluminum, as the vegetable minerals may react with the aluminum to give the stock a slightly metallic taste.
3. Add the onion and leeks and saute over medium heat until soft but not browned. Add celery and carrots and saute, being careful not to brown.
4. Add tomatoes, parsley, mushroom peelings, and thyme. Add 3 quarts cold water and bring to a boil. Boil for 5 minutes, skimming off any foam that might come to the top. Cover and gently simmer for 1 hour. Strain through a cotton cloth placed in a fine sieve.
5. The stock will keep 4 days in the refrigerator if the fat covering is left intact. It also may be frozen (see page 2).

Yield: 3 quarts   Preparation: Easy
Time: Fairly time consuming; may be frozen

Poaching Liquids

A nice way to cook fish, mussels, or shrimp is to poach them. Instead of poaching them in plain water, I use a poaching liquid—a seasoned liquid that provides an aromatic flavor to the food. In this section are recipes for poaching these seafoods.

You also will notice in this book recipes calling for poached mushrooms and mushroom poaching liquid. As poached mushrooms are lovely in a salad, I have placed my mushroom poaching liquid recipe in the salad chapter.

Fish Poaching Liquid

I have found that when I use this liquid for poaching white fish such as sole, haddock, cod, and pollock, it can be strained and frozen to be used later as a quick fish stock for soups and sauces. Read about poaching fish on page 220.

> 1 medium onion, thinly sliced
> 1 medium carrot, thinly sliced
> 4 cups water
> 1 cup dry white wine
> 1 small bay leaf
> pinch of ground mace (optional)
> 6 whole black peppercorns
> 1/2 teaspoon salt

1. Place all ingredients in a 2-quart stainless steel saucepan, bring to a boil, and gently simmer for 30 minutes. Strain it before poaching the fish in the liquid.
2. Freeze the liquid for a future use as a fish stock or poaching liquid.

Yield: 6 cups   Preparation: Easy
Time: Quick; may be frozen

Mussel or Shrimp Poaching Liquid

1 onion, thinly sliced
1 large carrot, thinly sliced
2 celery stalks, thinly sliced
2 cups dry white wine
4 cups cold water
1 bay leaf

1. Place all ingredients in a 2-quart stainless steel saucepan. Bring to a boil, lower the heat, and gently simmer for 40 minutes. Strain this liquid before using it to poach mussels or shrimp.
2. To poach shrimp, first devein the shrimp. (See illustration, page 250.) Add them to the gently simmering liquid, and gently simmer for 5 to 7 minutes, being careful not to boil. Do not overcook, as the shrimp will be rubbery in texture. Remove shrimp with a slotted spoon and cover as they cool so they do not dry out.
3. To poach mussels, first tap the open mussels on a hard surface. If they do not close, discard them, as they are dead. Carefully scrub and remove the beards. During this process also check the closed mussels for "mud" mussels; these will be full of mud and sand and during the cooking process will open and adversely affect the poaching liquid and the other mussels. These "mud" mussels will weigh two to three times more than the regular mussels and should be discarded. Poach the mussels in the gently simmering liquid until they open about ½-inch. Discard any that do not open. Remove mussels and strain the liquid through a cloth to screen any residual sand from the mussels. Use strained liquid as a base for mussel soup, if you wish.
4. This poaching liquid may be reused and refrozen up to 5 times. Before each use, add enough cold water to measure 4 to 5 cups.

Yield: 6 cups   **Preparation: Easy**
Time: Fairly time consuming; may be frozen

Sauces

With a ladle of sauce, an ordinary meal can become a surprisingly imaginative creation. As with anything special, the quality of a sauce will be determined by the quality of its stock. To stress the importance of making your own stocks, I offer a few words from Escoffier: "The basic component used in the production of sauces is a stock or gravy.... It is to the production of perfect stocks that the sauce cook should devote himself—the sauce cook who is, as the Marquis de Cuissy remarked, 'the enlightened chemist, the creative genius, and the cornerstone of the edifice of superlative cookery.' "

I also have selected several very fine sauces that do not require a stock, but depend on a high quality of ingredients.

Following these simple recipes you will be able to mix and match unusual combinations to your pleasure. Remember, rather than the "enlightened chemist," you are the "creative genius," so study, experiment, and most important, have fun discovering these new creations.

Tomato Sauce

This tomato sauce is light in both flavor and texture. If you prefer a denser, more acidic tomato flavor and a thicker consistency, add tomato paste. For best results, use vine-ripened tomatoes when they are readily available and freeze the sauce for future use. If you cannot find fully ripe vine-ripened tomatoes, let the tomatoes sit in a sunny window for 2 to 4 days to ripen. This sauce is used in a variety of recipes in this book, and also can be used on pasta or poached fish.

8 large vine-ripened tomatoes, peeled and seeded (juice reserved)
¼ cup olive oil
1 medium onion, very finely diced
3 medium garlic cloves, finely chopped or crushed
1 tablespoon dried basil
¾ cup red wine
1 to 2 tablespoons tomato paste (optional)

1. Place the tomatoes in a food processor and process medium-fine.
2. Bring the red wine to a boil in a saucepan. Ignite and let flame for 3 minutes. Set aside.
3. Heat the olive oil in a 2-quart stainless steel saucepan. Add the onion and garlic and saute on medium heat until the onion is clear, being careful not to brown. Add the tomatoes and tomato juice, then add the basil and red wine. Gently simmer, uncovered, for 40 minutes, stirring occasionally so the sauce does not scorch.
4. Whisk in 1 to 2 tablespoons tomato paste.
5. Add salt and freshly ground black pepper to taste. Cool.
6. Refrigerate for 3 days or freeze.

Yield: 4 cups   Preparation: Easy
Time: Fairly time consuming; may be frozen

Tomato Fennel Sauce

The fennel in this sauce imparts a light flavor of anise. The sauce is wonderful served with pasta dishes, grilled bluefish, mackerel, or fresh rabbit.

4 large vine-ripened tomatoes, peeled, seeded, and chopped (juice reserved)
1 medium fennel bulb (or 2 teaspoons fennel seeds ground in blender)
2 tablespoons unsalted butter
2 tablespoons olive oil
1 medium onion, finely chopped
2 medium garlic cloves, finely chopped or crushed
1 cup dry red wine
1 to 2 tablespoons tomato paste (optional)
¼ cup loosely packed fresh parsley leaves, finely chopped

1. Cut fennel bulb in half. Remove one coarse outside layer. Cut out the core and discard. Very finely chop the fennel.
2. Heat the butter and olive oil in a 2-quart stainless steel saucepan. Add the onion and garlic; saute over medium heat until the onion is clear, being careful not to brown.
3. Add the fresh fennel or fennel seeds and saute for 3 minutes. Add chopped tomatoes and tomato juice to the fennel.
4. Place the red wine in a 1-quart stainless steel saucepan, bring to a boil, and ignite. Flame for 3 minutes, then add it to the fennel mixture. Simmer sauce for 40 minutes, stirring occasionally to keep it from scorching. Add salt and freshly ground black pepper to taste. (For a stronger tomato flavor and thicker consistency, stir 1 to 2 tablespoons of tomato paste into the sauce, and gently simmer for 3 minutes.)
5. This sauce may be refrigerated for 2 to 3 days, or it may be frozen.
6. Just before serving, add the parsley and simmer for 3 minutes.

Yield: 3 to 4 cups   Preparation: Fairly easy
Time: Fairly time consuming; may be frozen

Tomato Coulis

This cold sauce is ideal served with poached shrimp or fish or vegetable terrines. It is especially important to use vine-ripened tomatoes.

6 small vine-ripened tomatoes, peeled and seeded
1 tablespoon tomato paste
¼ cup vegetable oil
2 tablespoons tarragon or basil vinegar

1. Place all ingredients in the food processor and process until very smooth, about 2 to 3 minutes. Add salt and freshly ground black pepper to taste.
2. This sauce may be refrigerated for 2 days before serving.
3. Whisk for 1 minute before serving. Serve it cold.

Yield: 1 cup   Preparation: Easy
Time: Quick; advance preparation possible

Tomato Ginger Coulis

This simple relish, which is thicker in consistency than my Tomato Coulis, is great served with grilled lamb, chicken, or shrimp. It can be served hot, warm, or chilled.

4 medium vine-ripened tomatoes, peeled and seeded (juice reserved)
1 ounce fresh ginger, peeled
3 tablespoons vegetable oil
⅓ cup loosely packed fresh mint or coriander leaves, coarsely chopped (optional)

1. Dice the tomatoes medium-fine.
2. Grate the ginger on a medium grater to measure one tablespoon.
3. Heat the vegetable oil in a 12-inch stainless steel saute pan. Add the tomato, tomato juice, and 1 tablespoon ginger, and saute over medium heat until the mixture is fairly thick. Stir occasionally so it does not scorch. Add more ginger to taste, if desired. Add salt and freshly ground black pepper to taste.
4. This coulis may be refrigerated for 2 days before serving.
5. A couple of hours before serving, add the fresh herbs.

Yield: 1½ cups   **Preparation: Easy**
Time: Quick; advance preparation possible

Pureed Vegetable Sauce

The carrots give this sauce a color like carrot puree, but it has a lovely, soft tomato flavor. It is wonderful served with cannelloni or manicotti, such as my Cannelloni Pesto (page 410). Vine-ripened tomatoes are preferable, but any fresh tomatoes may be used.

6 large vine-ripened tomatoes, peeled, seeded, and quartered
    (juice reserved)
2 medium leeks
6 tablespoons unsalted butter
1 medium onion, finely sliced
2 small carrots, thinly sliced (1 cup sliced carrots)

1. Remove and discard the coarse outside layer from the leeks. Cut the leek into thin slices up to the medium-green part and place the slices in a bowl of cold water for 30 minutes. Drain, rinse, drain well, and pat dry.
2. Heat the butter in a heavy 3-quart stainless steel pan, add the onion, and saute over medium heat until clear, being careful not to brown. Add the leeks and saute until soft.
3. Add the carrots, tomatoes, and tomato juice and simmer for 45 minutes, stirring occasionally to keep the sauce from scorching.
4. Pour the sauce into a blender or food processor and puree until very smooth. This may take a couple of minutes. Add salt and freshly ground black pepper to taste.
5. This sauce may be refrigerated for 3 days before serving, or frozen.
6. Reheat to serve.

Yield: 3 to 4 cups   Preparation: Easy
Time: Fairly time consuming; may be frozen

Red Pepper Puree

This sauce has a beautiful deep-red color. It can be made in the late summer when vine-ripened tomatoes and red peppers are plentiful and at their best, and frozen for use during the winter. The sauce is wonderful served with grilled steak, grilled bluefish, mackerel, or trout.

3 medium sweet red peppers
6 tablespoons unsalted butter
3 small vine-ripened tomatoes, peeled, seeded, and quartered
    (juice reserved)

1. Place whole peppers under a preheated broiler and broil until dark brown on all sides. Put into very cold water for 5 minutes, then peel off skin and remove core and seeds. Coarsely chop.
2. Heat the butter in a 12-inch stainless steel saute pan and add peppers, tomatoes, and tomato juice. Simmer for 10 to 15 minutes until mixture has reduced a little and is fairly thick.
3. Puree the mixture in a blender or food processor for 3 to 4 minutes until it is very smooth. Add salt and freshly ground black pepper to taste.
4. This sauce may be refrigerated for 2 days, or frozen.
5. Before serving, heat the sauce in a stainless steel pan, whisking in a little additional unsalted butter for richness, if desired.

Yield: 1½ to 1¾ cups   Preparation: Easy
Time: Fairly time consuming; may be frozen

Creole Sauce

This sauce is delicious with soft-shell crabs (see page 234), shrimp (see page 255), or broiled red snapper. I recommend 2 teaspoons of freshly ground black pepper for a medium to very spicy sauce, but you can adjust the spiciness to your taste. The ground sassafras leaves absolutely make this sauce, so do try to find them at a specialty food store. Other fresh tomatoes may be used instead of the vine-ripened tomatoes, if necessary.

4 medium vine-ripened tomatoes, peeled and seeded (juice reserved)
1 medium sweet green pepper
1/3 cup vegetable oil
1 medium onion, very finely chopped
1 large garlic clove, finely chopped or crushed
1/2 teaspoon freshly ground black pepper
1 teaspoon finely grated lemon rind
1 tablespoon fresh thyme leaves (or 1 1/2 teaspoons dried thyme)
1/2 cup strong chicken stock (or canned low-salt chicken broth)
1 tablespoon finely crumbled sassafras leaves (optional, but preferable)

1. Place green pepper under a preheated broiler and broil until medium brown on all sides. Put into very cold water for 5 minutes, then peel off skin and remove core and seeds. Chop medium-fine.
2. Puree tomatoes in food processor or blender, then add the reserved juice.
3. Heat oil in a 1- to 2-quart stainless steel saucepan, add onion and garlic, and saute over medium heat until clear, being careful not to brown. Add the freshly ground black pepper and saute on low heat for 2 minutes. Add tomatoes, lemon rind, green pepper, chicken stock, and thyme; gently simmer for 20 minutes. Add salt to taste.
4. The sauce may be prepared up to this point and stored in the refrigerator for 3 days, or it can be frozen.
5. Just before serving, reheat sauce. Add the sassafras and simmer for just 2 minutes. If sassafras is overcooked, the sauce could become bitter.

Yield: 4 cups   **Preparation: Easy**   **Time: Quick; may be frozen**

Catalan Sauce

Michela Larson's wonderful stories of Spain and discussions of its food inspired this sauce. It is great served with broiled swordfish or grilled fresh rabbit.

¾ cup blanched whole almonds
2 small or 1 large sweet red pepper
2 vine-ripened tomatoes, peeled and seeded
1 large garlic clove
½ cup mild olive oil
½ cup loosely packed fresh mint leaves

1. In a preheated 375-degree oven, toast almonds on a sheet pan, for 7 to 10 minutes, until they are light golden brown. Watch nuts carefully, as they easily burn. Remove nuts from oven and cool.
2. Place green peppers under a preheated broiler and broil until dark brown on all sides. Put into very cold water for 5 minutes, then peel off skin and remove core and seeds. Coarsely chop.
3. In a food processor, grind nuts to a medium-coarse consistency. Add chopped red peppers, tomatoes, garlic, and oil. Process until fairly smooth, scraping down the sides with a rubber spatula if necessary. Add mint and process until it is coarsely chopped. Add salt and freshly ground black pepper to taste.
4. This sauce may be refrigerated for 2 days before serving.
5. Reheat sauce before serving, but be careful not to boil it.

Yield: 1½ to 1¾ cups　　**Preparation: Easy**
Time: Quick; advance preparation possible

Mongolian Sauce

Mongolian Sauce has a wonderful rich taste. It is great served with beef, chicken, or poached shrimp. It is essential that you use fresh water chestnuts, which are available in Chinese markets.

2 medium vine-ripened tomatoes, peeled, seeded, and finely
    chopped
2 tablespoons vegetable oil
¼ teaspoon dried crushed red hot pepper
¾ cup homemade chicken stock (or low-salt canned chicken
    broth)
2 teaspoons cornstarch
3 tablespoons cold water
3 tablespoons low-salt soy sauce
8 fresh water chestnuts
1 tablespoon dark sesame oil
6 scallions

1. Heat 2 tablespoons oil in a 2-quart stainless steel saucepan. Add tomatoes and hot pepper and saute on medium heat for 5 minutes. Add the chicken stock and simmer for 5 minutes. Remove from heat.
2. Mix the cornstarch with the cold water. (If you desire a thicker sauce, increase the cornstarch to 1 tablespoon.) Add to the tomatoes, along with the soy sauce, and bring to a boil, stirring constantly.
3. The sauce may be prepared up to this point, if you wish, and refrigerated up to 3 days or frozen.
4. Before serving, peel the water chestnuts. Wash under cold water, pat dry, and slice them ⅛-inch thick. Remove and discard the coarse outside layer of the scallions. Slice the scallions on the diagonal into ½-inch pieces halfway up the green part.
5. Heat the sesame oil in a 10- to 12-inch stainless steel saute pan. Add scallions and toss over high heat for 1 minute. Add tomato sauce and water chestnuts; bring to a boil, and boil for 1 minute. Add salt to taste. Serve immediately.

Yield: 2 cups   Preparation: Easy
Time: Quick; some advance preparation possible

Sesame Sauce

Crunchy, with a wonderful flavor of sesame oil, this sauce is very good with steamed chicken, bluefish, or trout. Be certain you use the medium-brown or dark-brown sesame oil, found in Oriental food markets. This sauce should be made just before serving.

½ cup raw sesame seeds
1 tablespoon medium- to dark-brown sesame oil
1 cup strong chicken stock (or canned low-salt chicken broth)
6 scallions
3 tablespoons vegetable oil
2 tablespoons low-salt soy sauce

1. Place the chicken stock in a 1-quart saucepan and reduce to ½ cup.
2. Remove and discard the coarse outside layer of the scallions. Finely slice the scallions on the diagonal halfway up the green part.
3. Heat the vegetable oil in a 10-inch saute pan and add the sesame seeds. Toss them over high heat until they are light golden brown. Add scallions and toss over high heat for 2 minutes.
4. Add chicken stock, sesame oil, and soy sauce; bring to a boil. Add salt and freshly ground black pepper to taste. Serve immediately.

Yield: 1 cup   **Preparation: Easy**
Time: Quick

Mexican Walnut Sauce

Mexican Walnut Sauce is delicious served with sauteed chicken breasts or steamed bluefish. You will get much better results if you use freshly cracked walnuts. (Pecans may be substituted for walnuts.) You can adjust the spiciness of the sauce by adding more hot pepper.

> ¾ cup freshly cracked walnuts (or shelled pecans)
> 4 tablespoons unsalted butter
> 1 large onion, sliced
> ¼ teaspoon dried crushed red hot pepper
> ¾ to 1 cup homemade chicken stock (or canned low-salt
>   chicken broth)

1. Melt butter in a 12-inch saute pan. Add the onion and hot pepper and saute over medium heat until the onion is clear, being careful not to brown. The onion should be slightly crunchy. Add the walnuts and toss over high heat for 1 minute.
2. Process the onion-walnut mixture in a food processor until the nuts are fairly finely ground.
3. Place mixture in a 1-quart saucepan. Add ¾ cup stock and simmer the sauce for 5 minutes. If the sauce is very thick, add the remaining stock. Add salt to taste.
4. The sauce may be refrigerated for 3 days.
5. Before serving, reheat and simmer for 1 minute.

Yield: 1⅓ to 1½ cups   **Preparation: Easy**
Time: Fairly time consuming; advance preparation possible

Mexican Green Sauce

This sauce is good served with poached shrimp, sauteed and broiled swordfish, and chicken. Fresh coriander is available in Oriental food markets.

> 1 small head Romaine lettuce
> 1/3 cup blanched whole almonds
> 2 to 3 teaspoons very finely chopped fresh chili pepper (or 1 to 2 canned whole jalapeño pepper)
> 3 scallions (or 1/3 cup sliced onion)
> 1/3 cup loosely packed fresh coriander leaves
> 1/4 cup vegetable oil

1. Remove the dark green leaves from the lettuce and discard the coarse ones. For the sauce, use the medium- to light-green leaves; save the others for another use. Wash the lettuce leaves and drain, then pat very dry with paper towels. Remove the coarse center vein on each leaf, and coarsely slice the leaves.
2. Process the almonds in a food processor until very finely ground. Add 2 teaspoons chili peppers or 1 whole jalapeño pepper (add more if you want it highly spiced). If you are using sliced onion, add it at this point. Process until the mixture is a medium-fine consistency.
3. Add the sliced lettuce and process until it is medium-fine. Add the coriander leaves, process for 30 seconds, and slowly pour in the oil. Continue to process until the coriander is a medium-fine consistency.
4. If you are using scallions, remove and discard the coarse outside layer. Thinly slice scallions halfway up the green part.
5. Place the sauce in a bowl and add the scallions and salt and freshly ground black pepper to taste. If you want more coriander taste, finely chop more coriander leaves and add to sauce. Lay plastic wrap directly on the sauce to keep it from turning brown.
6. This sauce may be made 24 hours ahead of serving and stored in the refrigerator.
7. Serve the sauce chilled, at room temperature, or hot.

Yield: 1 1/3 cups   Preparation: Easy
Time: Quick; advance preparation possible

Agro Dolce

This slightly sweet and sour sauce is very good served with sauteed chicken breasts or steamed whole fish such as trout or carp.

¼ cup golden raisins
¼ cup white wine tarragon or basil vinegar
2 tablespoons vegetable oil
⅓ cup finely chopped blanched almonds
1 cup strong homemade chicken stock
2 teaspoons cornstarch
¼ cup cold water
⅓ cup loosely packed fresh coriander or mint leaves, coarsely chopped

1. Marinate raisins in vinegar for 1 to 4 hours.
2. Place the oil in a 1-quart saucepan and add the almonds. Stir over medium heat until they start to sizzle. Before they start to change color, add stock, raisins, and vinegar. Bring to a boil, stirring occasionally.
3. Mix cornstarch with the cold water until smooth. Pour ⅓ cup of the heated almond mixture into the cornstarch; stir. Remove the saucepan of almond mixture from heat and slowly stir in the cornstarch mixture. Return the pan to heat, stirring all the time, until the mixture starts to boil. Lower heat and gently simmer for 5 minutes, stirring occasionally.
4. The sauce may be prepared up to this point and refrigerated up to 2 days.
5. Just before serving, reheat sauce. Add coriander or mint, and salt and freshly ground black pepper to taste.

Yield: 1½ cups   Preparation: Easy
Time: Quick; some advance preparation necessary

Pesto

This is a slight variation of the classic pesto, as I find the use of parsley works better for the recipes in this book. Use an olive oil that suits your taste.

2 large garlic cloves
½ cup olive oil
2 cups loosely packed, sprigged, fresh parsley leaves
2 cups loosely packed, sprigged, fresh basil leaves
½ cup freshly grated Parmesan cheese

1. Make sure the herbs are well washed and very dry.
2. Process the garlic and olive oil in a food processor until the garlic is pureed.
3. Add the parsley and process until it is fairly fine. Add the basil and process until it is a fine consistency. Add the Parmesan cheese and process for 30 seconds.
4. Pour the pesto into a storage container and add salt and freshly ground black pepper to taste. Place plastic wrap directly on the pesto to prevent it from turning brown.
5. Pesto will keep up to 2 days in the refrigerator.

Variation 1: For a stiffer version of pesto, process ½ cup pine nuts or whole blanched almonds in the food processor until fairly fine. Then continue with the rest of the ingredients as described above. The yield will be 1¼ to 1½ cups.

Variation 2: Add ¾ cup sour cream to the prepared pesto and combine well. This version is wonderful served as a dip with lightly blanched fresh vegetables such as snow peas, broccoli, Jerusalem artichokes, yams, raw mushrooms, and endive. The yield will be 1¼ to 1½ cups.

Yield: 1 to 1¼ cups   Preparation: Easy
Time: Quick; advance preparation possible

Dill Mousseline

Dill Mousseline complements poached or grilled salmon, sole, haddock, and trout. It is similar to a hollandaise; but the sauce is lighter. Its preparation can be deceptive as it is quick to prepare, but it also carries a high risk of curdling. If you follow my directions carefully you will avoid that problem. (For more information, read about emulsifying in Appendix I.)

1 large egg
3 egg yolks
2 tablespoons white wine tarragon or basil vinegar
½ teaspoon salt
¼ teaspoon freshly ground black pepper
1 cup heavy cream
4 tablespoons unsalted butter, very soft, but not melted
⅓ cup loosely packed fresh dill sprigs, medium-fine chop

1. Use a saucepan that will hold a heavy 1- to 2-quart bowl securely, without letting the bowl touch the simmering water. Bring 3 inches of water to a simmering point in this saucepan.
2. Off the heat, place the egg, egg yolks, vinegar, salt, and pepper in the bowl. (The salt is used to help in the emulsification process.) Whisk until well emulsified. Very slowly beat in the heavy cream.
3. Place the bowl over the simmering water (be certain the bowl is not touching the water), whisking for approximately 10 minutes, until the mixture has a thick, mousselike consistency. (While whisking sauce, scrape down the edges with a plastic spatula, or the mixture will stick to the bowl and have a scrambled egg consistency.)
4. Once the sauce has thickened, remove the bowl from the pan immediately. Then, one tablespoon at a time, whisk in soft butter. Whisk in dill and add salt and freshly ground black pepper to taste.
5. The sauce may be made 30 minutes before serving: it should, however, be kept in a warm place.

Yield: 1½ cups   **Preparation: Fairly difficult**   **Time: Quick**

Dill Cucumber Mousseline

The addition of cucumber (preferably an English cucumber) makes this sauce even lighter. It is great served with poached or grilled trout or salmon.

Dill Mousseline (page 28)
1 medium cucumber
½ teaspoon salt

1. Peel cucumber and cut in half lengthwise. Scoop out the seeds with a teaspoon or tomato shark, and coarsely grate.
2. Bring 1 cup water to a boil in a 1-quart stainless steel saucepan, add cucumber and salt, and boil for 1 minute. Drain and immediately run under cold water. Squeeze dry. Leave in a warm place.
3. Make the Dill Mousseline. Stir in the cucumber.
4. The sauce may be made 30 minutes before serving; it should, however, be kept in a warm place.

Yield: 1¾ cups   **Preparation: Fairly difficult**
Time: Quick

Vermouth Madeira Sauce

This sauce is great served with a dish of veal and wild mushrooms. I use it in my Sweetbreads Champignons on page 374. Homemade stock or, even better, chicken consomme is highly recommended for this sauce.

¼ cup dry Vermouth
¼ cup dry Madeira
3 tablespoons unsalted butter
1 small onion, finely diced
1 celery stalk, finely diced
½ teaspoon dried thyme
1½ cups homemade chicken consomme or stock

1. Heat the butter in a 1-quart saucepan. Add the onion, celery, and thyme and saute until clear.
2. Add the stock, Vermouth, and Madeira and bring to a boil, then reduce on medium heat by 50 percent. Strain through a fine sieve.
3. This sauce may be refrigerated for 3 days or frozen.
4. Reheat the sauce to serve.

Yield: 1 cup   Preparation: Easy
Time: Quick; may be frozen

Horseradish Cream Sauce

This cold sauce is simple to prepare, sharp in flavor, and good served with smoked trout, cold roast beef, or gravlax.

1 cup heavy cream
1 tart apple, peeled and coarsely grated
⅓ cup white horseradish, drained

1. Whip cream until stiff. Gently fold apple and horseradish into cream. Be careful not to overfold the mixture, as cream will become too stiff. Add salt to taste. Refrigerate no longer than one hour.

Variation: Omit the apple and add ¼ cup chopped fresh dill.

Yield: 1¾ cup   **Preparation: Easy**
Time: Quick

Parmesan Sauce

I use this sauce in my Cannelloni Vitello on page 412. It is equally good with other pasta dishes. If you omit the Parmesan, you have a basic Béchamel (white sauce). I stress the use of cake flour as this will give the sauce a softer consistency. Should you require a thicker consistency, increase the butter to 4 tablespoons and the cake flour to 2 tablespoons.

> 1 cup milk
> ½ cup light cream
> 1 slice onion
> 1 slice carrot
> 1 small piece bay leaf
> 3 tablespoons unsalted butter
> 1 tablespoon + 2 teaspoons cake flour, sifted
> ⅓ cup freshly grated Parmesan

1. Place the milk, cream, onion, carrot, and bay leaf in a 1- to 2-quart heavy saucepan. Gently simmer over a low heat for 40 minutes.
2. Strain and reserve the milk. Discard the vegetables.
3. In a heavy saucepan, heat the butter, add the flour, and whisk until smooth. Gently cook for 1 minute. Remove from the heat and slowly add the milk, whisking all the time. Return to the heat and bring to a boil, whisking all the time. Then gently simmer for 5 minutes, stirring occasionally.
4. Remove from the heat and whisk in the Parmesan cheese until the sauce is smooth. Add salt and freshly ground black pepper to taste.
5. This sauce may be refrigerated for 2 days before serving. Keep it covered to prevent a skin forming on the surface.
6. When reheating the sauce, whisk occasionally; if it is too thick, add a little milk or cream to thin it.

Yield: 1½ cups   **Preparation: Easy**
Time: Quick

Beurre Blanc

Beurre blanc is a sauce made with white wine, vinegar (preferably home-made), fish or chicken stock (depending on what you are serving it with), and shallots. It is distinctive for its ability to blend with the flavor of the food it is served with, rather than to overpower the food. It is very versatile and may be used on a variety of foods.

Not an easy sauce to make, a beurre blanc can separate easily. This can be avoided if you balance the amounts of acid, butter, and heat as described in the recipes. If you have not made a beurre blanc before, I strongly advise that you start with tomato beurre blanc, as it tends not to separate because of the additional acid from the tomatoes. But if the beurre blanc should happen to break down, you may try to re-emulsify it. It is not quite as easy to re-emulsify as a mayonnaise as it takes longer, but frankly I think it's worth trying. The taste, however, will be a little more acidic. For this procedure, heat half the amount of wine, vinegar, stock, and shallots called for in the recipe, and reduce to 1 tablespoon of liquid. Slowly beat in 4 tablespoons soft butter, one tablespoon at a time, on a medium to low heat. Strain the shallots from the separated beurre blanc, then slowly beat in the separated beurre blanc. Add salt and freshly ground black pepper to taste. Should you decide not to try this, save the broken beurre blanc for up to 5 days in the refrigerator or freeze it. A broken or leftover beurre blanc should not be reheated but may be used in place of butter or oil when broiling fish. Do not try and halve a beurre blanc recipe as it probably will not work.

Once made, a beurre blanc will hold in a warm (not hot) place for up to one hour; it is very important, however, to avoid sudden cold drafts, which will cause the sauce to congeal and break down when it returns to room temperature.

All these beurre blanc recipes work well when doubled.

Basic Beurre Blanc

This beurre blanc is used in many of my recipes.

> ½ pound unsalted butter, room temperature, but not soft
> ½ cup homemade fish stock (or 1 cup homemade chicken
>   stock)
> ½ cup dry white wine
> ¼ cup white wine basil or tarragon vinegar
> 5 large or 10 small shallots, thinly sliced

1. Cut the butter into 1-inch pieces.
2. Place the fish stock, wine, vinegar, and shallots in a heavy 1-quart stainless steel saucepan. Bring to a boil and reduce until just 2 tablespoons of liquid remain. (As you are reducing it, watch carefully, as it can easily reduce too much and scorch.)
3. Lower the heat to medium to low and beat in the butter 1 tablespoon at a time, using a wooden spoon. Be very certain the butter is well incorporated before adding more.
4. Continue to beat until the sauce is hot, watching carefully that the butter does not separate. Strain the sauce through a fine sieve, return to the pan, and add salt and freshly ground black pepper to taste.
5. This sauce will hold in a warm, not hot, place for up to 1 hour before serving.

Yield: 1 cup   Preparation: Fairly difficult
Time: Fairly time consuming

Chive-Cucumber Beurre Blanc

Try this beurre blanc on poached or grilled salmon, trout, striped bass, sole, or halibut. Check that the cucumber you use in this recipe is not bitter, as it will impart an unpleasant flavor to the sauce.

½ pound unsalted butter, room temperature, but not soft
½ cup homemade fish stock
½ cup dry white wine
¼ cup white wine basil or tarragon vinegar
½ cup peeled, seeded, coarsely grated cucumber
5 large or 10 small shallots, thinly sliced
¼ cup finely snipped chives

1. Cut the butter into 1-inch pieces.
2. Place the fish stock, wine, vinegar, cucumbers, and shallots in a heavy 1-quart stainless steel saucepan. Bring to a boil and reduce until just 2 tablespoons of liquid remain. (As you are reducing it, watch carefully, as it can easily reduce too much and scorch.)
3. Turn down the heat to medium to low and beat in the butter, 1 tablespoon at a time, using a wooden spoon. Be very certain the butter is well incorporated before adding more.
4. Continue to beat until the sauce is hot, watching carefully that the butter does not separate. Strain the sauce through a fine sieve, return to the pan, and add salt and freshly ground black pepper to taste.
5. This sauce will hold in a warm, not hot, place for up to 1 hour before serving.
6. Just before serving, add the chives.

Yield: 1 cup   Preparation: Fairly difficult
Time: Fairly time consuming

Ginger-Lime Beurre Blanc

This beurre blanc is great with Soft-Shell Crabs Robert (see page 235) or with broiled red snapper. In this recipe I have substituted fresh lime juice for the traditional vinegar.

½ pound unsalted butter, room temperature, but not soft
½ cup homemade fish stock
½ cup dry white wine
¼ cup fresh lime juice
1 tablespoon peeled, coarsely grated fresh ginger
5 large or 10 small shallots, thinly sliced

1. Cut the butter into 1-inch pieces.
2. Place the fish stock, wine, lime juice, ginger, and shallots in a heavy 1-quart stainless steel saucepan. Bring to a boil and reduce until just 2 tablespoons of liquid are left. (Watch carefully as it reduces, so it doesn't reduce too much and scorch.)
3. Lower the heat to medium to low and beat in the butter 1 tablespoon at a time, using a wooden spoon. Make sure the butter is well incorporated before adding more.
4. Continue to beat until the sauce is hot, watching carefully that the butter does not separate. Strain the sauce through a fine sieve, return to the pan, and add salt and freshly ground black pepper to taste.
5. This sauce will hold in a warm, not hot, place for up to 1 hour before serving.

Yield: 1 cup   Preparation: Fairly difficult
Time: Fairly time consuming

Tomato Beurre Blanc

Tomato Beurre Blanc really enhances the taste of poached or grilled shrimp, salmon, or striped bass. The unpeeled tomatoes add extra flavor to the beurre blanc.

½ pound unsalted butter, room temperature, but not soft
½ cup homemade fish stock (or 1 cup homemade chicken
    stock)
½ cup dry white wine
¼ cup white wine basil or tarragon vinegar
3 small vine-ripened tomatoes, unpeeled and coarsely chopped
    (or 3 small fresh tomatoes coarsely chopped + 2 teaspoons
    tomato paste)
5 large or 10 small shallots, thinly sliced

1. Cut the butter into 1-inch pieces.
2. Place the fish stock, wine, vinegar, tomatoes, and shallots in a heavy 1-quart stainless steel saucepan. Bring to a boil and reduce until just 4 tablespoons of liquid remain. (As this reduces, watch carefully, as it can easily reduce too much and scorch.)
3. Turn down the heat to medium to low and beat in the butter 2 tablespoons at a time, using a wooden spoon. Make sure the butter is well incorporated before adding more.
4. Continue to beat until the sauce is hot, watching carefully that the butter does not separate. Strain the sauce through a fine sieve, return to the pan, and add salt and freshly cracked black pepper to taste.
5. This sauce will hold in a warm, not hot, place for up to 1 hour before serving.

Yield: 1 to 1½ cups   Preparation: Fairly difficult
Time: Fairly time consuming

Mayonnaises

When you try the mayonnaises in this section, you will find they have a flavor far superior to any purchased mayonnaise. If you are accustomed to commercial mayonnaise, you may find that my basic mayonnaise tastes a little thin.

All my mayonnaise recipes are made in a blender or food processor, so the egg white as well as the yolk is used. Homemade vinegar (page 61) is preferable in these recipes, but it is not required.

It is not difficult to make mayonnaise, but there are some very important points to keep in mind. It is essential that you put salt into the eggs in the beginning; it helps with the emulsification process. (You may want to read about emulsifying in Appendix I.) Yet you still may find the mayonnaise will not emulsify; it may seem to be very runny or separated. I have found that a mayonnaise will separate for one or more of the following reasons: 1) The eggs were not fresh. 2) The eggs were cold. 3) The oil was added too fast. 4) Lack of acid and or salt when beginning the procedure. 5) Incorrect agitation (this will probably only happen when you make the mayonnaise by hand whisking).

Should the mayonnaise separate, it is possible to rectify it, unless the eggs were not fresh. (Please see Appendix I for information about testing of eggs for freshness.)

Re-emulsification Method 1: When the mayonnaise has separated, remove it from the blender or food processor. Put one egg, a pinch of salt, and a tablespoon of vinegar in the blender. (The blender is preferred for this procedure, even if you were making the mayonnaise in a food processor.) Turn on blender and *very* slowly pour in 1 to 1½ cups of the separated mayonnaise. This should now emulsify; however, it might be thinner in consistency. If this is the case, thicken the mayonnaise by slowly pouring in ½ to 1 cup of oil. Of course, the balance of the flavors (fresh herbs or spices) will now need to be adjusted.

Re-emulsification Method 2: This method is very successful, but a little more time consuming. Place 1 egg yolk (2 egg yolks if the eggs are small) in a bowl with a pinch of salt. Whisk the mixture until the eggs are thick, add 1 teaspoon vinegar, and whisk for 1 minute. Add a few drops of the curdled mayonnaise, whisking all the time. When emulsified, add a few more drops—always whisking and not adding any more mixture until the mixture is well emulsified. Once ⅛ cup of the curdled mayonnaise has been added, whisk in 1 teaspoon vinegar, and continue to add more mayonnaise a couple of tablespoons at a time. Always be sure that before each addition the mixture is well emulsified. Once you have ½ to ¾ cup mixture in the bowl, beat with an electric hand beater on high speed as you slowly pour in the remaining mixture.

You have to be careful with storing and serving mayonnaise. Since it is made with raw egg, always store it in the refrigerator, and keep it for no longer than three days. Mayonnaise can be left out on a buffet table for a maximum of one hour; any leftovers must be discarded rather than refrigerated and reused. The best way to get around this problem is to put out only small portions of buffet food in which mayonnaise has been used and keep replenishing them.

Basic Mayonnaise

This is a very light mayonnaise, made with whole eggs in the food processor or blender.

> 2 large eggs, room temperature
> ½ teaspoon salt
> 3 tablespoons white wine vinegar
> 2 teaspoons Dijon mustard
> 1½ to 2 cups vegetable oil

1. Place the eggs, salt, vinegar, and mustard in a food processor or blender and blend for 1 minute. Slowly pour in 1 cup oil, stop the machine and stir with a plastic spatula. Turn on the machine and continue to add more oil until the mayonnaise is thick. (When making this in a blender, it will probably only take 1½ cups oil to make the mayonnaise very thick. In a food processor, it will take 2 cups oil before it is quite thick.) Add more salt and freshly ground black pepper to taste.
2. The mayonnaise may be stored in the refrigerator up to 3 days.

Yield: 2 cups   Preparation: Easy
Time: Quick; advance preparation possible

Mustard Mayonnaise

This is great served with cold roast beef or as a dip for poached shrimp. The mustard may be adjusted to your taste.

2 large eggs, room temperature
½ teaspoon salt
2 to 3 tablespoons Dijon mustard
3 tablespoons white wine vinegar
1½ cups vegetable oil
½ cup sour cream (optional)

1. Place the eggs, salt, vinegar, and 2 tablespoons mustard in a food processor or blender and blend for 1 minute. Slowly pour in 1 cup oil, stop the machine, and stir with a plastic spatula. Turn on the machine and continue to add more oil until the mayonnaise is thick. (If you are using a blender, it will probably take only 1½ cups oil to make the mayonnaise very thick. In a food processor it will take 2 cups oil before it is quite thick.)
2. Place sour cream in a bowl and whisk until smooth. Carefully stir in mayonnaise, but do not overmix as the mixture could become runny. Add salt and freshly ground black pepper to taste. Taste; if you desire a stronger mustard flavor, add more mustard.
3. This may be stored in the refrigerator for up to 3 days.

Yield: 2 cups   **Preparation: Easy**
Time: Quick; advance preparation possible

Curry Mayonnaise

This mayonnaise is great served with chicken salad or with cold poached shrimp. Your curry paste must be made with a Madras curry powder or homemade curry powder to give you the best results.

2 large eggs, room temperature
½ teaspoon salt
3 tablespoons white wine vinegar
1½ cups vegetable oil
2 to 3 tablespoons Curry Paste (page 65)
½ cup sour cream

1. Place the eggs, salt, vinegar, and oil in a food processor or blender and blend for 1 minute. Slowly pour in 1 cup oil, stop the machine and stir with a plastic spatula. Turn on the blender and continue to add more oil until the mayonnaise is thick. (If you are using a blender, it will probably take only 1½ cups oil to make the mayonnaise very thick. In a food processor it will take 2 cups oil before it is quite thick.)
2. Place 2 tablespoons curry paste and sour cream in a bowl and whisk until they are well blended. Then gently stir in the mayonnaise, being careful not to overmix or the mixture might become runny. Add more curry paste, salt, and freshly ground black pepper to taste.
3. This may be stored up to 3 days in the refrigerator.

Yield: 2 cups   Preparation: Easy
Time: Quick; advance preparation possible

Lemon Mayonnaise

This tart mayonnaise, with a velvety texture, is wonderful served with fresh asparagus, seafood salads, and cold poached chicken. It is best made in the blender.

> 2 large eggs, room temperature
> ½ teaspoon salt
> ¼ cup fresh lemon juice
> 2 teaspoons finely grated lemon rind (zest)
> 1½ to 2 cups vegetable oil
> ½ cup sour cream

1. Place the eggs, salt, lemon juice, and lemon rind in a blender and blend for 1 minute. Slowly pour in 1 cup oil, stop the machine, and stir with a plastic spatula. Turn the machine on and continue to add more oil until the mixture is thick.
2. Place the sour cream in a bowl and whisk until smooth. Gently whisk in the mayonnaise, being careful not to overmix, or the mixture will lose its thick consistency. Add more salt and freshly ground black pepper to taste.
3. The mayonnaise may be stored in the refrigerator for up to 3 days.

Yield: 2 cups   **Preparation: Easy**
Time: Quick; advance preparation possible

Black Pepper Mayonnaise

The aromatic, pungent flavor of this mayonnaise comes from pepper-corns that have been freshly ground in the blender. It is delectable served with a salad of Smithfield ham, pears, and watercress.

2 large eggs, room temperature
2 teaspoons whole black peppercorns
½ teaspoon salt
2 tablespoons white wine vinegar
1½ cups vegetable oil

1. Place the black pepper in a very dry blender and blend until the pepper has a coarse ground texture. (Do not try to make this in a food pro-cessor.) Add the eggs, vinegar, and salt, and blend for 1 minute. Slowly pour in ¾ cup oil, stop the motor, and stir the mixture. Then continue to blend, slowly pouring in the oil. Add salt to taste.
2. This mayonnaise may be stored up to 3 days in the refrigerator.

Yield: 2 cups   Preparation: Easy
Time: Quick; advance preparation possible

Green Mayonnaise

This is wonderful served with cold poached salmon, shrimp, or used in a chicken salad.

> 2 large eggs, room temperature
> ½ teaspoon salt
> ¼ cup white wine basil or tarragon vinegar
> 1 tablespoon Dijon mustard
> 1½ to 2 cups corn or safflower oil
> 1 cup loosely packed, sprigged fresh dill, washed and well dried
> 1 cup loosely packed, sprigged fresh parsley, washed and well dried
> 1 cup sour cream

1. Place eggs, salt, vinegar, and mustard in the food processor and process for 1 minute. Slowly pour in 1 cup oil, stop the machine, and stir with a plastic spatula. With motor on, continue to add more oil until the mixture is thick.
2. Add dill and parsley and process until herbs are very finely chopped.
3. Place sour cream in a bowl and beat until smooth. Carefully fold in the mayonnaise, making sure not to overmix, as the mixture will become runny. Add salt and freshly ground black pepper.
4. This mayonnaise will keep for 3 days in the refrigerator.

Yield: 3 cups   Preparation: Easy
Time: Quick; advance preparation possible

Pesto Mayonnaise

This is the perfect companion for steamed, broiled, or cold poached fish. It also may be combined with poached chicken to make a chicken salad; serve it with vine-ripened tomatoes and cucumbers.

2 large eggs, room temperature
½ teaspoon salt
3 tablespoons white wine vinegar
2 large or 4 small garlic cloves
1½ to 2 cups vegetable oil
½ cup loosely packed fresh basil leaves
½ cup loosely packed fresh parsley leaves
¼ cup freshly grated Parmesan

1. Make sure the herbs are dried well after being washed.
2. Place the eggs, salt, vinegar, and garlic in a food processor. Process for 1 minute. Slowly pour in 1 cup oil, stop the machine, and stir with a plastic spatula. Turn on the processor and continue to add more oil until the mixture is thick.
3. Add the basil and parsley and process until the herbs are chopped quite fine.
4. Pour the mayonnaise into a bowl and whisk in the Parmesan. Add salt and freshly ground black pepper to taste.
5. This may be stored up to 3 days in the refrigerator.

Yield: 2½ cups   **Preparation: Easy**
Time: Quick; advance preparation possible

Vermouth Mayonnaise

This mayonnaise does not have a very thick consistency. The flavor works well with chicken salad or cold roast veal.

2 large eggs, room temperature
4 tablespoons dry Vermouth
2 tablespoons white wine basil or tarragon vinegar
1 teaspoon salt
2 teaspoons grated orange rind (zest)
1 to 1½ cups vegetable oil

1. Place Vermouth, vinegar, eggs, salt, and orange rind in a blender, and blend for 1 minute. Slowly pour in 1 cup of oil, stop the machine, and stir with a plastic spatula. Turn on the blender and continue to add more oil until the mixture is thick. Add salt and freshly ground black pepper to taste.
2. This mayonnaise may be stored in the refrigerator for up to 3 days.

Yield: 1½ cups   **Preparation: Easy**
Time: Quick; advance preparation possible

Aïoli

This Aïoli is definitely for garlic lovers. Adjust the amount of garlic you add to this mayonnaise to suit your taste. It is great served with poached fish.

> *2 large eggs, room temperature*
> *½ teaspoon salt*
> *2 tablespoons white wine vinegar*
> *2 large or 4 small garlic cloves*
> *1½ to 2 cups vegetable oil*

1. Place the eggs, salt, vinegar, and garlic in a food processor or blender and blend for 1 minute. Slowly pour in 1 cup oil, stop the machine and stir with a plastic spatula. With the motor on, continue to add more oil until the mixture is thick. (When you are using a blender, it will probably only take 1½ cups oil to make the mayonnaise very thick. In a food processor it will take 2 cups oil before it is quite thick.) Add salt and freshly ground black pepper to taste.
2. Aïoli may be stored in the refrigerator up to 3 days.

Yield: 2 cups   Preparation: Easy
Time: Quick; advance preparation possible

Tomato Aïoli

This is an adaptation of the classic Spanish Aïoli. It is a very thick mayonnaise that goes well with broiled fish. It is important to use vine-ripened tomatoes.

> 3 egg yolks
> 2 vine-ripened tomatoes, peeled, seeded, and coarsely chopped
> 1 to 1½ cups light olive oil
> 2 tablespoons white wine vinegar
> ½ cup fresh, fine, white bread crumbs
> 2 medium or 3 small garlic cloves
> ½ teaspoon salt

1. Heat 4 tablespoons oil in a 10-inch stainless steel saute pan. Add the tomatoes and cook over high heat until well reduced and thick, stirring occasionally and scraping down the sides of the pan with a plastic spatula to keep the mixture from scorching. Cool.
2. Place the cooked tomatoes, vinegar, egg yolks, bread crumbs, garlic, and salt in the food processor and process for 1 minute. Slowly pour in ¾ cup oil. If it is very thick add 2 tablespoons water, then continue to add the rest of the oil. Add more salt and freshly ground black pepper to taste.
3. This may be stored in the refrigerator up to 3 days.

Yield: 2 cups   Preparation: Easy
Time: Quick; advance preparation possible

Compound Butters

A slice of compound butter placed on broiled meats or fish will add a delicious flavor to the food. Although compound butters are often overlooked, they add diversity and complexity to sauces, soups, and papillotes. If well organized, you can make compound butters in quantity and freeze them in small portions, such as 2-ounce packages. This is a great way to facilitate a quick but elegant last-minute dinner.

Green Butter

Although there is a lot of work involved in the preparation of Green Butter, you can make a large amount in the summer when parsley and dill are plentiful and freeze it in 2- to 4-ounce packages for use during the winter. It is a wonderful combination of herbs and is very good in Sole Papillote (page 259), or on broiled or grilled fish such as bluefish.

> *½ pound unsalted butter, very soft, but not melted*
> *5 scallions*
> *½ cup cooked, well-squeezed spinach*
> *½ cup loosely packed fresh parsley leaves*
> *⅓ cup loosely packed fresh dill leaves*
> *2 teaspoons finely grated lemon rind (zest)*

1. Remove and discard the coarse outside layer of the scallions. Slice the scallions into ¼-inch pieces halfway up the green part. Heat 4 tablespoons butter in a 10-inch saute pan. Add the scallions and toss over high heat for 2 to 3 minutes until just cooked. Cool.
2. Place the spinach, parsley, and dill in the food processor and process until the herbs are a medium chop, about 15 seconds.
3. Add the remaining butter and lemon zest and process for 15 seconds. Scrape down the sides and add the scallions and process for 30 seconds. Be careful to not overprocess, or the herbs will be overpureed.

4. Add salt and freshly ground black pepper to taste.
5. This may be refrigerated up to 4 days or frozen.

Yield: 1½ cups   Preparation: Easy
Time: Fairly time consuming; may be frozen

Celeste Butter

Celeste Butter is an ideal addition to poached salmon. It is equally delicious cooked en papillote with bluefish (see page 231). It is easy to prepare and can be made in batches and frozen in 2-ounce packages.

10 tablespoons unsalted butter, very soft but not melted
5 large or 10 small shallots, finely sliced
2 tablespoons white wine vinegar
1 tablespoon grated orange rind (zest)
3 tablespoons fresh tarragon leaves (or 1 tablespoon dried tarragon)

1. Heat 3 tablespoons butter in a 10-inch stainless steel saute pan. Add the shallots and saute on high heat until clear, being careful not to brown. Add the vinegar, orange rind and dried tarragon, if you are using it. Reduce on high heat until almost all the liquid has evaporated. Cool.
2. Beat the remaining butter until it is smooth, then beat in the shallot mixture. Add fresh tarragon at this time, if you are using it. Add salt and freshly ground black pepper to taste.
3. This may be refrigerated up to 4 days or frozen.

Yield: 1 cup   Preparation: Easy
Time: Quick; may be frozen

Jaffrey Butter

Be careful to stick to my measurement for turmeric, as this bright orange spice can overcome all other flavors if it is used too enthusiastically. It works most effectively in this butter, though, and wonderfully enhances the flavor of poached shrimp. (I use this butter in my Shrimp Jaffrey, page 252.) The 1 teaspoon of hot pepper will make a spicy butter; use ½ teaspoon if you prefer a medium spicy flavor.

12 tablespoons unsalted butter, very soft but not melted
½ to 1 teaspoon dried crushed red hot pepper
2 large or 4 medium garlic cloves
2 tablespoons peeled, coarsely grated fresh ginger
1½ teaspoons turmeric
1 cup loosely packed fresh coriander leaves

1. Process the hot pepper and garlic in a food processor until the garlic is finely chopped.
2. Scrape down the sides and add the butter, ginger, and turmeric. Process for 1 minute. Scrape down the sides. Add the coriander and process to a medium-fine chop. Add salt and pepper to taste.
3. Refrigerate up to 4 days or freeze.

Yield: 1½ cups   **Preparation: Easy**
Time: Quick; may be frozen

Ginger Garlic Butter

The strong, fresh, and delicious flavor of this compound butter makes it the perfect addition to shrimp or scallops or steamed carrots. It is simple to prepare and can be frozen in 2-ounce packages.

10 tablespoons unsalted butter, very soft but not melted
2 large or 4 small garlic cloves
2 tablespoons peeled, medium-grated fresh ginger

1. Process the garlic in a food processor until a fine chop. Add the ginger and butter and process for 1 minute. Add salt and freshly ground pepper to taste. Refrigerate up to 5 days or freeze.

Yield: ¾ cup   Preparation: Easy
Time: Quick; may be frozen

Saffron Butter

Even though saffron is expensive, you need only a small amount of it to get its full flavor in this lovely butter. I use Saffron Butter in my Sole Cala Llonga (see page 260) and also recommend it on poached or grilled sole, haddock, cod, or striped bass. You can make this butter in the summer when basil and parsley are easily obtainable and freeze it in 2-ounce packages.

12 tablespoons unsalted butter, very soft, but not melted
½ cup loosely packed fresh basil leaves
½ cup loosely packed fresh parsley leaves
2 medium garlic cloves
1 teaspoon saffron

1. Make sure you have thoroughly dried the herbs after washing them.
2. Place the garlic in the food processor and process for 30 seconds to a fine chop. Add the butter and process for 1 minute. Add the basil, parsley, and saffron and process for 30 seconds. Scrape down the sides and continue to process until the herbs are a medium to fine chop. Add salt and freshly ground pepper to taste.
3. Refrigerate up to 4 days or freeze.

Yield: ¾ to 1 cup   Preparation: Easy
Time: Quick; may be frozen

Garlic Butter

This garlicky compound butter is sure to delight garlic lovers. I use it in a variety of recipes, such as in the sauce for Parmesan Crêpes stuffed with Mushrooms (see page 390). It also is delicious when used for braising vegetables.

3 large garlic cloves
12 tablespoons unsalted butter, soft but not melted

1. Process the garlic in a food processor until it is a fine chop. Add the butter and process until smooth. Add salt and freshly ground pepper to taste.
2. Refrigerate up to 5 days or freeze.

Yield: ¾ cup   **Preparation: Easy**
Time: Quick; may be frozen

Marinades

Marinades were probably first used to extend the "edible" life of meats and fish, so they had a medium to high acid base, such as Ceviche. Later, marinades were used to tenderize meats and to impart additional flavors to some cuts of meat. The recipes I was introduced to twenty-four years ago were medium to high in acid and incorporated many aromatic herbs and spices to enhance the food.

So why are most of my marinade recipes made with an oil base rather than an acid base? I vividly remember reading a recipe that sounded like a wonderful treatment for venison. I put the recipe aside, ready to use it when venison was obtainable. Months later a friend of mine went on a shoot in Scotland and arrived back in London with a venison roast. He called me and asked what he should do with it. Excited, I recalled the recipe I had seen and offered to cook the venison. Since the recipe called for a four- to five-day marination period, a dinner party was planned. I carefully followed all the marinating instructions and five days later cooked the roast for our elegant dinner party. Everything went well except the venison; it was dry, shrunken, and not too appetizing. Years later, I realized my mistake: Meats, when subjected to a high acid marinade and then cooked, tend to toughen and become dry due to a change in the composition of protein caused by the acid in the marinade.

Now I use oil-based marinades for game, poultry, and meats. Although a little more expensive, since good oils are expensive, the end result is much more satisfying and successful. I find that oil gives a moist texture to the food and enhances the aromatic quality of the herbs in the marinade and is especially suitable for broiled, grilled, or barbecued foods. The marinade may also be used to baste the food while cooking.

Black Pepper Marinade

The key to the beautiful scent of this marinade lies in the freshly crushed black pepper. I use 2 teaspoons of peppercorns for a medium spicy taste; you may adjust the degree of pepperiness to suit your taste. Use this marinade to marinate chicken, lamb, beef, bluefish, or mackerel at least 4 hours before broiling.

2 teaspoons whole black peppercorns
1 cup vegetable or olive oil
½ cup loosely packed fresh Italian or curly parsley leaves
1 cup finely sliced onion

1. Place the pepper in a very dry blender and blend until it is coarsely ground. Add the oil and parsley and blend until the parsley is medium-chopped. Pour in a bowl and add the onion.
2. This marinade will keep for 2 days in the refrigerator.

Yield: ¾ cup   **Preparation: Easy**
Time: Quick; advance preparation possible

Fennel Marinade

Fennel has a flavor that is reminiscent of anise, which merges beautifully with the strong flavor of game. (You may use ¼ cup loosely packed fresh rosemary sprigs, coarsely chopped, instead of the fennel.) This marinade is especially suitable for pheasant or squab. Marinate the meat for 12 hours before broiling or roasting.

1 tablespoon dry fennel seeds
1 teaspoon whole black peppercorns
1 large or 2 medium garlic cloves
1 cup vegetable oil

1. Place the fennel and black peppercorns in a very dry blender and blend until the pepper has been coarsely ground. Add the garlic and oil and blend until the garlic is pureed.
2. This marinade will keep up to 4 days in the refrigerator.

Yield: 1 cup   **Preparation: Easy**
Time: Quick; advance preparation possible

Herb Marinade

The rosemary in this marinade lends a wonderful pungency. Enhance the flavor of swordfish or bluefish by marinating for one hour before cooking, or place poached shrimp in the marinade while they are still warm.

> 2 large or 4 medium garlic cloves
> ¾ cup olive oil
> 2 tablespoons fresh rosemary leaves
> ½ cup loosely packed fresh Italian or curly parsley leaves
> ¼ cup fresh lemon juice

1. Place the garlic in the blender and blend for 30 seconds. Add the oil, rosemary, and parsley and blend to a medium-chopped consistency.
2. Pour the mixture into a bowl and whisk in the lemon juice. Add salt and freshly ground black pepper to taste.
3. This will keep about 2 to 3 hours in the refrigerator. Do not keep it longer, as the lemon juice will make the herbs turn a brownish color. (If you want to keep it longer, or even freeze it, add the lemon juice just before using.)

Yield: 1¼ cups   **Preparation: Easy**
Time: Quick; advance preparation possible

Tandoori Marinade

Raj and Marjorie Bery not only introduced this wonderful marinade to me, but also taught me how to balance the spices perfectly, making this marinade very special. It is great used for bluefish, mackerel, and chicken, and I have also had great success using it as a salad dressing.

¼ cup cumin seeds
2 medium garlic cloves, sliced
¼ cup vegetable oil
1 tablespoon peeled and finely grated fresh ginger
1 teaspoon salt
¼ cup paprika
⅓ cup fresh lime or lemon juice
1 pint plain yogurt
Tabasco

1. Blend the cumin seeds in a very dry blender until a fine powder. Add the garlic and oil and blend until the garlic is smooth. Add the ginger, salt, paprika, and lime juice and blend for 30 seconds.
2. Pour into a bowl and whisk in the yogurt slowly until the whole mixture is well emulsified. Add the Tabasco to taste.
3. This marinade will keep for 3 days in the refrigerator.

Yield: 3 cups   Preparation: Easy
Time: Quick; advance preparation possible

Kashmir Marinade

This marinade is somewhat extravagant because of the saffron, but it has a beautiful, clean flavor and gives the food a brilliant color. It is excellent for bluefish, swordfish, and chicken, all of which should be marinated for one hour before cooking.

2 teaspoons saffron
1 cup finely sliced onion
¼ cup fresh lemon juice
1 teaspoon finely grated orange rind (zest)
¼ cup orange juice
¾ cup vegetable oil

1. Mix all ingredients together. Add salt and freshly ground black pepper to taste.
2. This marinade will keep for 24 hours in the refrigerator.

Yield: 1½ cups   Preparation: Easy
Time: Quick; advance preparation possible

Miscellaneous

Here are several recipes that can be made ahead of time and used in your general everyday cooking. I feel that they will add something special to your cooking.

White Wine Basil or Tarragon Vinegar

I personally find store-bought distilled, cider, and malt vinegars far too strong in acid, often taking away from the other flavors in a dish, not to mention ruining the wonderful taste of wines that accompany a meal. Here is a very simple vinegar, which has a lovely and mild flavor. I urge you to try making it to see how wonderful vinegar can taste. You will need six empty wine bottles. They do not need to be washed out, but should be free of mildew and not older than two weeks. Making six bottles at a time will take care of your needs for a couple of years. This recipe is simple, because it does not involve floating a "mother" (a slightly cloudy jellylike substance) in the white wine. This substance feeds on the alcohol and creates the acid in vinegar. The "mother" is not always successful, nor is it used in my recipe. I feel you will find a much more delicious, mild-flavored vinegar by omitting that step.

> *6 empty wine bottles with corks*
> *6 small bunches of basil or tarragon*
> *18 to 20 cups white wine distilled vinegar*
> *4½ cups inexpensive dry white wine*

1. If the herbs are dirty, wash and dry them well. Leave the stalks on.
2. With a chopstick, push 1 bunch of herbs into each bottle. Pour 3 cups of white distilled vinegar into each bottle. Then pour ¾ cup dry white wine into each bottle.
3. Cork each bottle and store in a cool place (a basement) for 1 month.
4. After 1 month, uncork each bottle and fill to the top with distilled vinegar and recork. Let rest in a cool place for at least 2 months or up to 24 months.

Yield: 6 bottles   Preparation: Easy
Time: Time consuming; advance preparation necessary

Clarified Butter

Clarified butter is butter with the milk solids (proteins) removed. The method I use for clarifying butter is a combination of two techniques: the French method and the Indian method for making ghee. This works very well; however, you must watch carefully during the process to make sure the butter does not burn. Clarified butter is used to sear foods. The process of removing the milk solids from butter increases the burning point; whole butter will burn at 250 degrees, while clarified butter can be heated up to 325 degrees without burning. In addition, the removal of the milk solids prevents the butter from turning rancid. In India, ghee is stored for months at room temperature without going rancid. I suggest making a 1-pound batch at a time, which can be stored in a sealed container in the refrigerator for at least 2 months.

1 pound unsalted butter, room temperature
1 cotton cloth

1. Place the butter in a heavy 2-quart saucepan and melt on low heat. Once it is melted, bring to a boil and boil on medium heat until the white foam (milk solids) that form on the top start to drop to the bottom of the pan.
2. Continue to boil until the residue on the bottom of the pan starts to turn a *very light* golden brown. Remove from the heat.
3. Place the cloth in a sieve, place the sieve over a bowl, and slowly pour the butter through it. Cool until warm.
4. Pour the butter into a container with a tightly fitting lid. Cool, then cover and refrigerate.

Yield: 1¾ cups   Preparation: Easy
Time: Fairly time consuming; advance preparation necessary

Garlic Paste

For garlic lovers, this recipe gives you a very soft-flavored paste that can be made ahead of time and refrigerated or frozen. A couple of tablespoons added to a sauce is a wonderful addition in many recipes. Try it, for example, whisked into some stock to make a sauce for roast chicken, or heat a little and pour on broiled mackerel or bluefish. The paste also can be made with olive oil instead of butter.

5 small or 4 medium whole garlic buds
10 tablespoons unsalted butter, soft

1. Break up each bud of garlic, but leave the skins on the cloves. Place all the garlic cloves in a 1-quart saucepan, cover with cold water, bring to a boil, and gently boil for 10 minutes.
2. Drain and run the garlic cloves under cold water until they are just warm. Peel the garlic and cut off the root end. Place the garlic and butter in a food processor and process until smooth, approximately 3 minutes.
3. This may be stored up to 5 days in the refrigerator or frozen in small batches.

Yield: Approximately 1 cup   Preparation: Easy
Time: Quick; may be frozen

Curry Powder

This unusual recipe combines the classic Indian method for making curry powder with a store-bought curry powder to produce a wonderful balance of spices. It is much better and much less acrid than any curry powder you can buy. By "burning" the spices you dispel the acrid quality of the curry powder, giving it a much smoother flavor. Be forewarned, however, that during the burning process a very strong odor is given off; do this step in a kitchen with good ventilation.

> ½ cup cumin seeds
> ½ cup coriander seeds
> 1 tablespoon fennel seeds
> 2 teaspoons whole black peppercorns
> 2 bay leaves
> 1 tablespoon peeled cardamom seeds
> ½ cup store-bought Madras curry powder

1. Place everything except the curry powder in a very dry blender and blend until the seeds are very fine. Pour into a medium sieve and press through. Any large bits left should be put back in the blender and blended until smooth. Mix this curry powder with the Madras curry powder.
2. Heat a 10- to 12-inch heavy saute pan. Add the curry powder and stir constantly to let the curry powder "burn" deeper in color. It is done when it is a medium-brown color. Pour into a bowl and cool.
3. Store in a jar with a tight cover. This will keep up to 12 months as long as the jar remains tightly sealed.

Yield: 1½ cups   Preparation: Easy
Time: Quick; advance preparation possible

Curry Paste

Curry Paste is used when you want to add a curry flavor to uncooked foods, such as mayonnaise or salads. Because it is cooked, it has a softer (not milder) and less acrid flavor than curry powder would have; curry powder is suitable for use in cooked dishes.

> *½ cup homemade curry powder (page 64) or ½ cup Madras*
> *curry powder*
> *½ cup vegetable oil*
> *2 small or 1 large onions, sliced*

1. Heat the oil in a heavy 10- to 12-inch saute pan. Add the onion and saute until clear, being careful not to brown. Stir in the curry powder, cover, and gently cook on a low heat for 10 minutes, stirring occasionally. Puree the mixture in the food processor or blender until very smooth.
2. Curry paste can be stored in the refrigerator for 5 days or it can be frozen.

Yield: ¾ to 1 cup   **Preparation: Easy**
Time: Quick; advance preparation necessary

Hors D'Oeuvres

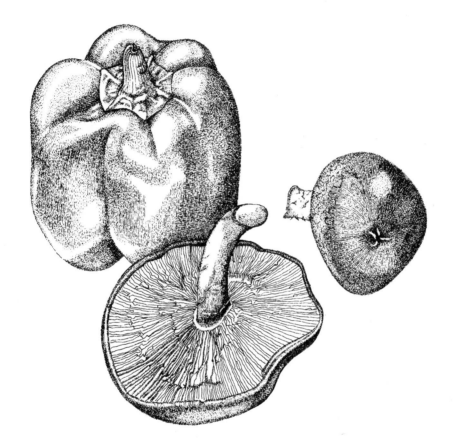

& Appetizers

Hors D'Oeuvres

Hors d'oeuvres are intended to stimulate the palate, not to satisfy the appetite. You will want to provide an interesting variety if you are giving a cocktail party, but if it's drinks before dinner, your aim is to excite your guests rather than sate them.

I am always unhappy when I am presented with a glorious array of cheeses with drinks before a dinner party, as I adore cheese and could easily make a meal out of it. Cheese, while convenient to serve, is just about the richest of foods; if it is to be served as an hors d'oeuvre, it should be selected with care from the lower-fat varieties and served with vegetables like cucumber slices, Belgian endive, and cherry tomatoes. The same rule of thumb applies to pâté when served as a predinner hors d'oeuvre.

When I was at the Cordon Bleu, and later, cooking in South Africa, I enjoyed whipping up complicated little canapes, puffs and vol-au-vents, all with savory fillings. I have not given you those recipes, because quite frankly, they require a lot of work and are better suited to those who have lots of time to cook. Since few of us can afford luxury, what we really need is a recipe that can be prepared ahead of time. The following hors d'oeuvres fit that bill. I am partial to my recipes for Tortes, which are ideal if you are giving a large cocktail party, as ten filled crêpes will yield about 100 canapes. They are tremendously versatile, as the fillings can be complemented by varying the ingredients of the crepe batter with the addition of parsley, thyme, or spinach. You will be delighted with the display you can make with a platter of three varieties of tortes, such as salmon, spinach, and black caviar.

I am partial, also, to crudités, in spite of the weary response I often get from customers when I suggest them for a cocktail party. I feel that the fresh, light taste of crudités is classic, and it takes only a little creativity to keep their appeal alive. With the fabulous variety of vegetables available today, there is never any excuse to be boring. Serve yams, sweet potatoes, turnips, parsnips, Chinese radishes, and Jerusalem artichokes. If you are using crisp, hard vegetables, such as green beans, broccoli, yams, carrots, or parsnips, you will greatly improve them with a very light blanching. They can be served with a dip such as my Pesto, Variation 2 (see page 27).

One of the hazards of serving hors d'oeuvres is the difficulty in keeping them fresh. To ensure that hors d'oeuvres and buffet foods always look appetizing, keep replenishing small servings throughout the party, rather than leaving stationary amounts to get crusted or droopy. There are few sights sorrier than a half-demolished pâté languishing on a messy platter. Be aware that the garnishes you use to decorate your hors d'oeuvres will be sitting around for an hour or two; you should choose them for durability as well as beauty. Watercress is one of my favorite greens, but it goes limp and looks awful after 30 minutes. Endive, fresh fennel greens, Italian parsley, raw sliced mushrooms, and fresh thyme sprigs will hold up for a long time. If you have an herb garden, you can add a truly special touch with flowering herbs, such as basil, thyme, and sage.

It is very hard to resist the wonderful taste combinations of hors d'oeuvres. I think you will find that the recipes in this chapter make them almost as much fun to make as to eat.

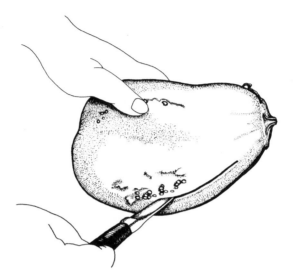

1. Score an eggplant half by running a small, sharp prep knife all around the edge.

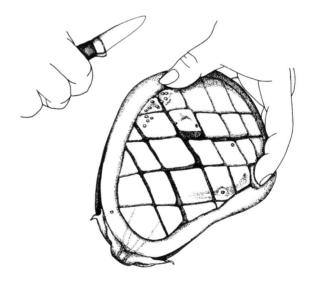

2. Make crisscross cuts through the flesh, being careful not to puncture skin.

Eggplant Caviar

Try Eggplant Caviar as a spread on either pumpernickel bread rounds or crackers. It also may be served as a chilled vegetable side dish to grilled lamb, serving 6 to 8 diners.

2 large eggplants, peeled
½ cup olive oil
2 garlic cloves, crushed
6 vine-ripened tomatoes, peeled and seeded
2 tablespoons tomato paste
⅓ cup loosely packed fresh parsley sprigs, finely chopped
1 tablespoon finely chopped onion
⅓ cup fresh lemon juice, or to taste

1. Dice eggplant into ½-inch pieces. Layer in a stainless steel colander, lightly sprinkling salt between each layer. Leave for 2 hours. Rinse well, then squeeze dry.
2. Heat the oil in a 12-inch stainless steal saute pan, add the eggplant, and cover. Gently saute until very soft, approximately 30 minutes, stirring occasionally. Add garlic and continue to cook an additional 3 minutes. Cool.
3. Meanwhile, finely dice the tomatoes. Mix with tomato paste, parsley, onion, and lemon juice to taste.
4. Once eggplant has cooled, mix with tomato mixture. Add salt and freshly ground black pepper to taste.
5. Refrigerate no longer than 2 days before serving.

Yield: 3 to 4 cups   Preparation: Easy
Time: Time consuming; advance preparation possible

Paillards of Beef Provençal

Pound the meat well to ensure a paper-thin thickness that makes this an easy and delicious hors d'oeuvre.

1 pound tenderloin of beef (or tips)
3 ounces chèvre cheese
⅓ cup olive oil
⅓ cup fresh lemon juice
⅓ cup loosely packed fresh mint leaves, finely chopped
fresh mint or basil leaves for garnish

1. Place the beef in the freezer for 30 minutes to make it easier to slice. Then very thinly slice the tenderloin. Gently pound until thin. Cut each slice in half.
2. Place one teaspoon of chèvre on each beef slice. Roll up each slice and place a layer of rolls, seam side down, in a glass or china dish.
3. Whisk together oil, lemon juice, and chopped mint in a bowl. Add salt and freshly ground black pepper to taste. Pour a little of the marinade over the layer of rolled beef slices, then lay another layer of meat on top, and pour on more marinade. Repeat procedure until all the marinade and meat are used up.
4. Leave to marinate in the refrigerator at least 10 hours, or up to 24 hours, before serving.
5. Before serving, remove the rolls from the marinade. Toothpick rolls and place on a serving platter. Garnish with mint or basil leaves.

Yield: 8 to 10   Preparation: Easy
Time: Fairly time consuming; advance preparation necessary

Mushrooms Stuffed
with Feta and Walnuts

The pungent taste of feta cheese, the wonderful Greek goat cheese, articulates this zesty hors d'oeuvre.

1½ pounds large mushrooms, cleaned
2 cups mushroom poaching liquid (page 171)
4 ounces feta cheese, crumbled
½ cup freshly shelled walnuts, finely chopped
⅓ cup loosely packed fresh basil or mint leaves, finely chopped
2 tablespoons olive oil
fresh basil or mint leaves for garnish

1. Remove and discard the stalks from the mushrooms. Bring mushroom poaching liquid to a boil in a 2-quart saucepan. Add mushroom caps and gently simmer for 5 to 7 minutes until cooked through. To test for doneness, remove 1 mushroom with a slotted spoon and cut it in half to check that the center is cooked. Be careful not to overcook or the mushrooms will shrink. Drain well. (Freeze the liquid for future use.)
2. Combine feta, walnuts, basil or mint, and olive oil in a bowl. Add salt and freshly ground black pepper to taste.
3. Stuff mushroom caps with mixture, leaving the stuffing level, not heaped.
4. The mushrooms may be prepared up to 6 hours ahead of serving.
5. For serving mushrooms at room temperature, arrange on a platter and sprinkle with a little olive oil. To serve them warm, preheat oven to 350 degrees. Place mushrooms on a sheet pan and bake for 7 minutes.
6. Garnish with mint or basil leaves.

Yield: Approximately 30 mushrooms   Preparation: Easy
Time: Fairly time consuming; advance preparation possible

Stuffed Mushrooms Verde

The combination of spinach and mint gives a very intense flavor to these delicious stuffed mushrooms.

24 large mushrooms
2 leeks (or ½ cup sliced shallots)
8 tablespoons unsalted butter
1 10-ounce package fresh spinach
2 tablespoons coarsely chopped fresh mint
6 ounces mild chèvre, crumbled (optional)

1. Remove and discard the coarse outside layer from leeks. Slice up to the medium-green part and place slices in cold water for 30 minutes. Drain, rinse, drain well and pat dry.
2. Clean the mushrooms. Remove and finely dice the stalks. Melt 3 tablespoons butter and brush mushroom caps inside and out with the butter.
3. Wash spinach. Remove and discard stalks. Bring 2 inches of water to a boil in a 3-quart saucepan, add the spinach, and cook for 40 seconds. Drain and run under cold water. Squeeze liquid from spinach until very dry. Finely chop by hand or in a food processor.
4. Heat 2 tablespoons butter in a large saute pan. Add leeks (or shallots), and toss over high heat until they are cooked but not brown and liquid has evaporated. Place in a bowl and add spinach and mint.
5. Heat the remaining 3 tablespoons butter in the pan used for the leeks. Add diced mushroom stalks and saute until all liquid has evaporated; do not allow mushrooms to brown. Cool them a little and add to spinach mixture. Add salt and freshly ground black pepper to taste.
6. Stuff spinach mixture into mushroom caps until level. Cover each mushroom cap with the chèvre. Put the mushrooms on a buttered heavy baking sheet.
7. The mushrooms may be refrigerated up to 24 hours, if you wish.
8. Just before serving, preheat oven to 375 degrees. Bake mushrooms for 10 to 15 minutes, until just cooked. Be careful not to overcook, as liquid will start to come out of the mushrooms, making them difficult to serve.

Yield: 24 mushrooms   Preparation: Easy
Time: Fairly time consuming; advance preparation possible

Stuffed Mushrooms with Bacon

Clark Rothhauser inspired this innovative combination of bacon and Aïoli.

1½ pounds large mushrooms, cleaned
2 cups mushroom poaching liquid (page 171)
1 tablespoon vegetable oil
4 slices of lean bacon (preferably not sugar-cured)
5 large or 10 small shallots, thinly sliced
1 cup loosely packed fresh parsley leaves, finely chopped
1 cup Aïoli (page 47)

1. Remove stalks from mushrooms and set aside. Bring poaching liquid to a boil in a 2-quart saucepan. Add mushroom caps and gently simmer for 5 to 7 minutes until cooked through. To test for doneness, remove 1 mushroom with a slotted spoon and cut in half to check that the center is cooked. Be careful not to overcook or they will shrink. Remove with a slotted spoon and drain well. Next poach mushroom stalks until done; remove with slotted spoon. Leave both to drain for 30 minutes. (The poaching liquid may be frozen for a future use.)
2. Heat oil in a saute pan, add bacon, and fry until golden brown. Remove from pan. Place the shallots in the same pan and saute until cooked; do not brown. Remove with a slotted spoon. Discard the bacon fat.
3. Place the shallots, mushroom stalks, and bacon in a food processor and puree until bacon is in approximately ⅛-inch fine bits. Put this mixture in a bowl. Add the parsley and salt and freshly ground black pepper to taste.
4. Stuff mixture into mushroom caps until level. Arrange on a serving platter. Chill at least 1 hour, or up to 24 hours, before serving.
5. Before serving, spoon a little of the aïoli onto each mushroom cap.

Yield: Approximately 30 mushrooms   **Preparation: Easy**
Time: Fairly time consuming; advance preparation necessary

Cheese Rounds

These rich cheese biscuits are great served hot or at room temperature. They can also be split and served as you would serve bread rounds or crackers as canapes.

> *1 cup finely grated cheddar cheese*
> *¾ cup freshly grated Parmesan cheese*
> *2 cups all-purpose unbleached flour*
> *8 tablespoons unsalted butter*
> *2 teaspoons baking powder*
> *½ teaspoon baking soda*
> *¼ teaspoon salt*
> *2 teaspoons fresh lemon juice*
> *¾ to 1 cup cold milk*

1. Place the flour in a bowl, cut the butter into small pieces, and add to the flour with baking powder, baking soda, and salt. Rub the butter into the dry ingredients until the mixture has the consistency of fine cake crumbs.
2. Very lightly mix both cheeses into the flour until well combined.
3. Add the lemon juice to the cup of milk and let stand for 3 minutes, until the milk begins to curdle. (You may not need to use all the milk.)
4. Mix ¾ cup of the sour milk into the flour mixture. Work the dough lightly with your hands, being careful not to overmix. Add more milk as necessary. The consistency of the dough should be soft, but not wet.
5. Lightly flour a marble slab or a Formica counter top. Roll out the dough ¼-inch thick. As you are rolling it out, pick up the dough and lightly reflour the surface two times. Keep the rolling pin clean by lightly flouring it 2 or 3 times.
6. Cut out the cheese rounds with a 1½- to 1¾-inch cookie cutter and place on buttered heavy cookie sheets.
7. These can be made up to this point and stored 3 hours in the refrigerator before cooking.
8. Preheat oven to 400 degrees. Bake cheese rounds for 10 to 15 minutes until golden brown and puffed.

Yield: 40 to 50 rounds   Preparation: Easy
Time: Fairly quick; advance preparation possible

Tortes

It was in Milan, Italy, that I first had tortes—thin crepes spread with exciting cream cheese mixtures that are then rolled up and sliced. When first looking at these recipes, you might find them time consuming; however, making tortes is an ideal way to make an enticing variety of canapes to serve a large number of guests. They may be prepared the day before serving and refrigerated.

In this book I have included only five torte fillings, but you can create so many more—for example, caviar, smoked salmon, black olives mixed with walnuts and herbs, all with a cream cheese base.

Although I realize that availability is limited, I suggest using a low-salt, low-gum cream cheese or farmer cheese, which are often available at some health food stores and specialty cheese shops.

2 large eggs
¾ cup cold water
¾ cup all-purpose unbleached flour
1 cup sprigged fresh parsley
unsalted butter

1. Place the eggs and water in a blender with a pinch of salt and blend for 30 seconds. Add flour, blending about 1 to 2 minutes, until smooth. Add parsley and blend until fairly smooth. Pour into a bowl, adding salt and freshly ground black pepper to taste. Cover and leave in the refrigerator at least 30 minutes, or up to 8 hours, before making crêpes.
2. To make crêpes, heat 2 teaspoons butter (1 teaspoon if using a Teflon pan) in a 10-inch sloping-sided iron pan, a heavy Teflon pan, or a heavy stainless steel-lined aluminum pan. When the butter bubbles, pour in just under ¼ cup batter. Roll the pan so its whole bottom surface is covered. Cook on medium heat until the bottom of the crêpe is a very light brown. Flip or turn it over with a round-ended metal spatula. Cook until the other side is a very light brown. Remove from the pan. The crêpe should be thin; don't be alarmed if the first crêpe does not work and sticks a little. (It can be discarded.) If the crêpe batter is too thick, add a little cold water to the batter before starting the next crêpe. Continue to make crêpes, lightly buttering the pan before making each crêpe. Stack crêpes on top of each other; cool. Cover when cool.

3. To fill, spread filling (see recipes) ¼-inch thick over the whole, cooled crêpe. Roll and rest with seam side down, then refrigerate for at least 3 hours, or up to 24 hours, covered with plastic wrap.
4. To serve, slice tortes ½-inch thick with a very sharp knife and arrange on a serving platter.

Yield: 6 to 8 crêpes   Preparation: Fairly difficult
Time: Fairly time consuming; advance preparation necessary

Chicken Tarragon Torte Filling

2 cups finely diced, cooked chicken
¼ cup loosely packed fresh tarragon leaves, finely chopped
8 ounces cream cheese, room temperature
sour cream

1. Combine chicken, tarragon, and cream cheese. The mixture will be fairly stiff; if it is very stiff add a little sour cream to soften. Add salt and freshly ground black pepper to taste. This makes enough filling for 4 to 5 tortes.

Shrimp and Cream Cheese Torte Filling

8 ounces peeled, cooked shrimp, finely diced
8 ounces cream cheese, room temperature
⅓ cup finely snipped chives
⅓ cup loosely packed fresh parsley sprigs, finely chopped
sour cream

1. Combine shrimp, cream cheese, chives, and parsley. If the mixture is very thick, add a little sour cream to soften. Add salt and freshly ground black pepper to taste. This makes enough filling for 4 to 5 tortes.

Salmon and Cream Cheese
Torte Filling

1 pound poached fresh salmon
8 ounces cream cheese, room temperature
⅓ cup chives, finely snipped
⅓ cup loosely packed fresh dill or parsley sprigs, finely chopped
sour cream

1. Remove any skin and bones from the salmon. Flake the salmon. Combine with cream cheese, chives, and dill or parsley. If the mixture is very stiff, add a little sour cream to soften. Add salt and freshly ground black pepper to taste. This makes enough filling for 3 to 4 tortes.

Prosciutto and Mushroom Torte Filling

¾ cup diced poached mushrooms (page 171), squeezed dry
4 thin slices prosciutto
8 ounces cream cheese, room temperature
¼ cup loosely packed fresh basil leaves, chopped

1. Combine cream cheese, mushrooms, basil, and salt and freshly ground black pepper to taste. Lay a slice of prosciutto on each crêpe, spread with the mushroom mixture, and roll up. This makes enough filling for 3 to 4 tortes.

Spinach, Mint, and Cream Cheese Torte Filling

½ cup cooked, drained, chopped, and well-squeezed fresh spinach
⅓ cup loosely packed fresh mint leaves, coarsely chopped
8 ounces cream cheese, room temperature
¼ cup finely snipped chives

1. Combine all the ingredients and add salt and freshly ground black pepper to taste. This makes enough filling for 3 to 4 tortes.

Appetizers

Like hors d'oeuvres, appetizers alert your palate to the joys of the meal to come. Since it is merely the overture, be careful to orchestrate the richness of the appetizer so that it does not overpower what follows. Actually, it is important to maintain this balance throughout the meal by monitoring the amount of butter, cream, and cheese you use.

The appetizer is pivotal to the meal. As the first course, it sets the tone for the entire meal, and even though you are unlikely to plan your menu around the appetizer, you will be giving your guests their first taste experience. Like most first impressions, it will be lasting. Your aim is to start the meal brightly, igniting it with a spark, so be creative. You will be considering eye appeal, as well as taste, texture, and richness. I discuss the balance of these elements in the section on entertaining, but it is worth mentioning here that the colors and tastes of your appetizer must blend well or contrast effectively with your other courses. Besides finding a variety of appetizer recipes in this chapter, you also might use one of the salads or fettucine dishes as appetizers.

Many of the recipes in this chapter work well as hors d'oeuvres. A number of them can be expanded to serve as luncheon or supper dishes. As usual, I have shown you how to do much of the preparation ahead of time to spread the workload for the busy cook.

Chilled Asparagus Mousse

You will not regret the time and attention that you will have to expend on this special mousse. It has the most beautiful green color accented by the orange of the carrots. A very strong chicken stock lends this delicacy all the more strength and subtlety.

> *1¼ pounds fresh asparagus*
> *6 thin carrot slices, blanched*
> *⅓ cup strong homemade chicken stock, cold*
> *1½ tablespoons (2 packets) gelatin*
> *1½ cups heavy cream*
> *1 tablespoon green peppercorns, drained and coarsely crushed*
> *2 egg whites*
> *fresh watercress for garnish*

1. Cut off ½-inch to 1 inch of the coarse asparagus stalks, then peel the asparagus halfway up the stalks.
2. Bring 3 quarts of water to a boil. Add asparagus and boil for 2 to 3 minutes until just tender (*al dente*), being careful not to overcook. Drain and place in ice water for 10 minutes; drain and dry well. Cut off 6 asparagus tips and set aside. Coarsely puree just half the asparagus in a food processor. Place it in a towel to squeeze out the excess liquid. Finely chop the remaining asparagus by hand. Place the pureed asparagus and the chopped asparagus in a bowl.
3. Brush a 5- to 6-cup mold with oil, then line it with plastic wrap. (The adhesion of plastic wrap to an oiled mold will give the mousse an even surface and will make the mousse easier to remove from the mold.) Arrange the 6 reserved asparagus tips and the 6 carrot slices in the mold. Refrigerate.
4. Place the cold chicken stock in a small heavy saucepan and sprinkle with gelatin. Let it stand 10 minutes until gelatin is absorbed and mixture is spongy. Meanwhile, beat cream until stiff and place in the refrigerator.

5. Over a gentle heat dissolve the gelatin until all granules have dissolved, being careful not to boil. Stir into the asparagus mixture. Place the bowl of asparagus over a bowl of ice water. Gently stir until the mixture starts to set. Remove the bowl from the ice water and put to one side.
6. Beat egg whites until stiff. Gently fold the whipped cream into the asparagus. Add peppercorns and salt and freshly ground black pepper to taste. Gently fold in the egg whites, being careful not to overwork or the mixture will lose its volume.
7. Pour the mixture into the prepared mold and place in the freezer for 20 minutes. Then refrigerate for at least 2 hours, or up to 24 hours, before serving.
8. To unmold, place a serving platter on top of the mold. Turn over. Gently remove the mold and the plastic wrap. Garnish the mousse with watercress.

Servings: 8   Preparation: Difficult
Time: Time consuming; advance preparation necessary

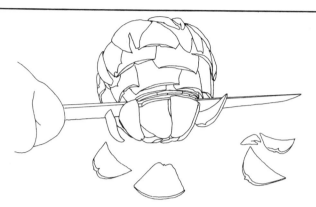

Top: With a sharp chef's knife or slicing knife, cut off the top of the cooked artichoke. Bottom: After you have scooped out the choke with a stainless steel teaspoon, the artichoke is ready for stuffing.

PREPARING ARTICHOKE FOR STUFFING

PREPARING ARTICHOKE BOTTOM FOR A SAUCE

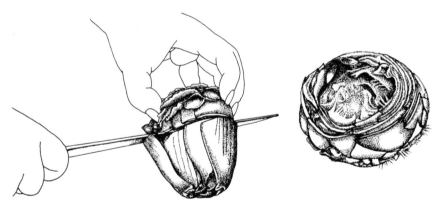

Left: Cut the cooked artichoke 2 to 2½ inches from the stem. Right: After you have scooped out the choke with a stainless steel teaspoon, the bottom is ready to be used.

Boiled Artichokes

This simple but very flavorful method for cooking artichokes may be used for a variety of dishes. The artichokes may be served hot or chilled with a sauce, such as Lemon Mayonnaise (page 42) or Mustard Mayonnaise (page 40). Or you can remove the leaves and choke and stuff the artichoke bottoms with a favorite stuffing; Eggplant Caviar is delicious (page 71). The poaching liquid may be frozen and used one more time; after that it will turn bitter. It is extremely important that you do not cook the artichokes in an aluminum pot, as it can impart an unpleasant flavor to them.

> *4 large artichokes*
> *¼ cup lemon juice*
> *1 bay leaf*
> *1 tablespoon dried basil*
> *1 tablespoon salt*
> *1 teaspoon freshly ground black pepper*
> *¼ cup olive oil*

1. If you plan to serve the artichokes whole, clip the leaves with kitchen scissors ½ inch down from the top. Cut off the stalk so it is even with the bottom of the artichoke.
2. Place 3 quarts water in a 4-quart stainless steel saucepan. Add the lemon juice, bay leaf, basil, salt, pepper, and oil, bring to a boil, and simmer for 5 minutes.
3. Add the artichokes and make sure they are completely submerged in the water; if there is not enough water, add more.
4. Gently boil the artichokes for 15 minutes, then take a small sharp knife and insert it in the stalk part to check for tenderness. The knife should go in easily; if it does not, continue to cook until tender, being careful not to overcook or the artichoke will be mushy. You should also test for tenderness by checking how easily you can pull out an artichoke leaf. If the leaf does not come out easily, cook the artichokes longer.
5. Remove from the water and if serving hot, drain for 3 minutes then serve. If serving cold, chill in the refrigerator.
6. If you are only using the artichoke bottoms or hearts, drain the artichokes until cool. Then remove two to three layers of artichoke leaves

until you come to the lighter-colored leaves. If you plan to use the artichoke bottoms for stuffing, slice through the artichoke ¼ to ½ inch from the top, using a very sharp knife; discard the leaves. Scoop out the choke with a stainless steel teaspoon. (See drawings on page 84.)

7. If you are using the artichoke bottom or heart for a sauce (as in my Pork Tenderloins with Artichoke Sauce (page 366), slice through the artichokes about 2 to 2½ inches from the bottom and scoop out the choke (see drawing).

Servings: 4   Preparation: Easy
Time: Fairly time consuming; advance preparation possible

Avocado Almond

Here is an appetizer that is wonderfully flavorful and nutritionally sound for the vegetarian (or anyone else who likes avocados).

3 small ripe avocados
¼ cup vegetable oil
¾ cup whole blanched almonds, coarsely chopped
1 medium carrot, coarsely grated
1 stalk celery, finely diced
½ cup loosely packed fresh mint or watercress leaves
1 cup plain yogurt
6 sprigs fresh mint or watercress for garnish

1. Heat the oil in a 10-inch saute pan, add the almonds, and saute until light golden brown. Pour them immediately into a bowl or they will continue to brown in the pan. Cool, then add carrot and celery. Add salt and freshly ground black pepper to taste.
2. Chill up to 24 hours if you wish.
3. Coarsely chop watercress or mint and mix into yogurt.
4. Just before serving, cut avocados in half lengthwise and remove the seed. Peel avocados. Cut a small slice off the bottom of each avocado

half so that it will stand steadily on a plate. Fill each half with the almond mixture. Place on individual serving plates and spoon the yogurt sauce on top. (If you are serving the avocados on one large platter, serve sauce separately.) Garnish with watercress or mint sprigs.

Servings: 6   **Preparation: Easy**
Time: Quick; some advance preparation possible

Avocado Noisette

I always take time to crack fresh walnuts, as their unique flavor and texture is not to be found in the canned or prepackaged variety.
   This recipe is also great served as a salad.

2 medium-sized ripe avocados
18 walnuts, cracked and shelled
1 large head of Belgian endive or 1 bunch watercress
½ pound poached mushrooms (page 171)
¼ cup fresh lemon juice
½ cup vegetable oil

1. Place walnuts on baking sheet in a preheated 400-degree oven. Toast for 5 to 7 minutes until light golden brown. Be sure to watch carefully, as nuts burn easily. Remove from oven and let cool. This procedure may be done 2 days ahead.
2. Just before serving, cut avocados in half lengthwise and remove seeds. Peel avocados and cut into ½-inch slices. Arrange the slices on a serving platter and surround with endive leaves or watercress. Arrange mushrooms on the platter.
3. Whisk lemon juice and oil together. Add salt and freshly ground black pepper to taste. Pour the dressing over the avocados and endive or watercress and sprinkle with walnuts.

Servings: 6   **Preparation: Easy**
Time: Fairly time consuming; some advance preparation possible

Vegetable-Stuffed Avocado

The radishes in the stuffing provide a nice, slightly peppery taste.

3 medium-sized ripe avocados
6 large or 9 small radishes
1 small zucchini (approximately 7 inches long)
1 small jar of marinated artichoke hearts or 3 cooked, fresh
*   artichoke hearts (page 85)*
⅓ cup balsamic vinegar
½ cup olive oil
¼ cup snipped fresh chives

1. Slice radishes ½-inch thick. Bring 1 quart water to a boil, add radishes, and boil for 2 minutes. Drain and place in cold water for 3 minutes. Drain well and pat dry.
2. Just before serving, grate zucchini on a coarse grater (grate around seeds and discard seeds). Cut artichoke hearts into ½-inch pieces. Place vinegar, oil, chives, zucchini, radishes, and artichokes in a bowl. Mix and add salt and freshly ground black pepper to taste.
3. Cut avocados in half lengthwise, remove seeds, and peel. Cut a small slice off the bottom of each avocado half so that it will stand steadily on a plate. Place the avocado halves on a serving platter or individual plates. Spoon the stuffing into each half.

Servings: 6   Preparation: Easy
Time: Quick

Eggplant Provençal

This appetizer is particularly delicious when it is redolent with thyme, so I use a lot of it. It may be served hot or cold.

3 small eggplants (approximately 8 inches long)
½ cup olive oil
1 medium onion, finely sliced
2 garlic cloves, finely chopped
1 tablespoon fresh thyme (or 2 teaspoons dried thyme)
4 vine-ripened tomatoes, peeled, seeded, and finely chopped
½ cup loosely packed fresh Italian parsley, finely chopped
½ cup freshly grated Parmesan cheese

1. Cut eggplants in half lengthwise through the stem end. Score by running a small sharp prep knife all around the edge. Then cut crisscrosses through the flesh, being careful not to puncture skin. (See diagrams on page 70.) Sprinkle with salt and allow to stand for 2 hours. Rinse under cold water and pat dry.
2. Preheat oven to 400 degrees. Brush eggplant halves with 2 tablespoons of oil and place on a heavy baking sheet. Bake for 40 to 50 minutes until eggplant is soft. Remove from oven. Let cool. Keeping skin intact, remove flesh, leaving a ¼-inch shell. Place flesh in a sieve for 5 minutes to drain off excess liquid.
3. Heat the remaining oil in a 12-inch stainless steel saute pan and add the onion and garlic, and dried thyme if you are using it. Saute until onion is clear.
4. Add tomatoes to onion and cook on high heat until tomatoes are reduced and thick. Scrape down the sides of the pan with a plastic spatula to keep the tomato mixture from scorching around the edges of the pan.
5. Place mixture in a bowl and chill about 30 minutes.
6. Coarsely chop eggplant and add it to the tomato mixture. Add parsley, fresh thyme (if you are using it), and salt and freshly ground black pepper to taste. Fill eggplant skins with mixture, sprinkle with Parmesan, then chill at least 30 minutes or up to 24 hours.
7. Serve chilled or, if heating, bake for 20 minutes in a 400-degree oven.

Servings: 6   **Preparation: Fairly easy**
Time: Time consuming; advance preparation possible

Stuffed Peppers Tierney

This colorful appetizer is named for my great friend, Michael Campbell Tierney, who has influenced my cooking style. If you like Roquefort cheese, it may be substituted for the feta.

> *4 medium red or green sweet peppers*
> *¾ cup feta cheese*
> *½ cup ricotta cheese*
> *½ cup olive oil*
> *fresh thyme or basil sprigs for garnish*

1. Place whole peppers under a preheated broiler and broil until dark brown on all sides. Leave in very cold water for 5 minutes, then peel off skin, being careful that the peppers do not break apart. Remove core and seeds; pat dry.
2. Crumble feta until quite fine. Place in a bowl, then fold in ricotta, adding freshly ground black pepper to taste.
3. The above procedures can be done 24 hours before serving. Refrigerate peppers and cheese.
4. Just before serving, stuff peppers with cheese mixture. Pour oil onto a serving platter and arrange peppers on oil. Garnish with thyme or basil sprigs.

Servings: 4   Preparation: Easy
Time: Quick; advance preparation possible

Herb Rouli

This chilled Herb Rouli is an extremely brilliant green color with a strong herb flavor. Filled with sauteed mushrooms, it is a delicious appetizer for 10 (or vegetarian entree for 6), but it is also good with a filling of chicken salad, shrimp salad, or ratatouille. It is a time-consuming dish to make; however, after preparing it once, you will find it much quicker the second time. It is important to use cake flour in the recipe, as it gives the rouli a much softer texture. If Shiitake mushrooms are not available, substitute 2 cups of cultivated mushrooms.

10 large eggs, separated
1 cup cooked fresh spinach, squeezed very dry
½ cup loosely packed fresh dill sprigs
½ cup loosely packed fresh parsley sprigs
¼ cup finely snipped fresh chives
⅓ cup + 1 tablespoon sifted cake flour
½ cup freshly grated Parmesan cheese

FILLING:
4 tablespoons unsalted butter
2 cups mushrooms, sliced ½-inch thick
2 cups Shiitake mushrooms, sliced ½-inch thick
1 cup crème fraîche or sour cream
cherry tomatoes or vine-ripened tomatoes for garnish

1. Preheat oven to 350 degrees. Lightly oil a 12x17-inch sheet pan, then line it with aluminum foil. Butter and dust with all-purpose flour; knock out the excess.
2. Place the spinach in the food processor and process to a coarse chopped consistency. Check that the herbs are very dry, then add them to the spinach and process to a medium-fine consistency.
3. Whisk the egg yolks in a large bowl with a pinch of salt and freshly ground black pepper until they begin to thicken. Add the spinach, dill, parsley, and chives and whisk until smooth. Whisk in the flour until smooth. Stir in ⅓ cup cheese.

4. Beat the egg whites with an electric mixer until very stiff. Gently fold one-third into the spinach mixture and continue to fold until well mixed. Then very gently fold in the remaining egg whites. Be very careful not to overmix, as the mixture will lose volume and become very runny. There might be pockets of egg whites; as long as these are not more than one inch in diameter, do not worry about them.

5. At this point, try to work very fast. Pour the mixture into the prepared sheet pan and spread fairly evenly. Here again, don't overwork the mixture or it will lose volume. Bake at 350 degrees for 15 minutes, until the rouli is very light golden brown on top and firm.

6. Lightly sprinkle a cloth with the remaining cheese, flip the rouli onto the cloth, and remove the aluminum foil. Gently roll up the rouli and the cloth together; do not roll tightly. Allow to cool on a cooling rack.

7. For the filling, heat 2 tablespoons butter in a large saute pan. Over high heat saute two cups of mushrooms until light golden brown. Place mushrooms in a colander and cool. Saute the Shiitake mushrooms in the remaining butter.

8. Chop mushrooms in a food processor until medium-fine (approximately 15 to 30 seconds). Place in a bowl and stir in the crème fraîche or sour cream and salt and freshly ground black pepper to taste. Unroll rouli, spread with mushroom mixture, and roll up. Place on a serving plate and refrigerate 2 hours or up to 24 hours.

9. To serve, slice the rouli into ¾-inch slices. Garnish each serving with cherry tomatoes or thin slices of vine-ripened tomatoes. Another wonderful garnish is a teaspoon of fresh American caviar per serving.

Servings: 10   Preparation: Difficult
Time: Time consuming; advance preparation possible

Roquefort Walnut Mousse

Roquefort is a French cheese made from ewes' milk. Its somewhat stringent flavor responds beautifully to a garnish of pears, apples, or cucumbers. Besides making a nice appetizer served on individual appetizer plates, it can be served as an hors d'oeuvre. The apple, pear, or cucumber slices then are used to dip into the mousse.

½ pound Roquefort cheese
¼ cup cold water
1 tablespoon gelatin
2 tablespoons unsalted butter
6 scallions, thinly sliced halfway up
½ cup dry white wine
1 cup heavy cream
½ cup freshly cracked walnuts for garnish
1 pear, tart apple, or cucumber, thinly sliced, for garnish

1. Lightly oil or butter a 6-cup mold, then line it with plastic wrap. (The adhesion of plastic wrap to an oiled mold will give the mousse an even surface and will make the mousse easier to remove from the mold.)
2. Place the cold water in a small heavy saucepan and sprinkle in the gelatin. Watch that the gelatin is fully absorbed; if any white crystals remain, sprinkle on a little cold water. Let stand for 10 minutes.
3. In the meantime, crumble Roquefort into small pieces in a bowl. Heat butter in a 10-inch saute pan, add scallions, and saute on high heat until soft but not browned. Add wine, bring to a boil, then pour over Roquefort, stirring until cheese becomes smooth. Put the mixture into a bowl.
4. Beat the cream until stiff and refrigerate.
5. Dissolve gelatin over a very low heat. Place the bowl of Roquefort mixture over a bowl of ice water. Add the gelatin and stir until it starts to set. Gently fold in whipped cream. Be careful not to stir too much, or the mixture will lose its volume.

6. Pour the mixture into the prepared mold and refrigerate at least 2 hours, or up to 2 days, before turning out and serving.

7. Toast the walnuts in a 375-degree oven for 7 to 10 minutes until light golden brown. Watch carefully that they do not burn. Remove from oven and cool.

8. To unmold the mousse, place a serving platter on top, turn over, and carefully remove the mold and the plastic wrap. The mousse will not be very stiff. Garnish with pear, apple, or cucumber slices and toasted walnuts, and serve.

Servings: 6 to 8   Preparation: Fairly easy
Time: Fairly time consuming; advance preparation necessary

Chèvre Mousse

Make this creamy, rich appetizer two days ahead and serve it garnished with lots of vegetables. Unlike the Roquefort Walnut Mousse, it is a very dense mousse.

6 ounces Montrachet or other mild creamy chèvre
3 large eggs, room temperature
3 egg yolks, room temperature
2 cups light cream
watercress, cucumber slices, and slices of red pepper for garnish

1. Preheat oven to 325 degrees. Butter six to eight 4- to 6-ounce individual molds.
2. Cut off any rind on outside of chèvre. Crumble chèvre into small pieces and place in a bowl.
3. With an electric mixer, beat eggs into the chèvre one at a time, making sure each is well incorporated before adding the next egg. Add yolks and beat for 1 minute, then slowly pour in the cream, beating all the time. Add freshly ground black pepper to taste. (Although mixture might need salt, be careful not to add too much, as when the custard is cooked, the saltiness of chèvre tends to come through.)
4. Pour into buttered molds. Place molds in a roasting pan and add enough hot water to cover three-fourths of the sides of the molds. Bake for 1 hour and 30 minutes at 325 degrees. Test for doneness by lightly pressing in the center; the mousses should be firm but not rubbery. If they are runny in the center, return to the oven, cook another 15 minutes, and test again.
5. Chill the mousses in the refrigerator for at least 2 hours, or up to 48 hours, before turning out.
6. To turn out, run a knife around the edge of the molds and turn onto a serving plate. Garnish with watercress, cucumber slices, and thin slices of red pepper.

Servings: 6 to 8   Preparation: Fairly easy
Time: Fairly time consuming; advance preparation necessary

Beef Milanese

This recipe was inspired by Jeffrey Starr's wonderful stories of his experiences in Italy. It is easy to prepare and a joyous combination of flavors. If you love your beef rare, you are only a step away from enjoying it raw. The recipe also works well with lamb; however, use Romano cheese instead of Parmesan and garnish with mint leaves instead of basil. I suggest you serve this appetizer when you're serving fish for the main course.

1 pound beef tenderloin
⅓ cup olive oil
2 ounces fresh Parmesan cheese
¼ pound mushrooms, sliced ¼-inch thick, for garnish
1 cup pitted black olives, halved lengthwise, for garnish
12 large fresh basil leaves, for garnish

1. Place the beef in the freezer for 30 minutes. This will make it easier to slice very thin.
2. Slice tenderloin as thinly as possible, cutting across the grain. Pound slices until very thin, being careful they do not break apart. If desired, cut into pieces approximately 1½-inches by 2½-inches. Chill in the refrigerator for a few hours.
3. Just before serving, arrange beef on appetizer plates. Sprinkle each serving with the oil and freshly ground black pepper. Thinly shave or coarsely grate the Parmesan cheese on top. Garnish each plate with mushrooms, olives, and basil.

Servings: 8   Preparation: Easy
Time: Quick; some advance preparation possible

Chicken Liver Pâté

This is a fairly unusual way to make a pâté, and it may be made a couple of days before your party. Its flavors combine beautifully and its texture is smoother and lighter than most pâtés. Serve it as an appetizer or hors d'oeuvre. The recipe can easily be doubled if you're making it for a large party. Leftover pâté may be frozen, but its texture will change considerably; I recommend you use frozen pâté only for cooking, such as in Chicken Rouennaise (see page 307).

> 1 1/4 pounds fresh chicken livers
> 1/2 cup heavy cream
> 2 tablespoons unsalted butter
> 5 medium shallots, sliced
> 1/4 cup loosely packed fresh tarragon leaves (or 1 teaspoon
>   dried tarragon)
> 2 egg yolks
> 2 large eggs
> 1/2 cup crème fraîche or heavy cream
> fresh watercress or parsley, or raw mushrooms for garnish

1. Remove center gristle and as much skin as possible from livers. Do not worry if they break up. Put them in a bowl with the cream and refrigerate for at least 3 hours, but no longer than 12 hours.
2. When the livers have been in the cream the necessary amount of time, preheat the oven to 300 degrees. Brush a Pyrex mold—9 inches long, 3 inches high, 5 inches across—with a little melted butter. Line bottom with wax paper and brush it with butter.
3. Heat the butter in a 10- to 12-inch saute pan and gently saute shallots and dried tarragon, if you are using it, on low heat until they are soft but not browned. Place warm shallots and tarragon in a food processor. Process until finely diced. If you are using fresh tarragon, add it now and process until fine. Remove from processor and put in a bowl.
4. Drain livers, reserving cream. Puree livers in food processor until very smooth, for at least 3 minutes.

5. Whisk yolks, eggs, and a pinch of salt in a bowl until well blended. Add crème fraîche, continuing to whisk until well blended. Add diced shallots, pureed livers, and cream marinade reserved from livers; whisk until well blended. Add salt and freshly ground black pepper to taste. (It is very important to taste a tiny amount to determine salt and pepper level. If you do not want to taste the liver raw, lightly saute a small amount of liver in oil or unsalted butter, then sample.)
6. Pour into the prepared mold. Cover with aluminum foil, then place in a 3- to 4-inch deep roasting pan. Add enough hot water to come three-fourths of the way up the sides. Bake for 1½ to 2 hours until internal temperature reads 155 degrees. (To check the temperature, insert an instant thermometer.) Remove pâté from roasting pan; let cool. Refrigerate at least 3 hours, or up to 2 days, before unmolding and serving.
7. To unmold, run a metal spatula or knife around mold. Place a serving platter on top, then turn over. Remove mold and peel back paper. Garnish with watercress, parsley, or slices of raw mushroom. Slice and serve.

Servings: 8   Preparation: Fairly easy
Time: Fairly time consuming; advance preparation necessary

Country Pâté

The lower-than-usual fat content of this pâté gives it a slightly grainy texture, but does nothing to minimize its rich flavor. It is a coarser pâté than the Chicken Liver Pâté.

> *¾ pound chicken livers*
> *1 teaspoon dry fennel seeds*
> *½ teaspoon whole black peppercorns*
> *2 large eggs*
> *2 medium garlic cloves*
> *1 teaspoon salt*
> *¾ pound ground veal*
> *1 medium onion, finely chopped*
> *1 teaspoon dried thyme leaves*
> *¾ pound hot Italian sausage*
> *6 ounces bacon slices (preferably not sugar-cured)*
> *⅓ cup homemade chicken stock, cold*
> *1 teaspoon gelatin*
> *fresh watercress for garnish*

1. Preheat oven to 300 degrees.
2. Place the fennel seeds and black peppercorns in a blender and blend until a medium-coarse grind. Add the eggs, garlic, and salt, and blend for 1 minute. While blender is on, add livers and slowly blend until a smooth puree.
3. Mix the liver puree in a bowl with the veal, onion, and thyme. Test the mixture for salt and pepper level by sauteeing one tablespoonful in a teaspoon of oil in a small saute pan; do not brown. Taste, and add more salt and freshly ground black pepper if necessary.
4. Flatten bacon, so as to stretch it, with the back of a knife. Line a Pyrex mold—9 inches long, 3 inches high, 5 inches across—with the bacon. Remove casing from sausage. Break up sausage and place on the bottom of the lined mold. Pour in the veal and liver mixture. Cover tightly.
5. Bake at 300 degrees for 1¾ hours. Test for doneness with an instant thermometer. When the internal temperature reaches 160 degrees, the pâté is done. (If it has not reached this temperature, cook for an additional 20 minutes, then take temperature again.) Remove from oven when cooked.

6. Place the chicken stock in a small saucepan, sprinkle the gelatin over it, and let stand for 10 minutes. Then dissolve the gelatin over a gentle heat until all the granules are dissolved, being careful not to boil. Pour it over the pâté.
7. Let cool. Refrigerate at least 3 hours, or up to 3 days, before unmolding and serving.
8. To unmold, run a knife around outside of the pâté and turn onto a platter. If the pâté is difficult to remove, dip the bottom of the mold in hot water for 1 to 2 minutes before turning out. Garnish with watercress and serve.

Servings: 8 to 10   Preparation: Fairly difficult
Time: Fairly time consuming; advance preparation necessary

Chicken Terrine

The pureed chicken livers added to the chopped chicken mixture gives this terrine a really rich flavor. I find it best to chop the chicken by hand, as chopping it in a food processor can give the terrine a dry consistency.

1 2½-pound chicken
2 small onions, sliced
1 carrot, sliced
1 stalk celery, sliced
1 bay leaf
¼ pound fresh chicken livers
4 tablespoons unsalted butter
2 tablespoons finely snipped fresh chives
¼ cup loosely packed fresh parsley sprigs, finely chopped
2 teaspoons fresh thyme leaves (optional)
1 cup heavy cream
fresh watercress for garnish

1. Line an oiled 5- to 6-cup mold with plastic wrap.
2. Place the chicken in a 4-quart saucepan, add one of the onions, the carrot, the celery, and bay leaf. Cover with cold water, bring to a boil, then simmer gently until just cooked, approximately 40 minutes. Be careful not to overcook chicken, as this will give the mousse a dry consistency. Remove chicken from liquid and cool thoroughly. (Reduce the liquid by 50 percent and freeze for use as chicken stock.)
3. While chicken cools, remove as much gristle as possible from livers. Heat butter in a 12-inch saute pan, add the remaining onion, and saute until clear. Add livers and toss over high heat until cooked through, again being careful not to overcook. Puree livers and onion in a food processor until very smooth. Place puree in a bowl and let cool.

4. Remove the meat from the cooled chicken and discard the skin, gristle, and bones. Very finely chop the chicken meat by hand. Add to the pureed livers along with the fresh herbs.
5. Whip cream until stiff. Place the bowl of chicken mixture over a bowl of ice water and stir until it is quite cold. If the mixture becomes too stiff, remove from ice water immediately. Gently fold in the whipped cream. Add salt and freshly ground black pepper to taste.
6. Spoon the chicken mixture into the mold and refrigerate for at least 2 hours, or up to 2 days, before turning out and serving.
7. To turn out, place a serving plate on top of the mold. Turn upside down, remove the mold, and gently remove the plastic wrap.
8. Garnish the terrine with watercress and serve with brioche toast, whole wheat toast, or crackers.

Servings: 6 to 8   Preparation: Fairly difficult
Time: Time consuming; advance preparation necessary

Sauteed Chicken Livers with Shallots

It is preferable to use chicken livers that have not been frozen and a good, strong stock in this dish. For a beautiful effect, serve on a bed of attractive fresh greens, such as radicchio, spinach, and Italian parsley. Besides being an interesting appetizer, it also makes a delicious supper dish.

1 pound chicken livers
½ cup red wine
½ cup strong homemade chicken stock
5 tablespoons unsalted butter
5 large or 10 small shallots, thinly sliced
2 tablespoons balsamic or red wine vinegar
fresh watercress for garnish

1. Divide livers in half and remove the center gristle without tearing the livers.
2. Bring the red wine to a boil in a 1-quart stainless steel or enamel pan. Ignite and allow to flame for 3 minutes. Add the stock and boil until the liquid has reduced to ⅓ cup.
3. Heat the butter in a 12-inch heavy stainless steel saute pan until it turns light golden brown. Add livers and toss over high heat until they are cooked but slightly rare in the middle. Do not overcook. Remove from the pan with a slotted spoon and place on a serving platter. Keep warm.
4. Add shallots to the saute pan and toss over high heat until they are clear but not brown. Add the wine and stock reduction and vinegar. If the sauce has a thin consistency, reduce it a little more. Add livers and toss over high heat for 2 minutes. Add salt and freshly ground black pepper to taste and, if necessary, a little more vinegar to taste.
5. Pour onto individual appetizer plates and garnish with watercress.

Servings: 4 to 6   **Preparation: Fairly easy**
Time: Quick

Chicken Livers with Celery Root

The combination of celery root and chicken livers makes an unusual but very appetizing dish.

1 pound chicken livers
about ½ pound celery root
½ cup red wine
½ cup homemade chicken stock
4 tablespoons unsalted butter
3 tablespoons chopped fresh parsley (optional)
1 bunch fresh watercress for garnish

1. Divide livers in half and remove the center gristle without tearing livers.
2. Peel celery root and coarsely grate. Measure 1 cup and set aside.
3. Bring the red wine to a boil in a 1-quart stainless steel saucepan. Ignite and let flame for 3 minutes. Add the stock and boil until the liquid has reduced to ½ cup.
4. Heat the butter in a 12-inch heavy saute pan until it starts to turn a light golden brown. Saute livers over high heat until cooked but still slightly rare in middle. Transfer the livers with a slotted spoon to a serving platter and keep warm.
5. Add the grated celery root to the pan. Toss over high heat for 3 minutes. Add wine mixture. Reduce the liquid over high heat until the mixture has the consistency of heavy cream. Add the livers and toss over a high heat for 1 minute. Add salt and freshly ground black pepper to taste.
6. Stir in the parsley and arrange on individual serving plates. Garnish with watercress.

Servings: 4 to 6   **Preparation: Easy**
Time: Quick

Lobster Mousse

This mousse is so rich that it has been described as "dessert-like." There is a lot of work involved in preparation, but you can save yourself some time by buying precooked lobster.

1 live 2-pound lobster
2 tablespoons unsalted butter
2 ripe tomatoes, peeled and seeded
¼ cup cognac
1 cup heavy cream
1 tablespoon gelatin
¼ cup cold water
fresh watercress or parsley for garnish

1. Bring 4 quarts water to a simmer (170–180 degrees) in a 3-gallon stainless steel or enamel pot. Add the lobster and gently simmer, covered, until cooked, approximately 40 to 50 minutes. Do not allow the water to boil, as this will toughen lobster. (Lobster should have turned red and long front feelers will come out easily when pulled, indicating lobster is cooked.) Remove lobster from water, cool, then refrigerate for at least two hours.
2. While the lobster cools, heat butter in a saute pan, add tomatoes, and cook over medium heat until all liquid has evaporated and tomatoes have a thick consistency (about 5 to 10 minutes), stirring occasionally. Add cognac, ignite, and let flame. Remove from heat and cool.
3. Cut the cooled lobster in half lengthwise. Remove the sack at the top of the head and discard. Remove meat, including the tomali and roe (coral). Puree tomali and roe with tomatoes in a blender. Finely dice the lobster meat; mix with pureed tomato mixture.
4. Whip cream until stiff; refrigerate.
5. Put the cold water in a small saucepan. Sprinkle the gelatin over the water. Let it stand for 10 minutes until gelatin is absorbed. Then dissolve gelatin over very low heat, being careful not to boil. When all granules are dissolved, pour into lobster and tomato mixture.
6. Meanwhile, lightly oil a 4- to 5-cup mold, and line it with plastic wrap. (The adhesion of plastic wrap to an oiled mold will give the mousse an even surface and makes the mousse easier to remove from the mold.)

7. Place the bowl of lobster mixture over a bowl of ice water. Gently stir until the mixture starts to set. Fold in cream, being careful not to overfold. Add salt and freshly ground black pepper to taste.
8. Pour the mixture into the prepared mold and refrigerate at least 2 hours, or up to 24 hours, before turning out. To unmold, place serving plate over mold, turn over, and remove mold and plastic wrap. Garnish with watercress or parsley and serve.

Servings: 6 to 8   **Preparation: Fairly difficult**
Time: Time consuming; advance preparation necessary

Lobster Salad with Caviar

Caviar and fennel have such strong, clear flavors that I use tomali to intensify the lobster in this dish. The result is a sensational medley of tastes with crème fraîche giving a lovely texture. If you cannot find crème fraîche, you may use sour cream.

> 1 live 2-pound lobster (or 2 1¼-pound lobsters)
> ¼ cup vegetable oil
> ½ cup finely diced onion
> 1 cup finely diced (⅛-inch to ¼-inch) carrot
> 1 cup finely diced fresh fennel (or 1 cup finely diced celery with
>   1 teaspoon coarsely ground dried fennel seeds)
> ½ cup loosely packed fresh parsley leaves, chopped
> ½ cup crème fraîche
> 1 ounce fresh American or red salmon caviar for garnish

1. Bring 4 quarts water to a simmer (170–180 degrees) in a 3-gallon stainless steel or enamel pot. Put in lobster; gently simmer, covered, until cooked (40 to 50 minutes), being careful that water does not boil, as this will toughen lobster meat. (To check for doneness, make sure lobster is completely red and that the long front feelers can be pulled out easily.) Remove lobster from water; let cool. Refrigerate for at least 2 hours before removing from shell.
2. While the lobster cools, heat oil in a 12-inch saute pan, add onion and toss or stir over high heat for 2 minutes. Add carrot and fennel (or celery and dried fennel) and continue to stir or toss over high heat until vegetables are *al dente*. Cool, place in a bowl, and chill.
3. Cut the cooled lobster in half lengthwise. Remove the sack at the top of the head and discard. Remove meat, including the coral (roe) and tomali. In a blender, blend roe and tomali until smooth; finely dice lobster meat. Add lobster, roe and tomali, and parsley to vegetables; add salt and freshly ground black pepper to taste. Chill at least 1 hour, or up to 6 hours, before serving.
4. To serve, arrange on chilled appetizer plates. Place 1½ tablespoons crème fraîche and a garnish of caviar on each portion.

Servings: 4 to 6   **Preparation: Fairly easy; advance preparation necessary**
Time: Time consuming; advance preparation necessary

Mussels Florentine

This is a time-consuming recipe, but well worth the effort. What makes this dish so special is the unusual use of seafood with vegetables, a combination that makes for a strong flavor and pleasing texture. A delightful appetizer, it also is a lovely seafood salad on a warm day.

3 pounds raw mussels in their shells
2 cups mussel poaching liquid (page 12)
1 10-ounce package fresh spinach, washed
½ pound mushrooms, sliced ½-inch thick
1 quart mushroom poaching liquid (page 171)
⅓ cup vegetable oil
1 cup Mustard Mayonnaise (page 40)
1 lemon, cut into wedges, for garnish

1. Check that mussels are alive by lightly tapping any opened ones on a counter. Discard those that do not close. Remove beards from mussels. Thoroughly scrub the shells under running cold water.
2. Boil poaching liquid in a 4-quart stainless steel saucepan, add half the mussels, and simmer gently until cooked, about 5 minutes. Mussels should open about one-half inch. (Discard any that do not open.) Remove with a slotted spoon, and allow to cool. Cook the remaining mussels. Remove all but 12 mussels from their shells. Freeze the liquid for a future use. The mussels may be refrigerated up to 4 hours.
3. Remove coarse stalks from spinach and discard. Bring 1 quart of water to a boil in a 2- to 3-quart saucepan and cook spinach for 2 minutes. Drain, then run under cold water. Drain well, then squeeze out as much water as possible.
4. Place mushroom poaching liquid in a 2-quart stainless steel saucepan and bring to a boil. Add half the mushrooms and simmer for 3 to 4 minutes. Remove with a slotted spoon. Repeat procedure with remaining mushrooms. Let mushrooms cool. Freeze liquid for future use.
5. Place spinach, mushrooms, and oil in a bowl and mix together. Add salt and freshly ground black pepper to taste. Refrigerate up to 4 hours.
6. Just before serving, arrange spinach and mushroom mixture on a platter. Place mussels on top. Spoon the mustard mayonnaise on top. Garnish with the mussels still in the shells and lemon wedges.

Servings: 6 to 8   Preparation: Fairly easy
Time: Time consuming; advance preparation necessary

Mussel Fennel Salad

Here is a wonderful dish for fall, when fennel is in season and we are just bidding mussels a fond farewell. Lightly poached bay scallops may be substituted for the mussels.

3 pounds raw mussels
2 cups mussel poaching liquid (page 12)
2 small fennel bulbs
1/3 cup loosely packed fresh parsley leaves, coarsely chopped
1/4 cup olive oil
1 cup Mustard Mayonnaise (page 40)

1. Check that the mussels are alive by lightly tapping any opened ones on a hard surface. Discard those that do not close. Remove beards from mussels and scrub the shells under running cold water. (See also page 12.)
2. Boil the mussel poaching liquid in a 4-quart stainless steel saucepan, add half the mussels, and simmer gently until cooked, about 5 minutes. Mussels should open about ½-inch. (Discard any that remain closed.) Remove with a slotted spoon and allow to cool. Repeat procedure with remaining mussels. Remove all but 12 mussels from their shells. Freeze the liquid for a future use. The mussels may be refrigerated up to 24 hours.
3. Cut the fennel bulbs in half and remove core. Remove and discard coarse outside leaves; thinly slice fennel. Cook in 2 quarts boiling water for 2 to 3 minutes. Make sure the fennel retains an *al dente* crunchiness. Drain, then run under cold water until cool. Drain well and pat dry.
4. Place fennel, parsley, oil, and freshly ground black pepper to taste in a bowl. Refrigerate up to 24 hours.
5. Before serving, arrange fennel mixture on appetizer plates. Arrange mussels on top of fennel. Spoon the Mustard Mayonnaise on top. Garnish each serving with 2 mussels still in the shell.

Servings: 6   Preparation: Fairly easy
Time: Time consuming; advance preparation necessary

Scallops Moutarde

Scallops Moutarde is a very popular dish in the restaurant. A delicious appetizer, it is also excellent as a seafood salad.

1 pound bay scallops
2 leeks
2 tablespoons vegetable oil
½ pound mushrooms
2 cups mushroom poaching liquid (page 171)
1 cup Mustard Mayonnaise (page 40)

1. Remove and discard the coarse outside layer from the leeks. Cut the leeks into thin slices up to the medium-green part. Place in a bowl of cold water for 30 minutes. Drain, rinse, drain well, and pat dry.
2. Remove side muscles from scallops and discard.
3. Heat the oil in a 12-inch saute pan, add leeks, and toss over high heat until cooked. Add scallops, continuing to toss over high heat, being very careful not to overcook them as they will become rubbery. When the scallops are cooked, transfer with a slotted spoon to a bowl. Reduce the scallop liquid over high heat by 50 percent, being careful to scrape down the sides of the pan with a spatula so that the liquid does not scorch. Pour reduced liquid over scallops. Add salt and freshly ground black pepper to taste. Chill.
4. Slice mushrooms ¼-inch thick. Bring the poaching liquid to a boil in a 2-quart stainless steel saucepan, add the mushrooms, and cook for 3 minutes. Drain and chill the mushrooms. Freeze the liquid for a future use.
5. Up to this point, the dish can be prepared 6 to 8 hours ahead of time.
6. Just before serving, place scallop mixture in center of a serving platter. Spoon Mustard Mayonnaise on top. Arrange mushrooms around outside of platter.

Servings: 6   Preparation: Easy
Time: Fairly time consuming; advance preparation necessary

Coquilles Noir

Although this scallop appetizer is time consuming to prepare, much of the work can be done a day before serving. It is very colorful and provides a very interesting combination of complementary flavors.

1 pound bay or small sea scallops
1 pound young, fresh green beans
2 cups mushroom poaching liquid (page 171)
½ pound mushrooms, sliced ¼-inch thick
1 onion, finely chopped
1 bay leaf
½ cup loosely packed fresh parsley leaves, chopped
⅓ cup corn or safflower oil
⅓ cup sour cream
¾ cup Mustard Mayonnaise (page 40)
2 ounces fresh American black caviar, for garnish (optional)

1. Cut green beans in half and remove tips. Bring 2 quarts water to a boil and cook beans until tender. Drain, run under cold water until cold, and drain well. Refrigerate.
2. Bring mushroom poaching liquid to a boil in a stainless steel pan. Add mushrooms and simmer for 3 minutes. Drain well and refrigerate. Freeze poaching liquid to use another time.
3. Bring 1 cup of water to a boil in a 10-inch stainless steel saute pan, add onion and bay leaf, and gently simmer for 10 minutes. While this simmers, remove side muscles from scallops and discard. Add scallops to poaching liquid and gently simmer until scallops are tender (about 3 to 7 minutes), being very careful not to overcook. Remove scallops and onion with a slotted spoon. Refrigerate. Freeze the liquid for another use.
4. The beans, mushrooms, scallops, and mayonnaise can be refrigerated, separately, for 24 hours.

5. Just before serving, mix the beans, mushrooms, parsley, and oil. Add salt and freshly ground black pepper to taste.
6. Place the sour cream in a bowl, whisk until smooth, then gently stir in the mayonnaise.
7. Arrange bean and mushroom mixture on a serving platter. Place scallops on top. Spoon mayonnaise over scallops.
8. If using the caviar, arrange the salad on individual plates and garnish with the caviar.

Servings: 6   Preparation: Fairly easy
Time: Time consuming; advance preparation necessary

Salade Celeste

This is simple to prepare and a joy to eat! The scallop mixture should be prepared 24 hours before serving.

1 pound bay scallops
2 oranges
1 small red onion
1 small hot chili pepper (or Tabasco to taste)
¼ cup fresh lemon juice
¼ cup fresh lime juice
½ cup loosely packed fresh parsley leaves, finely chopped
2 avocados

1. Remove and discard side muscles of scallops. Put scallops in a Pyrex or ceramic dish.
2. Grate the rind of the oranges on a fine grater to get 2 teaspoons, being careful to only grate the rind and not the pith (white part), which can be quite bitter. Cut onion in half; slice one half into very thin slices. Cut off the stalk of the hot red pepper and discard stem. Cut the pepper in half lengthwise, remove the inside fibers, then finely dice.
3. Combine the orange rind, lemon and lime juices, sliced onion, hot pepper to taste, and parsley. Add salt to taste. If hot pepper is mild, add a little Tabasco to taste. Pour this dressing over the scallops. Cover and place in refrigerator for 24 hours to marinate.
4. Before serving, thinly slice the remaining half of onion. Remove pith and rind from the oranges; slice across. Peel avocado, cut in half, and remove the seed. Slice the avocado into ½-inch lengthwise slices.
5. On individual plates, arrange scallop mixture with avocado, onion, and orange slices around the edges.

Servings: 6   Preparation: Easy
Time: Quick; advance preparation necessary

Sauteed Shrimp Caribbean

Brutas, the chef at Drake's Anchorage in the Virgin Islands where I found this recipe, makes his sauce by pureeing green, soft coconuts just off the tree. These coconuts are just not available here, but I have found you can use fresh coconut or even the prepared kind, as long as it is unsweetened.

1 pound shrimp (16 to 20 count), peeled and deveined
1 small head red leaf lettuce
1 whole coconut (or ½ cup dried unsweetened coconut and 3
   tablespoons water)
1 small hot chili pepper
⅓ cup fresh lime juice
5 tablespoons unsalted butter
lime wedges for garnish

1. Wash lettuce, dry it well, then place in refrigerator. Very finely dice hot pepper and set aside.
2. Drill 3 holes in the eyes of the coconut. Drain coconut milk and reserve 3 tablespoons. Crack coconut, peeling off dark shell and skin with a knife. Grate the fruit medium-fine and set aside 1 cup.
3. Just before serving, heat the butter in a 12-inch saute pan. Add the shrimp with a little hot pepper. Cover and very gently cook on a low heat, until shrimp start to turn pink on the underside. Turn them over and cover, continuing to cook. (You will be cooking the shrimp a total of 5 to 8 minutes.) Be careful not to overcook the shrimp, as they will become rubbery.
4. While the shrimp are cooking, arrange lettuce on appetizer plates. When the shrimp are cooked, remove them from pan with a slotted spoon, and arrange on the lettuce.
5. Return the pan to the burner and over medium heat add the lime juice, 3 tablespoons coconut milk or water, and grated coconut. Whisk for 2 minutes. Add a little salt and hot pepper to taste. Whisk sauce on high heat for 2 minutes, then spoon over the shrimp. Serve immediately, garnished with wedges of lime.

Servings: 4 to 6   Preparation: Easy
Time: Fairly time consuming

Escabeche of Shrimp

This light and zesty appetizer is ideal for a hot summer day. It is delightful garnished with avocado in addition to the fresh orange slices. It is of the utmost importance that the shrimp are extremely fresh.

1 pound shrimp (16 to 20 count), in shell
1 small carrot
1 orange
¼ cup olive oil
1 small onion, thinly sliced
¼ cup fresh orange juice
¼ cup fresh lemon juice
2 tablespoons white wine vinegar

1. Peel and devein shrimp. (See illustration, page 250.) To butterfly shrimp, make a deep incision from one end to the other, but do not cut all the way through the shrimp.
2. Cut carrot into very thin julienned strips. Remove the zest from half the orange with a vegetable peeler, being careful not to remove any of the pith. Cut orange zest into very thin julienne strips.
3. Heat the oil in a 10- to 12-inch stainless steel saute pan, add onion, and saute until half-cooked. Add orange zest, carrot, vinegar, and orange and lemon juices. Simmer for 1 minute. Add shrimp and very gently simmer for 1 to 2 minutes on each side just until they have turned color. Do not cook through, as shrimp will continue to "cook" in marinade.
4. Pour into a Pyrex or ceramic bowl and add salt and freshly ground black pepper to taste. Cool. Chill at least 4 hours, or up to 24, before serving.
5. Before serving, remove the rest of the rind and pith from the orange. Slice across. Arrange the shrimp on a platter and garnish with the orange slices.

Servings: 4 as main course; 6 as appetizer   Preparation: Easy
Time: Quick; advance preparation necessary

Ceviche

In *The Cuisines of Mexico,* Diana Kennedy tells us, "One of the leading gastronomes of Mexico, Don Armando Farga, says the word cebiche (ceviche) comes from the verb cebar, using its meaning 'to saturate.' " Other sources have led me to believe that ceviche, called "caveah" in Arabic countries, was brought to Spain and later introduced to the rest of Europe by the Spanish. Still, other sources claim the origin was Oriental. Regardless of its origin, I feel that it is a delightful treatment of fresh fish.

The term applies to marinating seafood in a high acid mixture. During the marination period the acid "cooks" the fish, and therefore no heat is required. It is extremely important to purchase very fresh seafood and to cut the fish into ¼-inch slices so that the marinade can penetrate. Scallops should not be too large, and shrimp should be butterflied so that the marinade will penetrate the inside. My preference is to omit both garlic and onion from most of these recipes, as I do not like the flavor they impart after a couple of hours of marinating. However, I realize that this is my taste, and of course you should experiment to determine your own taste.

Ceviche of Shrimp and Scallops

This ceviche is simple and quick to prepare and is excellent garnished with avocado.

1 pound shrimp (16 to 20 count), in shell
1 pound bay or small sea scallops
⅓ cup fresh lemon juice
⅓ cup fresh lime juice
1 or 2 small fresh hot chili peppers, very finely diced (or Tabasco
*   to taste)*
⅓ cup loosely packed fresh coriander leaves, coarsely chopped
1 ripe avocado for garnish

1. Peel and devein shrimp. To butterfly shrimp, make a deep incision from one end to the other to cut the shrimp almost in half, but do not cut all the way through the shrimp.
2. Mix together in a large Pyrex or ceramic dish lemon and lime juices, hot pepper or Tabasco, and salt to taste.
3. Bring 2 quarts water to a boil. Add shrimp and cook for 1 minute until they just start to turn color. (Be careful not to overcook, as they are going to "cook" in the marinade.) Immediately drain and put into the lemon-lime mixture. Cool.
4. Remove and discard side muscles from scallops. Add scallops and coriander to shrimp. Cover; refrigerate the mixture for at least 10 hours, or up to 24 hours, before serving.
5. Just before serving, peel and remove pit from avocado. Slice. Arrange ceviche on serving platter and garnish with avocado.

Servings: 6 to 8   Preparation: Easy
Time: Quick; advance preparation necessary

Ceviche of Halibut

The flavors are sublime in this ceviche. Be certain that the halibut is very fresh; it should have a slightly translucent quality.

> 2 pounds halibut steaks (or 1¼ pounds halibut fillet)
> ⅓ cup fresh lemon juice
> ⅓ cup fresh lime juice
> ½ cup loosely packed fresh mint leaves, finely chopped
> ¼ cup freshly snipped chives
> 2 small fresh hot chili peppers, very finely chopped
> fresh mint sprigs for garnish

1. Mix together lemon and lime juices, mint, and chives. Add salt and hot peppers to taste.
2. Skin and bone halibut steaks, then slice ¼-inch thick. Place one layer of halibut in a Pyrex or ceramic dish. Spoon a little of the marinade on top. Repeat this procedure until all the halibut and marinade are used up.
3. Cover and refrigerate for at least 8 hours or up to 24 hours. Just before serving, place on serving plates and garnish with mint sprigs.

Servings: 6   Preparation: Easy
Time: Quick; advance preparation necessary

Ceviche of Salmon

We serve this ceviche a lot at the restaurant. Marinating the salmon gives it an absolutely lovely and interesting texture. Unlike other ceviches, this one only needs a few hours to marinate and should be served within 24 hours.

> 1½ pounds skinless salmon fillets
> ¼ cup fresh lemon juice
> ¼ cup fresh lime juice
> ½ cup loosely packed fresh parsley sprigs, finely chopped
> 2 small fresh hot chili peppers, very finely chopped (or Tabasco)
> 1 ripe avocado for garnish

1. Cut salmon into very thin slices, ⅛-inch thick; it is easier to cut the salmon if it is very cold.
2. Combine lemon and lime juices with parsley. Add salt and hot peppers or Tabasco to taste.
3. Place a layer of salmon in a ceramic or Pyrex dish and spoon a little of the marinade over it. Repeat this procedure until all salmon and marinade are used.
4. Refrigerate, covered, at least 6 hours or up to 24 hours.
5. Just before serving, peel the avocado. Cut in half, remove the pit, and slice lengthwise into ⅛-inch-thick slices. Arrange the salmon on 6 plates. Garnish with the avocado.

Servings: 6 to 8   Preparation: Easy
Time: Quick; advance preparation necessary

Terrine of Seafood

This extremely delicate and delicious terrine takes a while to prepare the first time. Once mastered it is very easy. The success of this recipe relies on the use of fresh fish. Do not omit the salt; it is necessary for the coagulation process to take place.

> 2 pounds grey sole fillets, petrale sole, or striped bass
> ½ teaspoon salt
> 2 teaspoons fresh lemon juice
> 4 egg whites
> 1½ cups heavy cream, chilled
> 2 tablespoons finely chopped fresh parsley sprigs
> 2 tablespoons finely chopped fresh dill sprigs
> Basic Beurre Blanc (page 34)

1. Butter a Pyrex mold that is 9 inches long, 4 to 5 inches wide, and 3 inches high. Line with wax paper.
2. Remove all bones and bits of skin from the sole and discard. Place half the sole in a food processor with half the salt, half the lemon juice, and half the egg whites. Puree until mixture is very smooth and stiff, about 2 to 4 minutes. During the processing, turn off the machine, scrape down the sides, and then process again. Place the mixture in a metal bowl. Repeat this procedure with the remaining sole, salt, lemon juice, and egg whites. Chill mixture in the freezer for 30 to 40 minutes. (Be sure to clean out the inside of the processor blade; see Appendix II.)
3. Chill the cream in the freezer for 20 minutes.
4. Using an electric mixer set on high speed, very slowly beat the cream into the sole mixture until consistency resembles soft ice cream. Do not add the fibers that adhere to the beaters as they will give the mixture a coarse texture. Check for level of salt and pepper by cooking a small spoonful in boiling water. Add salt and freshly ground black pepper to taste.
5. Divide the mixture into three parts. Add the parsley and dill to one part. Spread one part of the white sole mixture on the bottom of the mold, spread on the herb mixture, then top with the remaining white sole mixture.

6. Preheat oven to 350 degrees.
7. Cover mold with buttered wax paper, then cover tightly with aluminum foil. Place mold in a 10-inch pan and pour in enough hot water to come two-thirds of the way up the mold. Cook for 1 to 1½ hours until internal temperature on an instant thermometer reads 145 degrees.
8. The terrine should rest at least 10 minutes before the mold is removed. If left in the mold, it will stay warm up to 30 minutes. Remove aluminum foil and wax paper, then turn out onto a serving platter and remove the remaining wax paper.
9. Slice and serve warm with Beurre Blanc.

Servings: 8 to 10   **Preparation: Fairly easy to prepare**
Time: Time consuming

Pescado en Escabeche

This versatile dish wonderfully serves the function of appetizer, supper dish, or summer salad. Whether you use sole, haddock, cod, or perch, this combination guarantees a delightful piquancy. This dish is good served hot, room temperature, or chilled.

1 pound grey sole or petrale sole fillets
4 tablespoons olive oil
1 small onion, thinly sliced
1 large garlic clove, thinly sliced
1 small carrot, thinly sliced on diagonal
½ bay leaf
1 tablespoon peeled and thinly sliced fresh ginger
⅓ cup white wine vinegar
3 tablespoons fresh lemon juice
¼ cup water
2 tablespoons unbleached all-purpose flour
fresh Italian parsley sprigs for garnish

1. Heat 2 tablespoons oil in an 8-inch stainless steel saute pan; gently saute onion and garlic until clear but not brown. Add carrot and gently saute, covered, for 3 minutes. Add bay leaf, ginger, vinegar, lemon juice, and ¼ cup water. Bring to a boil, then turn heat down, and gently simmer, covered, for 5 minutes. Add salt and freshly ground black pepper to taste. If less than ½ cup liquid remains, add a little more water to measure ½ cup liquid.
2. Cut sole fillets in half down one side of the fine, bony spine; remove bone. Cut sole into 3-inch diamonds. Lightly dust the diamonds with flour seasoned with salt and freshly ground black pepper.
3. Heat the remaining 2 tablespoons oil in a 12-inch saute pan until very hot but not smoking. Add half the sole and saute on high heat until light golden. Turn over. (It is important that each diamond is turned over within 3 minutes; when overcooked, fish is apt to break apart when turning.) Cook for 2 to 3 more minutes until the fish is done, then arrange in a large Pyrex or ceramic dish. Repeat procedure with remaining sole, adding more oil to the saute pan if necessary.
4. Pour the onion mixture over the sole in the dish. If serving hot, let fish stand in this mixture at least 10 minutes prior to serving. If you're serving it chilled, it can be refrigerated for 2 days.
5. Just before serving, garnish with Italian parsley sprigs.

Servings: 6   Preparation: Easy
Time: Fairly time consuming; advance preparation possible

Soups & Breads

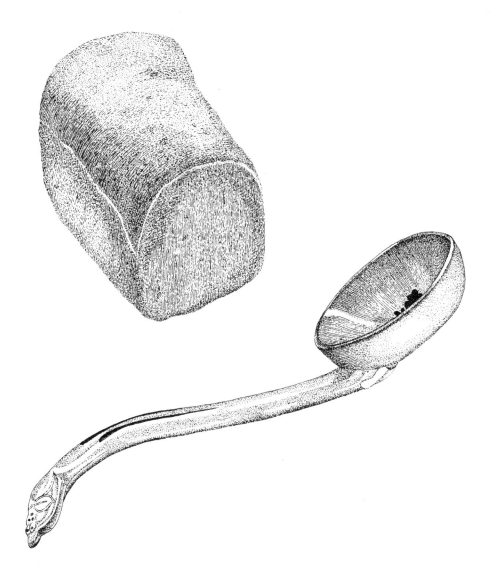

Soups

I love soup. One of my earliest memories is of the wonderful vegetable and pureed soups my mother made at home. She always made her own stock, skimmed off every trace of fat, and turned the fine variety of vegetables and fresh herbs from our garden into soups that were unforgettably delicious.

I cannot think of a better way to start a meal than with a small bowl of soup. In spring and early fall, a clean but richly flavored soup is ideal; summer calls for a refreshing iced soup, and in winter and late fall, a dense, hearty soup blankets you with warmth and flavor.

The soups I have included in this chapter are rich and varied in flavor. Since the essence of a good soup is the stock, I recommend that you make your own. I have a plentiful supply of freshly made stock available in the kitchen of my restaurant, so I always have a prepared base for my soups. It is not reasonable, however, to expect you to have fresh stock on hand at all times, so I have included a number of recipes in which canned broth can be substituted to excellent effect. (Always be careful to choose a good quality brand that is low in salt.) I have given you some useful guidelines on preparation and freezing of stocks on page 2, so do turn to them before you approach the soup recipes.

Bearing in mind the hectic schedules on which most of us are operating, I have included recipes for soups that can be prepared—totally or in part—several days ahead of time. I have also tested all the soups for freezing and have indicated those that freeze well. This is useful both as a timesaver and for preserving the excess when the recipe is designed to feed four to six and you are cooking for two.

Almond Garlic Soup

Treat your guests to a first course of this rich and rare soup. Take care to blend it well to a smooth consistency, then serve it garnished with large parsley sprigs.

Be sure that the almonds you use are whole, blanched, and not rancid.

> *¾ cup whole blanched almonds*
> *1 large leek*
> *5 large garlic cloves*
> *4 tablespoons unsalted butter*
> *1 medium onion, thinly sliced*
> *¼ cup converted raw rice*
> *5 cups homemade chicken stock (or canned low-salt chicken broth)*
> *⅛ teaspoon almond extract*
> *fresh mustard and cress greens (or Italian parsley) for garnish (optional)*

1. Remove and discard the coarse outside layer from the leek. Slice the leek up to the medium-green part. Place slices in a bowl of cold water for 30 minutes. Drain, rinse, drain well, and pat dry.
2. Bring 1 cup of water to a boil in a 2-quart saucepan. Add the garlic, with the skins still on, and boil for 3 minutes. Drain well, then peel.
3. Heat the butter in a 3- to 4-quart heavy saucepan. Add the onion and saute over medium heat until clear. Be careful it does not brown. Add the leek slices and saute until cooked; do not brown. Add the garlic, rice, and stock and bring the mixture to a boil. Lower the heat and simmer for 40 minutes.
4. Add the almonds and almond extract and simmer 10 minutes. Puree in the blender until very smooth.
5. The soup can be made 2 days ahead of time and stored in the refrigerator.
6. Reheat the soup before serving. If it is very thick, add a little water. Add salt and freshly ground black pepper to taste.
7. Garnish each serving with mustard and cress greens or parsley.

Servings: 6   Preparation: Easy
Time: Quick; advance preparation possible

Potage Longvielle

All the delights of a French country garden are to be found in this hearty winter soup.

2 small leeks
4 tablespoons unsalted butter
1 small onion, chopped
1 medium potato, peeled and cut into ⅛-inch dice
3 cups homemade chicken stock (or canned low-salt chicken broth)
1 cup frozen peas, thawed (or young, fresh peas)
2 cups stemmed, washed, and shredded raw spinach
1 cup light cream

1. Remove and discard the coarse outside layer from the leeks. Thinly slice the leek up to the medium-green part. Place slices in cold water for 30 minutes. Drain, rinse, drain well, and pat dry.
2. Heat butter over medium heat in a 3-quart saucepan, add onion, and saute until clear. Add leeks and continue to saute for 5 minutes, being careful not to brown. Add diced potato and chicken stock. Bring to a boil, reduce heat, and simmer for 10 minutes.
3. You may set this soup base aside for a couple of hours.
4. Just before serving, add peas and spinach and simmer, uncovered, for 5 more minutes. Add cream. Reheat, being careful not to boil as the soup may curdle. Add salt and freshly ground black pepper to taste.

Servings: 6   Preparation: Easy
Time: Quick; some advance preparation possible

Crème Élysée

This hearty winter soup might just convert you to the seldom-celebrated pleasures of the turnip!

2 cups peeled yellow turnips in ¼-inch dice
4 tablespoons unsalted butter
1 medium onion, thinly sliced
2 medium carrots, thinly sliced
3 cups strong homemade chicken stock (or canned low-salt chicken broth)
1 medium leek
1 small carrot, finely diced
1 small turnip, finely diced
1 cup light cream

1. Heat the butter in a heavy 2-quart saucepan, add the onion, and saute over medium heat until soft but not browned. Add carrots, turnips, and stock. Cover and gently simmer for 40 minutes.
2. Puree in a blender until very smooth. At this point, the base may be refrigerated for up to 2 days or frozen.
3. Cut the leek in half lengthwise, then cut in half again lengthwise, and thinly slice up to the medium-green part. Place slices in cold water for 30 minutes. Drain and pat dry.
4. Just before serving, reheat the soup base. Add the leeks and diced vegetables. Gently simmer for no longer than 10 minutes, or the vegetables are apt to become mushy. Add cream and reheat, being careful that soup does not boil or it might curdle. Add salt and freshly ground black pepper to taste.

Servings: 6 to 8   Preparation: Easy
Time: Fairly time consuming; soup base may be frozen

Solferino

The orange zest adds something very special to this soup. Try garnishing the soup with a spoonful of crème fraîche; it is a lovely addition.

> 4 large or 6 small vine-ripened tomatoes, peeled and seeded
> 4 tablespoons unsalted butter
> 1 medium onion, sliced
> 1½ cups thinly sliced carrots
> 3 cups homemade chicken stock or consomme
> finely pared rind (zest) of ½ orange
> crème fraîche or orange slices for garnish

1. Heat the butter in a 2-quart saucepan and gently saute onion until clear, approximately 8 to 10 minutes, being careful not to brown. Add tomatoes, carrots, orange zest, and chicken stock. Cover and simmer for 40 minutes.
2. Puree in the blender until very smooth.
3. At this point you may freeze the soup if you wish. If it should separate on defrosting, whisk while reheating and ingredients will come together.
4. Reheat and add salt and freshly ground black pepper to taste. Garnish each serving with crème fraîche or a slice of orange.

Servings: 6   Preparation: Easy
Time: Fairly time consuming; may be frozen

Potage Savoyarde

With its wonderful flavor of celery root, this soup is hearty and perfect for a cold fall day.

2 leeks
4 tablespoons unsalted butter
1 medium onion, thinly sliced
1 medium potato, peeled and thinly sliced
2 medium celery roots, peeled and thinly sliced
5 cups milk
whole fresh Italian parsley sprigs for garnish

1. Remove and discard the coarse outside layer from the leeks. Thinly slice the leek up to the medium-green part, and place the slices in cold water for 30 minutes. Drain, rinse, drain well, and pat dry.
2. Heat the butter in a heavy 3-quart saucepan. Add leeks and onion. Cover and gently saute over low heat for 15 minutes, being careful that they do not brown. Stir occasionally.
3. Add potato and celery root. Cover and gently saute for 15 minutes more. Add milk and bring the mixture to a simmer. Let it simmer 30 minutes. The soup may look as if it has curdled, but once it is pureed it will emulsify.
4. Puree in the blender until very smooth. Add salt and freshly ground black pepper to taste.
5. You may refrigerate the soup for 2 days.
6. Reheat, stirring occasionally, being careful not to boil, before serving. Garnish with whole Italian parsley sprigs.

Servings: 8   **Preparation: Easy**
Time: Fairly time consuming; advance preparation possible

Potage Bresilienne

Serve this velvety, rich, vegetarian bean soup with a tossed salad, French bread, and cheeses for a delightful light meal. Be sure to pick over the beans carefully and remove any stones.

> 1 cup dried black beans, well washed
> 4 tablespoons vegetable oil
> 1 medium onion, sliced
> ¼ teaspoon dried crushed red hot pepper
> 3 medium garlic cloves, sliced
> 4 medium tomatoes, peeled, seeded, and sliced
> 4 cups water
> ¼ bay leaf
> 2 teaspoons salt
> 1 carrot, finely diced
> 1 celery stalk, finely diced
> 1 small turnip, peeled and finely diced (optional)
> 2 tablespoons chopped fresh coriander leaves (optional)
> 6 tablespoons crème fraîche for garnish (optional)

1. Heat 2 tablespoons oil in a 3-quart heavy stainless steel saucepan. Add onion, hot pepper, and garlic and gently saute until onion is soft, being careful not to brown. Add tomatoes and cook for 5 minutes. Add beans, water, bay leaf, and salt. Cover and gently simmer for 2 hours, stirring occasionally, until beans are cooked and tender. Once in a while, check that water has not evaporated; if it has reduced, add more water.
2. When beans are soft, remove bay leaf and puree mixture in a blender until smooth.
3. Soup may be made ahead to this point and either stored in the refrigerator for up to 3 days or frozen.
4. Just before serving, heat remaining 2 tablespoons oil in a 10-inch saute pan and saute carrot, celery, and turnip over medium heat until soft; do not let them brown; add to the soup. Add water if soup is too thick. Add salt and freshly ground black pepper to taste. Reheat the soup and stir in coriander.
5. Garnish with a tablespoon of crème fraîche in each bowl.

Servings: 6 to 8   Preparation: Easy
Time: Time consuming; soup base may be frozen

Soup Mazur

The use of red rather than brown lentils gives this soup a lighter texture. You will find them in health food or Indian food stores. One cup of shredded fresh spinach is a nice alternative to the parsley.

1½ cups dried red lentils
3 tablespoons unsalted butter
1 tablespoon peeled, julienned fresh ginger
1 carrot, sliced
1 medium onion, sliced
1 stalk celery, sliced
6 cups homemade chicken stock or consomme (or canned
    low-salt chicken broth)
½ cup loosely packed fresh parsley sprigs, chopped

1. Heat the butter in a 3-quart heavy saucepan and add the ginger, carrot, onion, and celery. Cover and allow to gently saute over a very low heat for 10 minutes, being careful not to brown.
2. Meanwhile, pick over the lentils to remove any small stones.
3. Add the lentils and chicken stock to the sauteed vegetables. Bring to a boil, then turn down the heat and gently simmer for 1 hour, stirring occasionally. If the soup becomes very thick, add a little more water.
4. Puree in a food processor or blender.
5. This soup may be refrigerated for 2 days or frozen.
6. Before serving, reheat soup and add parsley. Add salt and freshly ground black pepper to taste.

Servings: 8   Preparation: Fairly easy
Time: Fairly time consuming; may be frozen

Soup Piment

Add a garnish of crème fraîche and fresh American caviar or chives to the rich color and opulent flavor of this soup, and you have perfection. Make the soup in large amounts during the summer when tomatoes and peppers are abundant and freeze it for the winter.

4 small or 3 large sweet red peppers
2 large or 3 medium vine-ripened tomatoes, peeled and seeded
    (juice reserved)
4 tablespoons unsalted butter
1 medium onion, thinly sliced
3 cups homemade chicken stock or consomme (or canned
    low-salt chicken broth)
crème fraîche for garnish
2 tablespoons snipped fresh chives or fresh American caviar for
    garnish

1. Place whole peppers under a preheated broiler and broil until dark brown all over. Leave in very cold water for 5 minutes. Peel and remove core and seeds. Slice peppers coarsely.
2. Over medium heat, melt butter in a large stainless steel saute pan. Add onion and saute until clear. Add peppers, tomatoes, tomato juice, and stock. Simmer for 30 minutes. Puree in a blender until the consistency is very smooth.
3. The soup may be frozen at this point, or refrigerated for 3 days.
4. Just before serving, reheat the soup and add salt and freshly ground black pepper to taste.
5. Garnish each serving with crème fraîche and chives or caviar.

Servings: 6   Preparation: Easy
Time: Fairly time consuming; may be frozen

Tomato, Mushroom, and Thyme Soup

The next time your garden is full of vine-ripened tomatoes, make this soup and freeze it for use during the winter. It is a very satisfying cold-weather soup with an unusually clean taste. The soup is especially wonderful when you make it with homemade chicken consomme.

3 large vine-ripened tomatoes, peeled and seeded (juice reserved)
6 tablespoons unsalted butter
1 medium onion, very finely chopped
1 tablespoon cake flour
2 cups homemade chicken stock or consomme (or canned low-salt chicken broth)
1½ tablespoons fresh thyme leaves (or 1 teaspoon dried thyme)
½ pound mushrooms

1. Slice the tomatoes into very thin strips.
2. Heat 2 tablespoons butter in a 3-quart stainless steel saucepan, add onion, and saute on medium heat until clear. Remove from heat and stir in flour until well incorporated. Return to low heat and cook for 1 minute.
3. Add chicken stock all at once to onion mixture. Bring to a boil, stirring constantly. Add tomatoes, tomato juice, and, if using dry thyme, add it at this time. Lower heat and gently simmer, uncovered, for 30 minutes.
4. This tomato-onion base may be made ahead of time and frozen or refrigerated.
5. Just before serving, cut the stalks level with the mushroom caps, then cut the caps and stalks into ⅛-inch slices. Heat 2 tablespoons butter in a large saute pan. Over high heat, stir in half the mushrooms, tossing until very light golden brown. Remove from pan and add to the soup base. Repeat this step with the remaining butter and mushrooms.
6. Bring the soup to a boil and, if using fresh thyme, add it at this time. Gently simmer for 5 minutes. Add salt and freshly ground black pepper to taste before serving.

Servings: 6   Preparation: Easy
Time: Fairly time consuming; soup base may be frozen

Mussel Fennel Soup

Mussel Fennel Soup, accompanied by a tossed salad and warm bread, makes a marvelous light meal. Farmed mussels are preferable to shore mussels because they are much cleaner; if you must use shore mussels, just be sure to check them thoroughly as discussed on page 12.

5 pounds mussels, in shells
1 cup white wine
5 cups water
1 medium onion, finely chopped
1 small bay leaf
2 teaspoons fennel seeds
1 ounce pancetta, very finely diced
2 tablespoons cake flour
1 cup light cream

1. Scrub mussels well and remove the beards. Discard any dead mussels. (If mussels are open, tap them lightly; if they close they are alive. Discard all mussels that do not close when tapped.)
2. Place the wine, water, onion, and bay leaf in a 4-quart stainless steel pan, and gently simmer for 20 minutes. Add one-third of the mussels and gently poach, uncovered, until the mussels have opened and shrunk away from the shell. Be careful not to overcook. Discard any mussels that do not open. Remove the mussels with a slotted spoon, and repeat this procedure with the remaining mussels, one-third at a time.
3. Pour the poaching liquid through a dampened cotton cloth (or several layers of cheesecloth) that has been placed in a sieve. Discard bay leaf and onion. Measure the liquid. If it is less than three cups, add more water.
4. Remove mussels from their shells and refrigerate.
5. Coarsely crush the fennel seeds in a blender or with a knife.
6. Place pancetta in a heavy 3- to 4-quart saucepan, and cook on medium heat until light golden brown. Stir in flour and fennel. Cook for 1 minute on low heat, stirring constantly. Slowly stir in the mussel liquid and bring it to a boil, stirring all the time. Turn down heat and gently simmer for 5 minutes.

7. The soup base and the mussels may be refrigerated for several hours at this point.
8. Just before serving, stir in the cream, add the mussels, and add salt and freshly ground black pepper to taste. Reheat soup, being careful not to boil, as the cream might curdle and the mussels might toughen if overcooked.

Servings: 8   Preparation: Easy
Time: Time consuming; advance preparation possible

Crabmeat Gumbo

An exciting mélange of flavors with a peppery tang that you can adjust to suit your taste. For a milder soup, decrease freshly ground black pepper to 1 teaspoon.

1 cup fresh, cooked crabmeat
1 sweet green pepper
⅓ cup vegetable oil
1 onion, very finely chopped
2 garlic cloves, finely chopped
1 tablespoon fresh thyme leaves (or 2 teaspoons dried thyme leaves)
1 tablespoon finely grated lemon rind (zest)
1 to 2 teaspoons freshly ground black pepper
4 small or 3 medium vine-ripened tomatoes, peeled, seeded, and diced
2 cups homemade chicken stock (or canned low-salt chicken broth)
1 cup fresh or frozen okra, sliced ⅛-inch thick

1. Preheat broiler. Broil green pepper until it is dark brown on all sides. Leave it in very cold water for 5 minutes. Remove and discard peel and seeds; finely dice the pepper.
2. Heat oil in a 3- to 4-quart stainless steel saucepan. Add onion and garlic and saute gently until clear, about 5 minutes. Add thyme, lemon zest, and 1 teaspoon black pepper. Cook on low heat for 2 minutes, being careful not to brown. Add tomatoes, stock, and green pepper and simmer gently for 20 minutes.
3. This base may be prepared to this point 3 days ahead of serving time and refrigerated. It may also be frozen.
4. Just before serving, add okra and crabmeat to the base. Gently simmer for 5 minutes. Add salt and freshly ground black pepper to taste.

Servings: 6   Preparation: Easy
Time: Fairly time consuming; soup base may be frozen

Shrimp Bisque

The use of a shrimp stock in this soup really adds to the flavor. You may make the shrimp stock any time you have raw shrimp shells, then freeze. The addition of tarragon is only for those tarragon lovers.

1 pound (16 to 20 count) shrimp, with shells
6 tablespoons unsalted butter
1 small onion, thinly sliced
1 small carrot, thinly sliced
4 vine-ripened tomatoes
½ bay leaf
2 cups water
2 small leeks
1 tablespoon cake flour
2 teaspoons dried tarragon (or 1 tablespoon fresh thyme leaves)
1 cup light cream

1. Peel the shrimp and devein. Refrigerate the shrimp, or if you're planning to freeze the soup, use the shrimp for another purpose. Save the shells.
2. Peel the tomatoes and save the skins. Remove the seeds. Puree the tomatoes and set aside.
3. To prepare stock, heat 3 tablespoons butter in a 3-quart stainless steel saucepan. On low heat, saute onion and carrot until soft, but not brown. Add tomato skins, bay leaf, shrimp shells, and 2 cups water to onion and carrot. Simmer gently, uncovered, for 40 minutes. Strain the shrimp stock and reserve. Discard the shells and vegetables.
4. Remove and discard the coarse outside layer from the leeks. Thinly slice leeks up to the medium-green part. Place in cold water for 30 minutes, then drain, rinse, drain well, and pat dry.
5. Heat the remaining 3 tablespoons butter in a 3-quart stainless steel saucepan. Add the leeks and saute on medium heat until soft; do not brown. Should water accumulate, continue to saute until all the liquid has evaporated.

6. Remove leeks from heat while you stir in flour. Then cook for 2 minutes on low heat, stirring constantly. Slowly stir in shrimp stock, pureed tomatoes, and tarragon or thyme. Bring to a boil, stirring constantly, then lower the heat and gently simmer for 15 minutes.
7. The soup can be prepared to this point and refrigerated for 6 hours or frozen.
8. Cut shrimp in half lengthwise. Add them to the soup and gently simmer until shrimp are cooked, about 3 to 5 minutes. Do not boil or overcook, as the shrimp will become rubbery in texture. Add cream. Gently reheat but do not boil, as the soup may curdle. Add salt and freshly ground black pepper to taste, and serve.

Servings: 4 to 6   **Preparation: Fairly easy**
Time: Fairly time consuming; soup base may be frozen

Spanish Fish Stew

You may be creative with this stew by combining different types of fish. Always be sure, though, to choose fish which contrast well in texture and taste. Make a meal of the stew accompanied by a tossed green salad and crusty warm bread.

1 pound skinless bluefish fillets, cut into 1-inch pieces
4 small vine-ripened tomatoes, peeled and seeded (juice reserved)
¼ cup olive oil
1 small onion, finely chopped
2 medium garlic cloves, thinly sliced
3 cups cold water
½ cup loosely packed fresh parsley leaves, coarsely chopped
½ cup loosely packed fresh basil leaves, coarsely chopped, or 2 teaspoons dried basil (optional)
pinch of saffron

1. Slice the tomatoes into thin julienne strips.
2. Heat olive oil in a 4-quart stainless steel or enamel saucepan over medium heat. Add garlic and onion and gently saute until onion is clear; be careful not to brown. Add tomatoes, tomato juice, and water. Bring to a boil, then lower the heat and gently simmer for 15 minutes.
3. This soup base may be refrigerated for 2 days or frozen.
4. Before serving, reheat base. Add bluefish, parsley, basil, and saffron. Simmer for 10 minutes. Add salt and freshly ground black pepper to taste. Serve immediately.

Servings: 6   Preparation: Easy
Time: Quick; soup base may be frozen

Crème d'Or

The splendor of a sunset is reflected in this glorious golden soup. The lemon and orange give it a light, lovely, and tart flavor. The soup is lovely served hot or cold.

2 cups thinly sliced carrots
4 tablespoons unsalted butter
1 medium onion, thinly sliced
2 tablespoons cake flour
4 cups homemade chicken stock (or canned low-salt chicken broth)
pared rind (zest) of ½ orange
3 to 4 tablespoons fresh lemon juice
1 cup light cream
orange slices or snipped fresh chives for garnish

1. Heat butter in a 3-quart saucepan. Gently saute onion on medium heat until clear, being careful not to brown. Turn heat down to low, stir in flour, and cook for 1 minute. Add stock and bring to a boil, stirring constantly.
2. Add orange rind and carrots. Turn down to a medium simmer, cover, and cook for 40 minutes, stirring occasionally.
3. Puree mixture in a blender until very smooth. Add 3 tablespoons lemon juice.
4. The soup may be frozen or refrigerated up to 2 days at this point; should it separate on reheating, whisk occasionally to emulsify.
5. To serve the soup chilled, add cream, lemon juice, and salt and freshly ground black pepper to taste to the soup base just before serving.
6. To serve hot, reheat soup and add cream, being careful not to boil, or the soup could curdle. Add lemon juice, salt, and freshly ground black pepper to taste.
7. Garnish with orange slices or snipped chives.

Servings: 6   Preparation: Easy
Time: Fairly time consuming; may be frozen

Mint and Pea Soup

This is a soup of exceptional color, delicious hot or cold. Children love it!

2 10-ounce packages frozen tiny peas, thawed and drained
2 tablespoons unsalted butter
1 medium onion, sliced ¼-inch thick
1 medium potato, peeled and sliced ¼-inch thick
3 cups homemade chicken stock (or canned low-salt chicken broth)
1 cup light cream
2 tablespoons chopped fresh mint leaves

1. Heat the butter in a 3-quart saucepan, add the onion, and gently saute over medium heat until soft but not brown. Add potato and stock and simmer for 40 minutes.
2. Add peas. Simmer an additional 5 minutes. Strain off 1½ cups of the liquid and set aside. Puree the remaining mixture in a blender until very smooth and all the pea skins are finely ground. Remove from blender and add the reserved liquid.
3. The soup may be prepared up to this point and refrigerated up to 2 days or frozen.
4. To serve hot, reheat. Add cream and reheat, being careful not to boil. Add the mint and salt and freshly ground black pepper to taste.
5. To serve cold, chill the soup for at least 2 hours. Just before serving, mix in the cream and mint. Add salt and freshly ground black pepper to taste.

Servings: 6 to 8   Preparation: Easy
Time: Fairly time consuming; may be frozen

Cauliflower and Watercress Soup

This delicately flavored soup, peppered with the tang of watercress, may be served hot or chilled. Cauliflower may not be one of your favorite vegetables, but it is lovely in this soup.

1 small cauliflower
2 tablespoons unsalted butter
1 medium onion, sliced
3 to 4 cups homemade chicken stock (or canned low-salt
  chicken broth)
1 cup light cream
1 small bunch watercress

1. Heat the butter in a 3-quart stainless steel saucepan, add the onion, and gently saute over medium heat until soft, being careful not to brown. Add chicken stock and bring up to a gentle simmer.
2. Cut flowerettes from cauliflower, leaving just ½-inch of stalk on them. Discard core. Add the flowerettes to stock and continue to gently simmer, uncovered, for 40 minutes. (Cauliflower should be uncovered so that sulphur will evaporate with the steam.)
3. Puree mixture in a blender until very smooth. This soup base may be refrigerated for 2 days or frozen.
4. Remove coarse stalks from watercress and discard. Chop watercress medium-fine.
5. For hot soup, reheat soup base. Three minutes before serving add cream, being careful not to boil soup as it might curdle, and watercress. Add salt and freshly ground black pepper to taste.
6. For chilled soup, add cream, watercress, and salt and freshly ground black pepper to taste to the cold soup base just before serving.

Servings: 6   Preparation: Easy
Time: Fairly time consuming; may be frozen

Asparagus Soup

Capture the heady flavor of spring in this bold, tasty soup. Try serving it hot or cold. If freezing or refrigerating this soup, the asparagus tips should be added immediately after pureeing.

1½ pound fresh asparagus
4 tablespoons unsalted butter
1 medium onion, thinly sliced
1 small carrot, thinly sliced
2 tablespoons cake flour
3 cups homemade chicken stock (or canned low-salt chicken
*   broth)*
1 cup light cream

1. Trim asparagus of any woody ends, then peel if the stalks seem tough. Cut off asparagus tips and set aside. Slice stalks into ½-inch pieces.
2. Heat butter in a 3-quart saucepan. Very gently saute onion until clear, being careful not to brown. Add carrot and gently saute, covered, for 5 more minutes, being careful not to brown. Remove the pan from the heat and stir in flour.
3. Add chicken stock all at once and bring to a boil, stirring constantly.
4. Add asparagus stalks, turn down heat, and gently simmer for 5 to 8 minutes. Be careful not to overcook the asparagus, as the soup will lose its fresh taste and appetizing color. Puree mixture in blender until smooth.
5. The soup may be prepared up to this point, then cooled and refrigerated for up to 3 days. It may also be frozen. If the soup separates on defrosting, whisk to emulsify.
6. To serve the soup hot, heat the puree to simmering. Coarsely chop the reserved asparagus tips and add them to the soup. (This may also be done before you refrigerate or freeze the soup.) Simmer for 5 minutes. Add cream and salt and freshly ground black pepper to taste. Reheat, but do not boil, as soup might curdle once cream has been added.
7. To serve the soup chilled, blanch the asparagus tips, run under cold water, drain well, dry, and finely chop. Add to the chilled soup along with the cream and salt and freshly ground black pepper to taste. Chill the soup at least 1 hour before serving.

Servings: 6   Preparation: Easy
Time: Fairly time consuming; soup base may be frozen

Chilled Consomme with Caviar

The distinct flavors of this elegant but light soup combine quite pleasantly. Serve it as a first course for a grand dinner party. Toasted brioche (page 152) is a delicious accompaniment.

3 cups jellied, homemade consomme or 6 cups liquid
    homemade consomme (see page 5)
1 ounce fresh American caviar
6 tablespoons crème fraîche or sour cream
2 tablespoons very finely snipped chives

1. If your consomme is not jellied, use 6 cups of consomme and reduce it by 50 percent on a high heat, then chill.
2. Chill six serving bowls.
3. Just before serving, place ½ cup well-chilled consomme in each bowl. Top each serving with 1 tablespoon crème fraîche. Sprinkle with chives, then arrange caviar on top of crème fraîche.

Servings: 6   **Preparation: Fairly easy**
Time: Time consuming; advance preparation necessary

Chilled Rumanian Crabmeat Soup

Don't be put off by the unusual combination of ingredients in this recipe, because it is such a flavorful soup. It is a summer soup that is satisfying enough to be a light meal unto itself. One cup of coarsely diced cooked shrimp may be substituted for the crabmeat.

1 cup fresh, cooked crabmeat
½ medium cucumber, peeled and coarsely grated
1 small boiling potato (preferably Maine), unpeeled
1 cup plain yogurt
1 cup strong, homemade chicken stock or consomme (or
*   canned low-salt chicken broth)*
⅓ cup loosely packed fresh mint leaves, finely chopped
2 tablespoons diced dill pickles
1 hard-boiled egg, peeled and finely chopped, for garnish

1. Place a layer of cucumber in a colander and lightly sprinkle with salt. Repeat until all cucumber is used up. Allow to sit for 1 hour. Rinse well under cold water and let drain for 10 minutes.
2. Place the potato in a 2-quart saucepan, cover with water, and gently boil until cooked. The potato is done when a knife is easily inserted into the middle. Leave potato in a bowl of cold water for 10 minutes, then remove and peel. Once potato is cooled, grate coarsely.
3. Place the yogurt in a bowl and whisk until smooth. Slowly whisk in stock or consomme, then stir in cucumber, potato, and crabmeat. Add mint, pickles, and salt and freshly ground black pepper to taste. Chill.
4. To serve, ladle into bowls and sprinkle with the egg.

Servings: 4   **Preparation: Easy**
Time: Fairly time consuming; advance preparation necessary

Chilled Avocado and Zucchini Soup

Here's an ideal opportunity to use those home-grown zucchini in a gorgeously green, mild-flavored soup.

1 small ripe avocado
3 small zucchini (7 to 7½ inches long)
2 tablespoons unsalted butter
1 medium onion, coarsely chopped
2 cups homemade chicken stock (or canned low-salt chicken broth)
2 tablespoons chopped fresh basil or mint leaves
¼ cup heavy cream (optional)
6 fresh basil or mint leaves for garnish

1. Heat the butter in a 3-quart saucepan, add the onion, and saute on a very low heat until clear. Add stock and gently simmer for 10 minutes.
2. Slice zucchini into ¼-inch-thick slices. Add the slices to the stock, bring to a boil, and simmer for 3 minutes, being careful not to overcook. (If the zucchini cooks longer, the soup may become unpleasantly bitter.)
3. Puree the mixture in a blender until smooth. Pour into a bowl and chill 2 hours or up to 2 days.
4. Just before serving, add chopped basil or mint and salt and freshly ground black pepper to taste. Peel avocado and cut into ¼-inch dice. Add diced avocado to soup. Ladle into soup bowls and pour a swirl of cream into each bowl. Garnish with a basil or mint leaf.

Servings: 6   Preparation: Easy
Time: Quick; advance preparation necessary

Chilled Crabmeat Corn Soup

You may be surprised by this recipe, but the exceptional blend of ingredients results in a fine soup. It makes good use of leftover boiled corn or frozen corn.

1 cup fresh, cooked crabmeat
1 cup cooked corn kernels
3 cups homemade chicken stock (or canned low-salt chicken broth)
¼ cup soy sauce, preferably low-salt
¼ cup loosely packed fresh mint leaves, chopped
¼ cup finely snipped fresh chives
Tabasco

1. In a food processor, process corn to a medium-puree consistency. There should still be some texture left.
2. Mix all ingredients together; add Tabasco to taste.
3. Chill for 1 hour before serving or up to 6 hours.

Servings: 6   Preparation: Easy
Time: Quick; advance preparation necessary

Chilled Cucumber and Tomato Soup

This tart and refreshing soup is best when made with vine-ripened tomatoes and English cucumbers.

½ English cucumber or 1 medium cucumber
3 very ripe, medium, vine-ripened tomatoes
1 cup plain yogurt
1 cup homemade chicken consomme or stock (or canned
low-salt chicken broth)
⅓ cup loosely packed fresh mint leaves, chopped
2 tablespoons finely snipped chives (optional)

1. Peel cucumber, then halve lengthwise and scrape out seeds. Coarsely grate cucumber. Peel and seed tomatoes; reserve the juice. Finely dice tomatoes.
2. Place yogurt in a bowl. Slowly whisk in stock. Add mint, chives, tomatoes, reserved tomato juice, and cucumber. Add salt and freshly ground black pepper to taste. Chill about 2 hours before serving, or up to 2 days.

Servings: 4   Preparation: Easy
Time: Quick; advance preparation necessary

Gazpacho

In my version of this Mexican classic, the coriander, cumin, and lime juice add some real zip.

> 4 large vine-ripened tomatoes, peeled and seeded (juice reserved)
> 1/4 cup vegetable oil
> 2 teaspoons cumin seeds
> 1 small onion, thickly sliced
> 1/4 to 1/2 teaspoon dried crushed red hot pepper
> 1 cucumber, peeled, halved lengthwise, seeded
> 1 cup lightly packed fresh coriander leaves, coarsely chopped
> 2 tablespoons fresh lime juice
> Tabasco (optional)
> 1 small avocado for garnish

1. Heat the oil in a 10-inch saute pan, add the cumin seeds, and saute over medium heat until they turn a more golden brown. Add onion and hot pepper and toss over high heat for 2 minutes until onion is semicooked. Puree mixture in blender. Pour into a bowl and cool.
2. Puree the tomatoes and juice in a blender and combine with onion mixture.
3. Grate cucumber on medium-sized grater. Add to the tomato-onion mixture. Add coriander and lime juice and salt to taste. Add Tabasco until soup is of desired spiciness. Chill at least 2 hours and up to 2 days.
4. Just before serving, peel and slice avocado. Serve soup garnished with avocado.

Servings: 4   Preparation: Easy
Time: Fairly time consuming; advance preparation necessary

Breads

There is nothing more inviting than the smell of freshly baked bread. It is the beginning, the middle, and the end of every great meal. Not only is it pleasing to the taste, but it is nutritious, satisfying at completion, and a wonderful therapy from the kneading to the rising and baking.

All but one of the following recipes are yeast breads. They may be made by hand, but the Whole Wheat, Onion Rosemary, Black Pepper, Hazelnut, and Walnut Cumin breads may be partially made in a mixer if it has a dough hook attachment. I strongly advise that you do not make a double batch of dough in your mixer unless your mixer bowl can hold 6 quarts or more, because large quantities put a strain on the motor of the mixer. To use the mixer, follow these steps:

1. Place the sugar and water in the mixer bowl, sprinkle in the yeast and let stand until light and frothy.
2. Place the bowl in the mixer and add the butter, salt, nuts, herbs, onions, or black pepper.
3. Turn the mixer to low speed and slowly add the flour until stiff, but not dry.
4. Continue to knead in the mixer for 3 to 5 minutes until the dough is smooth and slightly resilient to the touch.
5. Remove from the mixer and follow the remaining steps in the recipe.

Please read about flour and yeast in Appendix I before you begin making bread.

It is my preference not to freeze bread, as it tends to become dry when frozen. Therefore, if you feel you do not want to have two loaves of bread on hand, you can halve the recipe.

Cornbread

This fairly dense, non-yeast bread is ideal to make when you have a couple of leftover ears of corn. Or you may use canned or frozen corn in the recipe. The addition of the corn gives the bread a nice texture and a richer taste. My preference is for an unsweet, or savory cornbread, but if you prefer a sweeter taste, increase the sugar to 3 tablespoons. This bread is wonderful served with chicken salads, cold roast beef, and spicy fish dishes.

1 cup cooked fresh corn kernels (or 1 cup canned or frozen corn)
1 cup yellow cornmeal
1 cup all-purpose unbleached flour
1 tablespoon baking powder
1 tablespoon sugar
2 teaspoons salt
2 large eggs
¾ cup milk
½ cup melted unsalted butter, room temperature

1. Preheat oven to 375 degrees. Butter an 8x8x2-inch square pan.
2. Place the corn kernels in a food processor or blender and process to a medium coarse puree.
3. Place the cornmeal, flour, baking powder, sugar, and salt in a bowl. Mix well. Make a well in the center of the mixture and place the pureed corn, eggs, milk, and melted butter in it. Start gently whisking the liquid ingredients in the center, gradually whisking in the dry ingredients. When all the dry ingredients are whisked in, gently whisk the mixture until smooth.
4. Pour the batter into the pan and bake for 30 to 35 minutes or until light golden brown.
5. Remove the pan from the oven; leave the bread in the pan to cool. Serve warm or cold with unsalted butter.

Servings: 6   **Preparation: Easy**   **Time: Quick**

Brioche with Brie

Brioche with Brie is an ideal addition to buffets as it does not need to be served with butter. It is superb at room temperature and even more delightful fresh from the oven. You can also use this recipe for a delicious, rich brioche; note the variations at the end of the recipe.

4 to 5 cups all-purpose unbleached flour
1 tablespoon + 1 teaspoon dry active yeast
¾ cup water at 90–100 degrees
1 teaspoon sugar
7 large eggs
6 ounces unsalted butter, room temperature
2 teaspoons salt
8 ounces Brie

1. Pour the water into a large bowl, add the sugar, and sprinkle in the yeast. Let it stand until it is light and frothy.
2. Place the butter in a separate bowl and beat until it is smooth and very soft.
3. With an electric mixer, beat the eggs into the yeast mixture until frothy. Add the salt. Slowly add 2 cups of flour to the yeast mixture on a low speed. Beat in the butter, 2 tablespoons at a time, on a low speed. Beat in the remaining 2 to 3 cups flour on a low speed until the dough is fairly stiff, yet slightly sticky.
4. Lightly oil a large bowl, place the dough in the bowl, and turn the dough over. Cover the bowl. Leave the dough to rise in a warm place until it has doubled in size (30 to 60 minutes).
5. Cut the rind off the Brie and discard. Cut the Brie into ½-inch cubes.
6. Spread half the dough over the bottom of a buttered 10-inch cake pan. Place the Brie cubes in the center of the dough, leaving a 1-inch border uncovered. Spread the remaining dough on top. Tightly crimp the upper and lower edges together.
7. Allow the dough to rise in a warm place for 30 to 40 minutes or until doubled in size. Just before baking, brush with a little beaten egg.
8. Meanwhile, preheat oven to 400 degrees.
9. Place the brioche on the middle shelf in the preheated oven. Bake for 40 to 50 minutes or until the dough is dark golden brown and has

pulled away from the edges of the pan. Cool in the pan for 10 minutes before turning out and serving.

Variation: For a plain brioche, increase the sugar to ¼ cup and add with the eggs in step 3. After step 4, spread one-third of the dough evenly over the bottom of the buttered cake pan. Then divide the rest of the dough into 5 pieces, shape them into flat balls, and fit them evenly over the dough. Continue with step 7.

Yield: 1 large round loaf   **Preparation: Fairly easy**
Time: Time consuming

Savarin with Dried Apricots

This is a first-rate bread for toasting. I find it delightful as a tea bread, spread with unsalted butter. It is best served the day it is baked. This also is the dough that is used for rum babas, as it can be soaked in a rum syrup after it is baked. This variation will keep up to 2 days and is lovely served with whipped cream and strawberries.

4 cups all-purpose unbleached flour
½ cup water at 90–100 degrees
1 tablespoon dry active yeast
3 tablespoons sugar
1 teaspoon salt
8 large eggs, room temperature
1 cup finely diced dried apricots
1 tablespoon finely grated orange rind (zest)
10 ounces unsalted butter, soft but not melted

1. Place the warm water in a large bowl, add the sugar, and sprinkle in the yeast. Let it stand until light and frothy.
2. Whisk in the orange zest, apricots, salt, and eggs. Slowly beat in the flour with a wooden spoon; although the mixture may be lumpy, continue to beat in the flour. Then beat until smooth.

3. This step should be done with your hands. Slowly beat in the butter 4 tablespoons at a time, being careful that the butter does not melt. If your hands are warm, run them under cold water, dry well, then continue to beat in the butter until it is well incorporated.
4. Put the dough in a large, lightly oiled bowl and turn it over. Cover the bowl and allow the dough to rise in a warm place until it has doubled in size.
5. Punch down the dough. Place it into a buttered 2½-quart tube pan and leave it to rise in a warm place until it has doubled in size.
6. Meanwhile, preheat the oven to 400 degrees.
7. Lightly butter the top of the dough. Bake it in the preheated oven for 40 to 50 minutes until the dough is golden brown and starts to pull away from the sides of the pan. Turn onto a cooling rack and cool or serve warm.

Variation: Place 1 cup water and 1 cup sugar in a 1-quart saucepan. Allow the sugar to dissolve while you stir gently. When all the sugar has dissolved, bring the liquid to a boil and boil for 5 minutes. Remove from the stove and add ⅓ cup rum. Allow the syrup to cool down until it is warm.

Place the warm (not hot) Savarin in a 4- to 5-inch-deep china or Pyrex bowl or stainless steel pan. Slowly spoon half the syrup over it. Allow it to sit for 30 minutes, then turn it over and spoon the remaining syrup on top. Let it stand for at least 30 more minutes before slicing.

Yield: 1 large round loaf   **Preparation: Fairly easy**
Time: Time consuming

Fennel Bread

The addition of fennel gives this bread a flavor reminiscent of anise. It is lovely served toasted with smoked salmon or Gravlax. This recipe may be cut in half.

7 to 9 cups all-purpose unbleached flour
1 medium fennel bulb
1 tablespoon fennel seed
8 tablespoons unsalted butter
1 tablespoon + 1 teaspoon dry active yeast
1½ cups water at 90–100 degrees
2 teaspoons salt
1 cup water

1. Remove and discard the coarse outside layer from the fennel. Cut the bulb in half through the core, cut out the core, then finely dice the fennel. Coarsely grind the fennel seed in a very dry blender.
2. Heat the butter in a 12-inch saute pan, and add the fennel and fennel seed. Saute the fennel over medium heat for 3 to 5 minutes until it is almost soft, being careful not to let it overcook or brown. Cool.
3. Place the warm water in a large mixing bowl and sprinkle in the yeast. Leave in a warm place until the mixture is light and frothy. Add the remaining water.
4. Add the cooked fennel and salt to the yeast. Beat in the flour with a wooden spoon until the dough is stiff but not dry.
5. Place dough on a lightly floured board; knead until smooth, approximately 5 to 10 minutes. (If you have a mixer with a dough hook, knead in the mixer for 3 minutes.)
6. Clean the bowl, then lightly oil it. Form dough into a ball, put it in the bowl, then turn over. Cover the bowl with a damp cloth and leave it in a warm place until the dough has tripled in volume.
7. Place dough on a lightly floured board and gently knead until smooth. Divide in half. Roll each half into a 14-inch by 10-inch oblong, and then tightly roll it up. Lightly dampen the ends and crimp the edges. Place each loaf on a lightly floured sheet pan, seam side down. Brush each loaf with a little oil and cut ¼-inch-deep slashes 2 inches apart along

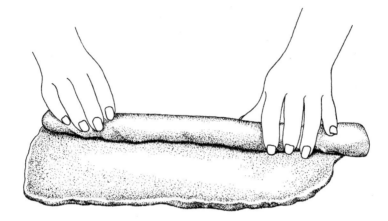

1. After rolling the dough into a 14- by 10-inch rectangle, roll it up tightly.

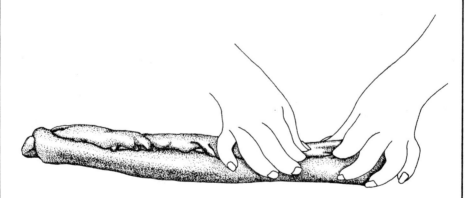

2. Crimp the edges together tightly. The crimped edges should be on the underside when the bread dough is placed on the sheet pan.

the top. Leave the loaves to rise in a warm place 1 hour until they have almost doubled in size.

8. Meanwhile, preheat oven to 400 degrees.
9. Place the loaves in the preheated oven and bake for 30 to 40 minutes until light golden brown. Remove the loaves from oven and cool, or serve slightly warm.

Yield: 2 loaves   **Preparation: Fairly easy**
Time: Time consuming

Whole Wheat Bread

You can make two delicious loaves of whole wheat bread with this recipe, or one pizza crust and one loaf of bread. The recipe also works well with all whole wheat flour, which gives a very dense bread with a lovely nutty flavor. This recipe may be cut in half.

3¾ cups whole wheat flour
3 to 4 cups all-purpose unbleached flour
1 cup warm water at 90–100 degrees
1 tablespoon + 2 teaspoons dry active yeast
1 teaspoon sugar
1 cup water
5 tablespoons unsalted butter, melted, at room temperature
2 teaspoons salt

1. Place the warm water in a large mixing bowl and sprinkle in yeast. Add sugar. Leave in a warm place until the mixture is light and frothy. Add remaining cup of water.
2. Add butter and salt to the yeast. Beat in the flour with a wooden spoon until the dough is stiff but not dry.
3. Place dough on a lightly floured board; knead until smooth, approximately 5 to 10 minutes.
4. Clean the bowl, then lightly oil. Form dough into a ball, put it into the bowl, then turn over. Cover the bowl with a damp cloth. Leave in a warm place until the dough has tripled in volume.

5. Place dough on a lightly floured board and gently knead until smooth. Divide in half. Roll each half into a 14-inch by 10-inch oblong, and then tightly roll up. Lightly dampen the ends and crimp the edges. Place each loaf on a lightly floured sheet pan, seam side down. Brush each loaf with a little oil and cut ¼-inch-deep slashes 2 inches apart across the top. Leave the loaves to rise in a warm place for 1 hour until they have almost doubled in size.
6. Meanwhile, preheat oven to 400 degrees.
7. Place the loaves in the oven and bake for 30 to 40 minutes until light golden brown. Remove from oven and cool, or serve slightly warm.

Yield: 2 loaves   Preparation: Fairly easy
Time: Time consuming

Black Pepper Bread

Grinding the pepper in the blender just before adding it to the dough adds an exquisitely aromatic flavor to this bread. Black Pepper Bread is wonderful served with cheeses and cream soup. The recipe may be cut in half, if you wish.

> *8 to 9 cups all-purpose, unbleached flour*
> *1 tablespoon black peppercorns*
> *1 cup warm water at 90–100 degrees*
> *1 tablespoon + 1 teaspoon dry active yeast*
> *1 teaspoon sugar*
> *1 cup water*
> *5 tablespoons unsalted butter, melted, at room temperature*
> *2 teaspoons salt*

1. Put the peppercorns in a very dry blender and grind coarsely.
2. Place the warm water in a large mixing bowl and sprinkle in yeast. Add sugar. Leave in a warm place until the mixture is light and frothy. Add remaining cup of water.
3. Add butter and salt and pepper to the yeast. Beat in flour with a wooden spoon until dough is stiff but not dry.
4. Place the dough on a lightly floured board and knead until smooth, approximately 5 to 10 minutes.

5. Clean the bowl and lightly oil it. Form the dough into a ball, put it into the bowl, and turn over. Cover the bowl with a damp cloth. Leave it in a warm place to rise until the dough has tripled in volume.
6. Place the dough on a lightly floured board and gently knead until smooth. Divide it in half. Roll each half into a 14-inch by 10-inch oblong and tightly roll up. Lightly dampen the ends and crimp the edges. Place each loaf, seam side down, on a lightly floured sheet pan. Brush each loaf with a little oil and cut ¼-inch-deep slashes 2 inches apart across the top. Leave the loaves to rise in a warm place for 1 hour until they have almost doubled in size.
7. Meanwhile, preheat oven to 400 degrees.
8. Place the loaves in the preheated oven and bake for 30 to 40 minutes until light golden brown. Remove from oven and cool, or serve slightly warm.

Yield: 2 loaves   Preparation: Easy
Time: Time consuming

Onion Rosemary Bread

This wonderful smelling bread is delicious served with unsalted butter. It also makes excellent toast. The recipe may be cut in half, if you wish.

8 to 9 cups all-purpose unbleached flour
6 tablespoons unsalted butter
1 large or 2 medium onions, finely diced
1½ tablespoons fresh rosemary, coarsely chopped
1 cup warm water at 90–100 degrees
1 tablespoon + 1 teaspoon dry active yeast
1 teaspoon sugar
1 cup water
2 teaspoons salt

1. Heat the butter in a 10- to 12-inch saute pan, add onion, and saute until clear, being careful not to brown. Add rosemary and continue to cook for 1 minute. Cool the mixture to room temperature before proceeding.
2. Place the warm water in a large mixing bowl and sprinkle in yeast. Add the sugar. Leave in a warm place until the mixture is light and frothy. Add remaining cup of water.

3. Add onion-rosemary mixture and salt to the yeast. Beat in the flour with a wooden spoon until dough is stiff but not dry.
4. Place dough on a lightly floured board and knead until smooth, approximately 5 to 10 minutes.
5. Clean the bowl; lightly oil. Form dough into a ball, put it into the bowl, then turn over. Cover the bowl with a damp cloth. Leave it in a warm place until the dough has tripled in volume.
6. Place the dough on a lightly floured board and gently knead until smooth. Divide in half. Roll each half into a 14-inch by 10-inch oblong and tightly roll up. Lightly dampen the ends and crimp the edges. Place each loaf, seam side down, on a lightly floured sheet pan. Brush each loaf with a little oil and cut ¼-inch-deep slashes 2 inches apart across the top. Leave the loaves to rise in a warm place for 1 hour until they have almost doubled in size.
7. Meanwhile, preheat oven to 400 degrees.
8. Place the loaves in the oven and bake for 30 to 40 minutes until they are light golden brown. Remove from oven and cool, or serve slightly warm.

Yield: 2 loaves   Preparation: Fairly easy
Time: Time consuming

Hazelnut Bread

If you are careful to ensure that the nuts you use are not at all rancid, you will get a delightfully sweet flavor from this bread. The recipe may be cut in half, if you wish.

3 to 4 cups whole wheat flour
3 cups all-purpose unbleached flour
1 cup water, 90–100 degrees
1 tablespoon + 2 teaspoons dry active yeast
1 teaspoon sugar
1 cup water
1 cup hazelnuts
5 tablespoons unsalted butter, melted, room temperature
2 teaspoons salt

1. Place the warm water in a large mixing bowl and sprinkle in the yeast. Add the sugar. Leave in a warm place until the mixture is light and frothy. Add the second cup of water.
2. Place the hazelnuts in a food processor and process until they are chopped medium fine.
3. Add the butter and salt to the yeast, then the hazelnuts. Beat in flour with a wooden spoon until the dough is stiff but not dry.
4. Place the dough on a lightly floured board and knead until smooth, about 5 to 10 minutes.
5. Clean the bowl and lightly oil it. Form the dough into a ball, put it in the bowl, then turn over. Cover the bowl with a damp cloth. Leave it in a warm place until the dough has tripled in volume.
6. Place the dough on a lightly floured board and gently knead for 2 to 3 minutes until smooth. Divide in half. Roll each half into a 14- by 10-inch oblong and tightly roll up. Lightly dampen the ends and crimp the edges. Place each loaf on a lightly floured sheet pan. Brush each loaf with a little oil and cut ¼-inch-deep slashes 2 inches apart across the top. Leave the loaves to rise in a warm place for 1 hour until they have almost doubled in size.
7. Meanwhile, preheat the oven to 400 degrees.
8. Place the loaves in the oven and bake for 30 to 40 minutes until light golden brown. Remove from the oven and cool, or serve slightly warm.

Yield: 2 loaves   **Preparation: Fairly easy**   **Time: Time consuming**

Walnut Cumin Bread

I strongly recommend freshly cracked walnuts for this bread. You might be concerned that they will taste too strong, but I assure you that the flavors come together very well when the bread has baked. The recipe may be cut in half.

3 to 4 cups whole wheat flour
3 cups all-purpose unbleached flour
1 cup warm water at 90–100 degrees
1 tablespoon + 2 teaspoons dry active yeast
1 teaspoon sugar
1 cup water
1 cup freshly cracked walnuts
5 tablespoons melted unsalted butter, room temperature
2 teaspoons ground cumin
2 teaspoons salt

1. Place the warm water in a large mixing bowl and sprinkle in the yeast. Add the sugar. Leave in a warm place until the mixture is light and frothy. Add the second cup of water.
2. Place the walnuts in a food processor and process until they are a medium-fine chop.
3. Add the butter and salt to the yeast. Beat in the flour, walnuts, and cumin with a wooden spoon until the dough is stiff but not dry.
4. Place the dough on a lightly floured board and knead until smooth, which takes about 5 to 10 minutes.
5. Clean the bowl and lightly oil. Form the dough into a ball, put it in the bowl, then turn over. Cover the bowl with a damp cloth and leave it in a warm place until the dough has tripled in volume.
6. Place the dough on a lightly floured board and gently knead until smooth. Divide it in half. Roll each half into a 14- by 10-inch oblong, and then tightly roll up into a loaf. Lightly dampen the ends, crimp the edges, and place each loaf on a lightly floured sheet pan. Brush each loaf with a little oil and cut ¼-inch-deep slashes 2 inches apart across the top. Leave the loaves to rise in a warm place for 1 hour until they have almost doubled in size.

7. Meanwhile, preheat oven to 400 degrees.
8. Place the loaves in the oven and bake for 30 to 40 minutes until light golden brown. Remove from the oven and cool, or serve slightly warm.

Yield: 2 loaves   Preparation: Fairly easy
Time: Time consuming

Salads

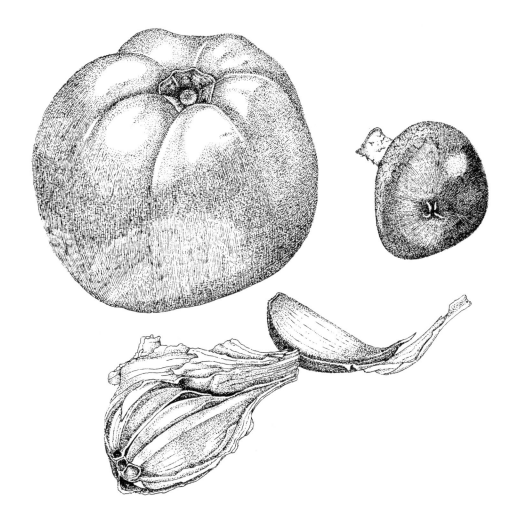

Salads

Take the best of the farmer's garden, a touch of the Orient, a dash of the sea, a pinch of imagination, and a spoonful of creativity, and before you will appear what we call a salad.

In this chapter are some of the creations that I have discovered in my travels through Europe and across America. From California—where the combinations of ingredients are served with such great imagination and simplicity and the wonderful West Coast climate lends itself to the growing and preparing of fresh vegetables and greens—to the farms of Massachusetts, where seasons are shorter and varieties are smaller, there are mixtures of wonderful ingredients that will make your meals exciting as well as nourishing.

I have included in this chapter recipes that can be an addition to any meal or a complete meal in themselves. Many of them can be served as an appetizer course. There are salads using fresh greens or fresh vegetables, fish salads, meat salads, and poultry salads.

Before you start here are a few helpful hints:

Once you have picked the freshest greens, do not wash them until several hours before you serve them. To further enhance your creation, dry the greens well before preparing your salad. I use English cucumbers, also called seedless cucumbers, as I prefer their flavor and texture. When it comes to tomatoes, if you have read more than ten pages of this book, you will know by now that I always recommend vine-ripened tomatoes. As far as I am concerned, they are the only kind of tomato worth considering; their flavor is superior. But I am pragmatic enough to concede that they are not always available. If you buy hothouse or artificially ripened tomatoes, let them ripen for 4 to 5 days in a sunny indoor spot and you will find their flavor will improve slightly.

Once assembled, a beautiful, fresh salad can be complemented with a lovely dressing. I have included three of my favorite dressings in this chapter. I also suggest that you make your own vinegar (see page 61). You will find that you can create salad dressings that are not only original, but also refreshing and delicious. Be aware, however, that you should not serve a highly acidic dressing when you are serving salads with fine wines. The vinegar is likely to taint the taste of the wine.

You will notice that many of my green vegetable salads have no acids added to them. Acids like vinegar or lemon juice will change the color of the vegetable from a bright green to an unappetizing brown, unless added just before serving. I also feel that the amount of acid added to green vegetables should be adjusted to one's own taste. Therefore, I garnish my green vegetable salads with wedges of lemon, which adds a lovely contrast in color as well as providing a means of flavoring the salad.

As my friend Steven Marsh once said, "A salad is allowed to be as exciting as its combinations of fresh ingredients, mixed with its unusual assortment of liquids, served from a bowl or a plate, terrifying with so many wines, but oh so wonderful!"

Hazelnut Dressing

I really love this salad dressing because the nuts give it a beautiful, rich flavor. It is very popular in the restaurant. It is especially good on a salad of lettuce, avocado, cucumber, and watercress. The base of the dressing keeps well in the refrigerator, but the nuts can only be added 2 hours before serving as they tend to get soggy if they soak longer. Be certain nuts are not rancid.

> 1 cup whole hazelnuts
> ¾ cup vegetable oil or peanut oil
> 5 large shallots
> ⅓ cup balsamic vinegar

1. Preheat oven to 400 degrees. Roast nuts on a sheet pan for 7 to 10 minutes, until skins start to crack and nuts turn slightly darker color. Watch nuts carefully, as they burn easily. Remove from oven, let cool, then rub off skins. (Some skin may stay on, which is fine.) Place in a food processor and work to a coarsely chopped consistency.
2. Thinly slice the shallots. Heat the oil in a 12-inch saute pan, add the shallots, and saute until clear but not brown. Pour shallots into a bowl and add vinegar. Chill.
3. Two hours before serving, mix the nuts into the shallot mixture. Add salt and freshly ground black pepper to taste. Chill, if you wish. If the dressing is a little too sharp for your tastes, add a little more oil.
4. Whisk well just before serving.

Yield: 2 cups   Preparation: Easy
Time: Quick; some advance preparation possible

Creamy Herb Dressing

This is a light, creamy salad dressing in which the flavor of the herbs comes through beautifully. I suggest you use it for Salad Chaya (page 214) and Watercress, Cucumber, and Mushroom Salad (page 181). It is also nice served with a tossed green salad.

3 tablespoons tarragon or basil vinegar (preferably homemade; page 61)
1 tablespoon chopped fresh tarragon leaves (or finely snipped fresh chives, or 2 tablespoons chopped fresh basil leaves or fresh dill sprigs)
⅓ cup vegetable oil
½ cup heavy cream

1. Whisk together vinegar, herbs, and oil until well blended. Slowly whisk in cream. Add salt and freshly ground black pepper to taste. Add to salad and serve.

Yield: ¾ cup   **Preparation: Easy**
Time: Quick

Sesame Dressing

This wonderful dressing was created by Gary Pfahl, a chef at Another Season. It is great served with a simple salad of mixed greens, cucumber and raw sliced mushrooms. Hoisin sauce and sesame oil are sold at Oriental food markets.

2 tablespoons Hoisin sauce
2 tablespoons medium-dark sesame oil
1 medium garlic clove, finely chopped or crushed
1 tablespoon peeled, finely grated ginger
¼ cup rice vinegar (or ⅓ cup white wine vinegar)
¾ cup vegetable oil
2 tablespoons finely snipped fresh chives (or 3 tablespoons
    finely sliced scallions)
sesame seeds for garnish

1. Place all the ingredients except the sesame seeds in a bowl and whisk until well emulsified.
2. Refrigerate up to 4 days.
3. Whisk or shake well before serving. Garnish the salad with sesame seeds.

Yield: 1 cup   Preparation: Easy
Time: Quick; advance preparation possible

Poached Mushrooms

Poached mushrooms are nice to use in salads, appetizers, and hors d'oeuvres where you don't want sauteed and buttery mushrooms. During the poaching process the vinegar and water turn the mushrooms a nice, light color. The mushroom poaching liquid may be frozen for use in recipes, such as Mushrooms Stuffed with Feta and Walnuts (page 73).

1 pound medium mushrooms
1 onion, sliced
½ cup white wine herb vinegar
2 cups water
1 bay leaf
1 teaspoon salt

1. Combine onion, vinegar, water, bay leaf, and salt in a 2-quart stainless steel pan. Add a little freshly ground black pepper. Cover and gently simmer for 30 minutes.
2. Cut mushroom stalks level with caps. (The stalks may be discarded or saved for another use.) Gently simmer the mushroom caps in poaching liquid for 5 minutes. To check for doneness, remove a mushroom with a slotted spoon and cut it in half to make sure it is cooked through. Remove remaining mushrooms with a slotted spoon. Chill before using.
3. The mushroom poaching liquid may be frozen and used 4 to 5 more times. Before using it each time, measure liquid and add enough water to come up to 3 to 4 cups of poaching liquid.

Yield: 2 cups   Preparation: Easy
Time: Fairly time consuming; advance preparation necessary

Green Bean Salad

This is a perfect salad for hot summer weather. It goes wonderfully with a chicken, beef, or seafood salad. You will notice I use no vinegar or lemon juice in the dressing; this is because the acid turns the beans an unattractive brown. So besides using the lemon wedges as garnish, they are also used to squeeze onto the beans before eating. The sun-dried tomatoes are optional because you may not be able to find them in your local store.

1 pound fresh young green beans
½ cup olive oil
2 red onions, finely sliced
4 sun-dried tomatoes, sliced very fine (optional)
½ cup loosely packed fresh parsley sprigs, finely chopped
1 lemon for garnish

1. Remove the tops from the green beans. Half fill a 2-quart saucepan with cold water and bring to a boil. Add the beans and boil until just tender. Drain and immediately run under cold water until cool. Leave in the colander to drain for 30 minutes.
2. Heat the olive oil in a 12-inch saute pan, add the onions, and toss over high heat until clear. Be careful not to overcook the onions, as they should be slightly crunchy. Pour the onions and oil into a bowl and cool.
3. Pat the green beans dry. Cut them in half on the diagonal. Add them to the onions along with the tomatoes, parsley, and salt and freshly ground black pepper to taste.
4. Refrigerate 1 hour or as long as 8 hours.
5. Just before serving, arrange the salad on a serving platter. Cut the lemon into wedges and garnish the platter.

Servings: 6   Preparation: Easy
Time: Fairly time consuming; advance preparation necessary

Green Bean and Cucumber Salad

This crisp green vegetable salad is lovely with a rich chicken or seafood salad.

1 pound fresh young green beans
1 English cucumber
⅓ cup olive oil
⅓ cup loosely packed fresh mint, coarsely chopped
⅓ cup loosely packed fresh parsley sprigs, coarsely chopped
1 lemon for garnish

1. Peel cucumber and slice it very thin. Line a colander with one layer of cucumber and lightly sprinkle with salt. Cover with another layer of cucumber, sprinkle with salt, and continue until all the cucumber is used up. Allow it to stand for 1 hour; then run the colander under cold water for 3 minutes. Let it drain for 30 minutes.
2. While cucumber drains, remove the ends from the green beans and cut the beans in half. Bring 2 quarts water to a boil in a 3-quart saucepan, add beans, and boil until they are just tender. Drain and immediately run under cold water until cool. Drain well; pat dry.
3. Thirty minutes to 1 hour before serving (or as much as 24 hours), mix oil, mint, and parsley in a bowl. Add cucumber and green beans; toss. Add salt and freshly ground black pepper to taste. Chill.
4. Cut lemon into wedges. Place salad on a serving platter and arrange the lemon wedges around the edge. Serve a lemon wedge with each serving of salad so that diners can squeeze the lemon onto the beans.

Servings: 4   Preparation: Easy
Time: Fairly time consuming; advance preparation necessary

Fagiolini Verdi con Prosciutto

The prosciutto really comes through in flavor in this green bean salad. No salt is needed because of the prosciutto, and I do not use any vinegar or lemon juice because they will turn the beans brown. The tomatoes add flavor but are not essential to the salad. This salad is really good served with a seafood salad.

1 pound fresh, young green beans
3 ounces prosciutto, sliced medium thin
⅓ cup olive oil
4 sun-dried tomatoes, very finely sliced (optional)
½ cup loosely packed parsley sprigs, finely chopped

1. Cut stalks off the beans, then slice the beans on a very heavy diagonal cut so that each piece is about 2 inches long.
2. Bring 2 quarts water to a boil in a 3-quart saucepan. Add the beans and cook until tender. Drain, then immediately run under cold water until cool. Drain well and pat dry. Refrigerate up to 24 hours.
3. Cut prosciutto into ⅛-inch julienne strips. Refrigerate up to 24 hours.
4. Two hours before serving, mix the oil, tomatoes, and parsley in a large bowl. Add the green beans, prosciutto, and freshly ground black pepper to taste. Refrigerate or leave at room temperature, as you wish.

Servings: 6   Preparation: Easy
Time: Quick; advance preparation necessary

Beet and Pear Salad

For those of you who do not like beets, I suggest you try this recipe. It may be the one to change your mind.

1 large or 2 medium beets, peeled and coarsely grated
3 tablespoons raspberry or red wine vinegar
⅓ cup vegetable oil
1 small head Boston lettuce, washed and dried
1 medium-sized ripe pear

1. Place the vinegar and oil in a bowl with a little salt and freshly ground black pepper; whisk until well emulsified. Add the beets and refrigerate for at least 1 hour, or as long as 24 hours.
2. Just before serving, arrange the lettuce on 4 salad plates. Place the beet dressing on top.
3. Peel the pear, cut into quarters lengthwise, remove the core, and slice. Arrange the slices on top of the beets and serve immediately.

Servings: 4   Preparation: Easy
Time: Quick; some advance preparation necessary

Cole Slaw

The process of lightly salting and weighting the cabbage gives it a very crunchy texture, quite different from the usual cole slaw. Try to find a firm, white cabbage; when you slice it, make an effort to cut it into very thin slices.

1 cabbage, approximately 1 to 1½ pounds
½ cup vegetable oil
¼ to ⅓ cup fresh lemon juice

1. Remove the coarse outside leaves from the cabbage. Cut the cabbage into quarters and cut off the core.
2. Very finely slice the cabbage. Place a layer of slices in a colander, just enough to cover the bottom. Lightly sprinkle with salt, cover with another layer of cabbage, and lightly sprinkle with salt. Continue with this procedure until all the cabbage is used. Place a heavy plate or a couple of plates on top of the cabbage to weight it down. Place the colander in a bowl and allow it to stand for 2 to 3 hours.
3. Rinse the cabbage under cold running water for 3 to 5 minutes until all the salt is washed off. Let it drain 30 minutes, then pat dry.
4. Place the oil and ¼ cup lemon juice in a bowl, whisk for a minute, and then add the cabbage. Add salt, freshly ground black pepper, and more lemon juice to taste.
5. The coleslaw must be made one hour, or as long as 24 hours, before serving, and refrigerated.

Servings: 8   Preparation: Easy
Time: Time consuming; advance preparation necessary

Late Summer Salad

This salad makes wonderful use of corn that is a little too old to eat off the cob.

> 3 ears of corn, shucked
> 1 cup whole radishes
> ½ pound young okra
> 2 tablespoons white wine basil or tarragon vinegar
> ½ cup vegetable oil
> 3 tablespoons finely snipped fresh chives

1. Bring 3 quarts of water to a boil in a 4-quart saucepan. Add the corn and cook for 3 to 7 minutes until it is tender. Drain immediately and run under cold water until cool. Drain.
2. Remove roots and stems from the radishes and slice ⅛-inch thick. Bring 1 quart of water to a boil, add the radishes, and boil for 1 minute. Drain and run under cold water until cool. Drain.
3. Bring 2 quarts of water to a boil, add the okra, and boil for 3 to 5 minutes. Drain, run under cold water until cool, then drain well. Remove and discard the coarse tops from the okra, then slice the okra into ¼-inch slices.
4. Cut the corn from the cob.
5. Mix the vinegar with the oil, add the corn, radishes, and okra, and add salt and freshly ground black pepper to taste. This may be made 4 hours before serving.
6. Add the chives just before serving.

Servings: 6   Preparation: Easy
Time: Fairly time consuming; advance preparation possible

Cucumber and Watercress with Tomato-Yogurt Dressing

This light and tart salad is easy to prepare, but it must be made at the last minute. It is wonderful as an accompaniment to any curried dish. For the best results vine-ripened or hothouse tomatoes are a necessity. The dressing is also great on a tossed green salad or on an avocado salad.

1 English cucumber, peeled
1 bunch watercress
1 cup plain yogurt
4 small vine-ripened tomatoes, peeled, seeded, and finely diced

1. Cut the cucumber in half lengthwise and thinly slice.
2. Arrange half the watercress and all the cucumber slices on a platter and refrigerate while you complete the recipe.
3. Remove most of the stems from the remaining watercress. Chop leaves medium-fine. Mix the yogurt, tomatoes, and chopped watercress together. Add salt and freshly ground black pepper to taste.
4. Either spoon the dressing over the cucumber-watercress just before serving, or serve separately.

Servings: 6   Preparation: Easy
Time: Quick

Cucumber Raita

This cool and slightly sharp relish provides a wonderful contrast to curried dishes.

2 large English cucumbers, peeled
⅓ cup homemade white wine herb vinegar (page 61)
½ cup loosely packed fresh mint leaves, chopped medium-fine
1 teaspoon sugar

1. Coarsely grate the cucumber. Place a layer of cucumber in a colander, very lightly sprinkle with salt, cover with another layer of cucumber, lightly sprinkle with salt, and continue this procedure until all the cucumbers are used up.
2. Let stand for 1 hour, then rinse well, and drain in colander for 30 minutes.
3. Place the cucumbers, mint, sugar, and vinegar in a bowl and mix well.
4. Refrigerate a minimum of 1 to 2 hours or up to 3 days.

Servings: 6 to 8   Preparation: Easy
Time: Time consuming; advance preparation necessary

Creamy Cucumber Salad

This salad is great served with poached shrimp or cold roast beef.

1 large English cucumber
1 cup crème fraîche or sour cream
2 to 3 tablespoons Dijon mustard
fresh parsley or mint sprigs for garnish

1. Peel the cucumber and slice it very thin. Line a colander with one layer of cucumber and lightly sprinkle with salt. Cover with another layer of cucumber, sprinkle with salt, and continue until all the cucumber is used. Let it stand for 1 hour, then run under cold water for 3 minutes. Let it drain for 30 minutes.
2. Place crème fraîche, 2 tablespoons mustard, and freshly ground black pepper in a bowl and whisk. Add more mustard to taste, if you wish.
3. Add the cucumber slices and toss. Cover and chill for 1 hour, or as long as 24 hours.
4. Before serving, garnish with parsley or mint sprigs.

Servings: 4 to 6   Preparation: Easy
Time: Quick; advance preparation necessary

Watercress, Cucumber, and Mushroom Salad

A simple but elegant salad for special occasions.

1 English cucumber, peeled and thinly sliced
1 large bunch watercress
6 mushrooms, thinly sliced
Creamy Herb Dressing (page 169)

1. Place a layer of cucumber in a colander, lightly sprinkle with salt, and repeat procedure until all the cucumber slices have been used. Leave to drain for 1 hour. Then run under cold water for 3 minutes and drain for 30 minutes.
2. Arrange watercress, cucumber, and mushrooms in a salad bowl. Refrigerate 30 minutes.
3. Make dressing and toss with salad. Serve.

Servings: 6   Preparation: Easy
Time: Fairly time consuming; some advance preparation necessary

Eggplant Salad with Roasted Red Peppers

This eggplant salad has an interesting combination of a light smoky flavor and a tart flavor. It is great served with grilled lamb on a warm summer night.

> *2 large eggplants*
> *2 red or green sweet peppers*
> *½ cup olive oil*
> *juice of 1 to 1½ lemons*
> *2 large garlic cloves, crushed or finely chopped*
> *¼ cup loosely packed fresh parsley, chopped*

1. Preheat broiler. Place the eggplant on a broiler pan 6 inches away from the heat and broil until very soft and slightly charred on one side. Turn over and continue to broil until slightly charred on the other side. (Slightly charring the skin gives the eggplant a smoky flavor.) Cool the eggplant.
2. Broil peppers until dark brown all over. Leave in very cold water for 5 minutes. Peel off skin and remove the cores and seeds. Slice peppers into ¼-inch slices and mix with 2 tablespoons oil. Add salt and freshly ground black pepper to taste. Refrigerate.
3. Cut the eggplant in half lengthwise and scoop out all the flesh. Discard the skins. Place eggplant pulp in a sieve or colander for 5 minutes to drain.
4. Combine in a large bowl the remaining oil, juice from one lemon, and garlic. Whisk for 1 minute. Coarsely chop the eggplant and add to the dressing. Add salt, freshly ground black pepper, and more lemon juice to taste.
5. The salad may be served at this point, or refrigerated up to 2 days before serving.
6. Just before serving combine parsley with the eggplant, and place in a shallow serving bowl. Garnish the top with the marinated peppers.

Servings: 6   Preparation: Easy
Time: Fairly time consuming; advance preparation possible

Greek Eggplant Salad

This wonderful eggplant salad recipe was inspired by Rebecca Caras. Do not be put off by the unusual method of cooking the eggplant, as it works extremely well.

>*1 large eggplant*
>*1 large zucchini*
>*1 large onion*
>*1 large sweet green pepper*
>*2 teaspoons salt*
>*1 teaspoon dried rosemary*
>*1½ teaspoon dried thyme*
>*1 teaspoon dried sweet basil*
>*⅓ cup olive oil*
>*¼ pound feta cheese*

1. Peel and dice eggplant into ½-inch cubes. Place a layer of eggplant in a colander and lightly sprinkle with salt. Repeat this procedure until all the eggplant is used up. Let stand for 1½ to 2 hours. Rinse under cold water and allow to drain 30 minutes.
2. Cut zucchini and onion into ½-inch cubes.
3. Place the pepper under a preheated broiler and broil until dark brown all over. Leave in very cold water for 5 minutes. Remove skin, core, and seeds; slice into ¼-inch pieces.
4. Boil 1½ quarts water with the 2 teaspoons salt in a 3-quart stainless steel saucepan. Add diced onion and zucchini, bring the water to a boil again, and boil for 1 minute. With a slotted spoon transfer the onion and zucchini to a colander. Run under cold water until cool and let drain for 30 minutes to 1 hour. Pat dry if still wet.
5. Add herbs and half the oil to the vegetable water. Simmer for 5 minutes. Add eggplant, then simmer for 10 to 12 minutes or until the eggplant is soft. Drain well and cool; do not run under cold water.
6. When eggplant has cooled, combine it with the peppers, onion, zucchini, remaining oil, and crumbled feta cheese. Add salt and freshly ground black pepper to taste.
7. This salad should be made and refrigerated 4 hours ahead of serving, or as much as 24 hours ahead.

Servings: 6 to 8   Preparation: Easy
Time: Time consuming; advance preparation necessary

Mushrooms Gascony

This very light and flavorful mushroom salad is delicious with Chicken Almond Salad (page 195). It is also good as a vegetarian summer appetizer.

1½ pounds mushrooms
4 cups mushroom poaching liquid (page 171)
½ cup olive oil
5 large or 10 small shallots, thinly sliced
4 tablespoons white wine tarragon or basil vinegar
¼ cup finely snipped fresh chives
⅓ cup loosely packed fresh mint leaves, finely shredded
1 English cucumber
fresh mint sprigs for garnish

1. Remove and discard stalks from the mushrooms. Bring mushroom poaching liquid to a boil in a 2-quart stainless steel saucepan. Gently simmer mushroom caps for 5 to 7 minutes until cooked through. To test for doneness, remove a mushroom with a slotted spoon and cut it in half to check that the center is cooked. Be careful not to overcook or they will shrink. Drain well. Freeze the liquid for a future use.
2. Heat 3 tablespoons oil in a 10-inch saute pan, add the shallots, and saute on medium heat, stirring all the time. Be careful not to brown. Saute until clear. Place them in a large bowl. Immediately add vinegar. Cool.
3. When cool, add remaining oil, chives, and mint. Add salt and freshly ground black pepper to taste, then add mushrooms and toss. Chill until ready to serve; this will keep up to 4 days in the refrigerator.
4. Just before serving, peel the cucumber and cut it in half lengthwise. Slice cucumber ¼-inch thick. Add to mushroom mixture. Toss well. Add salt and freshly ground black pepper to taste.
5. Arrange in a serving bowl. Garnish with mint sprigs.

Servings: 8 to 10   Preparation: Easy
Time: Fairly time consuming; some advance preparation possible

Mushroom Rice Salad

Do not be put off by the bland appearance of this salad, as it tastes wonderful with simple cold meats or fish.

> 1 cup raw converted rice
> 3 tablespoons tarragon or basil white wine vinegar (preferably homemade; page 61)
> 1/4 cup loosely packed fresh tarragon or basil leaves, finely chopped
> 1/3 cup vegetable oil
> 1/2 cup heavy cream
> 2 cups poached mushrooms (page 171), sliced 1/4-inch thick
> 1/2 cup finely snipped fresh chives

1. Place rice in a 2-quart saucepan. Cover with cold water, bring to a boil, stir, and gently simmer, covered, for 30 to 40 minutes until the rice is very tender. Drain and run under cold water until the rice is quite cold. Let drain at least 1 hour.
2. Combine the vinegar, tarragon or basil, and oil. Whisk well, then slowly whisk in the cream. Add salt and freshly ground black pepper to taste.
3. Combine the dressing, the rice, mushrooms, and chives. Taste and add more salt and pepper as necessary. Chill for 1 to 2 hours before serving.

Servings: 8   Preparation: Easy
Time: Fairly time consuming; advance preparation necessary

Potato Salad Provençal

Here is an interesting, colorful, and delicious departure from the usual mayonnaise-based potato salads. It is good served with simple meat or fish salads.

1½ pounds red russet potatoes
2 tablespoons white wine herb vinegar
6 tablespoons olive oil
1 garlic clove, finely chopped
3 medium vine-ripened tomatoes, peeled, seeded and sliced
¼ cup sliced, pitted, black olives
¼ cup loosely packed fresh basil leaves, finely shredded
fresh basil leaves for garnish

1. Combine the vinegar, oil, and garlic in a large bowl. Whisk thoroughly and add salt and freshly ground black pepper to taste.
2. Scrub potatoes well and leave on the skins. Slice ¼-inch thick.
3. Bring 2 quarts water to a boil in a 4-quart saucepan. Add the potatoes and boil for 10 to 15 minutes until tender, being very careful not to overcook.
4. Allow the potatoes to drain for 3 minutes. Then, while they are still hot, place in the dressing, stirring gently once in a while. When the potatoes are cooled, add the tomatoes, olives, and shredded basil. Check the seasoning and add more salt and freshly ground black pepper to taste.
5. Refrigerate for 2 hours, or as long as 24 hours, before serving.
6. Garnish the salad bowl with fresh basil leaves before serving.

Servings: 6   Preparation: Easy
Time: Fairly time consuming; advance preparation necessary

Spinach Coconut Salad

This spinach salad is unusual because the spinach is slightly cooked and it tastes hot and spicy. It makes a wonderful accompaniment to Crabmeat Salad Indian (page 211), Chicken Almond Salad (page 195), or a curried chicken salad. Fresh coconut really makes the difference in this salad.

12 ounces raw spinach, washed and trimmed
½ cup grated fresh coconut
½ cup finely diced sweet red pepper
1 to 2 teaspoons finely diced fresh hot pepper
4 tablespoons vegetable oil
1 lime for garnish

1. Bring 2 cups water to a boil in a 3-quart saucepan. Add the spinach and cook for 2 minutes. Drain and run under cold water until cool.
2. Squeeze excess liquid from spinach, and coarsely chop. Combine spinach with the other ingredients. Add salt to taste.
3. This salad must be refrigerated a minimum of 2 hours, or up to 8 hours, before serving. Garnish each serving with a slice of lime.

Servings: 4 to 6   Preparation: Easy
Time: Quick; advance preparation necessary

Spinach and Zucchini Salad

As you will see, there is no acid in this salad, which means that the vegetables retain their vibrant green color. Enhance the beauty of the dish by garnishing it with wedges of lemon around the platter.

> *½ pound raw spinach, washed and trimmed*
> *2 cups shelled fresh peas (or frozen peas)*
> *3 small zucchini*
> *½ cup olive oil*
> *½ cup crumbled feta cheese*
> *⅓ cup loosely packed fresh parsley, chopped*
> *3 scallions, thinly sliced*
> *2 small garlic cloves, crushed or finely chopped*
> *1 lemon for garnish*

1. Bring 2 cups of water to a boil in a 3-quart saucepan. Add the spinach and cook for 2 minutes. Drain and immediately run under cold water until cool. Drain for 30 minutes, then squeeze out any excess water. Coarsely chop the spinach.
2. Cut the ends off the zucchini, cut in half lengthwise, and scoop out the seeds with a teaspoon or tomato shark. Cut into ¼-inch slices.
3. Place 1 quart of water in a 2-quart saucepan and bring to a boil. Add the sliced zucchini, bring to a boil, and cook for 3 minutes or until just tender. Remove the zucchini with a slotted spoon and place it in a colander. Immediately run under cold water until cool, then drain again. Pat dry with kitchen paper towels or a towel.
4. Bring the water back to a boil. Add the peas, bring to a boil, and cook for 3 to 5 minutes or until just tender. Drain and immediately run under cold water until cool. Drain for 20 minutes.
5. Place the oil, cheese, parsley, scallions, and garlic in a large bowl and whisk for 1 minute. Add the spinach, peas, and zucchini. Toss the mixture well and add salt and freshly ground black pepper to taste.
6. This should be made and refrigerated 1 hour, or as long as 8 hours, before serving.
7. Arrange on a serving platter and garnish with lemon wedges.

Servings: 6 to 8   Preparation: Easy
Time: Fairly time consuming; advance preparation necessary

Tomato, Avocado, and Watercress Salad

The interesting contrast of textures gives this salad a distinctive quality.

1 large ripe avocado
¼ cup balsamic vinegar
½ cup olive oil
2 large vine-ripened tomatoes, peeled, seeded, and finely diced
1 bunch watercress

1. Place the vinegar and oil in a bowl. Whisk for one minute, then stir in the tomatoes, and add salt and freshly ground black pepper to taste. This may be made up to 8 hours before serving.
2. Just before serving, peel the avocado, remove and discard the seed, and slice ½-inch thick. Arrange avocado slices on a platter with the watercress. Whisk the dressing and pour it on top.

Servings: 4   Preparation: Easy
Time: Quick; some advance preparation possible

Tomato Avocado Relish

This recipe does not work well if you do not use vine-ripened tomatoes. It is a wonderful accompaniment to broiled swordfish or poached shrimp.

4 medium vine-ripened tomatoes, peeled and seeded (juice reserved)
1 tablespoon finely chopped onion
⅓ cup loosely packed fresh coriander leaves
1 large very ripe avocado
1 to 1½ teaspoons Tabasco

1. Place the tomato and tomato juice and onion in a food processor and process until smooth. Add the coriander and process for 30 seconds until the coriander is coarsely chopped. Pour into a bowl.
2. Peel the avocado and cut into ¼-inch dice. Add to the tomato mixture. Add salt and Tabasco to taste. Refrigerate.
3. This recipe should be prepared at least 30 minutes, but no more than 2 hours, before serving.

Servings: 4 to 6   Preparation: Easy
Time: Quick; advance preparation necessary

Pasta Salad with Marinated Carrots

This colorful pasta salad has a bright flavor to match. Most of the zesty taste comes from marinating the carrots and the pasta the day before serving. This salad may also be made with couscous.

½ pound of any small dry pasta
2 tablespoons vegetable oil
1 teaspoon salt
3 medium carrots, grated medium to fine
⅓ cup fresh lemon juice
½ cup olive oil
⅓ cup loosely packed fresh dill sprigs, coarsely chopped
¼ cup fresh finely snipped chives
lemon slices for garnish

1. Bring 2 quarts water to a boil in a 3-quart saucepan and add the vegetable oil and salt. Add the pasta. Stir for 30 seconds. Gently boil until tender. Drain and run under cold water until cool, then let drain for 30 minutes.
2. Meanwhile, place carrots, lemon juice, and olive oil in a bowl and mix together. Let stand for 30 minutes, then stir in pasta.
3. Refrigerate for 24 hours (or a minimum of 2 hours) before serving.
4. Just before serving add the dill, chives, and salt and freshly ground black pepper to taste. Arrange salad in a serving bowl and garnish with the lemon slices.

Servings: 6   **Preparation: Easy**
Time: Fairly time consuming; advance preparation necessary

Tabouli

Tabouli is one of my most favorite things to eat in the summertime. I make it without any vinegar or lemon juice because I feel this gives the ingredients a more distinctive flavor. I prefer to use coarse bulgur wheat because it is nuttier and crunchier, but if you cannot find it, any bulgur wheat will suffice. Couscous may be substituted for bulgur.

2 cups coarse bulgur wheat
½ cup olive oil
*3 small or 2 large vine-ripened tomatoes, peeled, seeded, and
    finely diced*
1 small cucumber, peeled, halved, and coarsely grated
*⅓ cup finely snipped fresh chives (or 3 tablespoons finely diced
    onion)*
½ cup loosely packed mint leaves, finely chopped

1. Place the bulgur wheat in a 2-quart saucepan; add enough water to come 2 inches above bulgur. Bring to a boil, then turn down heat and gently simmer for 5 to 15 minutes until tender. Be careful not to overcook; it should be tender, not mushy. The water should have evaporated by the time the bulgur wheat is done; if it evaporates before the bulgur is tender, add a little more water. Once it is cooked, pour it into a bowl and cool.
2. Place oil, tomatoes, cucumber, chives, and mint in a bowl. Mix well, add bulgur, continuing to mix well. Add salt and freshly ground black pepper to taste.
3. This salad can be stored up to 24 hours in the refrigerator, although I prefer to serve it almost immediately, as I feel the flavors are fresher and more distinctive.

Yield: 5 cups   Preparation: Easy
Time: Fairly time consuming; advance preparation possible

Couscous with Mint

This salad is wonderful served with Barbecued Lamb (page 332) and Greek Eggplant Salad (page 183).

2 cups couscous
½ cup olive oil
1 large or 2 small onions, finely chopped
½ cup loosely packed fresh mint leaves, finely chopped
⅓ cup finely snipped fresh chives

1. Heat the oil in a 2-quart saucepan, add the onions, and gently saute on medium heat until clear but not browned. Add couscous and 3½ cups water or enough to come 1 inch above couscous. Bring the pan up to a simmer. Gently simmer, stirring occasionally, for 5 to 10 minutes until couscous is tender.
2. Immediately pour into a bowl and whisk with a fork to make sure there are no lumps. Cool the couscous completely, then add mint and chives. Add salt and freshly ground black pepper to taste.
3. This salad may be made 8 hours ahead of serving time and stored in the refrigerator, or it may be eaten as soon as the couscous is fully cool.

Servings: 6 to 8   Preparation: Easy
Time: Quick; advance preparation necessary

Salad Pistou

This is a dish from the South of France, where dried beans are used to great effect. All the textures in the salad are soft and combine in a subtle and satisfying way. The salad makes a filling lunchtime meal.

½ pound dried small white beans
3 large ripe tomatoes, peeled, seeded, and diced
2 ounces prosciutto, diced into ⅛-inch cubes
½ cup vegetable oil
½ cup loosely packed fresh parsley sprigs, chopped
½ cup loosely packed fresh basil leaves, chopped
1 avocado

1. Wash and pick over beans. Soak beans for 2 hours; drain well. Put them in a 2-quart saucepan, adding enough cold water to come 4 inches above beans. Simmer for 1 to 1½ hours, until tender. (If too much water evaporates during boiling, add more.) Drain beans, then run under cold water for 30 seconds. Drain well; cool.
2. Combine beans, tomatoes, prosciutto, and oil. Add salt and freshly ground black pepper to taste.
3. The salad may be prepared to this point 6 hours ahead of serving time and stored in the refrigerator. The salad may be served chilled or at room temperature.
4. Just before serving, mix in the parsley and basil. Place the salad on a serving platter.
5. Peel the avocado. Cut in half lengthwise, slice ¼-inch thick, and arrange around the bean salad.

Servings: 8   Preparation: Easy
Time: Fairly time consuming; advance preparation possible

Chicken Almond Salad

I recommend poaching chicken for this salad and my other chicken salads because it will be moister and more flavorful. You may use leftover roast chicken or turkey, however, if you wish. Chicken Almond Salad is medium-hot in spiciness. If jalapeño peppers are not readily available, Tabasco may be substituted to taste. This salad is lovely served with fresh orange slices, if you want a variation from the avocado slices.

1 3- to 3½-pound chicken
1 stalk celery, sliced
1 carrot, sliced
1 onion, sliced
1 small bay leaf

DRESSING
⅓ cup vegetable oil
½ cup blanched almonds, coarsely chopped
¼ cup fresh lime juice
1 tablespoon chopped fresh or canned jalapeño pepper
½ cup loosely packed fresh mint leaves, coarsely chopped
2 small ripe avocados for garnish

1. Place chicken in a 4-quart saucepan with the celery, onion, carrot, and bay leaf. Cover the chicken with water, bring to a boil, then gently simmer for 40 to 50 minutes until cooked. To check for doneness, pull the thigh away from the breast and insert a knife into the thickest part of the thigh to check that the chicken is cooked through. If it is not, continue to simmer for another 10 minutes.
2. Remove the chicken from the liquid and cool. You may save the stock for a future use; first reduce it by 50 percent, then freeze.
3. While the chicken is cooling, heat the oil in a 10-inch saute pan and add the almonds. Toss over medium heat until light golden brown, then immediately pour the almonds and oil into a bowl and cool.
4. When the almonds are cool, add the lime juice and jalapeño peppers.

5. Remove the chicken meat from the bones, discard the skin and gristle, and dice the chicken into 1-inch pieces. Add the still-warm chicken to the almond dressing with the mint, and add salt and freshly ground black pepper to taste.
6. The salad should be refrigerated for 4 hours, or for as long as 24 hours, before serving.
7. Just before serving, cut the avocados in half lengthwise and remove and discard the pit. Peel and slice into ¼-inch slices lengthwise.
8. Toss the chicken gently, then arrange in the center of a platter and garnish with the avocado slices.

Servings: 6   **Preparation: Easy**
Time: Time consuming; advance preparation necessary

Chinese Chicken Salad

This wonderful recipe was given to me by Jack Milan of Different Tastes. I love its variety of flavors and textures. The recipe works equally well with poached shrimp. You will find raw peanuts at a health food store.

1 3- to 3½-pound chicken
1 carrot, sliced
1 onion, sliced
1 stalk celery, sliced
1 bay leaf
1 small cucumber

DRESSING
½ cup white wine vinegar
1 cup raw peanuts
1 to 2 hot chili peppers, finely diced (or 1 to 2 teaspoons dried
*   crushed red hot pepper)*
1 onion, finely diced
½ cup vegetable oil
8 ounces fresh bean sprouts for garnish

1. Place chicken in a 4-quart saucepan with the carrot, onion, celery, and bay leaf. Cover with cold water, bring to a boil, then gently simmer for 40 to 50 minutes until chicken is cooked. To test for doneness pull the thigh away from the chicken and insert a knife into the thickest part of the thigh to check that the chicken is cooked through. If it is not, continue to simmer for another 10 minutes.
2. Remove the chicken from the liquid and cool. You may save the stock for a future use; first reduce it by 50 percent, then freeze.
3. Meanwhile, peel the cucumber and cut in half lengthwise. Remove the seeds with a teaspoon. Slice ⅛-inch thick. Place a layer of cucumber slices in a colander, lightly sprinkle with salt, cover with another layer of cucumber slices, salt, and continue until there is no cucumber remaining. Let stand for 1 hour. Rinse the cucumbers under running cold water for 2 minutes. Drain for 30 minutes. Pat dry and place in the vinegar for ½ hour to 24 hours. Refrigerate.

4. Roast raw peanuts in a preheated 400-degree oven until light golden brown, approximately 5 to 10 minutes. Be careful they do not burn. Cool. Chop coarsely in a food processor.
5. Heat the oil in a 10-inch saute pan, add the onion and pepper, and saute until onion is clear. Pour into a bowl and add salt, more pepper to taste, and peanuts.
6. After chicken has completely cooled, remove meat from bones, discard skin and gristle, and cut the meat into thin julienne strips.
7. All the above steps may be done 24 hours before serving, in which case the cucumbers, chicken, and peanut dressing must be refrigerated. Or you may serve the salad as soon as the chicken has cooled to room temperature.
8. Just before serving, place bean sprouts on a platter, covering them with the vinegar and cucumber mixture, and arrange the chicken on top. Spoon the peanut dressing over the chicken. Garnish around the platter with watercress.

Servings: 6   Preparation: Fairly easy
Time: Time consuming; advance preparation possible

Chicken, Walnut, and Orange Salad

If you like a salad on the sweet side, this rather rich chicken salad is made with freshly cracked walnuts (or pecans), golden raisins, and oranges.

1 3- to 3½-pound chicken
1 onion, sliced
1 carrot, sliced
1 stalk celery, sliced
½ bay leaf
2 oranges
⅓ cup fresh lemon juice
¼ cup corn or peanut oil
½ cup freshly cracked walnuts
⅓ cup golden raisins or currants
1 cup Vermouth Mayonnaise (page 46)

1. Place chicken, onion, carrot, celery, and bay leaf in a 4-quart saucepan. Add enough cold water to cover the chicken. Bring to a boil, then gently simmer for 40 to 50 minutes until cooked. To check for doneness, pull the thigh away from the breast and insert a knife into the thickest part of the thigh to check that the chicken is cooked through. If it is not, continue to simmer for another 10 minutes.
2. Remove from liquid and cool. You may save the stock for a future use; first reduce it by 50 percent, then freeze.
3. Remove the chicken meat from the bones, discard the skin and gristle, and cut the chicken into 1-inch pieces.
4. Finely grate the rind of half an orange. Cut the rind and pith from the remaining oranges and discard. Slice the oranges and refrigerate.
5. Place the grated orange rind, lemon juice, and oil in a bowl. Whisk, add salt and freshly ground black pepper to taste, then add the still-warm chicken, walnuts, and raisins or currants. Add additional salt and pepper to taste. Chill for one hour or up to 24 hours.
6. Just before serving, toss the salad and place it on a serving platter. Spoon Vermouth Mayonnaise on top. Arrange the orange slices around the chicken and serve.

Servings: 4 to 6   Preparation: Easy
Time: Time consuming; advance preparation necessary

Smoked Chicken Salad

This is a powerful salad with a strong flavor and visual appeal. The smoked chicken is what gives it a distinctive flavor, so the substitution of fresh chicken substantially changes the taste of the salad. The addition of the glazed shallots adds a wonderful ending touch. Besides being delicious, the salad also looks beautiful with its bright reds and oranges. Try serving it as an appetizer.

> *1 2½-pound smoked chicken (or 3 3½-pound cooked chickens)*
> *1 orange*
> *2 sweet red peppers (or 5 sun-dried tomatoes)*
> *¼ cup finely snipped fresh chives*
> *½ cup peanut or safflower oil*
> *10 shallots*
> *½ cup homemade chicken stock*
> *2 tablespoons balsamic vinegar*

1. Peel half the rind from the orange, being careful to remove only zest, not pith. Very finely julienne zest and set aside.
2. Place whole peppers under a preheated broiler and broil until dark brown all over. Leave in ice water for 5 minutes. Peel, remove the core and seeds, then julienne finely.
3. Remove chicken meat from bones and julienne finely. Place chicken, red pepper, julienned orange zest, chives, and one-third of the oil in a bowl. Mix, adding salt and freshly ground black pepper to taste. Refrigerate for 1 to 8 hours before serving.
4. Remove skin from shallots. If the outer layer seems tough, remove and discard. Divide shallots in half, lengthwise, through root, where there is usually a natural division. Trim off the dark part of the root, being careful not to cut off root, as shallots will fall apart when cooking.
5. Heat remaining oil in a saute pan, add shallots, and saute until they are light golden brown. Add stock and vinegar. Cook on high heat until almost all liquid is evaporated and shallots are glazed. (Steps 4 and 5 may be done several hours ahead of serving, if you wish.)
6. Before serving remove the remaining zest and pith from the orange. Slice the orange. Place chicken on a platter and arrange shallots around the edge. Garnish with orange slices.

Servings: 4   Preparation: Easy
Time: Fairly time consuming

Chicken Roulades

This wonderful dish makes an excellent summertime salad. You also can serve it as an hors d'oeuvre by using small chicken breasts, rolled tightly and sliced very thin.

4 12-ounce chicken breasts, boned, with the skin left on
1 cup Pesto, Variation 1 (page 27)
1 cup strong homemade chicken stock
4 medium vine-ripened tomatoes for garnish
½ cup black olives for garnish
8 anchovy fillets (optional)
⅓ cup virgin olive oil
fresh basil leaves for garnish

1. Bone the chicken breasts. Instead of starting the boning at the top of the breast, start at the rib cage. Bone very carefully down to the breast bone on one side; turn around and repeat on the other side. Then gently pull the bone away from the breast. Pound the breasts, skin side up, until very thin.
2. Preheat oven to 300 degrees.
3. Spread each chicken breast with pesto and roll up. Toothpick to hold and put in an ovenproof dish. Or put the rolls, seam side down, in the dish, placing them close together so they do not spring open as they cook.
4. Add the chicken stock to the dish. Cover and bake for 40 to 60 minutes until the internal temperature (tested on an instant thermometer) is 160 degrees. Remove from the oven and cool.
5. Refrigerate at least 4 hours, or up to 24 hours, before serving.
6. Pit the olives and cut them in half lengthwise. To serve, thinly slice the tomatoes and arrange on a platter. Slice the chicken rolls about ½-inch thick and arrange on the platter. Cut the anchovies in half lengthwise and arrange on the chicken. Arrange the sliced olives and basil leaves around the platter. Sprinkle everything with the virgin olive oil and freshly ground black pepper.

Servings: 8   Preparation: Easy
Time: Fairly time consuming; advance preparation necessary

Duck Salad New York

Hilary Southern Nanda remembers roast duck being the highlight of her grandmother's seaside picnics at home in England. Just as no self-respecting British lamb would be served without mint, so too may the duck benefit from its favors! I find that many people do not think of using duck for salads, but it is truly delicious. This very interesting salad is well worth the effort needed to make it. It is also delicious as an appetizer.

> *1 4- to 5-pound duck*
> *3 to 5 tablespoons balsamic vinegar*
> *½ cup vegetable oil*
> *½ cup loosely packed fresh mint leaves, finely chopped*
> *2 cups poached mushrooms, thinly sliced (page 171)*
> *½ pound sweet or tart cherries for garnish*

1. Preheat oven to 450 degrees.
2. Cut excess fat from around the cavity of the duck and discard. On the diagonal, so as not to puncture the meat, prick the duck all over with a small sharp knife. (This procedure helps release the fat.) Tie the legs together with natural fiber string. (See drawings on page 322.)
3. You will need a deep roasting pan to keep the duck fat from making a mess of your oven, and a cake rack or roasting rack that fits inside the pan. Put the duck on the rack. Roast the duck at 450 degrees for 30 minutes. Reduce the heat to 350 degrees and cook the duck for one hour. Be sure not to overcook the duck, as it is apt to become tough. To check for doneness, insert an instant thermometer into the thickest part of the thigh, being careful not to touch the bone. Leave it in for at least 30 seconds to get a reading. The temperature should read 155 degrees.
4. Remove the duck from the oven and cool. Remove the meat from the bones, save the crisp skin, and discard the rest of the skin with the fat. Cut duck meat and skin into julienne strips, approximately 2 inches long and ⅛-inch thick. Chill in the refrigerator up to 2 days or, if serving immediately, leave at room temperature, depending on your preference for warm or chilled salad.

5. Just before serving, place 3 tablespoons vinegar, the oil, and the mint in a bowl and whisk. Mix in mushrooms and combine with julienned duck. Add more vinegar, salt, and freshly ground black pepper to taste.
6. Pit the cherries. Arrange salad on a platter and garnish with the cherries.

Servings: 4 to 6   Preparation: Fairly easy
Time: Time consuming

Swiss Country Salad

This is my own version of a chef's salad. It is great served with hot French bread or Black Pepper Bread (page 158). I have occasionally substituted cold roast chicken for the ham and have found it works very well.

½ pound good quality boiled ham, sliced ⅛-inch thick
1 medium carrot, coarsely grated
1 celery stalk, very finely sliced
¼ pound Gruyère or Emmenthal cheese, coarsely grated
3 tablespoons white wine herb vinegar
⅓ cup vegetable oil
1 tablespoon Dijon mustard
⅓ cup sour cream
2 heads Belgian endive
1 small bunch watercress

1. Slice the ham into ⅛-inch julienne strips.
2. Place the vinegar, oil, and mustard in a bowl, and whisk until well emulsified. Slowly whisk in the sour cream and add salt and freshly ground black pepper to taste.
3. The dressing and ham may be prepared just before you serve the salad or chilled up to 6 hours.
4. Just before serving, cut the core away from the endive, and arrange the leaves around the outside of a platter. Remove the coarse stems from the watercress and arrange on top of the endive.
5. Mix the carrot, cheese, and celery together and arrange in the center of the platter. Arrange the ham on the top and serve the dressing separately.

Servings: 6   Preparation: Easy
Time: Quick; some advance preparation possible

Autumn Salad

You may choose to use either pork or veal for this robust salad, but when it comes to freshly cracked walnuts, there is no choice! This is also good with cooked sliced chicken or very lean cold roast pork. I like to serve it for a Sunday lunch, preceded by a hot soup.

2 veal tenderloins (1¼ to 1½ pounds) or pork tenderloin
2 tablespoons vegetable oil
3 ounces Roquefort cheese
⅓ cup boiling water
½ cup sour cream
2 pears, peeled, sliced ¼ inch thick
1 bunch watercress, trimmed
½ cup freshly cracked walnuts

1. Preheat oven to 350 degrees. Remove any heavy sinews from the outside of the veal tenderloins.
2. Heat the oil in a 12-inch saute pan. Saute veal or pork tenderloin until light golden brown all over. Place in a roasting pan and roast for 15 to 25 minutes. Insert an instant thermometer into the thickest part of the meat; it has finished cooking when the internal temperature reaches 145 degrees for veal or 155 degrees for pork. Remove from the oven and allow to cool for at least 1 hour.
3. Crumble Roquefort into small pieces into a bowl, add the boiling water, and mix well until quite smooth. Stir in sour cream, adding freshly ground black pepper to taste.
4. The meat and the dressing may be refrigerated up to 8 hours, if you wish.
5. Just before serving, thinly slice the veal. Cut pears into quarters, remove the cores, and slice ¼-inch thick.
6. Arrange veal, pears, and watercress on a platter. Sprinkle with walnuts. Serve sauce separately.

Servings: 6   Preparation: Easy
Time: Fairly time consuming; advance preparation possible

Haitian Pork Salad

I was given this very special recipe by Edner Cayemite, who brought it with him from Haiti. As you might imagine, it is the perfect dish for a hot, sultry day.

2 pounds pork stew meat
3 tablespoons all-purpose unbleached flour
1 teaspoon salt
¼ teaspoon freshly ground black pepper
⅓ cup vegetable oil
⅓ cup fresh lemon juice
⅓ cup fresh lime juice
½–1 teaspoon dried crushed red hot pepper, or to taste
1 avocado
1 grapefruit

1. Cut pork into 1-inch cubes. Cut off almost all fat and discard.
2. Place flour on a plate and add salt and freshly ground black pepper. Very lightly dust the pork with flour; shake off any excess flour.
3. Heat the oil in a heavy 12-inch heavy stainless steel saute pan, add a third of the pork, and saute on medium to high heat until golden brown all over. Remove the meat from the pan with a slotted spoon. Repeat with the remaining pork.
4. When all pork is sauteed, drain excess oil from pan. Return the pork to the pan and add lemon juice, lime juice, and hot pepper. Cover and very gently simmer for 1 to 1½ hours until pork is tender. Check occasionally; if the liquid has evaporated, add a little water. Once the pork is cooked, cool it to room temperature for about one hour and add salt and freshly ground black pepper to taste.
5. Arrange the pork and juices in the center of a platter.
6. Remove rind and pith from grapefruit with a serrated knife. Cut into sections. Cut the avocado in half, remove the pit, and peel. Slice it into ½-inch slices.
7. Arrange avocado and grapefruit around the edge of the serving platter.

Servings: 6   Preparation: Easy
Time: Fairly time consuming; advance preparation possible

Smoked Trout Salad

You will find the combination of flavors in this dish irresistible. The rich hazelnut dressing highlights the smoky taste of the fish and the redolence of the Jerusalem artichoke and watercress. If Jerusalem artichokes are not available, thin slices of cucumber can be substituted.

3 smoked trout (approximately 6 to 8 ounces each)
½ pound Jerusalem artichokes
Hazelnut Dressing (page 168)
1 bunch watercress

1. Remove the skin from the trout, gently remove top fillet and place it on a salad or appetizer plate. Remove its small bones. Remove the center bones and then remove the small bones in the bottom fillet. The trout may flake or break in half; in this case, just piece the fish back together when placing them on plates.
2. Cover the plates of trout fillets with plastic wrap, and store in the refrigerator for up to 6 hours.
3. Just before serving, make the dressing. If the Jerusalem artichokes are not too knobby, peel them; however, if they are knobby, just scrub them very well. Slice them ⅛-inch thick.
4. Arrange the sliced artichokes on one side of the trout and the watercress on the other side. Spoon the dressing over the watercress and artichokes, but not on the trout. Serve immediately.

Servings: 6   Preparation: Easy
Time: Quick; some advance preparation possible

Seafood Salad Citron

This is a delightfully mild dish, given a refreshing tartness by the lemon in the sauce. Serve it with fresh asparagus for the perfect summer meal.

1½ pounds haddock or pollock fillet, skin on
2 cups fish poaching liquid (page 11)
1 pound shrimp (21 to 25 count), peeled and deveined (see page 250)
1½ cups Lemon Mayonnaise (page 42)
fresh mint or watercress sprigs for garnish

1. Place poaching liquid in a 2-quart stainless steel pan and bring to a simmer.
2. Cut fish into 4 pieces. Add to the liquid and gently poach, covered, until cooked through, approximately 7 to 10 minutes, being careful not to overcook. The fish will break up into smaller pieces as it cooks. Remove with a slotted spoon and let cool. Remove skin.
3. Add shrimp to the liquid and gently poach, covered, approximately 5 to 7 minutes, until cooked through. Remove with slotted spoon and let cool.
4. Place sour cream in a bowl and whisk until smooth. Fold in the mayonnaise, being careful not to overstir, as the mixture could become runny.
5. The dressing, fish, and shrimp may be chilled for 1 hour.
6. Arrange the fish in the center of a serving platter, spoon the lemon mayonnaise over it, and arrange the shrimp around the edge of the platter. Garnish with the mint or watercress.

Servings: 6   Preparation: Easy
Time: Fairly time consuming

Italian Seafood Salad

The addition of the prosciutto adds a very interesting touch to this seafood salad. It is great with a salad of vine-ripened tomatoes, sliced cucumbers, and fresh greens. My preference is to make the salad no more than 1 hour before serving and to serve it at room temperature, but it can be chilled if you prefer. Shrimp may be substituted for the scallops, or the salad is fine made with just two pounds of fish.

1 pound haddock or cod fillets, skin on
1 pound bay scallops
1 cup fish poaching liquid (page 11)
2 thin slices prosciutto
½ cup olive oil
1 tablespoon fresh thyme leaves
⅓ cup loosely packed fresh parsley sprigs, finely chopped
1 lemon for garnish

1. Cut the fish into 3- to 4-inch pieces. Remove the side muscle from the scallops.
2. Bring the poaching liquid to a boil in a 12-inch stainless steel saute pan. Add the fish, cover, and gently simmer for 7 to 10 minutes or until the fish is cooked through. Be careful not to overcook the fish. Remove the fish with a slotted spoon and cool. Remove the skin.
3. Add the scallops to the poaching liquid and gently simmer for 3 to 5 minutes or until cooked through. Do not overcook the scallops or they will have a rubbery consistency. Remove the scallops with a slotted spoon. The poaching liquid may be frozen for a future use.
4. While the seafood is cooking, finely dice the prosciutto and place it in a bowl with the olive oil, thyme, and parsley. Mix well.
5. Add the fish and scallops to the prosciutto dressing with salt and freshly ground black pepper to taste. Gently mix, being careful not to overmix, so the fish doesn't break up too much. It should stay in 1- to 2-inch pieces.
6. Cut the lemon into 6 wedges or slices and remove the seeds. Place the salad on a serving platter and garnish with the lemon wedges. It may be held at room temperature for one hour before serving.

Servings: 4 to 6   Preparation: Fairly difficult
Time: Fairly time consuming; advance preparation necessary

Crabmeat Salad Dana

This salad is assembled just before you want to serve it, as the rice tends to harden in the refrigerator. Freshly grated nutmeg really finishes this salad to perfection.

12 ounces cooked fresh crabmeat
1 cup raw converted rice
2 sweet green peppers
½ pound mushrooms, sliced ⅛-inch thick
½ cup vegetable oil
⅓ cup fresh lemon juice
2 medium garlic cloves, finely chopped
½ teaspoon freshly grated nutmeg

1. Place the rice in a 2-quart saucepan. Add 4 cups of cold water, bring to a boil, stir, and gently simmer, covered, for 30 to 40 minutes until the rice is very tender. Drain in a colander and run under cold water until the rice is quite cold. Leave to drain at least 1 hour.
2. While the rice is boiling, place peppers under a broiler and broil until they are dark brown all over. Leave them in very cold water for 5 minutes. Peel and remove stem and seeds. Cut in half, and then into ⅛-inch slices.
3. Remove any shells from the crabmeat. If wet, drain for 20 minutes in a colander.
4. Just before serving, place the oil, lemon juice, and garlic in a bowl and whisk. Whisk in the nutmeg. Add crabmeat, peppers, mushrooms, and rice, toss. Add salt and freshly ground black pepper to taste. Serve.

Servings: 6   Preparation: Easy
Time: Fairly time consuming; some advance preparation possible

Crabmeat Salad Indian

The spiciness of this salad is wonderful on a hot summer day. It is also nice as an appetizer at any time of the year. The salad dressing is equally delicious on poached shrimp and garnished with avocado slices instead of the Cucumber Raita.

1½ pounds cooked fresh crabmeat
⅓ cup snipped fresh chives
¾ cup Curry Mayonnaise (page 41)
Cucumber Raita for garnish (page 179)

1. Remove any pieces of shell from the crabmeat. (If the crabmeat is wet, drain for 20 minutes in a colander.)
2. Place crabmeat in a bowl with the chives. Add the mayonnaise and mix gently. Add salt to taste. Arrange the salad on a platter. Garnish around the edge with the Cucumber Raita.

Servings: 6   Preparation: Easy
Time: Fairly time consuming

Shrimp Venetian Style

The prosciutto and shrimp make a wonderful combination of flavors in this extremely attractive salad. It is also wonderful as an appetizer or hors d'oeuvre.

1 pound shrimp (16 to 20 count), peeled and deveined
1 carrot, thinly sliced
1 onion, thinly sliced
1 bay leaf
6 black peppercorns, coarsely crushed
2 cups water
¼ pound prosciutto, thinly sliced
1 head Bibb or Boston lettuce, washed and dried
⅓ cup olive oil or virgin olive oil
1 lemon for garnish

1. Place the onion, carrot, bay leaf, crushed peppercorns, and water in a 2-quart stainless steel pan. Cover and gently simmer for 20 minutes. This is your poaching liquid.
2. Add shrimp and very gently simmer for 4 to 7 minutes until they are just cooked. Be careful not to overcook, as the shrimp will become rubbery. Remove from poaching liquid and cool. (The poaching liquid can be frozen and used again.) Strain out the vegetables and reserve.
3. Cut each slice of prosciutto in half lengthwise. Wrap a piece of prosciutto around the top of each shrimp, leaving the tail exposed.
4. The above steps may be done just before serving, or you may refrigerate the shrimp and the vegetables reserved from the poaching liquid up to 8 hours.
5. Just before serving, arrange the lettuce on a serving platter. Arrange the shrimp on the lettuce. Place the vegetables in the center. Sprinkle with the olive oil and some coarsely crushed black pepper.
6. Cut the lemon into wedges and remove the seeds. Garnish the platter with the lemon wedges and serve.

Servings: 4   Preparation: Easy
Time: Fairly time consuming; advance preparation possible

Brazilian Shrimp Salad

Fresh coconut is wonderful in this dish inspired by Cameron Watson. It gives a lighter, fresher taste than dried coconut. The coriander is a wonderful addition; however, it is not always readily available so mint may be substituted. The end result will be quite different; you may want to choose the herb according to your taste preference. The salad is good with a simple rice salad tossed with a little oil and fresh herbs. It is also excellent with crabmeat substituted for the shrimp.

2 pounds shrimp (21 to 26 count), peeled and deveined
2 cups shrimp poaching liquid (page 12)
¾ cup raw cashews, whole or broken
3 medium vine-ripened tomatoes, peeled and seeded
¼ cup loosely packed fresh coriander or mint leaves, finely chopped
⅓ cup grated fresh coconut (or dried unsweetened coconut)
3 tablespoons fresh lime juice
½ cup vegetable oil

1. Bring the shrimp poaching liquid to a boil in a 12-inch stainless steel saute pan. Add the shrimp and gently simmer for 3 to 5 minutes until cooked through, being careful not to overcook. Remove with a slotted spoon and cool. Refrigerate up to 8 hours before serving.
2. In a preheated 375-degree oven, toast the cashews for 5 to 7 minutes until light golden brown. Watch them carefully so they do not burn. Remove and cool.
3. Meanwhile, dice tomatoes medium-fine.
4. Place tomatoes, coriander or mint, coconut, lime juice, and oil in a bowl and mix. Add salt and freshly ground black pepper to taste. The dressing may be made 8 hours before serving and refrigerated.
5. Just before serving, add all but 6 to 8 shrimp (depending on the number of people you are serving) to the dressing. Add salt and freshly ground black pepper to taste. Arrange on a serving platter and garnish with cashews and the reserved shrimp.

Servings: 6 to 8   Preparation: Easy
Time: Fairly time consuming; some advance preparation possible

Salad Chaya

It is preferable to use tarragon in the Creamy Herb Dressing, because it adds a very distinctive flavor to the salad, but if you cannot obtain tarragon, basil or chives will be satisfactory. This salad is delicious as an appetizer or main dish.

1½ pounds shrimp (16 to 20 count), peeled and deveined
1 cup shrimp poaching liquid (page 12)
Creamy Herb Dressing (page 169)
2 heads Belgian endive
1 grapefruit for garnish

1. Cut shrimp in half lengthwise. Bring poaching liquid to a boil, add shrimp, and poach very gently in barely simmering water until just cooked. Be careful not to overcook or the shrimp will become rubbery. Remove the shrimp from the liquid and refrigerate up to 8 hours. The liquid may be frozen for a future use.
2. Just before serving, cut one endive in half lengthwise. Remove the core and discard. Finely shred the endive. Add the shredded endive and shrimp to the dressing and gently mix, being careful not to overmix or the dressing could separate.
3. With a serrated knife, remove the rind, pith, and skin from the grapefruit. Cut it into sections.
4. Arrange the whole leaves from the one remaining endive around the edge of a platter. Place shrimp in the center and garnish with the grapefruit sections.

Servings: 4 to 8   Preparation: Easy
Time: Fairly time consuming; some advance preparation possible

Stuffed Zucchini Greek Style

Great on a hot summer's day with vine-ripened tomatoes!

3 small zucchini (about 6 inches long)
16 medium shrimp (21 to 26 count), cooked (see Brazilian
  Shrimp, page 213)
1/2 cup crumbled feta cheese
1/4 cup olive oil
2 tablespoons coarsely chopped fresh mint
1/4 cup loosely packed fresh parsley springs, finely chopped

1. Cut zucchini in half lengthwise; scoop out seeds and flesh, leaving a 1/4-inch shell. Discard seeds. Bring 2 quarts of water to a boil. Add a little salt and boil shells 3 to 4 minutes, until *al dente.* Drain, run under cold water until cool, drain well, and pat dry.
2. Slice 10 of the cooked shrimp 1/8-inch thick. Combine them with feta, oil, mint, and parsley. Mix well and add salt and freshly ground black pepper to taste.
3. This part of the recipe should be done 1 hour ahead of serving time, or as long as 8 hours, and refrigerated.
4. Just before serving cut the remaining shrimp in half lengthwise.
5. Stuff the zucchini shells with the feta-shrimp mixture and place on a serving platter. Garnish with the remaining shrimp halves.

Servings: 6   Preparation: Easy
Time: Fairly time consuming; advance preparation necessary

Seafood Entrees

Seafood

When I was a child growing up in England, seafood was a very important part of my diet. I remember catching shrimp on the beach in Sussex, the excitement of finding an occasional tiny plaice caught in the nets, and the journey to the docks where my father purchased live lobster, fresh from the traps to make a salad that still remains a sweet memory. The pâté he made from the tomali, which we served simply with lettuce, vine-ripened tomatoes, and cucumber, created a taste that I would always look forward to. After I graduated from the Cordon Bleu, my parents took me on a trip to Paris and the shores of Brittany, where I spent three memorable days tasting—and many times overeating—their exquisite, yet simple seafood dishes. This was to be the start of my appreciation and my later preference for seafood.

To understand the basic facts about purchasing and cooking fish, you should be aware that there are two categories that fish fall into. "Non-oily fish" are those in which the oil is confined to the skin and the liver; cod is the best example of this, hence cod liver oil. Other examples are sole, flounder, haddock, halibut, and pollock. As a general rule, the fish in this category have a white flesh and the oil is less than 5.7 percent. In "oily fish" the oil is 5.7 percent or more, and runs through the entire body of the fish. Bluefish, mackerel, swordfish, and salmon are the best examples. In general, the flesh of the fish in this category is darker than in the non-oily variety.

Purchasing Seafood

I have made seafood a larger part of my diet than red meat. In a restaurant or at home, I prefer to have an entree of seafood; however, I caution you that if it is not fresh it may be unappetizing. Much like poultry, seafood should be smelled and carefully inspected before it is purchased. I offer the following hints to help make that purchase an easier task.

Choosing a whole fish is easier than choosing fillets. Check the eyes of the fish, which should be bright and clear, and the body should be firm to the touch. There should be little or no odor and the smell should be sweet. Another way to tell if your whole unscaled fish is fresh is the harder it is to scale, the fresher the fish.

When purchasing seafood, look for a translucent quality to both fish and scallops. The best example of this is gray sole. When it is extremely fresh it will have a clear quality; the more opaque, the older the fish. This is not necessarily bad, but remember, the older the fish, the less moist and the stronger the flavor.

Another important point to keep in mind is the odor of fish. You probably will be embarrassed to ask the salesperson if you can smell the fish, but the odor is one of the best indicators of the freshness of the fish. So try, at least, to smell the fish before you leave the store to avoid a return trip. There should be little or no odor; it should not be strong or fishy or overpowering. In the case of oily fish, such as bluefish, salmon, or swordfish, there will be some odor, but it should not be very strong. Shrimp should have no strong odor and no trace of ammonia.

Once you have purchased the fish, use it as soon as possible. If it is stored in the refrigerator, it should be kept in the coldest part, and not near the door where it is accessible to warm drafts and temperature changes.

In Boston, we are extremely fortunate to have a fine selection of fresh fish available. Although my preference is to not use frozen fish, I realize that there are parts of the country where the selection of fish is limited, and that the alternative is frozen fish. Therefore, I am including these hints to help in assuring a satisfactory experience when you use frozen fish.

In the process of freezing fish, the intricate (fine) cell structure of the fish is punctured. When the fish defrosts, the cell structure breaks down, and liquid is released. Therefore, when the fish cooks, it is very dry. If you cook the fish with a sauce, it will moisten the fish and make it more appetizing. Oily fish tend to freeze better because they are more moist, yet it is important to be sure they were flash frozen and that they have not been frozen too long. When an oily fish is frozen more than three or four months, the oils tend to impart a rancid flavor to the fish.

Cooking Seafood

In general, fish and shellfish require a shorter cooking time than meats, although the tendency has been to overcook, which creates a drier, less appetizing, dish. As with meats, fish cooked on the bone retains more moisture and has a better flavor; however, I have found that many people prefer filleted fish, partly because it is free of bones and partly because few people know how to debone a cooked fish.

In this book, I have included a recipe for whole, baked, stuffed fish (see page 232). I think it is absolutely delicious, as well as inexpensive, and an elegant dinner entree. I urge you to try it, as once cooked, the bones are easily removed from the fish. The method of cooking is so easy that I am sure once you have tried it, you will want to experiment with different flavorful ingredients for stuffing the fish.

Also, you should be aware that fish fillets sometimes have hidden bones in them, so you should check them carefully before cooking. These bones are difficult to remove without tearing the flesh; however, one implement, surgical hemostats, work wonders in removing them. They have a fine serrated edge on the inside and should be slightly curved at the end, making it easy to get a good grip on the bones. Pull gently and the bone will come away with ease. They are especially helpful with salmon fillets where the bones are embedded and difficult to grip, and bluefish fillets where the bones are particularly tough to pull out. For a small investment you will find this instrument extremely useful.

There are six methods of cooking fish and shellfish that I feel are important to discuss. Note that in general, non-oily fish, such as sole, should not be overcooked. The drier texture will be extremely unappetizing. Oily fish are not as prone to drying out, as the oil helps maintain the moisture.

Baking: When baking, it is important that the fish be lightly brushed with a little oil or butter to prevent it from drying out. Sauces and stuffings will also prevent this. (See Sole English's Style on page 263.)

Whole fish should be cooked with the skin on (as in all my trout recipes) to retain the moisture.

Broiling: Before broiling, the fish should be lightly brushed with butter or oil to keep it from drying out. Thin—¼-inch or less—pieces should be placed close to the heat source and thicker pieces farther away. This ensures that the fish does not overbrown before being cooked all the way through. With trout and bluefish, once the fish is golden brown, it is easier to finish the cooking by baking it in the oven so it won't brown too much.

Frying: Do not confuse frying with sauteing or light frying. It is important when frying fish that the pieces you use are not too thick (up to 1 inch is preferable), to ensure that the inside is cooked to the required doneness while the outside remains a crisp golden brown. Before frying, the fish or shellfish should be coated with a light outer layer of bread crumbs or batter to give the protective coating necessary to ensure a moist inside. This also adds a lovely texture to fried fish.

Poaching: Poaching is cooking a fish or shellfish in liquid without boiling it. For whole fish, such as salmon, I find one can obtain the best results by poaching it in the oven in a tightly covered pan at 300 degrees. It should be poached in a poaching liquid (see page 11), which will impart a lovely flavor to the fish. Sole fillets, salmon fillets, and so on also benefit from the same treatment.

I prefer poaching fillets for 4 to 6 servings on top of the stove, as they are easier to check for doneness, and the pan juices may be reduced as a base for a sauce. However, for 6 to 12 servings it is much easier to poach the fish in the oven (double the fish poaching liquid recipe on page 11) and choose a non–pan-reduced sauce such as a buerre blanc or mousseline.

Scallops and shrimp should be gently poached on top of the stove. It is ideal to cook them in a poaching liquid, imparting a flavor of its own. Since the sizes of these fish are small, you should watch them to check for doneness. A temperature less than simmering results in a better texture in the fish.

Sauteing: This is the process of lightly frying fish or shellfish in butter or oil. Scallops should be tossed while they saute, so they cook evenly. It is important that shrimp be cooked gently over a low heat so they do not become tough and rubbery in texture. For the best results, I suggest cooking them in a covered pan over low heat (in essence, poaching them in butter). It is important to not overcook a lean fish like sole or flounder, and you may find it is difficult to remove from the pan without it falling apart. Should you wish to turn it over, I find it easier to achieve if they are sauteed in a fairly hot pan and turned within 1 to 2 minutes, while the fish is still firm.

It is not advisable to saute over 1-inch thick pieces of fish unless the fish is cut into smaller pieces. If it is not cut up, the fish will brown before the inside cooks all the way through.

Steaming: This is the method of cooking fish or shellfish in a moist heat. The fish should be placed on a perforated rack over gently boiling water. The water should be kept at a constant gentle boil and the lid should be kept on the pan so the steam can circulate around the fish. Be careful when you remove the lid, as steam produces water on the lid that will drip on the fish. Lifting the lid will release a burst of steam that could scald your face and hands.

Testing Fish for Doneness

I always recommend that you test a piece of fish for doneness by inserting a small sharp knife into the thickest part of the fish. Look inside; when fish is cooked, it turns from translucent to opaque. In the case of haddock, cod, or salmon, a tiny amount in the center of a thick fillet that looks slightly translucent is actually fine and will ensure that the fish is still moist.

The following seafood recipes are for fish and seafood that I find readily available in the Boston area. Most of them can be adapted to similar fish found in other parts of the country. You also will find fish and seafood recipes in the Appetizers chapter and the Salads chapter.

Bluefish

I was unfamiliar with bluefish until I came to America, and initially I was put off by its strong flavor. Over the years, however, I have grown to appreciate bluefish, since by its very nature it works beautifully with powerful sauces.

Bluefish is classified as an oily fish, which means that oil runs through the entire body; but with a 5.7-percent fat content, even bluefish can hardly be accused of being fatty. Recently I have been getting bluefish from Florida in the winter, and these are even lower in fat content. They are smaller than usual, more delicate in flavor, and I recommend them highly. No matter which kind of bluefish you choose, however, the key to good fish is always freshness.

Generally in the following recipes the skin is left on the fish as it cooks. I find it tends to stick to the cooking pan, and in removing the fillets from the pan, the skin comes away easily.

Bluefish with Apples

Dr. Mitchell Rabkin loves the bluefish dishes we make at Another Season, and this is one of his favorites. It has become one of the most popular bluefish dishes served at the restaurant. Fresh mackerel or herring may be substituted for the bluefish.

> *4 6-ounce bluefish fillets (or approximately 1½ pounds fillet)*
> *½ cup quick fish stock (page 9)*
> *3 tablespoons unsalted butter*
> *1 small red onion, thinly sliced*
> *1 tart apple, peeled and thinly sliced*
> *1 to 2 tablespoons Pommery mustard (or any coarse-grained mustard)*
> *⅓ cup heavy cream*
> *fresh Italian parsley or watercress for garnish*

1. If you are portioning the fish, cut it into 4 equal portions, cutting off and discarding 2 inches of the tail end and cutting slightly on the diagonal. Remove any bones. If there is any skin on the fillet, leave it on.
2. Reduce the fish stock to ¼ cup in a 1-quart stainless steel saucepan. Set aside.
3. Preheat a broiler.
4. Butter the bluefish with 1 tablespoon butter and place on an oiled broiler pan. Broil the fish 6 inches from the heat until the top of the fillets is a light golden brown. To check for doneness insert a small sharp knife into the thickest part of each fillet. If the fish is not cooked through, but already brown, turn off the broiler and bake at 350 degrees for 3 to 6 minutes until done.
5. Meanwhile, heat 2 tablespoons butter in a 10-inch saute pan. Add the onion and toss over high heat until soft. Add the apple and toss for 3 minutes. Place on a serving platter and keep warm.
6. Add the reduced fish stock to the saute pan. Whisk in 1 tablespoon mustard and reduce the sauce to a medium syrupy consistency. Add the cream and reduce until the sauce is thick enough to coat a spoon. Add salt, freshly ground black pepper, and more mustard to taste.
7. When you remove the fillets from the broiler pan, do not be concerned if the skin stays stuck to the pan. Place the fillets over the onion-apple mixture and spoon over the sauce. Garnish with Italian parsley or watercress.

Servings: 4   Preparation: Easy
Time: Fairly time consuming

Bluefish Tandoori

Tandoori food has a beautiful color and distinctive flavor. Most Americans are familiar with Tandoori Chicken. I love to cook Bluefish Tandoori for my Indian cousins, the Nanda family. Besides broiling the bluefish, you can bake it or cook it on a grill.

4 6-ounce bluefish fillets (or approximately 1½ pounds fillet)
1 cup Tandoori Marinade (page 59)
3 tablespoons melted unsalted butter
fresh coriander sprigs for garnish (optional)

1. If you are portioning the fish, cut it into 4 equal portions, cutting off and discarding 2 inches of the tail end and cutting slightly on the diagonal. Remove any bones. Do not remove the skin from the fillets.
2. Place the fillets in a Pyrex or china dish, pour the marinade over them, and leave them to marinate for 6 to 24 hours in the refrigerator.
3. Thirty minutes before cooking, remove the fish from the refrigerator.
4. Preheat broiler.
5. Butter a broiler pan. Remove the fillets from the marinade and place them on the pan.
6. Broil the fillets 6 inches from the heat source for 5 minutes, then spoon the rest of the marinade and the 3 tablespoons of butter over them. Continue to broil for 5 to 10 minutes until the bluefish is a light golden brown. To check for doneness, insert a small knife into the thickest part of each fillet to ensure it is cooked through. If they are not, but already golden brown, turn off the broiler and continue to cook the fish in a 350-degree oven until cooked through.
7. Place the fillets on four dinner plates and garnish with coriander sprigs.

Servings: 4   Preparation: Easy
Time: Fairly time consuming; advance preparation necessary

Bluefish Moutarde

The combination of the mustard and the aromatic thyme works well with a strongly flavored fish like bluefish. This sauce is also great served with broiled swordfish, mackerel, or herring. Cabbage with Prosciutto (see page 427) goes well with this dish.

> 4 6-ounce bluefish fillets (or approximately 1½ pounds fillet)
> 1 tablespoon unsalted butter
> 1 to 2 tablespoons Pommery mustard (or any coarse-grained mustard)
> ¼ cup quick fish stock (page 9)
> ¼ cup heavy cream
> 1 tablespoon fresh thyme leaves
> ⅛ cup finely snipped fresh chives
> ¼ cup loosely packed fresh parsley sprigs, finely chopped
> fresh thyme sprigs for garnish

1. If you are portioning the fish, cut it into 4 equal portions, cutting off and discarding 2 inches of the tail end and cutting slightly on the diagonal. Remove any bones.
2. Preheat broiler.
3. Place the bluefish on an oiled broiler pan and butter the bluefish with the 1 tablespoon butter. Broil the bluefish 6 inches from the heat source until the top of the fillets is a light golden brown. Check that they are cooked through by inserting a small sharp knife into the thickest part of each fillet. If they are not cooked through, but already brown, turn off the broiler and bake at 350 degrees for 3 to 6 minutes until done.
4. While the bluefish is cooking, place 1 tablespoon mustard and fish stock in a 10-inch saute pan. Bring to a boil, whisking the mustard into the fish stock. Add the cream and thyme leaves and reduce a little over high heat until the sauce is thick enough to coat a spoon. Remove from the heat. Add salt and freshly ground pepper to taste.
5. When the fillets are cooked, arrange them on dinner plates. Return the sauce to the heat and add the chives and parsley and bring to a boil. If necessary, add more mustard to taste. Spoon the sauce over the fish and garnish with the thyme sprigs.

Servings: 4   **Preparation: Easy**
Time: Quick

Bluefish en Papillote Celeriac

Cooking *en papillote* involves wrapping fish or meat in parchment paper with a compound butter or an herb mixture so that the food cooks in its own juices and all the flavors are retained. This is an ideal way to cook for a dinner party, as the papillotes may be prepared up to six hours ahead of dinnertime and stored in the refrigerator. (Read more about papillotes in Appendix I.) In this recipe, you will be making a delicious celery root compound butter; you can substitute mackerel or salmon for the bluefish.

6 6-ounce, skinless bluefish fillets (or 2¼ pounds fillet)
8 tablespoons unsalted butter, room temperature
1 medium celery root, peeled
1 tablespoon Dijon mustard
2 tablespoons snipped fresh chives
2 tablespoons chopped fresh parsley leaves
6 parchment hearts

1. If you are portioning the fish, cut it into 6 equal portions, cutting off and discarding 2 inches of the tail end and cutting slightly on the diagonal. Remove any bones.
2. Coarsely grate the celery root just before cooking. Heat 2 tablespoons butter in a large saute pan. Add the celery root and toss over medium heat until cooked, being careful not to brown. Put to one side to cool.
3. Beat the remaining butter until smooth. Gradually beat in the mustard and herbs. Add the cooled celery root. Season with salt and freshly ground black pepper, slightly stronger than your taste, as this also seasons the fish.
4. Brush the hearts with vegetable oil, leaving a half-inch margin all the way around without oil. Place one bluefish fillet on one half of one heart. Spread the top with one-sixth of the butter mixture, fold over the other side of the heart, and secure the edges (see diagrams on page 228). Repeat with the other fillets.
5. These can be made up to this point and refrigerated for 6 hours. Remove them from the refrigerator 30 minutes before cooking to bring them up to room temperature.

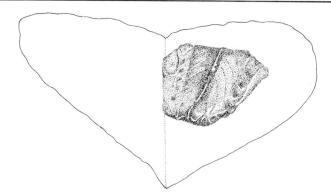

1. Place the bluefish fillet on the buttered parchment heart.

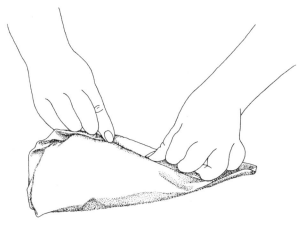

2. Fold the paper over the fillet. Starting at the top of the lobe, twist the paper over and over again, in very tight, overlapping folds.

MAKING
PAPILLOTES

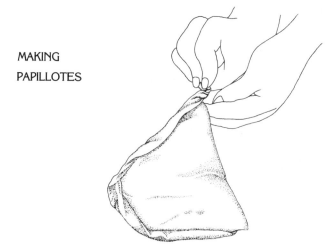

3. Be sure to twist the bottom of the lobe very tightly over and over again.

6. Preheat oven to 425 degrees.
7. Place the papillotes on a heavy sheet pan and bake for 25 to 30 minutes. They probably will have browned and puffed.
8. Place on a serving platter. Take the unopened papillotes directly to the table and open each one with a sharp knife as you serve it onto a dinner plate.

Servings: 6   **Preparation: Fairly easy**
Time: Fairly time consuming; advance preparation possible

Bluefish Provençal en Papillote

Perhaps you do not like anchovies; still, you should try them in this recipe anyway. You will hardly notice them, but you are sure to appreciate the really lovely intense flavor they provide. You may substitute striped bass, grey sole, or a thick piece of haddock for the bluefish.

> 4 6-ounce skinless bluefish fillets (or approximately 1½ pounds fillet)
> 10 tablespoons unsalted butter, soft
> 3 medium vine-ripened tomatoes, peeled, seeded, and coarsely chopped
> 1 medium garlic clove, finely chopped
> ½ cup loosely packed fresh basil leaves, finely shredded
> 1 teaspoon finely grated lemon rind (zest)
> 4 anchovy fillets (optional)
> 4 parchment hearts

1. If you are portioning the fish, cut it into 4 equal portions, cutting off and discarding 2 inches of the tail end and cutting slightly on the diagonal. Remove any bones.
2. Heat 2 tablespoons butter in a 10-inch stainless steel saute pan, add the chopped tomatoes, and reduce over high heat until thick. Remove and cool.
3. Beat the rest of the butter in a bowl until smooth. Add garlic, basil, and lemon rind, then slowly beat in the cool tomato mixture. Add salt and freshly ground black pepper slightly stronger than your taste, as this seasoning will also flavor the fish.
4. Brush the hearts with vegetable oil, leaving a half-inch margin all the way around without oil. Place one bluefish fillet on one half of one heart. Spread the top with one-fourth of the butter mixture, place one anchovy on top, fold over the other side of the heart, and secure the edges (see diagrams on page 228).
5. These can be made up to this point and refrigerated for 6 hours. Remove them from the refrigerator 30 minutes before cooking to bring up to room temperature.
6. Preheat oven to 425 degrees.

7. Place the papillotes on a heavy sheet pan and bake for 25 to 30 minutes. They probably will have browned and puffed.
8. Place on a serving platter. Take the unopened papillotes directly to the table and open each one with a sharp knife as you serve it onto a dinner plate.

Servings: 4   Preparation: Fairly easy
Time: Fairly time consuming; some advance preparation possible

Bluefish en Papillote Celeste

If you have made the Celeste Butter in advance, this entree will be fairly quick to prepare. It also works well with salmon.

> *4 6-ounce skinless bluefish fillets (or approximately 1½ pounds fillet)*
> *8 tablespoons Celeste Butter (page 50)*
> *4 parchment hearts*

1. If you are portioning the fish, cut it into 4 equal portions, cutting off and discarding 2 inches of the tail end and cutting slightly on the diagonal. Remove any bones.
2. Brush the hearts with vegetable oil, leaving a half-inch margin all the way around without oil. Place one bluefish fillet on one half of one heart. Spread the top with 2 tablespoons of the compound butter, fold over the other side of the heart, and secure the edges. (See diagrams on page 228.) Repeat with the other three fillets.
3. These can be made up to this point and refrigerated up to 6 hours. Remove them from the refrigerator 30 minutes before cooking to bring them up to room temperature.
4. Preheat oven to 425 degrees.
5. Place the papillotes on a heavy sheet pan and bake for 25 to 30 minutes. They probably will have browned and puffed.
6. Place on a serving platter. Take the unopened papillotes directly to the table and open each one with a sharp knife as you serve it onto a dinner plate.

Servings: 4   Preparation: Fairly easy
Time: Fairly time consuming

Baked Stuffed Haddock

This method of cooking a whole fish on the bone is simple, and absolutely delicious. You get a better quality of fish when you buy a whole fish, and since it is cooked on the bone, it will give you a very moist dish. For garlic lovers, Aïoli (see page 47) is a great accompaniment. The best place to find pancetta is in an Italian market, but bacon also will work. Bluefish may be substituted for the haddock.

1 4- to 5-pound whole haddock
2 leeks
1 medium carrot
2 thin slices pancetta (or 3 slices bacon)
⅓ cup olive oil
1 cup loosely packed fresh parsley sprigs, finely chopped
2 tablespoons fresh thyme leaves (or 1 teaspoon dried thyme)
1 lemon
2 garlic cloves

1. Remove and discard the coarse outside layer from the leeks. Cut the leeks into thin slices up to the light-green part. Place in cold water for 30 minutes. Drain, rinse, drain well, and pat dry.
2. Peel and coarsely grate the carrot.
3. Finely dice the pancetta. Place it in a heavy pan with 1 tablespoon oil and saute until light golden brown. Add the leeks and carrots, and cook for 3 minutes. Cool the mixture and add the parsley, thyme, and freshly ground black pepper to taste.
4. Refrigerate stuffing up to 24 hours.
5. Preheat the oven to 400 degrees.
6. Cut the lemon in half lengthwise. Cut the lemon into thin slices and remove the seeds. Slice the garlic thin.
7. Clean the cavity of the fish by rubbing a little salt into the bloody parts, washing with cold water, and pat dry. Stuff the cavity with the vegetable and pancetta mixture and close the cavity with toothpicks. (Toothpicking is not absolutely necessary, and sometimes is difficult to do.)

8. Place the fish on an oiled, heavy sheet pan and cut seven ¼-to ½-inch-deep slashes across the fish. Stud the slashes with the lemon and garlic. Heat the remaining olive oil until very hot, but not smoking. Pour it over the fish and bake the fish at 400 degrees for 40 to 50 minutes. To test for doneness, insert an instant thermometer into the thickest part of the fish. Leave it in for 30 to 60 seconds to get a reading; it should read 150 to 155 degrees.
9. Place the fish on a serving platter and serve immediately.

Servings: 4   Preparation: Easy
Time: Fairly time consuming; some advance preparation possible

Soft-Shell Crabs

In May, when soft-shell crabs are first shipped to Boston alive and beautifully packed in straw, I serve them as a special treat to my clientele and take pleasure in preparing them for those who are unfamiliar with them. I have included here two recipes for soft-shell crabs. For an easy and elegant entree, you should also try lightly sauteing them whole in butter with freshly ground black pepper and serving them on Italian parsley sprigs. Then sprinkle crabs with chives.

When purchasing them, note that they should be (preferably) alive. Soft-shell crabs that are not alive should be checked for freshness. The smell should not be strong (actually it is a very unpleasant odor). If the odor is strong, discard them, as they are bad. It is also important to make sure that the shells are soft; the larger soft-shell crabs have a heavy, papery, top shell that is not easy to eat.

Soft-shell crabs (at least in New England) are available frozen all year. I do not like their flavor or texture. I recommend that you wait to purchase them as a special treat when they are fresh and in season.

To clean soft-shell crabs, turn over on the back and remove the triangular apron. Lift flaps on each end and remove spongy lungs, exposing cartilage. With sharp kitchen scissors, cut off the head just behind the eyes. Squeeze the body to release the sack. Discard the sack, head, and lungs. If this sounds complicated, it really isn't; it can be done in just a few minutes. Ask the salesperson at the fish market to demonstrate the method for you.

Soft-Shell Crabs Louisiana Style

Lightly sauteed fresh soft-shell crabs and deep-fried soft-shell crabs served with a wedge of lemon are sublime. However, for those of you who would like an interesting departure, please try this dish. I suggest serving it with plain boiled rice and a steamed green vegetable.

> *12 soft-shell crabs*
> *4 tablespoons clarified butter (page 62)*
> *1½ to 2 cups Creole Sauce (page 20)*

1. Clean the soft shells as described on page 234.
2. Heat the clarified butter in two 12-inch saute pans. (A 10-inch pan and a 12-inch pan also will suffice.)
3. Place 6 soft-shell crabs in each pan, shell side (upper side) down, and saute on medium heat until the crabs turn a pink color. Turn the crabs over and continue to saute, covered, until they are cooked, about 3 to 5 minutes.
4. With a slotted spoon transfer the crabs to a dish and keep warm. Combine the pan juices of both pans in one pan.
5. Add the Creole Sauce to the pan juices, bring to a boil, and add salt and freshly ground black pepper to taste.
6. Pour the sauce onto a warm serving platter and arrange the crabs on top.

Servings: 4   Preparation: Easy
Time: Fairly time consuming; some advance preparation possible

Soft-Shell Crabs Robert

The rich flavor of these crabs blends well with the tart and slightly spicy sauce in this recipe given to me by Robert Mahon. Do not serve them with anything rich; a simple steamed green vegetable will be perfect.

18 soft-shell crabs
4 tablespoons clarified butter (page 62)
Ginger-Lime Beurre Blanc (page 36)
fresh Italian parsley or coriander sprigs for garnish

1. Clean the soft-shell crabs as described on page 234.
2. Heat the clarified butter in two 12-inch saute pans.
3. Place 9 soft-shell crabs in each pan, shell side (upper side) down, and saute on medium heat until the crabs turn a pink color. Turn the crabs over and continue to saute, covered, until they are cooked, about 3 to 5 minutes.
4. While the crabs are cooking, warm 6 dinner plates. Warm the beurre blanc in a small saucepan.
5. Spoon the beurre blanc onto the dinner plates and arrange the crabs on top. (There will be leftover beurre blanc.) Garnish with the parsley or coriander.

Servings: 6   Preparation: Fairly easy
Time: Fairly time consuming

Red Snapper

A tropical and semitropical fish, red snapper is not readily available in seafood markets around Boston, but it is available in the South. When you do find it in your market, be sure to buy it! It's a very special fish, with a beautiful flavor and a nice, resilient flesh. It is excellent served broiled or steamed with fresh herbs, or as prepared in both of the following recipes.

Blackened Red Snapper

This wonderfully flavorful dish is ideal for those who enjoy highly seasoned dishes. Although I call it "Blackened," I don't actually blacken the fish because it imparts a bitter taste. I like a medium spicy flavor; you may adjust the amount of spices according to your tastes. Thin swordfish steaks may be substituted for the red snapper. A tossed green salad and warm cornbread (page 151) would be excellent with this entree.

4 5-ounce red snapper fillets
2 teaspoons fennel seeds
1 teaspoon whole black peppercorns
2 teaspoons dried thyme
½ teaspoon salt
1 teaspoon dried basil
¼ teaspoon cayenne pepper
2 tablespoons vegetable oil
4 tablespoons unsalted butter

1. Place the fennel seed and black peppercorns in a very dry blender and blend until fine. Add the thyme, salt, cayenne, and basil, and blend for 30 seconds until fairly fine, but not a powder.
2. Just before serving, brush each fillet lavishly with the oil.
3. Melt the butter in a large cast-iron or heavy saute pan until it gently bubbles. At the same time, lightly coat the fish with the spices. I find the

best way to do this is to hold the fish in one hand as I sprinkle on the spice mix. Place the fillets in the pan, flesh side down.

4. Saute fillets over medium heat until they are a light golden brown. Turn them over and continue to saute until cooked through (about 10 minutes total cooking time). When the fillets are cooking they might start to curl, not lying flat in the pan. This is a problem because they will not cook evenly. When this happens, make a couple of ¼- to ½-inch-deep slashes around the outer edge of each fillet and lightly press them down to flatten them out.

5. Test the fish for doneness by inserting a small knife in the thickest part. Remove from the pan when cooked and serve immediately.

Servings: 4   **Preparation: Easy**
Time: Quick

Red Snapper Oriental Style

Here is a low-calorie preparation for red snapper that has a mildly spicy and rich flavor. I recommend you serve it with a steamed green vegetable such as asparagus, broccoli, or green beans. Haddock or cod may be substituted for the red snapper.

1½ pounds red snapper fillets
4 scallions
4 tablespoons unsalted butter (or 3 tablespoons vegetable oil)
1 tablespoon peeled and grated fresh ginger
2 tomatoes, peeled, seeded, and sliced (vine-ripened preferred)
½ cup loosely packed fresh coriander leaves, coarsely chopped
8 lime wedges for garnish

1. Remove and discard the coarse outer layer from the scallions. Slice them on the diagonal and include 1 inch of the green portion.
2. Cut the snapper into 3-inch pieces.
3. Heat the butter in a 12-inch saute pan. Add the scallions and ginger and toss for 2 minutes on high heat. Add the tomatoes and toss for 1 minute on high heat.
4. Place the snapper over the tomato mixture, cover, and braise over medium heat until the snapper is cooked, about 5 minutes. To check for doneness, insert a small sharp knife into the thickest part of the fish to check that it is cooked through.
5. With a slotted spatula, remove the fish from the pan and arrange on a serving platter. Reduce the sauce on high heat to a fairly thick consistency, add the coriander and salt and freshly ground black pepper to taste. Spoon the sauce over the fish and garnish the platter with lime wedges.

Servings: 4   Preparation: Easy
Time: Fairly time consuming

Salmon

I remember with delight those special dinners during the summer months when my mother cooked salmon. She served it with tiny new potatoes, seasoned with fresh mint, and fresh asparagus or peas. In the fall she would occasionally serve salmon with an egg sauce (chopped hard-boiled eggs in a white sauce) that was a wonderful addition to the salmon. At the Cordon Bleu I learned to prepare Cold Poached Salmon with a Chaud-froid Sauce. This took hours to prepare and looked absolutely beautiful, but I must admit that the simple salmon dishes that my mother prepared still linger in my memory.

My mother always used a Scottish salmon, not too oily, very moist, and very delicate. In the United States I have found many different varieties of salmon. The variety you use will undoubtedly be determined by what is available where you live. Living in Boston, I find East Coast salmon to be an absolute treat, but it has a very short season. I also like Norwegian salmon, which fortunately is available almost all year round. It is a little more oily than East Coast salmon, but very moist and delicate. It is wonderful poached or broiled.

Being an oily fish, salmon has an extremely strong taste if it is not very fresh. For this reason, I highly recommend you look carefully for the translucent qualities of this fish. There should not be a strong odor. If you purchase a whole salmon, the eyes should be clear and bright and the flesh fairly firm to the touch. Seven-ounce salmon steaks may be substituted for fillets.

Salmon with Basil Mushroom Sauce

The fresh basil adds a wonderful flavor to the sauce. Sole or halibut may be substituted for the salmon.

4 6-ounce boneless salmon fillets, with skin
¼ pound mushrooms
4 tablespoons unsalted butter
⅓ cup quick fish stock (page 9)
3 tablespoons dry white wine
⅓ cup heavy cream
⅓ cup loosely packed fresh basil leaves, finely shredded
4 fresh basil leaves for garnish

1. Cut the mushroom stalks even with the caps and slice 1/8-inch thick.
2. Heat the butter in a 12-inch stainless steel saute pan, add the mushrooms, and saute on high heat, tossing all the time, until light golden brown.
3. Add the fish stock, wine, and salmon, skin side up. Cover and gently simmer for 7 to 10 minutes until the salmon is cooked through. To check for doneness, insert a small sharp knife into the thickest part of each fillet to check if it is cooked through. Be careful not to overcook or the salmon will be dry.
4. Remove the salmon from the pan with a slotted spatula and remove and discard the skin. Keep the fillets warm.
5. On a high heat, reduce the pan juice to a light syrupy consistency. Add the cream and shredded basil and continue to reduce until the mixture is thick enough to coat a spoon. Add any juices that have accumulated from the salmon and continue to reduce for a minute more. Add salt and freshly ground black pepper to taste.
6. Arrange the salmon on four dinner plates and spoon the sauce on top. Garnish each fillet with a basil leaf.

Servings: 4   Preparation: Easy
Time: Fairly time consuming

Salmon with Tarragon Sauce

There are probably as many recipes for Salmon with Tarragon Sauce as there are salmon in the sea. You will find my version a rich and wonderfully velvety sauce. Sorrel may be substituted for the tarragon if you wish.

> 4 6-ounce boneless salmon fillets, with skin
> 1/3 cup quick fish stock (page 9)
> 2 tablespoons dry white wine
> 5 tablespoons softened unsalted butter
> 1/4 cup heavy cream
> 1/4 cup loosely packed fresh tarragon leaves (or 3/4 cup loosely
>   packed, finely shredded sorrel leaves)
> fresh tarragon sprigs for garnish

1. Place the fish stock, white wine, and 2 tablespoons butter in a 12-inch heavy stainless steel saute pan and bring to a boil.
2. Place the salmon in the pan, skin side up. Cover and gently simmer for 7 to 10 minutes until the fillets are cooked through. To check for doneness, insert a small knife into the thickest part of each fillet to ensure that they are cooked through. Be careful not to overcook the salmon or it will be dry.
3. Remove the fillets from the pan with a slotted spatula and remove and discard the skin. Keep the fillets warm.
4. Turn up the heat and reduce the pan juices to a medium syrupy consistency. Add the cream and continue to reduce until the sauce is thick enough to coat a spoon. Add the tarragon and slowly whisk in the remaining butter a little at a time over medium heat. Should the sauce start to separate, add 1 tablespoon of white wine and continue to whisk over a low heat for a minute or two. Add salt and freshly ground black pepper to taste.
5. Arrange the salmon on four warm dinner plates, spoon the sauce on top, and garnish with the tarragon sprigs.

Servings: 4   Preparation: Easy
Time: Fairly time consuming

Salmon Condercet

This is my favorite fish sauce, but I must caution you that you should use vine-ripened tomatoes to give the sauce the special touch it needs.

4 6-ounce boneless salmon fillets, with skin
2 tablespoons unsalted butter
3 small vine-ripened tomatoes, peeled, seeded, and sliced
½ cup fish stock (page 9)
½ small English cucumber, peeled, seeded, and very thinly sliced
½ cup heavy cream
¼ cup loosely packed fresh parsley leaves, finely chopped

1. Cut the salmon slightly on the diagonal into 4 portions.
2. Heat the butter in a 12-inch heavy stainless steel saute pan, add the tomatoes, and reduce on high heat for 5 minutes. Add the stock and salmon, skin side up, and gently braise, covered, until the fillets have cooked approximately 7 to 10 minutes. To check for doneness, insert a knife into the thickest part of each fillet to ensure that the fish is cooked through. Be careful not to overcook or the salmon will be dry.
3. Remove the fillets with a slotted spatula and place on a serving platter. Remove and discard the skin. Keep the fillets warm.
4. Add the cucumber to the pan juices and reduce the sauce over high heat until it has a thick consistency. Keep scraping down the sides of the pan to prevent the sauce from scorching. Add the cream and parsley and reduce to a fairly thick consistency. Add salt and freshly ground black pepper to taste and pour the sauce over the salmon.

Servings: 4   Preparation: Easy
Time: Fairly time consuming

Salmon Tart

This tart is wonderful for lunch or supper, served with a tossed green salad. It is also good for brunch. The tart is best when you use a mild English cheese—Caerphilly or Wensleydale.

½ pound boneless salmon fillet, with skin
6 cups fish poaching liquid (page 11)
1 uncooked 12-inch pâte brisée shell (page 482)
3 large eggs
1½ cups light cream
4 ounces Wensleydale or Caerphilly cheese, finely grated
3 tablespoons finely snipped chives

1. Bring the poaching liquid to a boil. Add the salmon, cover, and very gently poach for 10 to 15 minutes until it is cooked through. Remove with a spatula, cover, and cool. Freeze the poaching liquid for a future use.
2. Preheat oven to 375 degrees.
3. Line the pie shell with wax paper and weight with rice (see Baking Blind in Appendix I). Bake 7 minutes, remove the paper, bake the pie shell for 5 more minutes, and remove from the oven.
4. While the pie shell is baking, place the eggs in a bowl with a pinch of salt and whisk for one minute. Add the cream, cheese, and chives.
5. Remove any skin and bones from the fish and flake into ½- to 1-inch pieces. Add to the cream mixture. Add salt and freshly ground black pepper to taste.
6. Both the filling and pie shell can be prepared 6 hours before serving; refrigerate the filling.
7. Thirty minutes before cooking, bring the filling up to room temperature. Pour the filling into the pie shell and bake at 375 degrees for 40 to 45 minutes until the custard is set.
8. Remove the tart from the oven and let it rest for 5 minutes before cutting.

Servings: 6 to 8   Preparation: Fairly difficult
Time: Time consuming; advance preparation possible

Salmon with Orange Madeira Sauce

The exquisite color of this sauce gives it a visual appeal to match the lovely flavor provided by the rare combination of ingredients. This dish may be served with sauteed green vegetables (see page 439).

> 4 6-ounce boneless salmon fillets, with skin
> 1 orange
> 1/3 cup quick fish stock (page 9)
> 2 tablespoons fresh lemon juice
> 4 tablespoons unsalted butter
> 2 tablespoons dry Madeira
> 1/4 cup heavy cream

1. Finely grate the rind (zest) of the orange to measure one teaspoon. Set aside. Remove the remaining rind and pith and slice the orange crosswise into 1/4-inch slices. Reserve for garnish.
2. Just before serving, place the fish stock, lemon juice, orange zest, butter, and Madeira in a 12-inch heavy stainless steel saute pan. Bring to a boil, then reduce a little.
3. Add the salmon fillets, skin side up. Cover and very gently simmer them for 7 to 10 minutes until they are cooked through. To check for doneness, insert a small sharp knife into the thickest part of each fillet.
4. Remove the salmon from the pan with a slotted spatula, then remove and discard the skin. Keep the salmon warm.
5. Turn up the heat under the pan juices and reduce them to a light syrupy consistency. Add the heavy cream and continue to reduce until the sauce is thick enough to coat a spoon. Add salt and freshly ground black pepper to taste.
6. Arrange the fillets on four dinner plates and spoon the sauce on top. Garnish with the orange slices.

Servings: 4   Preparation: Easy
Time: Fairly time consuming

Scallops

At the end of the summer I always look forward to the availability of fresh scallops in Boston. I use scallops only in the fall and winter when they are fresh; I find them disappointing during the rest of the year when they are frozen. Frozen scallops, when cooked, are rubbery in texture and lacking the lovely sweet flavor of fresh scallops. When purchasing fresh scallops, look for ones with a translucent appearance, which are not sitting in a "milky" liquid in the store.

New England is known for its wide assortment of scallops; cape, bay, and sea scallops. You will note that each of my recipes calls for specific scallops; this is because of their size. Cape scallops are tiny and tend to cook very quickly. Sea scallops are so large they tend to take a long time to cook, but they're perfect for Scallops en Brochette because a smaller size would fall through the openings in the grill or dry out too quickly. Bay scallops are intermediate in size, so they tend to cook more evenly.

Scallops en Brochette

The tart flavor of the marinade, combined with the smokiness of the bacon, makes my Scallops en Brochette stand out from similar recipes. Try grilling them outside on that last warm fall day; sheer delight. Besides serving this dish as an entree, you may also serve it as an hors d'oeuvre to a larger gathering of friends. Do not use smaller scallops as they will dry out as they cook.

1½ pounds sea scallops
¼ cup dry white Vermouth
¼ cup dry white wine
¼ cup fresh lemon juice
1 teaspoon dry thyme leaves (or 1 tablespoon fresh thyme)
2 tablespoons vegetable oil
¼ cup loosely packed fresh parsley leaves, finely chopped
¼ pound thin-sliced bacon (preferably not sugar cured)
1 lemon for garnish
fresh Italian parsley for garnish

1. Place the Vermouth, wine, lemon juice, thyme, oil, and freshly ground black pepper in a bowl. Remove the muscle on the side of the scallops. Place the scallops and chopped parsley in the marinade. Toss gently, being careful not to break the scallops. Refrigerate for at least an hour but not more than 3 hours.
2. Cut the bacon into 1-inch-wide strips. Divide the scallops into 6 portions. Lightly brush 6 skewers with oil and put the scallops on them, alternating each with the bacon.
3. Preheat broiler.
4. Brush a broiler pan lightly with oil, place the skewers on the pan, and place the pan 4 inches from the broiler.
5. Cook until the scallops are light golden brown, turn them over, and cook until the other side is light golden brown.
6. Place the skewers on a serving platter and garnish with lemon wedges and Italian parsley.

Serves: 6   Preparation: Easy
Time: Quick; advance preparation necessary

Scallops Verona

This special recipe was inspired by Betsy West. It is not an easy dish to make because you must work very quickly. Be very careful not to overcook the scallops, and careful also not to let the beurre blanc boil, as it will separate. Nevertheless, the combination of textures and flavors is luxurious and it is well worth the time it takes to prepare. It is extremely important to use very fresh scallops. It is also important to make your beurre blanc just before starting this dish (there will be some sauce left over). The vegetables to accompany the scallops should be easy to prepare; my preference is steamed asparagus.

1¼ pounds cape or bay scallops
⅓ cup pine nuts
2 tablespoons unsalted butter
¼ cup quick fish stock (page 9)
⅓ cup loosely packed fresh parsley, very finely chopped and dry
¾ cup Basic Beurre Blanc (page 34)

1. Toast the pine nuts in a preheated 375-degree oven for 5 to 8 minutes, watching carefully that they do not burn. Remove from the oven and cool.
2. Remove side muscle from scallops.
3. Heat the 2 tablespoons butter in a 12-inch heavy stainless steel saute pan. Add scallops and toss over high heat until just cooked. Be very careful not to overcook as they will become rubbery in texture.
4. Remove with a slotted spoon, then arrange on a serving dish. Keep warm.
5. Add the fish stock to the pan. Reduce it over high heat for 1 to 2 minutes until almost all the liquid has evaporated; be careful not to burn.
6. Add to the fish stock any juices that have accumulated from the scallops. Add the parsley and pine nuts and continue to reduce until almost all the liquid has evaporated, being careful not to burn.
7. Stir in the beurre blanc and reheat over a low heat; be careful not to overheat or the sauce might break.

8. Drain off any more juices that have accumulated from the scallops; discard. (Do not add them to the beurre blanc.) Add the scallops, toss over high heat for 1 minute, being careful not to overcook so the beurre blanc does not break down. Add salt and freshly ground black pepper to taste. Serve immediately.

Servings: 4   Preparation: Difficult
Time: Fairly time consuming

Sauteed Scallops with Pesto

If you like pesto, you will love this dish. Its vibrant green color is wonderful and its taste is glorious. If you make the pesto ahead of time, the dish can be quickly put together at the last minute.

> *1¼ pounds bay or cape scallops*
> *2 tablespoons unsalted butter*
> *¾ cup Pesto (page 27)*
> *1 lemon for garnish*

1. Remove the side muscles from the scallops.
2. Heat the butter in a 12-inch saute pan until bubbling. Add scallops and stir or toss over high heat for 3 minutes until almost cooked; be careful not to overcook them. Remove scallops with a slotted spoon. Reduce any liquids in the pan to just a couple of tablespoons, being careful not to scorch.
3. Add the pesto to the pan and heat, being careful not to boil.
4. Drain off and discard any liquid that has accumulated from the scallops.
5. Toss the scallops in the pesto for 1 minute. Add salt and freshly ground black pepper to taste.
6. Place scallops on a serving dish. Garnish with the lemon wedges.

Servings: 4   Preparation: Easy
Time: Fairly time consuming; advance preparation possible

Shrimp

The shrimp I use in my restaurant are quite different from the strong, salty shrimp I used to eat in England, but now, as then, I find them versatile and easy to prepare. They are always a popular seafood.

Fresh shrimp have a wonderful flavor and a soft, pleasing texture; however, they are extremely perishable and difficult to obtain, at least in New England. The shrimp we use in the restaurant has been frozen and defrosted. I find them to be very satisfactory. However, you must be extremely careful when you purchase shrimp that they smell sweet and have no trace of ammonia or iodine smell.

The size of a shrimp is measured by the number there are in a pound, so that the large ones, which come fewer by the pound, are more expensive than the smaller. The larger shrimp also have the disadvantage of taking longer to cook all the way through, so that often by the time they are done inside, the outsides are tough. For best results, I suggest you take the middle-of-the-road approach and buy shrimp that are 16 to 20 count (formerly 15 to 20 count) or 21 to 25 count.

I recommend that you buy unpeeled shrimp, then peel and devein them at home.

PREPARATION OF SHRIMP

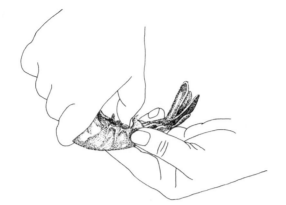

1. Remove the feelers of the shrimp with your thumb.

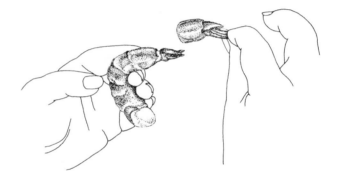

2. Remove the shell with your fingers. It will probably come off in a few pieces.

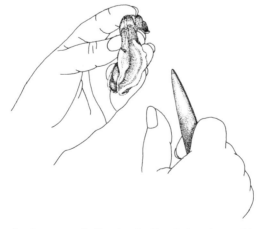

3. With a small, sharp prep knife, devein the shrimp by making an incision on the top side (opposite of where the feelers were). When the incision is deep, as shown here, this technique is called butterflying.

Italian Shrimp

Simple to prepare, this is an absolutely delicious dish where the cognac really highlights the sauce. The recipe was inspired by Phyllis Briskin. It is ideal served on fresh pasta.

1½ pounds (16 to 20 count) shrimp, with shells
1 large sweet green pepper
12 fairly firm cherry tomatoes
6 tablespoons Garlic Butter (page 54)
2 tablespoons cognac or brandy
¼ cup dry white wine
¼ cup loosely packed fresh basil leaves, finely shredded
¼ cup loosely packed fresh parsley sprigs, finely chopped

1. Peel and devein the shrimp.
2. Place whole pepper under a preheated broiler and broil until dark brown all over. Put into very cold water for 5 minutes, then peel and remove the core and seeds. Cut into fine julienne pieces.
3. Cut the cherry tomatoes in half.
4. The above procedures may be done 6 hours ahead of serving time. Refrigerate shrimp, peppers, and tomatoes.
5. Thirty minutes before cooking, remove the shrimp, peppers, and tomatoes from the refrigerator and bring up to room temperature.
6. Melt the garlic butter in a heavy stainless steel saute pan. Add the shrimp and saute over a very low heat (to be certain the shrimp do not toughen) for 3 to 5 minutes until the underside turns pink. Turn the shrimp over and continue to cook for another 3 to 5 minutes, being very careful not to overcook or the shrimp will be rubbery. Remove the shrimp from the pan with a slotted spoon and keep warm.
7. Turn up the heat under the saute pan and add the cognac, wine, peppers, and tomatoes. Stir over high heat for 3 to 5 minutes until the tomatoes start to soften.
8. Add the fresh herbs and salt and freshly ground black pepper to taste.
9. Arrange the shrimp on 4 dinner plates and top with the sauce.

Servings: 4   Preparation: Easy
Time: Fairly time consuming; some advance preparation possible

Shrimp Jaffrey

Here is an adaptation of one of Madhur Jaffrey's wonderful recipes from India. It is extremely colorful and medium spicy in taste. The fresh coriander adds flavor, but it is optional because it may be difficult to purchase. The Jaffrey Butter may be made in advance.

> *1 pound (16 to 20 count) shrimp, peeled and deveined*
> *1 small zucchini*
> *8 tablespoons Jaffrey Butter (page 51)*
> *2 small tomatoes, peeled, seeded, and diced (vine-ripened*
> *preferred)*
> *⅓ cup loosely packed fresh coriander leaves (optional)*

1. Coarsely grate the zucchini around the center seeds. Discard the seeds.
2. Place the Jaffrey Butter in a 12-inch saute pan and melt on low heat. Add the shrimp, cover, and gently saute on very low heat for 3 to 5 minutes. When the underside of the shrimp has turned pink, turn them over, re-cover, and continue to gently saute until cooked through. Be careful not to overcook or the shrimp will be tough. Remove the shrimp from the pan with a slotted spoon and keep warm.
3. Turn up the heat under the pan, add the grated zucchini and diced tomatoes, and toss over medium heat 3 to 5 minutes until the zucchini is lightly cooked. Add salt and freshly ground black pepper to taste.
4. Pour the sauce onto a warm serving platter, arrange the shrimp on top, and sprinkle with the coriander leaves.

Servings: 4   Preparation: Easy
Time: Fairly time consuming; some advance preparation possible

Ginger Shrimp

For a nice, light, summer dinner, or an unusual appetizer, try Ginger Shrimp. The marinade of ginger and garlic adds a delightful intensity of flavor. Leaving the shell on when broiling or grilling shrimp prevents them from becoming tough.

1¼ pounds (16 to 20 count) shrimp, with shells
1 small cucumber (English cucumber preferred)
¼ cup white wine basil or tarragon vinegar
2 teaspoons cumin seeds
2 tablespoons peeled and grated fresh ginger
2 medium garlic cloves, crushed
½ cup vegetable oil
¼ pound bean sprouts
1 small bunch watercress for garnish

1. Peel the cucumber and cut it in half lengthwise. Remove the seeds and slice it thin. Place a layer of cucumber slices in a colander, lightly sprinkle with salt, cover with a layer of cucumber slices, salt, and continue until all the cucumber is used up. Leave the cucumber for 1 hour, then run under cold water for 2 to 3 minutes. Drain well, pat dry, then put the slices into the vinegar. Refrigerate.
2. Remove the little feelers from the underside of the shrimp. With sharp kitchen scissors or a very sharp prep knife, make an ⅛-inch-deep incision down the back of the shrimp, leaving the shell on. Devein the shrimp.
3. In a preheated 350-degree oven, toast the cumin seeds on a small baking sheet for 7 to 10 minutes until they have turned a little darker. Remove the seeds from the oven and coarsely grind in the blender.
4. Mix the cumin seeds, ginger, garlic, and oil together to make a marinade. Place a layer of shrimp in a china or glass dish. Spoon the marinade over them and repeat this procedure until all the shrimp and marinade are used up.
5. Marinate at least 4 hours, or up to 8 hours, in the refrigerator.
6. Thirty minutes before serving, remove the shrimp from the refrigerator and bring up to room temperature.

7. Preheat broiler.
8. Place the shrimp with the marinade on the bottom part of a broiler pan. Broil until they turn pink on top. Turn the shrimp over and broil another 2 to 3 minutes until they turn a light golden brown. Be careful not to overcook the shrimp or they will be tough.
9. While the shrimp are broiling, arrange the bean sprouts on a platter. Cover with the sliced cucumber. Arrange the shrimp on top and spoon the juices from the broiler pan over the shrimp. Garnish with the watercress. My preference is to serve the shrimp in the shell; the shells are easily removed at the table.

Servings: 4   Preparation: Easy
Time: Fairly time consuming; advance preparation necessary

Shrimp Creole

If you have made and frozen Creole Sauce, you will find Shrimp Creole a delight to serve—and absolutely delicious to eat! Boiled rice and sauteed okra provide the perfect accompaniment.

1½ pounds shrimp (16 to 20 count), peeled and deveined
3 tablespoons unsalted butter
Creole Sauce (page 20)

1. Heat the butter in a heavy 12-inch saucepan. Add the shrimp, cover, and cook on a low heat for 3 to 5 minutes until the underside of the shrimp is pink. Turn the shrimp over, cover, and cook for 3 to 5 minutes, or until the shrimp is cooked through. Be careful not to overcook, or the shrimp will become rubbery. Remove the shrimp from the pan and keep warm.
2. Add the sauce to the pan juices and bring to a boil.
3. Spoon the sauce onto 6 warm dinner plates and arrange the shrimp on top.

Servings: 6   Preparation: Easy
Time: Fairly time consuming; advance preparation possible

Shrimp Mosco

Shrimp Mosco is a very aromatic dish. The hot pepper may be adjusted to your desired spiciness.

> 24 (16 to 20 count) shrimp, peeled and deveined
> ½ teaspoon dried crushed hot red pepper
> 1 bay leaf, finely crumbled
> ⅓ cup olive oil
> 2 medium garlic cloves, finely chopped or crushed
> 1 tablespoon fresh rosemary leaves (or 2 teaspoons dried
>   rosemary)
> 4 lemon wedges for garnish

1. Place the hot pepper and bay leaf in a heavy 1-quart saucepan with the oil. Heat slowly for 5 to 10 minutes, being careful not to burn. Remove from the heat, scrape into a bowl, and cool. Add the garlic and rosemary. Add the shrimp, stir to coat, and marinate for 24 hours in the refrigerator.
2. Remove the shrimp from the refrigerator 30 minutes before cooking.
3. Just before serving, remove the shrimp from the oil with a slotted spoon; set aside. Heat the oil in a 12-inch saute pan. Add the shrimp and cook on low heat for 2 minutes. Turn the shrimp over, cover, and cook until they are cooked through, being careful not to overcook.
4. Remove the shrimp with a slotted spoon and place them on plates. Add salt to taste to the pan and stir for 1 minute. Spoon this sauce over the shrimp and garnish each serving with a wedge of lemon.

Servings: 4   Preparation: Easy
Time: Quick, advance preparation necessary

Shrimp Rogowski

Patricia Buckley Rogowski put this vibrant dish together. I love the brilliance of the pink shrimp against the red sauce.

> 1½ pounds (16 to 20 count) shrimp, peeled and deveined
> 2 sweet red peppers
> 6 tablespoons unsalted butter
> 2 vine-ripened tomatoes, peeled, seeded, and coarsely chopped
>   (juice reserved)
> 3 scallions, thinly sliced on the diagonal
> 1 tablespoon chopped fresh coriander (optional)
> Tabasco
> fresh coriander sprigs for garnish

1. Place the whole red peppers on a sheet pan and broil until dark brown all over. Put them into very cold water for 5 minutes. Peel, remove the core and seeds, and coarsely chop.
2. Heat 2 tablespoons butter in a 10-inch stainless steel saute pan, add the tomatoes and juice, and saute over high heat, stirring, until thick. Add the chopped peppers and saute over high heat for 3 minutes. Puree the mixture in a blender or food processor until very smooth.
3. This tomato-pepper puree may be stored for 24 hours in the refrigerator.
4. Just before serving, heat 4 tablespoons butter in a 12-inch heavy saute pan, add the shrimp, and cover. Cook on low heat for 3 minutes. When the underside of the shrimp turns pink, turn shrimp over. Cover again and cook until the shrimp are done, being careful not to overcook or the shrimp will become rubbery. Remove the shrimp from the pan with a slotted spoon and keep warm.
5. Add the scallions to the saute pan and saute on high heat for 2 minutes. Add the tomato-pepper puree, chopped coriander, Tabasco, and salt to taste. Simmer the sauce until it has a medium-thick consistency.
6. Pour the sauce onto a serving platter and arrange the shrimp on top. Garnish with coriander sprigs.

Servings: 6   Preparation: Easy
Time: Fairly time consuming; some advance preparation possible

Sole

There are many varieties of sole, both on the East Coast and West Coast. On the East Coast, there are five major varieties: winter sole, lemon sole, yellowtail sole, gray flounder, and sea dab. I am particularly partial to gray flounder, which I call gray sole. I find the flesh to be firmer than the other East Coast varieties.

On the West Coast are found rex sole, petrale (petroli) sole, sand dab sole, and Dover sole. Dover sole is very special and very resilient in texture. When I was in Los Angeles in 1985 giving a cookery demonstration for *Seafood Leader,* I had a chance to use petrale sole. I really enjoyed it. The flesh was quite resilient, and I found that it made a particularly good fish terrine (see page 120).

Whatever the type of sole you purchase, just be sure that it is fresh. It should have a slightly translucent look and a mild odor or none at all. You will notice that the fillets come in many sizes (2- to 10-ounce fillets on the average). Should you only be able to purchase small fillets, use two per serving. When the recipe calls for folding it in half, still do so; this helps you remove the fillet from the pan without letting it break.

Sole en Papillote Verde

The next time you want to treat your guests to a unique and special food experience, cook fish *en papillote*. (Read about papillotes in Appendix I.) In this papillote recipe, the sole is enhanced with Green Compound Butter. Fresh oysters or shrimp (16 to 20 count, cut in half lengthwise), can be added to the papillote. I recommend using gray or petrale sole, because you need a firm sole.

4 6- to 7-ounce gray or petrale sole fillets
8 tablespoons Green Butter (page 49)
4 parchment hearts

1. Fold the sole fillets in half across.
2. Brush the hearts with vegetable oil, leaving a half-inch margin all the way around without oil. Place one sole fillet on one half of one heart. Spread the top with 2 tablespoons of the butter, fold over the other side of the heart, and secure the edges (see diagram on page 228). Repeat with the other three fillets.
3. If you are using oysters or shrimp, place on top of the sole, then put the butter on top.
4. These can be made up to this point and refrigerated up to 6 hours. Remove them from the refrigerator 30 minutes before cooking to bring them up to room temperature.
5. Preheat oven to 425 degrees.
6. Place the papillotes on a heavy sheet pan and bake for 20 to 25 minutes. They probably will have browned and puffed.
7. Place on a serving platter. Take the unopened papillotes to the table and open each one with a sharp knife as you serve it onto a dinner plate.

Servings: 4   **Preparation: Fairly easy**
Time: Fairly time consuming; advance preparation possible

Sole Cala Llonga

The combination of mussels, saffron, and basil makes a very rich and flavorful sauce for sole.

> *4 5-ounce sole fillets (approximately 1¼ pounds)*
> *2 pounds mussels in the shells*
> *2 cups mussel poaching liquid (page 12)*
> *6 tablespoons Saffron Butter, room temperature and soft (page 53)*

1. Scrub the mussels and remove the beards. Discard any open mussels that do not close when lightly tapped, as they are dead.
2. Boil the mussel poaching liquid in a 4-quart stainless steel saucepan. Add the mussels and simmer gently until cooked, about 5 minutes. Mussels should open about ½-inch. Remove with a slotted spoon and allow to cool. Discard any mussels that remain closed. Then remove all but 4 mussels from the shells. Strain ⅓ cup poaching liquid through a cloth and reserve. You may freeze the rest of the liquid for a future use.
3. The mussels and strained poaching liquid may be refrigerated up to 24 hours, if you wish.
4. Just before serving, fold each fillet in half across. Bring the unshelled mussels up to room temperature.
5. Warm the ⅓ cup mussel poaching liquid in a 12-inch heavy stainless steel saute pan. Add the sole fillets, cover, and gently poach until they are cooked. Be careful not to overcook them. (To check for doneness, insert a small sharp knife into the thickest part of a fillet.)
6. Remove the cooked fillets with a slotted spatula and place them on a warm serving platter. Turn up the heat and reduce the stock to 3 tablespoons, being careful not to scorch. Then, on medium heat, slowly add the Saffron Butter and whisk until it is well incorporated into the stock.
7. Add the shelled mussels and any liquid that has accumulated on the sole platter. Heat the mussels, then remove them with a slotted spoon, and place them over the sole. Reduce the sauce over medium heat until it has a light syrupy consistency; be careful not to over-reduce or the sauce could separate. Add salt and freshly ground black pepper to taste.
8. Pour the sauce over the sole and garnish with the 4 mussels in the shell.

Servings: 4   Preparation: Fairly difficult
Time: Fairly time consuming; advance preparation possible

Sole Verde

This dish is very light, and the ginger-vinegar sauce gives it a clean but flavorful touch. Large spinach leaves or Boston lettuce leaves may be substituted for the Romaine.

> 4 6-ounce sole fillets
> 2 tablespoons peeled, finely chopped or thinly julienned ginger
> 1/2 cup white wine basil or tarragon vinegar
> 2 medium leeks
> 2 carrots
> 1/4 pound Shiitake mushrooms
> 3 tablespoons corn, soy, or peanut oil
> 8 Romaine lettuce leaves
> 1/4 cup quick fish stock (page 9) (or water)

1. Combine the ginger and vinegar and marinate for at least 6 hours.
2. Remove and discard the coarse outside layer from the leeks. Cut the leeks into thin slices up to the light-green part. Soak them in very cold water for 30 minutes. Drain, rinse, drain well, and pat dry. Slice the carrot 1/8-inch thick on the diagonal and then cut into very thin julienne strips 1/8-inch thick.
3. Remove and discard the stems from the mushrooms and slice the caps 1/8-inch thick. Heat 2 tablespoons oil in a saute pan, add the mushrooms, and toss over high heat until cooked but not brown. Cool.
4. Fill a 2-quart saucepan with water and bring to a boil. Have a bowl ready with ice water. Using tongs dip the lettuce leaves in the water for 10 seconds, one at a time; place immediately in the ice water, then dry. Cut the center vein out of the leaves.
5. Steps 2 through 4 may be done up to 4 hours ahead of time and refrigerated.
6. Divide the Shiitake mushrooms into 4 parts. Lay one of these parts on a sole fillet, fold over, and wrap in 2 lettuce leaves. Repeat this process with all the sole.
7. Heat the remaining tablespoon of oil in a large stainless steel saute pan. Add the carrots and leeks, cover, and saute on a medium to low heat until they are slightly cooked, about 2 to 3 minutes. Be careful they do not overcook.

8. Place the sole on top of the vegetables and add the fish stock. Cover and gently steam for 7 to 12 minutes until the sole is cooked. To test, use an instant thermometer; the reading should be 155 to 160 degrees in the thickest part of the sole.
9. Arrange the sole and vegetables on a serving platter and serve the ginger-vinegar sauce separately.

Servings: 4   Preparation: Fairly easy
Time: Fairly time consuming; advance preparation necessary

Sole English's Style

This is inspired by a dish I had many years ago at English's Restaurant in Brighton, England. The dish relies on a very sharp cheddar cheese for its special flavor.

4 5-ounce sole fillets
12 shrimp (16 to 20 count), peeled and deveined
3 tablespoons unsalted butter
1 tablespoon + 1 teaspoon cake flour
½ cup quick fish stock (page 9)
½ cup light cream
½ cup finely grated very sharp cheddar

1. Cut the shrimp in half lengthwise.
2. With 1 tablespoon butter, butter a 9x13x3-inch ovenproof serving dish. Fold the sole in half across and place in the dish. Sprinkle with 2 tablespoons fish stock and cover the dish.
3. Heat the remaining butter in a 1-quart heavy saucepan, add the flour, and cook on low heat for 1 minute. Add the remaining stock all at once and bring to a boil, stirring all the time. At this point the sauce will be very thick. Remove from the heat immediately, cover so that the sauce does not form a skin, and put to one side.
4. Preheat oven to 350 degrees. Place the covered dish of sole in the oven and cook for 10 minutes. Remove the dish from the oven and pour off the liquid into a measuring cup.
5. Arrange the shrimp over the sole, re-cover, and bake for 10 more minutes.
6. While the sole and shrimp are baking, return the sauce to the heat and whisk in the sole juices. Reheat and slowly whisk in the cream.
7. Remove the sole from the oven. Adjust an oven shelf near the broiler. Preheat the broiler.
8. Pour the sauce over the sole. Sprinkle with the cheese and broil until light golden brown. Serve.

Servings: 4   Preparation: Easy
Time: Fairly time consuming

Sole Aurore

The rich red sauce in this dish highlights the best of the tomato and the richness of the cream. The quality of the sauce depends upon the use of vine-ripened tomatoes and crème fraîche, but you can substitute cream.

4 5- to 6-ounce sole fillets
¼ cup quick fish stock (page 9)
2 tablespoons unsalted butter
2 small vine-ripened tomatoes, peeled, seeded, and julienned
(juice reserved)
1 teaspoon fresh thyme leaves (or 1 teaspoon dried thyme)
¼ cup crème fraîche (or heavy cream)
fresh thyme sprigs for garnish

1. Fold the fillets in half across.
2. Place the sole, fish stock, butter, tomatoes, tomato juice, and dry thyme (if you are using it) in a 12-inch saute pan. Cover and very gently simmer for 3 minutes. Turn the fillets over and gently simmer for 4 to 6 more minutes until they are cooked through. To check for doneness, insert a small knife into the thickest part of the sole. Be careful not to overcook or the sole will be dry.
3. Remove the fillets from the pan with a slotted spatula and place them on a warm serving platter.
4. Turn up the heat under the pan juices and reduce, scraping down the sides with a plastic spatula to keep the sauce from scorching. When the liquid has reduced to a thick consistency, add the crème fraîche or cream, fresh thyme (if you're using it), and any juices that have accumulated on the sole platter. Reduce to the consistency of heavy cream.
5. Add salt and freshly ground black pepper to taste and pour the sauce over the sole. Garnish with the thyme sprigs.

Servings: 4   Preparation: Easy
Time: Fairly time consuming

Sole Caribbean Style

This dish is perfect for a dinner party as, aside from being delicious and attractive, it can be prepared ahead of time and baked in the oven while you and your guests are eating your first course.

This recipe also works well with cod or haddock.

4 5- to 6-ounce sole fillets
½ cup whole blanched almonds
3 tablespoons clarified butter (page 62) or vegetable oil
1 medium onion, very finely diced
2 tablespoons fresh lime juice
½ to 1 teaspoon Tabasco
fresh coriander leaves for garnish (optional)

1. Cook the almonds on a baking sheet in a preheated 375-degree oven for 7 to 10 minutes until light golden brown. Watch carefully that they do not burn. Cool.
2. Heat the butter or oil in a 10-inch saute pan, add the onion, and saute until clear, being careful not to brown.
3. Add the lime juice and ½ tablespoon Tabasco to the onion mixture. Cook over high heat, stirring all the time, until almost all the liquid has evaporated. Pour into a bowl.
4. Chop the almonds medium to fine in a food processor or by hand. Add to the onion mixture. Add salt and more Tabasco to taste.
5. This part of the recipe can be stored for 24 hours in the refrigerator.
6. Just before serving, remove the fillets from the refrigerator and bring them up to room temperature. Preheat oven to 375 degrees.
7. Butter or oil an 8x6x3-inch ovenproof serving dish. Fold the fillets in half across and place them in the dish. Cover each fillet with the almond mixture.
8. Bake the fillets at 375 degrees for 30 minutes. Check that the fish is cooked by inserting a small knife in the thickest part of each fillet. If not cooked, return the dish to the oven for another 5 minutes.
9. Garnish each serving with the coriander leaves.

Servings: 4   **Preparation: Easy**
Time: Fairly time consuming; advance preparation possible

Sole Linda

At first glance this may look like an overly strong sauce for sole, but I assure you that it works extremely well, making a rich and sumptuous dish.

4 5-ounce sole fillets
1½ pounds mussels in the shells
2 cups mussel poaching liquid (page 12)
2 tablespoons unsalted butter
1 tablespoon Dijon mustard
¼ cup heavy cream
2 tablespoons finely chopped fresh parsley

1. Scrub the mussels and remove the beards. Discard any open mussels that do not close when lightly tapped, as they are dead.
2. Heat the poaching liquid in a stainless steel pan, add the mussels, and gently poach until the mussels are open. (It is not necessary to cover the pan.) Be careful not to overcook, as this will toughen the mussels. The mussels should open about ½-inch; discard any that do not open. Remove mussels from the pan with a slotted spoon and cool. Then remove the mussels from the shells. Strain ⅓ cup poaching liquid through a cloth and reserve. You may freeze the rest of the liquid.
3. The mussels and strained poaching liquid may be refrigerated up to 24 hours, if you wish.
4. Just before serving, fold the fillets in half across and place them in a 12-inch stainless steel saute pan. Add the reserved poaching liquid and butter, cover, and gently poach on medium heat for 4 to 6 minutes until the sole is cooked. Remove the sole with a slotted spatula and place on a warm serving platter.
5. Turn up the heat under the saute pan, whisk in the mustard, and reduce the sauce until it has a light syrupy consistency. Add the cream and continue to reduce on high heat, scraping down the sides of the pan with a plastic spatula to keep the sauce from scorching on them.
6. Add the mussels and any liquid that has accumulated on the sole platter. While you heat the mussels, reduce the sauce until it is thick enough to coat a spoon. Add salt and freshly ground black pepper to taste and parsley. Spoon the sauce over the sole and serve.

Servings: 4   Preparation: Easy
Time: Fairly time consuming; some advance preparation possible

Fish Stew Sakonnet

This recipe was inspired by Lolly and Jim Mitchell of the Sakonnet Winery. The stew has a light balance and blend of flavors. Scallops may be substituted for the shrimp, and haddock or cod for the sole.

1 pound sole fillets
1 pound shrimp (21 to 25 count), peeled and deveined
½ cup olive oil
1 medium onion, finely chopped
4 tomatoes, peeled, seeded, and finely chopped (vine-ripened
    preferred)
½ teaspoon grated orange rind (zest)
1 medium fennel bulb, finely diced (or 2 celery stalks, finely
    diced + 1½ teaspoons crushed fennel seeds)
4 cups fish stock (page 7)
⅓ cup loosely packed fresh parsley leaves, finely chopped (or ⅓
    cup loosely packed fresh basil leaves, finely shredded, or 2
    teaspoons dried basil)

1. Heat the olive oil in a 3-quart stainless steel saucepan. Add the onion and saute over medium heat until clear. Add the tomatoes, orange rind, fennel (or celery and crushed fennel), and stock. If you are using dried basil, add it at this time. Gently simmer for 40 minutes.
2. The recipe may be made up to this point and refrigerated for 24 hours.
3. Cut the fish fillet into 1-inch pieces. Cut the shrimp in half lengthwise.
4. Before serving, reheat the soup base. Add the fish and shrimp and gently simmer for 10 minutes. Add the parsley or fresh basil and salt and freshly ground black pepper to taste.

Servings: 6 to 8   Preparation: Easy
Time: Fairly time consuming; some advance preparation possible

Sole Normandy

If possible, try to obtain a dry Normandy cider for this dish, as it really enhances the flavor of the sauce. If you cannot obtain Normandy cider, you can use a dry white wine, preferably a Bordeaux.

6 6-ounce sole fillets
1 cup quick fish stock (page 9)
2 tablespoons unsalted butter
¼ pound mushrooms, sliced ¼-inch thick
½ cup dry Normandy cider or dry white wine
18 large, shucked, raw oysters
½ cup heavy cream
1 tablespoon finely chopped fresh parsley

1. Place the fish stock in a 1-quart stainless steel saucepan and reduce over medium-high heat to ½ cup.
2. Meanwhile, heat the butter in a 12-inch saute pan, add the mushrooms, and toss over high heat until light golden brown and all the liquid has evaporated. Remove mushrooms from pan and put to one side.
3. Fold the sole fillets in half across and arrange in the saute pan. Pour the reduced fish stock and cider or wine over the fillets. Cover and gently poach 3 to 5 minutes until just cooked. To check for doneness, insert a small sharp knife into the thickest part of the fish. Remove the fillets from the pan and arrange on a serving dish. Keep warm.
4. Reduce the pan juices to ½ cup over high heat. Turn down the heat, add the oysters, and gently poach, covered, for 2 minutes. Turn over, cover, and continue to poach until cooked (about 2 to 3 minutes). Be very careful not to overcook them, as they will become rubbery and will shrink. Remove with a slotted spoon and arrange over the sole.
5. Add the cream and mushrooms to the pan juices and reduce over medium-high heat until the sauce is thick enough to coat a spoon.
6. Stir in the parsley. Add salt and freshly ground black pepper to taste. Add any juices that have accumulated on the sole platter, and continue to reduce a little more. Spoon the sauce over the sole and serve immediately.

Servings: 6   **Preparation: Easy**   **Time: Fairly time consuming**

Sole Piedmontese

The addition of lemon juice to the sauce gives this dish a clean, light flavor; fresh thyme gives a more aromatic flavor than basil. Broiled Polenta (page 442) is a wonderful accompaniment. Cod or haddock can be substituted for the sole.

4 6-ounce sole fillets
1/3 cup quick fish stock (page 9)
1 small garlic clove, finely chopped or crushed
4 tablespoons unsalted butter
2 small vine-ripened tomatoes, peeled, seeded, and diced
2 tablespoons fresh lemon juice
1 tablespoon fresh thyme leaves (or 1/4 cup loosely packed fresh basil leaves, finely shredded)

1. Fold the sole fillets in half across. Place them in a heavy 12-inch stainless steel saute pan. Add the stock, garlic, butter, tomatoes, and 1 tablespoon lemon juice.
2. Cover and gently poach on low heat for 3 to 5 minutes until the sole is cooked through. To check for doneness, insert a small knife into the thickest part of the fish. Be careful not to overcook or the sole will become dry.
3. Remove the fillets from the pan with a slotted spatula and place on a warm serving platter.
4. On high heat reduce the pan juices. Scrape down the sides of the pan once in a while with a plastic spatula, to prevent the sauce from scorching on them. Reduce the sauce until it has a medium-thick consistency and add the thyme, and salt, freshly ground black pepper, and more lemon juice to taste. Cook the sauce for 1 more minute and pour it over the fish. Serve.

Servings: 4   **Preparation: Easy**
Time: Quick

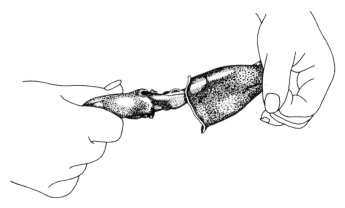

1. Detach the head and tentacles from the body.

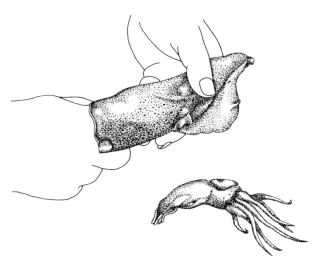

2. With your fingers, thoroughly remove the innards from the body. Note the head and tentacles on the work surface.

Squid

While I was in Spain on vacation, I discovered the wonder of fresh squid. The Spanish offer a simple dish: grilled fresh squid served with olive oil and lemon, accompanied by a salad of vine-ripened tomatoes and a little onion. To me, this is sublime.

Whenever possible you should use fresh, rather than frozen squid. I have discovered, however, that frozen squid works nicely in both recipes offered in this book, and strongly suggest that if time allows, you experiment with this product. If you do purchase frozen squid, try to buy them precleaned. Also, keep in mind that frozen squid will take longer to cook than fresh squid in some recipes, such as in my Stuffed Squid Italiano.

Cleaning squid looks like a messy operation, but it is really quite easy. First, detach the head and tentacles from the body. With your fingers, remove the innards from the body, being careful to remove everything, including the spine which looks like a piece of clear plastic. After you have cut off the tentacles, you may discard the head. (Refer to the drawings on page 270.) You will need the tentacles and bodies for my recipes.

Stuffed Squid Italiano

I really enjoy this squid recipe and find the rich stuffing quick and easy to prepare. It is the essence of Southern Italy, combining the flavor of a rich Parmesan with their finest olive oil and their delicious tomatoes.

> 1½ pounds cleaned small to medium-sized fresh or frozen squid
>   (or 2 pounds uncleaned)
> ¾ cup dry bread crumbs
> ½ cup olive oil
> 1 large garlic clove, finely chopped or crushed
> ½ cup freshly grated Parmesan cheese
> 1½ tablespoons dried basil
> 4 medium tomatoes, peeled, seeded, and diced fine (juice
>   reserved)

1. Clean the squid as described on page 271. Refrigerate the bodies and tentacles no longer than 6 hours.
2. Place the bread crumbs, ¼ cup of the olive oil, garlic, cheese, and basil in a bowl and mix well. The mixture should stick together; if it is still dry, add a little more oil.
3. The stuffing may be refrigerated up to 6 hours.
4. One hour before serving, carefully open the cavity of the squid bodies. With a small teaspoon, stuff each cavity three-fourths full with the bread crumb mixture.
5. Heat the remaining olive oil in a 12-inch heavy stainless steel saute pan and add the squid bodies. Cover and saute on medium heat for 3 minutes. With 2 large spoons, gently turn the squid over, being careful that the stuffing does not come out. Cover and cook 5 more minutes.
6. Add the tomatoes, tomato juice, and tentacles. Cover. If the squid is fresh, gently saute for 10 minutes and check that the squid is tender by slicing off a small part. If the squid is frozen, cook for 30 minutes and check for doneness in the same way.
7. Remove the squid from the pan with a slotted spoon and place on a warm serving platter.
8. Reduce the sauce over high heat until fairly thick and add salt and freshly ground black pepper to taste. Pour the sauce over the squid and serve.

Servings: 4   Preparation: Fairly easy
Time: Fairly time consuming; some advance preparation possible

Grilled Squid with Almonds

This squid dish looks lovely surrounded by fresh parsley sprigs. The taste is light, while the texture remains wonderfully simple.

1½ pounds cleaned fresh or frozen squid (or 2 pounds uncleaned)
4 tablespoons soft Garlic Butter (page 54)
4 tablespoons olive oil
½ cup coarsely chopped blanched almonds
½ cup loosely packed fresh Italian parsley sprigs, coarsely chopped
fresh parsley sprigs for garnish
1 lemon for garnish

1. Clean the squid as described on page 271. Cut the squid bodies into ¼-inch thick slices. The slices and the tentacles may be refrigerated for 4 hours until cooking time.
2. Thirty minutes before cooking, remove the squid from the refrigerator and bring up to room temperature. If any liquid accumulates from the squid, drain and discard before cooking.
3. Preheat broiler.
4. Place the garlic butter and olive oil in a shallow, 9x13-inch ovenproof dish. Add the squid and toss. Place the dish under the broiler, 3 inches from the heat source, and broil for 2 to 3 minutes. Remove and toss the squid so the undersides come to the top.
5. Continue to broil until the squid is almost cooked, then stir in the almonds. Continue to broil until the almonds turn a light golden brown, watching carefully that the almonds do not burn. The squid should be firm and white when cooked; be careful not to overcook or the texture will be rubbery.
6. Stir in the chopped parsley and salt and freshly ground black pepper to taste.
7. Garnish each serving with parsley sprigs and lemon wedges.

Servings: 4   Preparation: Fairly easy
Time: Fairly time consuming; some advance preparation possible

Swordfish

I had not eaten swordfish when I came to the United States. Now I find this a delightful fish. Since it has a fairly strong flavor, it will stand up well to strong sauces. One of my favorite methods of cooking swordfish is on a barbecue grill, outside, in the summer; I like to serve it with fresh corn. Since you all know how to do that, no recipe follows!

The bottom line on swordfish is that it should only be used fresh, not frozen. In choosing steaks, be careful not to get very thick ones. One-half-inch-thick (or less) steaks are preferable; any thicker steaks will need to cook longer, and the longer they cook the more they will dry out.

Swordfish Catalan

I like to serve Catalan Sauce on swordfish because it is very rich in flavor and has a nice crunchy texture. On a summer night, try barbecuing the swordfish and serving the sauce on the side.

> *4 5- to 6-ounce swordfish steaks*
> *1 cup Catalan Sauce (page 21)*
> *1 tablespoon unsalted butter, melted*

1. Thirty minutes before serving, remove the Catalan Sauce and swordfish from the refrigerator and bring up to room temperature.
2. Preheat broiler. Lightly brush a broiler pan with vegetable oil.
3. Place the swordfish steaks on the broiler pan and brush them with the butter. Place the pan three inches from the heat source. Broil for 3 to 5 minutes, then turn over and continue to broil for another 3 to 5 minutes. Check for doneness by removing the steaks from the broiler and cutting off a small piece of the thickest part to make sure the fish is cooked through. If not, return to the broiler and continue to cook for a few more minutes.

4. Place the swordfish steaks on 4 dinner plates and spoon the sauce over them.

Servings: 4   **Preparation: Easy**
Time: Fairly time consuming; some advance preparation possible

Swordfish with Mexican Green Sauce

This sauce, a vibrant green, is a wonderful blend of flavors. Besides broiling the fish, you can grill it on an outdoor grill and serve the sauce separately.

> *4 5- to 6-ounce swordfish steaks*
> *1 cup Mexican Green Sauce (page 25)*
> *1 tablespoon unsalted butter, melted*
> *fresh coriander leaves for garnish*

1. Thirty minutes before serving, remove the Mexican Green Sauce from the refrigerator and bring up to room temperature.
2. Preheat broiler.
3. Lightly brush a broiler pan with vegetable oil. Place the swordfish steaks on the broiler pan and brush with the melted butter. Place the pan 3 inches from the heat source. Broil for 3 to 5 minutes, then turn the steaks over and continue to broil for another 3 to 5 minutes. Check for doneness by removing the steaks from the broiler and cutting off a small piece of the thickest part to make sure the fish is cooked through. If not, return to the broiler and continue to cook for a few more minutes.
4. Place the swordfish steaks on 4 dinner plates and spoon or spread the sauce over the fish (you may need to spread it as the sauce may be quite thick).
5. Garnish with the coriander leaves.

Servings: 4   **Preparation: Easy**
Time: Fairly time consuming; some advance preparation possible

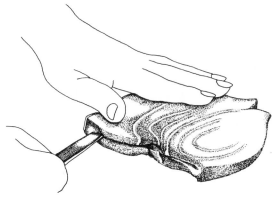

1. With a small, sharp prep knife, cut a pocket in each swordfish steak, being careful not to puncture the flesh.

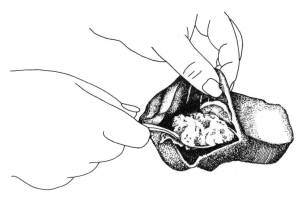

2. Gently insert the stuffing into the pocket.

Stuffed Swordfish Italian Style

This is a wonderful, rich dish. It is excellent served with the lemon butter, or you may use any beurre blanc, or a Red Pepper Puree (page 19).

> 4 7-ounce, ½-inch thick swordfish steaks
> 1 large leek
> 7 tablespoons unsalted butter
> 2 tablespoons finely chopped fresh basil
> ¼ cup loosely packed fresh parsley leaves, finely chopped
> 4 thin slices Mozzarella cheese
> juice of ½ lemon
> fresh basil leaves for garnish

1. Remove and discard the coarse outside layer from the leek. Cut the leek into thin slices up to the medium-green part, and place the slices in a bowl of very cold water for 30 minutes. Drain, rinse, drain well, and pat dry.
2. Heat 2 tablespoons butter in a saute pan. Add the sliced leek and saute until cooked and all the liquid has evaporated, being careful not to brown. Cool. Stir in the basil and parsley and add salt and freshly ground black pepper to taste. Cool.
3. This stuffing can be refrigerated for one day, if desired.
4. With a small sharp prep knife, cut a pocket in each swordfish steak, according to the drawing on page 276. Be careful not to tear the fish. Gently insert one-fourth of the stuffing and a slice of cheese into each steak pocket.
5. Brush the swordfish steaks with one tablespoon melted butter. Butter a broiler pan. Place the swordfish on the pan. Preheat broiler.
6. Place the broiler pan 3 inches from the broiler and broil until the steaks are light golden brown on one side. Turn over the steaks and continue to broil until light golden brown and cooked through. To check for doneness, insert a knife into the thickest part of the steaks. If they are not done, return to the broiler for a few more minutes.
7. While the steaks are cooking, heat the remaining 4 tablespoons of butter with the lemon juice. Add salt and freshly ground black pepper to taste. When the swordfish steaks are cooked, arrange them on a platter, garnish with basil leaves, and pour the lemon-butter over.

Servings: 4   Preparation: Fairly easy
Time: Fairly time consuming; some advance preparation possible

Broiled Swordfish Bahamian Style

This is a wonderful, simple preparation for swordfish. It yields a dish that tastes great garnished with fresh avocado slices, and accompanied by Black Bean Stew.

> 4 5- to 6-ounce swordfish steaks
> 1 small garlic clove, finely chopped
> 3 tablespoons fresh lime juice
> 1 teaspoon Tabasco
> 1/3 cup vegetable oil
> 1 1/2 cups Black Bean Stew (page 419) (optional)
> 1 small ripe avocado
> 1/4 cup loosely packed fresh coriander leaves for garnish
>   (optional)

1. Make a marinade by combining the garlic, lime juice, Tabasco, and oil in a bowl. Whisk.
2. Place the swordfish steaks in a china or glass dish and cover with the marinade. Leave to marinate at least 20 minutes before broiling, but no longer than 1 hour.
3. Warm the black bean stew in a 1-quart saucepan on low heat, stirring occasionally.
4. Preheat broiler. Lightly oil a broiler pan.
5. Remove steaks from marinade and place on the broiler pan. Place the pan 4 inches from the heat source. (The marinade may be discarded.) Broil for 3 to 5 minutes, then turn over and continue to broil for 3 to 5 minutes. Check for doneness by cutting off a small piece of the thickest part of the fish to make sure it is cooked through. If not, return to the broiler and continue to cook for a few more minutes.
6. Meanwhile, cut the avocado in half lengthwise and remove the pit, then peel and slice 1/8-inch thick.
7. To serve, arrange the swordfish on 4 plates. Place the avocado on top of the swordfish and sprinkle with the coriander leaves. Spoon the bean stew onto the plates.

Servings: 4   Preparation: Easy
Time: Quick; some advance preparation necessary

Swordfish Shiitake

The flavor of Shiitake mushrooms makes a wonderful sauce for swordfish. If Porcini mushrooms are available, however, they are even more delicious.

4 5- to 6-ounce swordfish steaks
¼ pound Shiitake or Porcini mushrooms
4 tablespoons unsalted butter
⅓ cup quick fish stock (page 9)
¼ cup heavy cream
fresh Italian parsley sprigs for garnish

1. Cut off and discard the coarse stalks from the mushrooms. Slice the caps ⅛-inch thick.
2. Preheat broiler and adjust the oven rack 6 to 8 inches from the heat.
3. Place the swordfish steaks on a lightly oiled broiler pan and brush them with 1 tablespoon melted butter. Broil for 5 to 7 minutes, turn over and continue to broil for 3 to 5 minutes. Check for doneness by removing the steaks from the broiler and cutting off a small piece of the thickest part to make sure they are cooked through. If not, return to the broiler and continue to cook for a few more minutes.
4. Meanwhile, heat the remaining butter in a 12-inch saute pan. Add the mushrooms, and toss them over medium heat until they turn a light golden brown and are cooked through. Add the quick fish stock, turn up the heat to high, and reduce the sauce until it has a light syrupy consistency. Add the cream and continue to reduce until the sauce is thick enough to coat a spoon. Add salt and freshly ground black pepper to taste.
5. Place the swordfish steaks on 4 dinner plates and spoon the sauce on top.

Servings: 4　　**Preparation: Easy**
Time: Quick

Trout

The history of man's fascination with trout can be traced as far back as the Roman Empire. The Romans' concern for the best trout was the reason for importing trout to the streams of Northern Italy, even though another species already existed there. This concern continued with the British, who seemed to take trout wherever they settled, even to the extent of moving the cold water fish to the hot climates of Africa. Later, when rainbow trout were discovered in the mountain streams of Idaho, there arose an immediate discussion as to which was better, the new-found American trout or the European variety.

Trout can be used in many combinations and variations, whether it is smoked, poached, grilled, broiled, or pan fried. I do always suggest fresh versus frozen. Frozen trout has a drier texture that can be unappealing. I feel that the quality of fresh trout is so superior it is worth any extra effort necessary to obtain it.

Trout Noisette

The marriage of hazelnuts, shallots, and parsley gives this dish a truly rich flavor. For a lighter touch, Tomato Coulis (page 16) may be substituted for the beurre blanc.

4 6- to 8-ounce boneless whole trout
½ cup hazelnuts
3 tablespoons unsalted butter
5 large or 10 small shallots, thinly sliced
¼ cup loosely packed fresh parsley leaves, finely chopped
1 cup Basic Beurre Blanc (page 34)

1. Place the hazelnuts in a food processor and process to a medium-coarse chop, or chop by hand.
2. Heat 2 tablespoons butter in a 10-inch saute pan, add the shallots, and saute on medium heat until clear, being careful not to brown. Place the shallots and hazelnuts in a bowl and cool. Add the parsley and salt and freshly ground black pepper to taste.
3. This stuffing may be stored in the refrigerator for 8 hours.
4. Just before serving, clip the fins and tails from the trout with a pair of kitchen scissors. Cut off the heads.
5. Preheat broiler.
6. Place one-fourth of the stuffing in the cavity of each trout.
7. Butter the trout with the remaining tablespoon of butter. Place on an oiled broiler pan, place the pan 4 to 6 inches from the heat source, and broil until light golden brown. Remove from the broiler and turn over each trout, being careful that the stuffing does not fall out. Return to the broiler and broil until light golden brown. To check for doneness, remove the trout from the broiler. Gently lift up the top fillet and check the cavity to make sure it is cooked through. If it is not cooked, turn the broiler off, return the trout to the oven, and bake at 350 degrees for 3 to 5 minutes until cooked.
8. To serve, pour the beurre blanc onto 4 warm dinner plates and place the trout on the sauce.

Servings: 4   Preparation: Fairly difficult
Time: Fairly time consuming; some advance preparation possible

Trout Piment

Trout looks beautiful when served on this bright red sauce. The sauce is attractive as well as convenient, as it can be made ahead of time.

Fresh chives, finely snipped, may be substituted for caviar.

4 6- to 8-ounce boneless whole trout
2 tablespoons all-purpose unbleached flour
1 cup Red Pepper Puree (page 19)
4 tablespoons unsalted butter
⅓ cup sour cream or crème fraîche for garnish
1 ounce fresh American caviar for garnish (optional)

1. Put flour on a plate and add salt and freshly ground black pepper.
2. With kitchen scissors, clip the fins and tails off the trout. Cut off the heads.
3. Warm the Red Pepper Puree in a 1-quart saucepan over low heat.
4. Just before serving, pat the fish dry, then lightly flour the trout, dusting off any excess flour.
5. Heat the butter in a heavy 12-inch stainless steel pan, add the trout, and saute over medium heat until golden brown on one side. Turn the trout over, cover, and gently saute until cooked through, approximately 4 to 7 minutes. To check for doneness, gently lift up the top fillet and check the cavity to make sure it is cooked through. Be careful not to overcook, or the fish will be dry.
6. Remove the trout from the pan and remove the skin from the top of each trout.
7. Spoon the sauce onto 4 warm dinner plates. Place the trout on top and garnish each one with the sour cream or crème fraîche and caviar.

Servings: 4   Preparation: Easy
Time: Fairly time consuming

Trout Moutarde

This delicious dish is simple to make, and uses a compound butter that can be made a couple of days ahead of time.

4 6- to 8-ounce boneless whole trout
5 tablespoons unsalted butter, room temperature
1 tablespoon Dijon mustard
1½ tablespoons coarsely chopped fresh tarragon leaves
2 medium vine-ripened tomatoes, peeled, seeded, thinly sliced
1 medium onion, thinly sliced
3 tablespoons vegetable oil
fresh parsley or tarragon leaves for garnish

1. Place the butter in a bowl and beat until smooth and soft. Beat in the mustard, then stir in the tarragon and add salt and freshly ground black pepper to taste.
2. This compound butter may be made two days ahead of serving and stored in the refrigerator.
3. One hour before serving, remove the butter from the refrigerator. Bring up to room temperature and soften. With kitchen scissors, clip the fins and tails off the trout. Cut off the heads.
4. Place the tomato slices in a bowl with the onion. Mix with 2 tablespoons oil and add salt and freshly ground black pepper to taste.
5. Stuff one-fourth of the butter into the cavity of each trout. Close the cavity with a toothpick. (This might be difficult, as the toothpicks sometimes break.) Brush the trout with the remaining tablespoon of oil.
6. Preheat broiler.
7. Place the onion and tomato in a 9- by 13-inch, shallow, ovenproof serving dish. Broil the onion and tomato for 2 to 3 minutes until they are a very light golden brown. Remove from the broiler and place the trout on the onion mixture, making sure the mixture is tucked under the trout. Broil 4 to 6 inches from the heat source.

8. Broil until the trout are light golden brown. Remove from the broiler and turn over, then continue to broil until light golden brown. To check for doneness, remove the pan from the broiler, insert a knife in the thickest part of each trout, and check to see that it is cooked through. If the trout are not cooked, return the pan to the oven and turn off the broiler. Bake at 350 degrees for 3 to 5 minutes until cooked.
9. Garnish with parsley or tarragon sprigs just before serving.

Servings: 4   Preparation: Easy
Time: Quick; some advance preparation possible

Trout Verona

This sophisticated dish gets its lovely, aromatic flavor from the rosemary.

4 6- to 8-ounce boneless whole trout
2 tablespoons all-purpose unbleached flour
3 tablespoons olive oil
4 tablespoons unsalted butter
1 small garlic clove, finely chopped or crushed
3 ounces (21 to 25 count) shrimp, peeled and deveined
1 tablespoon fresh lemon juice
¼ cup white wine
½ teaspoon coarsely chopped fresh rosemary
fresh rosemary sprigs for garnish

1. Place the flour on a plate and add a little salt and freshly ground black pepper to taste.
2. With kitchen scissors, clip the fins and tails off the trout. Cut off the heads. Pat the trout dry and dust lightly with flour, shaking off any excess flour.
3. Heat the olive oil in a 12-inch saute pan. Place the trout in the pan and saute on medium heat until light golden brown on one side. Turn over the trout, cover the pan, and gently saute for 4 to 7 minutes until the trout are cooked through. To check for doneness, gently lift up the top fillet of each trout and look into the cavity. Be careful not to overcook or they will be dry.
4. Remove the trout from the pan and place them on a serving platter or 4 dinner plates. Remove and discard the top skin. Keep the trout warm.
5. Add the butter, garlic, and shrimp to the pan. Saute on low heat for 3 to 4 minutes, being careful that the garlic does not brown and that the shrimp are not overcooked.
6. When the shrimp are cooked, remove them from the pan with a slotted spoon and place over the trout.
7. Add the lemon juice, white wine, and rosemary to the pan. Reduce on high heat for a minute, whisking all the time. The sauce should emulsify.
8. Pour the sauce over the trout and garnish with fresh rosemary sprigs.

Servings: 4   **Preparation: Easy**
Time: Quick

Poultry & Meat

Entrees

Poultry

My favorite way to prepare chicken is simply to roast it, but this satisfying meal is dependent on a high-quality product. Therefore, I offer the following information.

There are two types of chicken available in today's market: free range chickens (chickens that run free) and battery chickens (otherwise called commodity chickens). Range chickens are fed low levels of therapeutic antibiotic feed to prevent salmonella. Battery chickens are fed high levels of therapeutic antibiotic feed. Often the feed has fish meal and marigold petals in it, giving the battery chicken a yellowish color. It is for this reason that range chickens have a different and more appealing flavor than battery chickens. Range chickens are generally available in specialty stores; though more expensive, they are well worth the additional price. It is especially important to the quality of the product that it not be frozen. To emphasize my point, I often purchase chickens in Boston's Chinatown, where they offer live range chickens slaughtered at purchase to retain their quality and freshness.

If you purchase chicken in a supermarket, check to see if the skin is moist, but not slimy, and that there is little or no odor. To ensure quality, you should smell the chicken before leaving the store. (Just open the plastic wrap on the package before you have paid for the chicken; if the chicken does not seem to be fresh, ask for another package.) Certain stores will not be thrilled by this practice, but there is nothing more frustrating than getting home, opening your purchase, and discovering a poor quality product.

You will notice that most of the recipes in this chapter call for chicken breasts that are boned. I suggest that you bone the breasts yourself; it is easier than you might think. Once you have done this several times, it will become a quick simple procedure. Even if you tear or puncture the meat in your first attempts, don't give up; once the breast is cooked and masked with a sauce, no one will ever notice. Refer to the drawings on page 290.

There are two reasons why I urge you to try to master this technique. When chicken breasts have been boned no more than several hours before cooking, the breasts will be moist and tender; store-bought preboned breasts may have been boned for many hours, so they may be dry. Second, the bones can be frozen until you have accumulated a large quantity, which can be made into chicken stock. As I have noted on page 2, my preference is the use of homemade stocks in soups, casseroles, and especially sauces.

In almost all my recipes I have called for one-pound chicken breasts, before they are boned. I realize it's not always possible to obtain this exact weight, so I suggest you look for breasts ranging from 16 to 20 ounces. Breasts of this size are then split in half to provide two servings. If you can only find small chicken breasts, however, instead of serving half a breast per person, use two small breasts per person.

In addition to chicken recipes, you also will find two recipes for pheasant in this chapter. To quote the *American Heritage Cookbook,* published by Simon & Schuster, Inc. in 1964: "The pheasant came to America by way of England from China and the shores of the Black Sea. Richard Bache, an Englishman, who married Benjamin Franklin's only daughter, was (among) the first to attempt to raise pheasant in this country, on his estate in New Jersey." Wavery Root continues the history in his book *Food,* telling us that Bache was not successful and that it was not until 1880 that an American consul returned from Shanghai with Chinese ring-necked pheasants and was successful in breeding them.

When I arrived in the United States, I discovered there was a difference between the English and American varieties of pheasants. In my youth, my father would be given pheasants. Father would hang these beautiful birds in the garden shed for five to ten days, then pluck and draw them. The meat was dark in color, tender, and strong in flavor. The pheasant I purchased in Boston came as quite a surprise. The flesh was light in color, the flavor was mild, and the texture was dry.

Since that first purchase, I have discovered that the pheasant sold in this country are generally not wild, and that hanging them is not a customary practice. This accounts for the lighter color and the drier taste. Therefore, to compensate for this, I have offered a marinade of rosemary or fennel (see page 57), which is excellent with pheasant.

As a last comment on pheasant, you will find that if you bone a pheasant and a chicken of the equivalent size, the leg of the pheasant will have tougher sinews and tendons than that of the chicken. If you tie or truss the legs before roasting the bird it will ensure a moist finished product. Many of the early recipes in England also called for wrapping pheasant breasts in bacon to make up for the dryness of the meat. Of course, this will impart a flavor of its own, but the additional moisture is wonderful for the pheasant.

This chapter also includes a recipe for duck and mentions the possibility of substitution of Cornish game hens in several recipes. When at all possible, try to purchase fresh, not frozen, ducks and game hens, as you will find the flesh to be more moist and tender.

HOW TO BONE CHICKEN BREASTS

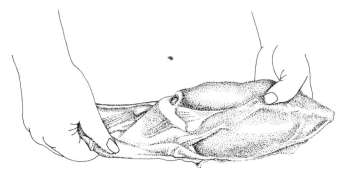

1. Pull the skin off the chicken breast.

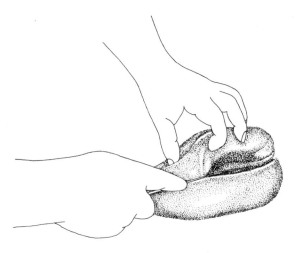

2. With a sharp, flexible boning knife, cut close into one side of the breast bone and work down, being certain the back of the knife is against the bone.

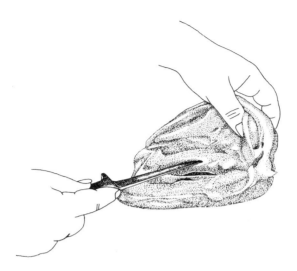

3. Turn the breast over and bone the other side.

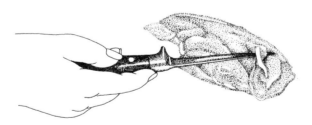

4. Now that the breast is boned, you have a fillet. Remove the coarse tendon that runs through the fillet with your knife.

Chicken Maurice

This recipe is named for my good friend Maurice Moore-Betty, who encouraged and guided me when I first arrived in America. It is an excellent dish to make in the summer and early autumn when plums are plentiful. A beautiful purple in color, it looks marvelous when it is served with a green vegetable, such as zucchini or Sauteed Cucumbers and Peas (page 429).

> *2 1-pound chicken breasts*
> *⅔ cup homemade chicken stock (or ½ cup low-salt canned chicken broth)*
> *2 medium-sized, ripe, Santa Rosa or Florentina plums*
> *4 tablespoons unsalted butter*
> *2 tablespoons vintage Port or good Tawny Port*
> *½ tablespoon fresh savory or thyme leaves, coarsely chopped*
> *1 teaspoon finely grated lemon rind (zest)*
> *4 thin lemon slices for garnish*

1. Skin and bone the chicken breasts (see page 290). Pound the thickest part of the chicken breast to a thickness even with that of the thinnest part.
2. Place the chicken stock in a 1-quart saucepan and reduce over high heat to ⅓ cup.
3. Cut the plums in half and remove the pits. Slice the plums into ¼-inch-thick slices. Put 4 slices aside for garnish.
4. Heat the butter in a 12-inch saute pan. Add the chicken breasts and saute on medium heat for 3 to 5 minutes. Turn them over and continue to saute until cooked through. Remove the chicken from the pan with a slotted spatula and keep warm.
5. Add the sliced plums to the pan and saute over high heat for 3 minutes. Add the reduced chicken stock, Port, savory or thyme, and lemon rind. Reduce over high heat until the sauce has a light syrupy consistency. Add salt and freshly ground black pepper to taste.
6. Arrange the chicken breasts on 4 dinner plates and spoon the sauce over them. Garnish each serving with a lemon slice topped with a plum slice. Serve immediately.

Servings: 4   **Preparation: Easy**
Time: Quick

Chicken Breasts Chapelle

This chicken entree has the most delightful visual appeal, with the reddish-brown sauce against the dark green of the spinach leaves. It also has a wonderful rich and tart flavor.

2 1-pound chicken breasts
1 cup red wine
1 cup strong homemade chicken stock
4 tablespoons unsalted butter
16 large fresh spinach leaves
1 tablespoon Dijon mustard
4 tablespoons crème fraîche or sour cream

1. Skin and bone the chicken breasts (see page 290). Pound the thickest part of the chicken breast to a thickness even with that of the thinnest part.
2. Bring the red wine to a boil in a 1- to 2-quart stainless steel saucepan. Ignite, then let it flame for 3 minutes. Add the chicken stock and boil until the liquid has reduced to ½ cup.
3. Heat the butter in a 12-inch stainless steel saute pan. Saute the chicken for 3 to 5 minutes on medium heat, then turn over. Continue to saute until cooked through, approximately 3 to 5 minutes. Be careful not to let the butter burn. Remove the chicken from the pan with a slotted spatula and keep warm.
4. While the chicken is cooking, bring 2 cups water to a boil in a separate saucepan. Add the spinach leaves and cook for 30 seconds. Gently remove the leaves with a slotted spoon and keep warm.
5. Add the reduced stock and red wine mixture to the pan used for the chicken and whisk in the mustard until smooth. Whisk over high heat until the sauce has reduced to ¼ cup, and has a light syrupy consistency. Whisk in the crème fraîche or sour cream. Continue to reduce until the sauce is thick enough to coat a spoon. Add salt and freshly ground black pepper to taste.
6. Arrange the spinach leaves on 4 warm dinner plates, and arrange the chicken breasts on the spinach. Spoon the sauce over the chicken and serve immediately.

Servings: 4   Preparation: Easy
Time: Fairly time consuming

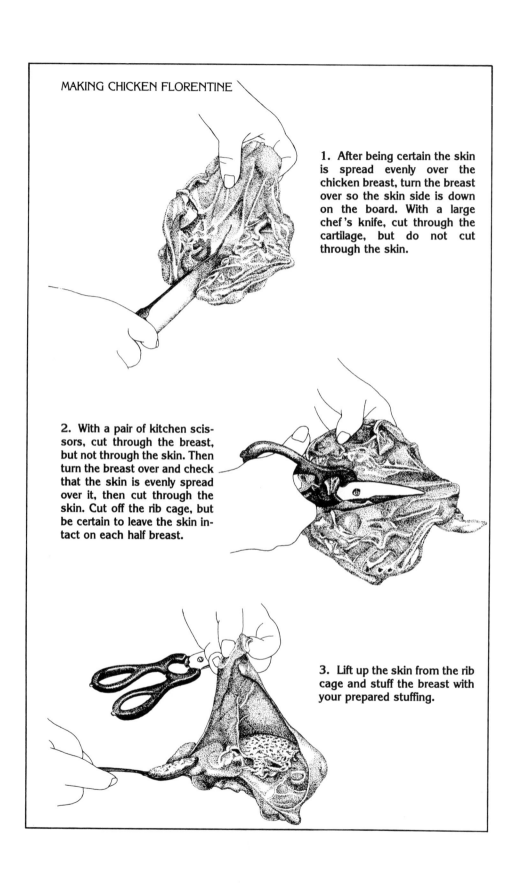

MAKING CHICKEN FLORENTINE

1. After being certain the skin is spread evenly over the chicken breast, turn the breast over so the skin side is down on the board. With a large chef's knife, cut through the cartilage, but do not cut through the skin.

2. With a pair of kitchen scissors, cut through the breast, but not through the skin. Then turn the breast over and check that the skin is evenly spread over it, then cut through the skin. Cut off the rib cage, but be certain to leave the skin intact on each half breast.

3. Lift up the skin from the rib cage and stuff the breast with your prepared stuffing.

Chicken Florentine

Chicken Florentine was inspired by Betsy West, whose simple but creative way with food is exemplified by this recipe. For variation, you may substitute Tomato Sauce (page 14) for the Madeira sauce used here.

2 1-pound chicken breasts
1 large egg
¾ cup ricotta cheese
½ cup loosely packed fresh basil leaves, finely shredded (or 2
    teaspoons dried basil)
½ cup cooked, squeezed dry, and finely chopped fresh spinach
1 tablespoon unsalted butter, softened
¾ cup homemade chicken consomme or stock
¼ cup dry Madeira
1 teaspoon finely grated lemon rind (zest)
2 teaspoons cornstarch
¼ cup water
lemon slices for garnish

1. Make sure the chicken breasts have a good skin covering and that the skin is even on both sides. Turn the chicken over so the breast side is down on the cutting board. Now refer to the drawings on page 294 as you cut away the rib cage from the breasts. It is essential that you leave the skin attached to the breasts.
2. Place the egg in a bowl with a little salt and freshly ground black pepper, whisk until well emulsified. Whisk in the ricotta. Add the basil, spinach, and salt and freshly ground black pepper to taste. Divide the stuffing into four portions.
3. These steps may be done 6 hours ahead of serving time; refrigerate the chicken and stuffing.
4. Preheat oven to 400 degrees.
5. Just before baking, stuff chicken. From the rib cage end, lift up the skin from the chicken and push the stuffing under the skin. With the tablespoon of butter, butter the top of each chicken breast. Lightly butter a sheet pan. Place the chicken breasts on the pan, skin side up. Bake at 400 degrees for 30 to 40 minutes. To test for doneness, insert an

instant thermometer into the thickest part of the meat; it should read 155 degrees.

6. While the chicken is cooking, place the chicken consomme or stock in a 1-quart saucepan with the Madeira and lemon rind. Bring to a boil and reduce to ¾ cup. In a bowl, mix the cornstarch with the ¼ cup water. Pour a little stock into the cornstarch mixture, then slowly pour it back into the pan, whisking all the time, off the heat. Return to the heat and bring to a boil, continuing to whisk constantly. Lower the heat and gently simmer for 5 minutes. Add salt and freshly ground pepper to taste.

7. Place chicken on a serving platter and garnish with lemon slices. Serve the sauce separately.

Servings: 4   Preparation: Fairly difficult
Time: Fairly time consuming; some advance preparation possible

Chicken with Chèvre

When you bite into this chicken, you get the most glorious task of warm, oozing chèvre. I happen to prefer the strong flavor of Bucheron, but milder chèvres work well in this recipe.

> 2 1-pound chicken breasts
> 6 tablespoons Montrachet, Bucheron, or a mild chèvre cheese,
>   rind removed
> ½ cup homemade chicken consomme or stock
> 4 tablespoons unsalted butter
> 1 to 2 tablespoons fresh lemon juice
> ¼ cup loosely packed fresh mint leaves, finely shredded
> Fresh mint sprigs for garnish

1. Skin and bone the chicken breasts (see page 290).
2. Cut a pocket with a small, sharp, prep knife into the thickest part of the chicken breasts. Divide the cheese into 4 equal portions and stuff into the chicken breasts. Secure the openings with lightly oiled toothpicks. (If you find the toothpicking step too difficult, you can eliminate this step.)
3. Reduce the consomme or stock over high heat to ¼ cup.
4. Heat the butter in a 12-inch stainless steel saute pan. Add the chicken breasts and saute on medium heat for 3 to 5 minutes. Turn and saute for another 3 to 5 minutes until the breasts are cooked through. Remove the chicken with a slotted spatula to a warm platter and keep warm.
5. Add the reduced chicken stock and 1 tablespoon lemon juice to the pan and reduce to a light syrupy consistency. Add the mint, and salt, freshly ground black pepper, and more lemon juice to taste.
6. Remove the toothpicks. Pour the sauce over the chicken breasts and garnish with the mint leaves.

Servings: 4   Preparation: Fairly easy to prepare
Time: Fairly time consuming

Chicken Breasts Clara

Jeffrey Starr inspired this marvelous dish. The sauce has the most wonderful rich flavor in which the nuttiness is highlighted by the garlic. Please be sure to check that hazelnuts are not rancid. I suggest serving this entree with a simple green vegetable. In the summer it is nice to garnish it with slices of fresh ripe peaches.

> 2 1-pound chicken breasts
> ½ cup hazelnuts
> 1 cup homemade chicken consomme or stock
> 3 tablespoons Garlic Butter, room temperature (page 54)
> ¼ cup heavy cream
> fresh parsley sprigs for garnish

1. In a preheated 350-degree oven toast hazelnuts on a heavy sheet pan for 10 to 15 minutes, until the skins start to crack off and the nuts are a medium brown. Watch them carefully, as they can easily burn. Remove from the oven, cool a little, and rub the skins off. Cool completely and grind until fairly fine in a food processor.
2. Skin and bone chicken breasts (see page 290). Pound the thickest part of the chicken breast to a thickness even with that of the thinnest part.
3. The above procedures may be done 6 hours ahead of serving time. Refrigerate the nuts and the chicken.
4. Place the consomme or stock in a saucepan. Boil until it has reduced to ⅓ cup.
5. Heat the garlic butter in a 12-inch heavy saute pan. Add the chicken and saute on medium heat for 3 to 5 minutes until cooked, being careful that the butter does not brown. Turn the chicken over and cook another 3 to 5 minutes until the chicken is cooked through. Remove from the pan with a slotted spatula and place on a warm serving platter.
6. Turn up the heat under the pan, add the stock and nuts, and reduce over high heat until fairly thick. Add the cream and continue to reduce until the sauce is thick enough to coat a spoon.
7. Spoon the sauce over the chicken and garnish with the parsley. Serve immediately.

Servings: 4   Preparation: Easy
Time: Fairly time consuming; some advance preparation possible

Sauteed Chicken Breasts Valentino

This chicken entree is very popular in the restaurant. It brings together some very distinctive flavors—in particular, the lemon juice and the Parmesan. I urge you to only use freshly grated Parmesan; it makes quite a difference in the dish.

2 chicken breasts, 16 to 18 ounces each [handwritten: 48]
3 tablespoons unsalted butter [handwritten: 36T ov 1'1⁄2#]
4 ounces mushrooms, sliced 1/8-inch thick [handwritten: 3 #]
1 cup homemade chicken stock (or 3/4 cup canned low-salt [handwritten: 1 2 c. = 3 p5.]
chicken broth)
1 to 2 tablespoons fresh lemon juice [handwritten: 1 2T = 4Lemon]
1⁄4 cup freshly grated Parmesan cheese [handwritten: 3 cups]
1⁄8 cup heavy cream [handwritten: 1'1⁄2 c.]
4 lemon slices for garnish

1. Skin and bone the chicken breasts (see diagram on page 290). Pound the thickest part of the chicken breast to a thickness even with that of the thinnest part.
2. Place the chicken stock in a 1-quart saucepan and reduce over high heat to 1⁄3 cup.
3. Heat the butter in a 12-inch saute pan. Add chicken and saute on medium heat until light golden brown, 3 to 5 minutes. Turn over and saute another 3 to 5 minutes, until the chicken is cooked through. Remove from pan with a slotted spatula and place on a warm platter.
4. If the pan has chicken juices in it besides the butter, turn up the heat and reduce the pan juices until only the butter remains. Then add the mushrooms and saute on medium to high heat until light golden brown, tossing all the time.
5. Add stock and 1 tablespoon lemon juice and simmer 1 minute. Then add the cream and reduce a little.
6. Turn down the heat to low and stir in the Parmesan, whisking all the time. Add salt and freshly ground black pepper and the additional lemon juice to taste. Pour the sauce over the chicken breasts and serve, garnished with lemon slices.

Servings: 4   **Preparation: Easy**
Time: Quick

Chicken Greek Style

This special chicken entree was created for Paul Calderone. The richness of the sauce is offset by the lemon. The addition of the egg yolk gives the sauce a wonderful velvety texture and glossy appearance. Steamed broccoli, asparagus, or green beans would be a good accompaniment.

> *2 1-pound chicken breasts*
> *1½ cups homemade chicken consomme or stock*
> *4 tablespoons unsalted butter*
> *⅓ cup heavy cream*
> *1 egg yolk*
> *2 tablespoons fresh lemon juice*
> *¼ cup loosely packed fresh mint or dill sprigs, medium-chopped fresh mint or dill sprigs for garnish*
> *4 thin lemon slices for garnish*

1. Skin and bone the chicken breasts (see page 290). Pound the thickest part of the breast to a thickness even with that of the thinnest part.
2. Place the consomme in a 1-quart saucepan and reduce to 1/2 cup.
3. Heat the butter in a heavy 12-inch stainless steel saute pan. Add the chicken breasts and saute on medium heat for 3 to 5 minutes. Turn over and saute another 3 to 5 minutes, until cooked through. Check for doneness by inserting a small sharp knife in the thickest part of the chicken. Remove the chicken with a slotted spatula to a warm platter and keep warm.
4. Whisk the cream and egg yolk together.
5. Add the consomme or stock to the pan with the lemon juice and reduce over high heat to a medium syrupy consistency. Remove the pan from the heat to whisk in the egg and cream mixture with the chopped mint or dill. Whisk over high heat until the sauce starts to thicken; the egg yolk needs to be brought almost to a boil to facilitate thickening, but you must be very careful not to boil, or the sauce will curdle. Add salt and freshly ground black pepper to taste.
6. Pour the sauce over the chicken and garnish with the herb sprigs and lemon slices.

Servings: 4   Preparation: Easy
Time: Fairly time consuming

Chicken Basque Style

If you like chicken livers, you'll love Chicken Basque Style. Even if they are not one of your favorite foods, try this dish anyway. They accentuate the flavor of the chicken, providing a very richly flavored sauce. The next time you buy a roasting chicken, freeze the livers until you're ready to make this dish.

> 2 12- to 16-ounce chicken breasts
> 4 tablespoons unsalted butter
> ½ medium onion, sliced
> 3 small garlic cloves, finely sliced
> 2 chicken livers
> ½ to ¾ cup homemade chicken stock (or ½ cup low-salt
>   chicken broth and ¼ cup water)
> ½ cup whole blanched almonds
> ¼ cup loosely packed fresh parsley sprigs, finely chopped
> 1 hard-boiled egg, finely chopped, for garnish

1. Skin and bone chicken breasts (see page 290). Pound the thickest part of the chicken breast to a thickness even with that of the thinnest part.
2. Heat 2 tablespoons butter in a 12-inch stainless steel saute pan. Add the onion and garlic and saute until clear. Add the chicken livers and saute for 3 minutes on a medium to high heat. Add ½ cup chicken stock and almonds, cover, and gently simmer for 10 minutes. Then while this mixture is still hot, puree it in the blender until smooth.
3. You may refrigerate the chicken and the sauce up to 6 hours.
4. Heat the remaining 2 tablespoons of butter. Add the chicken breasts and saute on one side on medium heat for 3 to 5 minutes, being careful not to brown the butter. Turn the chicken over and saute another 3 to 5 minutes until the breasts are cooked through. Remove the chicken with a slotted spatula and place on a warm serving platter.
5. Add the chicken liver puree to the pan juices and reheat. Add the parsley and a little more stock if the sauce is too thick. Add salt and freshly ground black pepper to taste.
6. Pour the sauce over the chicken on the platter and garnish with the chopped egg.

Servings: 4   Preparation: Easy
Time: Fairly time consuming; some advance preparation possible

Chicken with Brie

This great recipe was given to me by Chris Carron. The addition of the Brie gives the sauce a wonderful, rich, velvety consistency and, of course, a superb flavor.

For best results, use homemade chicken stock and Brie that is 60-percent butterfat. (Ask the cheese salesperson.) The Brie should be ripe. No salt should be added, but the addition of freshly ground black pepper gives a lovely aromatic finish to the dish. I like to serve this dish with a steamed green vegetable, such as asparagus, zucchini, broccoli, or beans.

> *2 1-pound chicken breasts*
> *3 ounces ripe 60-percent butterfat Brie*
> *3 tablespoons unsalted butter*
> *½ cup strong homemade chicken stock (or ⅓ cup canned*
> *low-salt chicken broth)*
> *2 tablespoons heavy cream*
> *2 teaspoons fresh thyme leaves*

1. Bone the chicken breasts (see page 290). Pound the thickest part of the breast to a thickness even with that of the thinnest part.
2. Remove and discard the rind from the Brie; break the Brie into small pieces.
3. These steps may be done 6 hours ahead of serving time; refrigerate the chicken and Brie.
4. One hour before serving, remove the Brie and chicken from the refrigerator to bring them up to room temperature.
5. Just before serving, heat the butter in a 12-inch heavy saute pan. Add the chicken breasts, and saute on medium heat for 3 to 5 minutes. Turn over and saute another 3 to 5 minutes, until the chicken is cooked through. Insert a small sharp knife in the thickest part of the chicken to check it is done. Remove the chicken breasts from the pan with a slotted spatula and place on a warm serving platter.
6. Add the chicken stock to the pan and reduce over high heat to 1/4 cup. Add the cream and any juices that have acccumulated from the chicken and reduce over high heat until the sauce lightly coats the back of the spoon. Remove the pan from the heat. Whisk in the pieces of Brie and

thyme and return the pan to low heat. Continue to whisk until Brie is melted. Add freshly ground black pepper to taste.

7. Pour the sauce over the chicken and serve immediately.

Servings: 4   Preparation: Easy
Time: Fairly time consuming; some advance preparation possible

Chicken Breasts Gingembre

Although I am not a great lover of the fish-meat combination, the unusual mix of flavors in this dish is very successful. Do try the marjoram in the sauce; even though it is so scented and aromatic, it really works well. Basil may be substituted if marjoram is not available.

2 8- to 10-ounce chicken breasts
8 shrimp (16 to 20 count), peeled and deveined
4 tablespoons Ginger Garlic Butter (page 52)
2 tablespoons fresh lemon juice
¼ cup dry white wine
⅓ cup strong homemade chicken stock
1½ tablespoons fresh marjoram leaves, coarsely chopped (or 2
    tablespoons fresh basil leaves, chopped)
sprigs of fresh marjoram or basil leaves for garnish

1. Skin and bone chicken breasts (see page 290). Pound the thickest part of the chicken breast to a thickness even with that of the thinnest part.
2. Cut the shrimp in half lengthwise.
3. Heat the Ginger Garlic Butter in a 12-inch heavy stainless steel saute pan, being careful that the butter does not brown. Add the chicken breasts and turn down the heat. Gently saute 3 to 5 minutes; turn them over and gently saute until cooked through, approximately 3 to 5 minutes. Insert a small sharp knife in the thickest part of the chicken to check it is done. Remove the chicken breasts with a slotted spatula and keep them warm on 4 dinner plates.

4. Add the shrimp to the pan. Cover and gently saute for 3 to 5 minutes until cooked through; be careful not to overcook the shrimp or they will become rubbery. Remove from the pan and arrange on the 4 dinner plates with the chicken breasts.
5. Add the lemon juice, wine, and chicken stock to the same pan and cook on a very high heat, constantly whisking, until you have reduced the liquid by 30 percent. Stir in the chopped marjoram or basil and salt and freshly ground black pepper to taste.
6. Spoon the sauce over the chicken and shrimp and garnish with marjoram sprigs or basil leaves. Serve immediately.

Servings: 4   Preparation: Easy
Time: Fairly time consuming

Chicken Lundi

This chicken entree is another Peter Pastan inspiration and a sheer delight. It has a nice, crisp and peppery outside and is excellent served with pureed parsnips or creamed spinach.

2 1-pound chicken breasts
1 tablespoon dried yellow mustard seeds
6 tablespoons dry bread crumbs
2 teaspoons dried thyme leaves
1 large egg
1 tablespoon water
4 tablespoons flour
6 tablespoons vegetable oil
fresh watercress sprigs for garnish (optional)

1. Skin and bone the chicken breasts (see page 290). Pound the thickest part of the chicken breast to a thickness even with that of the thinnest part.
2. Place the mustard seeds in a dry blender and blend until fairly fine. Add the bread crumbs and thyme and blend until well mixed, about 15 seconds. Be careful not to overblend or the bread crumbs will become a fine powder. Put this mixture on a plate.
3. Put the flour on another plate and add a pinch of salt and freshly ground black pepper.
4. Crack the egg into a bowl, add a pinch of salt and the tablespoon of water, and whisk until it is well emulsified.
5. Just before cooking the chicken, very lightly dust the chicken breasts with the flour, then coat with egg, and finally coat with the bread crumb mixture.
6. Heat the oil in a heavy 12-inch saute pan. Add the chicken and saute on medium heat until light golden brown on one side. Turn and continue to cook until light golden brown. If the chicken is not cooked through, at this point, finish the cooking in a 375-degree oven (about 3 to 5 minutes) to keep the bread crumb mixture from burning.
7. Arrange the chicken on 4 dinner plates and garnish with the watercress.

Servings: 4   Preparation: Easy
Time: Fairly time consuming

Autumn Chicken Casserole

This simple autumn casserole makes a good family dinner. It is easy to prepare and children always seem to like it. Hubbard squash may be substituted for the butternut.

9 chicken legs, thighs attached
4 small leeks
2 pounds butternut squash
4 tablespoons all-purpose unbleached flour
2 to 4 tablespoons vegetable oil
2 teaspoons dried thyme (or 1 tablespoon fresh thyme leaves)
fresh Italian parsley sprigs for garnish

1. Peel coarse outer layers from leeks and discard. Thinly slice leeks up to medium-green part. Leave in cold water for 30 minutes; drain; run under cold water. Drain again and pat dry.
2. Peel squash and remove seeds. Cut squash into 2-inch cubes.
3. Preheat oven to 400 degrees.
4. Place the flour on a plate, and add a little salt and freshly ground black pepper. Cut the chicken through the leg and thigh so they are detached. Lightly dust the chicken with the flour.
5. In a large saute pan, heat oil and add 6 pieces of chicken. Brown them on all sides on medium heat, then place in an ovenproof dish. Repeat with the remaining chicken, adding more oil if necessary.
6. Add leeks to saute pan and toss over high heat for 2 minutes, being careful not to brown. Add them to the chicken, along with the squash, thyme, and a little salt and freshly ground black pepper. Cover the dish and bake at 400 degrees for 40 minutes until chicken is cooked through.
7. Arrange the chicken and vegetables on a serving dish. Garnish with the parsley.

Servings: 6   Preparation: Easy
Time: Fairly time consuming

Chicken Rouennaise

The next time you have some leftover chicken liver pâté, freeze it and use it later in this very rich dish. It is an inexpensive and impressive dinner party dish.

8 chicken thighs
2 ounces chicken liver pâté (page 97)
1 medium leek
1 small carrot
2 tablespoons unsalted butter
3 tablespoons cognac or brandy
¼ cup homemade chicken consomme or stock
¼ cup heavy cream
¼ cup loosely packed fresh parsley sprigs, finely chopped
fresh watercress sprigs for garnish

1. Bone the chicken thighs, being careful to leave the skin intact. Stand a thigh on one end, holding it steady with one hand. Insert a small sharp prep knife just below the knuckle, slipping the knife carefully underneath the skin. Cut upwards in short strokes, cutting away the sinews attached to the knuckle. Then cut downwards with short strokes, with the back of the knife against the bone, to remove the meat from the bone. At the bottom where the sinews are still attached to the bone, just cut them away from the bone.
2. Remove and discard the coarse outside layer from the leek. Cut the leek in half lengthwise, then into 1½-inch pieces, and then into thin julienne pieces. Wash well, drain, and pat dry. Peel the carrot and slice it thinly on the diagonal, and then into thin julienne pieces.
3. Up to this point, the recipe may be prepared 4 hours ahead of time. Refrigerate the chicken and vegetables.
4. Just before serving, divide the pâté into 8 portions and stuff it into the thighs. Close the openings with lightly oiled toothpicks. (Toothpicking is not always easy to do and may be eliminated.)

5. Heat the butter in a 12-inch heavy saute pan. Add the thighs, skin side down, and saute over medium heat until light golden brown. Reduce the heat to low and cover the pan. Gently braise the chicken for 10 to 15 minutes until cooked through. Remove the thighs from the pan with a slotted spatula and place on a serving platter. Keep the chicken warm.
6. Add the leeks and carrots to the pan and saute on medium heat until cooked; be careful not to brown. Add the cognac or brandy and ignite. Add the chicken stock and simmer for 3 minutes. Add the cream and chopped parsley and simmer for 3 minutes. Add salt and freshly ground black pepper to taste.
7. Pour the sauce over the chicken. Garnish with the watercress sprigs.

Servings: 4   Preparation: Fairly difficult
Time: Fairly time consuming; some advance preparation possible

Curried Chicken

In many parts of India, chicken is a luxury meat, so it is treated very specially with a fine curry sauce. My Curried Chicken may be prepared in advance and is delicious with Cucumber Raita (page 179) and steamed rice. If you decide to use homemade curry powder instead of the Madras curry powder, omit the cognac. If you are watching your calories, the cream may be omitted. The coriander is optional because it is not essential to the dish and sometimes is difficult to find.

1 3½ pound chicken, quartered
2 tablespoons all-purpose unbleached flour
3 tablespoons unsalted butter
1 large onion, very finely diced
1 tablespoon Madras curry powder
1 cup homemade chicken stock (or canned low-salt chicken broth)
½ cup heavy cream
2 tablespoons cognac
½ cup loosely packed coriander leaves (optional)

1. Mix the flour with a little salt on a plate. Lightly coat each piece of chicken with the flour.
2. Heat the butter in a 12-inch saute pan and add the chicken, skin side down. Saute on medium heat until golden brown. Remove from the pan and put to one side.
3. Measure the fat in the pan and remove all but 3 tablespoons. Add the onion and saute until clear, being careful not to brown.
4. Add the curry powder and cook for 1 minute, then add the chicken and chicken stock. Cover and gently simmer for 30 to 40 minutes until the chicken is cooked through.
5. Remove the chicken from the pan. Place on a platter and keep warm. Add the cream to the sauce and bring to a boil, stirring all the time. Continue to boil until the sauce reaches the desired consistency. Add the cognac and simmer for 3 minutes. Add salt to taste. Pour the sauce over the chicken.
6. This dish may be cooked 24 hours ahead of time and stored in the refrigerator. To reheat, remove from the refrigerator 1 hour before

serving. Gently simmer, covered, for 10 to 15 minutes. If the sauce is too thick add a little more chicken stock.
7. Just before serving, cover the entire dish with the coriander leaves.

Servings: 4   Preparation: Easy
Time: Fairly time consuming; advance preparation possible

Chicken Provençal

This is a favorite flavor combination of mine. Fresh rosemary or basil may be used instead of thyme. Vine-ripened tomatoes are nice to use, but not essential.

1 2½–3-pound chicken
½ cup red wine
1 cup strong homemade chicken stock
4 tablespoons unsalted butter
1 small onion, finely chopped
1 medium garlic clove, finely chopped
2 medium tomatoes, peeled, seeded and chopped
1 teaspoon finely grated orange rind (zest)
1 tablespoon fresh thyme leaves (or 1 teaspoon dried thyme
    leaves)
fresh thyme sprigs for garnish

1. With a sharp knife, cut the chicken into quarters; then separate the legs from the thighs and cut the breast sections in half.
2. Bring the red wine to a boil in a 1-quart stainless steel saucepan. Ignite and flame for 1 minute. Add the chicken stock and reduce to ¾ cup. Pour it out of the saucepan and set aside.
3. Heat 2 tablespoons butter in the saucepan. Add the onion and garlic and saute until clear, being careful not to brown. Add the tomatoes, stock and wine mixture, and orange rind. If you are using dry thyme, add it at this time. Bring to a boil and simmer for 20 minutes.

4. Heat 2 tablespoons butter in a 12-inch saute pan. Add the chicken, skin side down, and saute until golden brown. Turn and saute until light brown. Add the sauce, cover, and gently simmer for 30 to 40 minutes until the chicken is cooked through. Transfer the chicken with a slotted spoon to a platter and keep warm.
5. If you are using fresh thyme, add it to the sauce at this time. Reduce the liquid to a light syrupy consistency. Skim off fat. Add salt and freshly ground black pepper to taste. Pour the sauce over the chicken.
6. This casserole may be made a day ahead of time and refrigerated. Remove it from the refrigerator 1 hour before reheating. Remove fat from the top of the chicken. Gently reheat the chicken and sauce in a covered pan on low heat for 10 to 15 minutes.
7. Garnish the chicken with thyme sprigs just before serving.

Servings: 4   **Preparation: Easy**
Time: Fairly time consuming; advance preparation possible

Mexican Chicken

I have stressed the use of freshly cracked walnuts repeatedly throughout this book. If you do not use fresh walnuts in this recipe the sauce will have a bitter, unpleasant flavor. If fresh hot peppers are available, use 2 to 3 teaspoons, chopped, according to your taste. Mexican Chicken is excellent with steamed rice and my Tomato, Avocado, and Watercress Salad (see page 189).

> *8 chicken thighs*
> *2 tablespoons vegetable oil*
> *2 medium onions, finely chopped*
> *1 teaspoon dried crushed red hot pepper*
> *½ cup homemade chicken stock (or canned low-salt chicken broth)*
> *¾ cup freshly cracked walnuts, finely chopped*
> *½ cup loosely packed fresh coriander leaves, coarsely chopped*
> *fresh coriander sprigs for garnish*

1. Remove any excess skin and fat from the thighs.
2. Heat the oil in a 12-inch saute pan. Add the thighs, skin side down, and saute over medium-high heat until golden brown. Turn them over and lightly brown the other side. Remove with a slotted spoon and put to one side.
3. Add the onions and ½ teaspoon hot pepper and saute over medium heat until the onions are clear, being careful not to brown. Add the chicken stock, walnuts, and chicken thighs. Cover and very gently simmer for 20 to 30 minutes or until the chicken is cooked through.
4. Remove the chicken from the pan and place on a serving dish. On high heat, reduce the pan juices to 1 cup. Add salt and hot pepper to taste. Pour the sauce over the chicken.
5. This dish may be made a day ahead of time. One hour before serving remove it from the refrigerator and bring it up to room temperature. Gently reheat, covered, for 15 to 20 minutes on low heat.
6. Just before serving, stir the chopped fresh coriander into the sauce. Garnish with the coriander sprigs.

Servings: 4   Preparation: Easy
Time: Fairly time consuming; advance preparation possible

Chicken Aromatique

Don Fields inspired this simple but aromatic dish. The beurre blanc adds the most wonderful richness, but may be eliminated by people who are watching their caloric intake. Don now resides in Hawaii and I look forward to hearing about his new creations.

2 2-pound chickens or 2 1½-pound Cornish game hens
3 tablespoons unsalted butter
4 large shallots, peeled and thinly sliced
1 carrot, coarsely grated
½ cup loosely packed fresh parsley leaves, finely chopped
1 tablespoon fresh rosemary leaves
1 cup Beurre Blanc (page 34) (optional)
fresh parsley or rosemary sprigs for garnish

1. With very sharp kitchen scissors, cut the chickens in half through the breasts. Then cut them through each side of the back bone. Discard the back bone.
2. Heat 2 tablespoons of butter in a 10-inch saute pan. Add the shallots and saute until clear, being careful not to brown. Add the carrot and toss over high heat for 2 to 3 minutes. Cool and add the parsley and rosemary and salt and freshly ground black pepper to taste. Divide this stuffing mixture into four portions.
3. You may prepare this dish up to this point 6 hours ahead of serving time; refrigerate the chicken and the stuffing.
4. Pull the skin of the chicken up from the thigh part, being careful not to tear the skin. Gently push a portion of the stuffing under the skin toward the breast. Place the chicken pieces on a broiler pan, skin side up. Spread the remaining tablespoon of butter on the chicken.
5. Preheat broiler.

6. Broil the chicken until it is light golden brown; then turn the oven to 375 degrees and roast the chicken for 20 to 30 minutes until each piece is cooked through. To check for doneness, insert a small knife into the thickest part of the thigh. If it is not cooked, return it to the oven for an additional 10 minutes.
7. While the chicken is cooking, make the beurre blanc.
8. Place the chicken on dinner plates and garnish with rosemary or parsley sprigs. Serve the beurre blanc separately.

Servings: 4   Preparation: Fairly difficult; some advance preparation possible Time: Time consuming

Chicken Mongolian Style

Here is a low-calorie chicken entree with a medium spicy taste. I strongly advise you to use the fresh water chestnuts. They are very crunchy with a sweet and wonderful taste—very different from canned. If you cannot find them in a Chinese food market or specialty stores, you may use canned, but the dish won't be as appealing. You may use chicken thighs or a combination of thighs and breast.

> 2 1-pound chicken breasts
> 1 cup strong homemade chicken stock
> 5 scallions
> 2 tomatoes, peeled and seeded
> 10 fresh water chestnuts
> 3 tablespoons vegetable oil
> 1 tablespoon medium to dark-brown sesame oil
> 2 tablespoons low-salt soy sauce (or 1 tablespoon regular soy
>   sauce)
> 1 teaspoon Tabasco
> 1 tablespoon cornstarch
> 1/4 cup cold water
> fresh coriander leaves for garnish (optional)

1. Bone the chicken breasts (see page 290). Cut the chicken into 1-inch pieces.
2. Place the stock in a 1-quart pan and reduce over high heat by 50 percent.
3. Remove and discard the coarse outside layer from the scallions. Slice them on the diagonal into 1-inch slices. Thinly slice the tomatoes.
4. Peel the water chestnuts. Wash under cold water, pat dry, then cut into 1/4-inch slices.
5. Heat the vegetable oil in a 12-inch saute pan. Add the chicken and cook on medium-high heat. Do not move the chicken pieces until they release easily from the pan; then turn them over with a spatula and continue to saute until they are cooked through. Be very careful not to overcook them. Remove from the pan with a slotted spoon and place on a warm serving dish.

6. Add the sesame oil and scallions to the same pan. Toss scallions over high heat for 1 minute. Add the tomatoes and toss over high heat until all the liquid has evaporated. Add the stock, soy sauce, and Tabasco; bring to a boil.
7. Mix the cornstarch with the cold water. Remove the pan from the heat. Slowly stir in the cornstarch mixture, then return the pan to the heat. Bring to a boil, stirring constantly, then gently simmer for 3 minutes. Add the chicken, chicken juices that have accumulated on the platter, and water chestnuts and heat for 2 minutes.
8. Pour onto the serving platter and garnish with coriander leaves.

Servings: 4   Preparation: Easy
Time: Fairly time consuming

Ms. Mead's Broiled Chicken Wings

Broiled or grilled chicken wings make a marvelous hors d'oeuvre, picnic dish, or family supper. I like the marinade in this recipe because it is really refreshing, tart, and extremely flavorful.

12 chicken wings
2 large garlic cloves, finely chopped
2 teaspoons Hungarian paprika
½ teaspoon cayenne pepper
½ cup white wine basil or tarragon vinegar
½ cup fresh lemon juice
2 tablespoons peeled and coarsely grated fresh ginger
2 teaspoons salt
2 tablespoons vegetable oil
1 lemon, sliced fine, for garnish

1. Cut off the wing tip and discard.
2. Make the marinade by combining the garlic, paprika, cayenne pepper, vinegar, lemon juice, ginger, and salt.
3. Place 1 layer of the wings in a china or Pyrex bowl and cover with a little of the marinade. Cover with another layer of chicken wings and some marinade. Repeat until all the chicken and marinade are used. Leave the chicken to marinate 14 to 24 hours in the refrigerator; turn over the wings in the marinade once during this time.
4. Remove the chicken from the refrigerator at least 1 hour before cooking. Oil a broiler pan and preheat broiler.
5. Remove the chicken wings from the marinade. Brush them with 2 tablespoons of oil and place them on the broiler pan. Broil the wings at least 6 inches away from the broiler until they are golden brown. Turn them over and broil the other side until golden brown. (It is not necessary to baste the wings as they broil.)
6. Place the wings on a serving platter and serve hot or at room temperature. Arrange the lemon slices around the chicken.

Servings: 4   Preparation: Easy
Time: Quick; advance preparation necessary

Pheasant Juniper

The combination of juniper berries with game is a superb marriage of flavors; I'm sure you will love this wonderfully aromatic dish. If you cannot get pheasant, chicken works well.

2 1½ pound fresh pheasants
4 tablespoons unsalted butter
1 medium carrot, finely diced
1 medium onion, finely diced
2 celery stalks, finely diced
2 tablespoons gin
2 teaspoons juniper berries, finely chopped
1 teaspoon dried sage
1 to 2 tablespoons Garlic Paste, page 63 (or 1 large garlic clove, crushed)
¾ cup homemade chicken stock
⅓ cup heavy cream

1. Cut the pheasants in half through the breasts. Then cut them through each side of the back bone. Discard the back bone.
2. Heat 2 tablespoons butter in a 12-inch saute pan. Add the diced carrot, celery, and onion, and toss over high heat for 3 minutes. (If you are using a garlic clove, add it now.) Be careful not to brown the vegetables. Add the gin and 1 teaspoon juniper berries, and toss over high heat until the gin has evaporated. Remove the vegetables and juniper berries from the pan and place in an ovenproof serving dish.
3. Preheat oven to 400 degrees.
4. Heat the remaining butter in the saute pan. Add the pheasant, breast side down. Saute until light golden brown. Remove from the pan. Arrange them breast side up on the vegetables.
5. Roast the pheasant halves at 400 degrees for 20 to 30 minutes until they are cooked to the desired doneness. (To check for doneness, insert a knife into the thickest part of the thigh and breast. Look toward the bone.) When they are cooked, remove the dish from the oven and let it stand for 5 minutes before serving.

6. While the pheasant is cooking, place the chicken stock, 1 tablespoon garlic paste, and 1 teaspoon juniper berries in a 10-inch saute pan. On high heat reduce the stock by 50 percent, scraping down the sides continually so the stock does not scorch. Add the cream and reduce over high heat for 3 to 5 minutes, constantly scraping down the edges of the pan so the sauce does not scorch. Add more garlic paste to taste. Add salt and freshly ground black pepper to taste.

7. Serve the sauce separately.

Servings: 4   Preparation: Easy
Time: Fairly time consuming

Pheasant Hunter's Style

You will impress your company with this hearty dish. It is also great with chicken, squab, or Cornish game hens, served with a mushroom rice pilaf. When vine-ripened tomatoes are plentiful the sauce may be made ahead of time and frozen. Fresh thyme or rosemary may be substituted for the sage.

4 ¾–1-pound fresh pheasants
1½ tablespoons shredded fresh sage
6 tablespoons unsalted butter, room temperature
4 bacon slices
1 cup dry red wine
1 cup strong homemade chicken stock
1 onion, finely diced
1 small carrot, finely diced
1 small celery stalk, finely diced
1 medium garlic clove, finely chopped
2 tomatoes, peeled, seeded, and diced

1. Preheat oven to 400 degrees.
2. Mix ½ tablespoon of sage with 2 tablespoons of butter and freshly ground black pepper. Divide into 4 equal portions. Gently loosen the pheasant skin over the breast and insert one portion of the sage butter between the breast and skin of each pheasant.
3. Tie the legs together on each pheasant. Put the pheasants in a buttered roasting pan. Cut each slice of bacon in half across and place two pieces over each pheasant.
4. Put the pheasants in the preheated oven. Roast for 40 to 50 minutes or until they are cooked through. To check for doneness, remove the pheasants from the oven and insert a knife into the thickest part of the thigh. If the meat is not cooked through, return the pheasants to the oven for an additional 10 minutes.
5. While the pheasants are roasting, place the red wine in a 1-quart stainless steel saucepan, bring it to a boil, and ignite. Allow it to flame for 2 to 3 minutes. Add the chicken stock and reduce over high heat until it measures 1 cup.

6. Heat 4 tablespoons of butter in a 1- to 2-quart stainless steel saucepan. Add the onion, carrot, celery, and garlic and saute until clear, being careful not to brown. Add the tomatoes, and reduced wine and stock mixture, and reduce over medium heat for 10 to 15 minutes. Add the remaining fresh sage.
7. When the pheasants are cooked, set them on 4 dinner plates.
8. Pour a little of the pan juices into the sauce and reduce until fairly thick. Skim off any excess fat. Add salt and freshly ground black pepper to taste. Pour the sauce over the pheasants or serve the sauce separately.

Servings: 4   Preparation: Easy
Time: Fairly time consuming

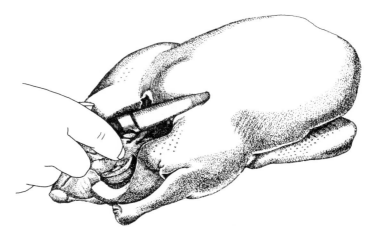

1. Pricking the skin of a duck helps release the fat as the duck cooks. Be sure to prick on the diagonal through the skin, being careful not to puncture the flesh. Use a small, sharp prep knife.

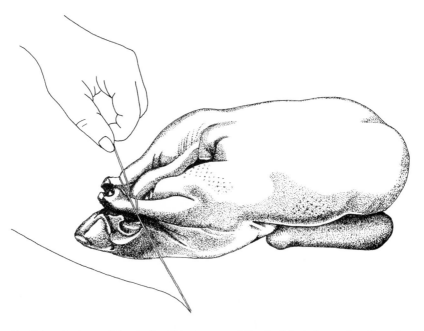

2. Tying the legs of the duck will help prevent the duck's drying out as it cooks. Use a natural fiber string, as synthetic fibers will melt during roasting.

Roast Duck Timkin

Ducks tend to be fatty, but the sauce in this recipe has a tartness that will offset the duck's richness. As you will note, I use prunes in the sauce. Unfortunately there is some stigma in this country against using them; nonetheless, I urge you to try them, as they add a beautiful fullness to the dish. If you are absolutely opposed, you may use 4 large dried apricots in their place. If possible, try to use a fresh duck.

> *1 5- to 6-pound duck*
> *1 small onion, thinly sliced*
> *1 cup homemade chicken stock (or canned low-salt*
> *   chicken broth)*
> *¾ cup dry red wine*
> *4 dried prunes*
> *5 medium shallots, thinly sliced*
> *1 tart apple, peeled*

1. Remove excess fat from around the cavity and cut off the back flap. Save the fat you remove from the duck. Check that the duck heart and giblets are removed from the cavity; put them to one side. On the diagonal, so as not to puncture the meat, prick the duck all over, using a small sharp prep knife. Pricking helps release the fat in the duck. Tightly tie the legs together, using a natural fiber string. Tying prevents the duck's drying out as it cooks.
2. Preheat oven to 450 degrees.
3. You will need a deep roasting pan so the fat will not make a mess of your oven, and a cake rack or roasting rack that fits inside the pan. Put the duck on the rack. Roast the duck at 450 degrees for 30 minutes, then reduce the heat to 350 degrees and roast the duck for 1 hour.
4. After you put the duck in the oven, take ¼ cup of the fat that was removed from the duck and place it in a heated 1-quart saucepan over medium heat. Saute for 5 to 10 minutes, being careful that it does not turn darker than a golden brown. Save 3 tablespoons of fat in the pan; discard the rest.
5. Add the onion to the 3 tablespoons fat and saute the onion until clear. Add the chicken stock, duck heart, and giblets. Bring to a boil, then

gently simmer for 5 minutes. Skim off and discard the grey foam with a metal spoon. Cover the pan and gently simmer the stock for 1 hour.

6. Bring the red wine to a boil in a 1-quart stainless steel saucepan, ignite, and allow to flame for 3 minutes; put to one side.

7. Strain the duck stock through a medium-fine sieve, add it to the red wine with the prunes, and simmer over high heat for 20 minutes. Puree the mixture in the blender.

8. Cut the apple into quarters, slice into ¼-inch pieces, then dice.

9. After the duck has cooked 1½ hours, check it for doneness by inserting an instant thermometer into the thickest part of the thigh, being careful that the thermometer is not touching the bone. The temperature should read 155 degrees for medium (my preference), 165 for medium to well-done, and 170 for well-done. If not cooked to desired doneness, return it to the oven for 10 to 15 minutes.

10. When the duck is cooked, set it on a platter and leave it to rest in a warm place for 10 to 15 minutes before serving. While the duck is resting, take 2 tablespoons duck fat from the roasting pan and place in a 12-inch saute pan. Add the shallots, and saute on medium heat until clear. Add the apples, toss over high heat for 3 minutes. Add the red wine puree and reduce over high heat until the sauce lightly coats a spoon. Add salt and freshly ground black pepper to taste.

11. Carve the duck, and serve the sauce separately.

Servings: 4   Preparation: Fairly easy
Time: Time consuming

Meat

Raw meat products should be stored in the refrigerator, lightly wrapped, leaving them slightly exposed to the air. This exposure will slow down the growth of bacteria. Although those areas exposed to the air will form a slight crust, this will not affect the cooked product. Should you store the cooked meat in the refrigerator, be aware that bacteria will grow faster if the meat is *not* tightly wrapped.

Before cooking, meats should be taken from the refrigerator and allowed to come to room temperature. Thirty minutes should be sufficient time for steak, chops, and casserole meats. Roasts and larger cuts will take approximately an hour. If they are left too long at room temperature (and especially if the kitchen is hot) the bacterial level will increase in the meats at a rapid rate. If meats are cooked when cold, they will tend to stew rather than saute, as the cold product will reduce the temperature of the pan. With a roast, the center will take longer (especially with a bone-in roast), producing an overcooked outside layer. By the time the center is cooked, the outside will be overcooked.

I feel it is important to not salt meats before sauteing, broiling, or grilling, as this will draw out the juices (dehydrate them), and therefore produce a very dry product. With roasts, a light sprinkling of salt on the fat areas releases the fat, adds to the flavor, and creates a crisp crust on the outside of the roast.

When broiling, sauteing, or roasting meats, leave a thin layer of fat covering the meat to help retain the moisture; however, this should not be in excess. If you purchase meats that have a large amount of fat, trim it to ⅛- to ¼-inch, using a sharp boning knife or a sharp prep knife.

Roasting Meats

Boneless roasts should be tied so they will hold their shape and to help prevent the center from becoming too dry. Always use natural fiber string for tying, as synthetic fibers will melt during roasting. Do not tie the meats too tightly, as during the cooking process the meat will expand and further increase the chance of losing juices. Lean roasts should be tied with a thin covering of fat to prevent them from losing too much moisture.

If you roast meats at a high temperature, 400 to 450 degrees, the roast will have a delicious crisp outside; however, at this temperature, the roast will shrink more and often will be quite dry. Roasting meats at 300 to 350 degrees will give you a moist roast, less shrinkage, and an unappetizing surface. Therefore, I recommend the following procedure: For small roasts, heat 1 tablespoon oil in a 12-inch saute pan, then saute the fat areas of the roast until light golden brown. (Do not brown the flesh parts, as this will tend to toughen the meat.) Then place the meat in the oven and roast at 300 to 350 degrees. For large roasts, preheat the broiler; place the meat in a roasting pan 6 inches from the heat source (if the roast does not fit in the broiler, brown it in a saute pan). Broil the fat areas of the meat until light golden brown. Turn the oven dial to 300 to 350 degrees, but leave the door open for 5 minutes to allow the temperature to drop; then close the door and roast the meat to required doneness.

Both the weight and shape of the roast will influence the amount of time it will take to cook. For example, a tenderloin of beef weighing 6 to 7 pounds, which is long in shape and has a diameter of 3 to 4 inches, will take approximately 30 to 40 minutes to cook. A shorter roast, 6 to 8 inches in diameter, will take 1 to 1½ hours to cook. Therefore, you should start checking the temperature of a long and narrow roast after 30 minutes of cooking; with a thicker roast, start checking after 1 hour.

To check for doneness, insert an instant thermometer into the thickest part of the meat, avoiding the fatty areas and any bones, as this could give you an incorrect reading. Leave the thermometer in for 30 to 60 seconds before reading the temperature. Try taking the temperature in three areas of the meat, from the thinnest to the thickest parts.

I recommend the following temperatures for doneness based on my assumption that you will let the meat rest 10 to 20 minutes in a warm part of the kitchen after taking the temperature. The outside temperature of the meat will slightly increase the internal temperature. This step (resting the meat) lets the juices settle, so you will retain more juices when you carve the meat and therefore have a moister product.

Beef
- rare: 127 to 135 degrees
- medium-rare: 135 to 140 degrees
- medium: 140 to 145 degrees
- well-done: 150 degrees

Lamb
- rare to medium-rare: 135 to 140 degrees
- medium: 140 to 145 degrees
- well-done: 155 to 160 degrees

Pork
- well-done: 155 to 160 degrees

Veal
- slightly pink in center: 137 to 147 degrees

To carve the roast, use a very sharp slicing or carving knife (read about knives in Appendix II), 8 to 10 inches long. Carve across the grain (typically the grain flows from the middle of the carcass to the limbs, head, and tail). If you are confused about this, ask your butcher how to carve the meat when you purchase it.

Sauteing Meats

For steaks and chops, follow these points to ensure a tender and moist product:
1. Make sure the meat is at room temperature before cooking.
2. Choose a heavy 12-inch saute pan for 4 steaks or chops, and a 10-inch saute pan for 2 to 3 steaks or chops. Be careful not to overcrowd or you will lower the heat of the pan, and the meats will not brown.
3. Use a small amount of oil or clarified butter as the burning point is higher than whole butter. (See Appendix I.)
4. To sear the meat, heat the pan and oil medium to hot, but not smoking. If the fat is smoking, the meat will toughen and be too brown before the center is cooked to required doneness.
5. When placing the meat in the pan, avoid moving it until it is light brown. As the meat cooks, it will come away from the pan. Moving it too early will tear the meat. Use a metal spatula or spoon to move the meat, not a fork or knife, which would puncture the meat and let the juices escape.
6. Choose meats ½ to 1 ½ inches thick; any thicker and the meat will be overcooked on the outside before the center is cooked to required doneness.

Broiling and Grilling Meats

The placement of meats from the direct heat depends on their thickness. Place thin pieces close to the heat source to cook them quickly until light golden brown on each side. Place 1½- to 2-inch steaks 6 inches from the heat source to ensure the outside of the meat is not overcooked before the center is cooked to required doneness.

For other thick pieces of meat, broil or grill 6 inches from the heat source until seared (light brown) on both sides, then bake in the oven to ensure the meat is cooked to required doneness without burning.

Stews and Casseroles

Much has been written as to whether one should sear (brown) stew meat or not, before adding the liquid. Having tried both methods numerous times, I find that if you brown the meat before adding the liquid, you get a slightly more moist product. It is advisable to very lightly dust the meat with seasoned, unbleached all-purpose flour first, being careful that there are no clumps of flour on the meat. The meat should be floured just before putting it in the pan. Do not move the meat until it has turned a light golden brown, to prevent tearing it. Use a spoon or spatula to keep from puncturing the meat. After the meat has been seared on both sides, add the liquid and cook the casserole or stew at a very low simmering point. If it is boiled, the meat will toughen. It is easier to do this cooking in the oven at 250 degrees rather than on top of the stove, which is harder to regulate.

Lamb

In America, a Sunday afternoon dinner used to mean a pot roast with an accompaniment of vegetables. In England the scene was the same, but the roast was not beef, it was lamb. Unlike Americans, the British have long cherished lamb; to quote Jane Garmey in *Great Britain Cooking: A Well Kept Secret*: "What could be more British than lamb . . ."

Although many times the English ate lamb because it was cheaper, there developed an appreciation for this meat. Given the fairly strong flavor of lamb (its odor is derived from the fat), I have found it blends well with strong sauces. As Jane Garmey reminds us, "Perhaps we can thank those unlucky cooks who were trying to pass off their 'mutton dressed as lamb' for the invention of that great English institution—Mint Sauce—without which no self respecting Briton would not presume to eat even lamb . . ."

The age of lamb varies according to the authority you read. Larousse says it is lamb until the age of one, after that is called a yearling and then mutton. Constance Spry calls lamb immature meat, and *Mastering the Art of French Cooking* says it is lamb only from 5 to 9 months of age. I agree with Harold McGee, who says in *On Food and Cooking—The Science and Lore of the Kitchen* lamb is less than 14 months.

Here are some tips on purchasing lamb. Fresh versus frozen? Fresh lamb is lovely, and I definitely prefer fresh lamb chops, but I have eaten frozen legs of lamb and they have been fine. How can you find a leg of lamb of the size I suggest? If the legs are running about 12 pounds, buy half a leg. Just be certain to buy the upper half (butt end), not the lower half (shank end). What is the difference between the different cuts of lamb chops? There are loin chops, rib chops, and shoulder chops. Loin chops have more meat than rib chops and are slightly more tender. They are also more expensive. Shoulder chops are the least expensive of the three types and a little tougher. In my lamb chop recipes you will notice we have specified loin or rib chops. You can use any of the three types of chops in these recipes, depending on what is available and what you like. When my recipe calls for 4 chops for 4 people, look at the size of the chops and determine if they will be enough for your needs and whether you want to buy 2 chops per person. (Refer to the drawings on page 337 for trimming fat from rib and loin lamb chops.)

If you like your beef cooked rare to medium, then I suggest you try lamb cooked to the same temperature. I do not feel cooking lamb medium-well- or well-done does justice to this meat, as it tends to dry out faster and becomes less appetizing. Nonetheless, lamb has long been overlooked in this country. I hope the recipes in this book will help you discover what a treat lamb can be.

Lamb Rosemary

I suggest that you roast a leg of lamb with the bone in, as this method gives a much better flavor and a moister product. The sauce for this entree is simple to make, but relies on vine-ripened tomatoes for its taste. Serve this lovely lamb dish with my Rice and Potato Pilaf (see page 436).

> 1 6- to 8-pound leg of lamb
> 3 tablespoons fresh rosemary leaves
> 3 to 4 medium garlic cloves, finely sliced
> 3 tablespoons olive oil
> ½ cup dry red wine
> 1 cup homemade chicken stock (or canned low-salt chicken broth)
> 3 vine-ripened tomatoes, peeled, seeded, and chopped (juice reserved)

1. Trim any excess fat off the lamb, leaving just a thin layer of fat. With a small sharp knife, make 20 1-inch-deep incisions all over the lamb.
2. Stud each incision with a leaf of rosemary and a thin slice of garlic. There should be some garlic and rosemary left over; put them aside to use for the sauce. Brush the lamb with one tablespoon olive oil. Put the lamb in a roasting pan.
3. Preheat broiler. Place the lamb 4 to 6 inches from the heat source.
4. Broil the lamb until the top is golden brown. Turn off the broiler and roast the leg at 325 degrees for 1½ to 2 hours until it reaches the desired doneness. To test for doneness, remove the roast from the oven and insert an instant meat thermometer into the thickest part of the meat; try to avoid the fatty parts and touching the bone. Leave the thermometer in 30 to 60 seconds to get a reading. For rare to medium-

rare meat the temperature should be 135 to 140 degrees; for medium the temperature should be 140 to 145 degrees; and for well-done meat the temperature should be 155 to 160 degrees.

5. While the lamb is roasting, bring the red wine to a boil in a 1-quart stainless steel pan. Ignite and allow to flame for 3 minutes, then add the chicken stock and reduce over high heat by 50 percent.

6. Finely chop the remaining garlic. Heat the remaining olive oil in a 2-quart stainless steel saucepan, add the chopped garlic, and gently saute it for 2 minutes on low heat, being careful not to burn. Add the tomatoes, tomato juice, 2 coarsely chopped teaspoons of the remaining rosemary leaves, and the red wine-stock mixture. Simmer for 15 minutes. Add salt and freshly ground black pepper to taste.

7. Before serving, let the leg rest in a warm part of the kitchen for at least 10 minutes, so that it will retain more of its juices. Slice the lamb and serve the sauce separately.

Servings: 8 to 10 **Preparation: Fairly easy**
Time: Time consuming

Barbecued Leg of Lamb

I love the slightly smoky flavor this dish takes on with barbecuing. My preference is that the lamb be served rare or medium-rare. It is important that the coals not be too hot or cool, and that the lamb be served hot to warm, not cold. This lamb is wonderful served with Tomato Ginger Coulis (page 17), Tabouli (192), Chick Peas with Spinach (432), Tomato Avocado Relish (190), or Green Bean Salad (172).

1 5- to 7-pound boned leg of lamb
½ cup olive or vegetable oil
1 cup loosely packed fresh mint, coarsely chopped
3 medium garlic cloves, finely chopped or crushed
2 teaspoons freshly ground black pepper

1. Trim any excess fat from lamb, leaving just a thin layer on the outside.
2. Lay the lamb in front of you, skin side down, so you're looking at the pocket where the bone was. Make an incision through the pocket and down the leg. Open it out and remove the heavy connective tissue with a sharp boning or prep knife. The meat will now be almost flat.
3. Mix together oil, mint, garlic, and pepper, and pour the mixture into center of the lamb leg where the bone was. Leave the lamb to marinate in the refrigerator at least 12 hours.
4. Remove the lamb from the refrigerator 1 hour before cooking.
5. Thirty to 40 minutes before cooking, light the coals in the barbecue. When they provide a low, even heat, place lamb on the grill, fat side down. Cover with a lid; barbecue for 10 to 15 minutes. While barbecuing, baste the meat with the marinade, trying to spoon it inside the leg. (Keep a pan of water nearby in case fat from the lamb catches fire. Wearing oven mitts and holding your head back, lightly sprinkle the coals with water, which should dampen the fire. Please be careful.)
6. Turn the meat over and continue to cook another 10 to 20 minutes, basting, until the meat reaches the desired doneness. To check for doneness, insert a small sharp knife or instant thermometer into the thickest part of the meat, move it to one side, and look inside to see how cooked this part of the meat is.
7. When the lamb has cooked to your satisfaction, remove it from the grill and let it rest 10 to 15 minutes before carving it into thin slices.

Servings: 8 to 10   Preparation: Easy
Time: Time consuming; some advance preparation necessary

Roast Leg of Lamb Persil

This is a simple roast leg of lamb with a mild garlic sauce, finished with masses of parsley.

1 6- to 8-pound leg of lamb
1 tablespoon vegetable oil
3 to 4 tablespoons Garlic Paste (page 63)
1 cup strong homemade chicken stock (or canned low-salt
*   chicken broth)*
1 cup tightly packed parsley sprigs, very finely chopped

1. Trim any excess fat off the leg, leaving just a ⅛-inch-thick layer of fat.
2. Preheat broiler.
3. Lightly brush the lamb with the oil. Place the lamb in a roasting pan and cover it with freshly ground black pepper. Broil the lamb about 8 inches away from the broiler until it is light golden brown.
4. Turn off the broiler and roast the lamb at 325 degrees for 1½ to 2 hours until it reaches the desired doneness. To test for doneness, remove the roast from the oven and insert an instant meat thermometer into the thickest part of the meat; try to avoid the fatty parts and touching the bone. Leave the thermometer in 30 to 60 seconds to get a reading. For rare to medium-rare meat the temperature should be 135 to 140 degrees; for medium the temperature should be 140 to 145 degrees; and for well-done meat the temperature should be 155 to 160 degrees.
5. When the lamb has cooked to your satisfaction, remove it from the oven. Let it rest in a warm place at least 10 minutes or up to 30 minutes so that it will retain more of its juices.
6. Pour any pan juices into a 1-quart saucepan, add the chicken stock, and bring to a boil. Skim off any fat with a shallow metal spoon and discard.
7. Turn down the heat to a gentle simmer and slowly whisk in 3 tablespoons garlic paste; taste, and add more garlic paste if desired. Add the parsley and salt and freshly ground black pepper to taste.
8. Carve the lamb and serve the sauce separately.

Servings: 8 to 10   **Preparation: Easy**
Time: Time consuming

Stuffed Leg of Lamb Florentine

This has been a favorite recipe in my cooking classes for many years. The wonderfully rich stuffing has a great flavor, yet it is light. It can be made the day before, but it should not be put into the lamb until just before cooking. I like to serve this dish with my White Bean Tomato Stew (see page 418).

> 1 5- to 6-pound boned leg of lamb
> 1 10-ounce package raw spinach, washed and sprigged
> 2 tablespoons unsalted butter
> 5 medium shallots or scallions, finely sliced
> ½ cup loosely packed fresh mint leaves, coarsely chopped
> ½ cup pine nuts (or blanched almonds)
> 2 large garlic cloves
> 1 tablespoon oil
> 1 cup homemade chicken stock (or canned low-salt chicken broth)
> ½ cup loosely packed fresh dill sprigs, coarsely chopped
> 1 to 2 tablespoons fresh lemon juice
> 2 teaspoons cornstarch (optional)
> ¼ cup water (optional)

1. Have ready a bowl of ice water. Bring 3 cups water to a boil in a 3-quart saucepan, add the spinach, and boil for 1 minute. Drain, then place spinach immediately in ice water. When the spinach is cold, drain, and squeeze out the water until it is dry. Chop the spinach fine.
2. Heat butter in a 10-inch saute pan. Add shallots or scallions and toss over medium heat until clear; do not brown. Add them to the spinach along with the mint and pine nuts. Add salt and freshly ground black pepper to taste and mix until well blended.
3. The stuffing can be refrigerated for 24 hours.
4. Trim the excess fat from lamb, leaving a covering of ⅛-inch-thick fat. Place stuffing inside leg just prior to cooking. Make 20 ½-inch-deep incisions all over the lamb. Slice garlic into very thin slivers and insert a piece into each incision. Brush the lamb with oil and put it into a roasting pan.
5. Preheat broiler. Broil the lamb 8 inches away from the broiler until it is light golden brown.

6. Turn off the broiler and cook the lamb in a 350-degree oven for 1½ to 2 hours. To test for doneness, remove the lamb from the oven and insert an instant meat thermometer into the thickest part of the meat; try to avoid the fatty parts and touching the bone. Leave the thermometer in for 30 to 60 seconds to get a reading. For rare to medium-rare meat, the temperature should read 135 to 140 degrees; for medium it should read 140 to 145 degrees; and for well-done meat it should read 155 to 160 degrees.
7. While the lamb is roasting, heat the chicken stock in a 1-quart saucepan and reduce to ¾ cup.
8. When the lamb is done, remove it from oven and pour the pan juices into a small bowl. Skim off and discard the fat; add the juices to the chicken stock, and boil for 5 minutes. Add dill, and lemon juice, salt, and freshly ground black pepper to taste. If the sauce seems thin, mix the cornstarch with the water, pour a little hot sauce into it, then return it to the pan, whisking all the time. Return it to a boil and boil one minute.
9. Thinly slice the lamb and serve the sauce separately.

Servings: 8   Preparation: Fairly easy
Time: Time consuming; some advance preparation possible

Lamb Chops Diane

The sauce in this dish is delightfully simple and clean. Choose a fairly firm type of pear for cooking. One tablespoon chopped mint and one to two tablespoons fresh lime juice can be substituted for the green peppercorns, if you wish.

> 4 loin lamb chops
> 2 pears, medium-ripe to firm
> 3 tablespoons unsalted butter
> 1 cup homemade chicken stock or consomme
> 1 tablespoon drained green peppercorns

1. Trim the fat off the lamb chops, leaving just a thin layer of fat. (See drawings on page 337.)
2. Cut the pears in quarters, remove the cores, and cut the quarters into ¼-inch slices lengthwise.
3. Preheat broiler. Lightly oil a broiler pan and place the chops on the pan.
4. Place the broiler pan 6 inches away from the broiler and broil the chops until they are golden brown on both sides and cooked to desired doneness. To check for doneness, insert a knife into the thickest part of the lamb.
5. While the chops are cooking, heat the butter in a heavy 12-inch saute pan, add the pears, and saute until they are light golden brown. With a slotted spoon, remove the pears and keep them warm. Add the consomme and peppercorns to the pan and reduce on a high heat to ½ cup. Add salt to taste.
6. Arrange the pears with the lamb chops on 4 dinner plates. Pour the sauce over them.

Servings: 4   **Preparation: Easy**
Time: Quick

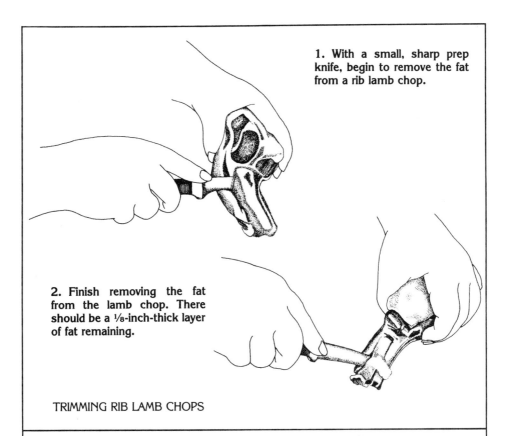

1. With a small, sharp prep knife, begin to remove the fat from a rib lamb chop.

2. Finish removing the fat from the lamb chop. There should be a ⅛-inch-thick layer of fat remaining.

TRIMMING RIB LAMB CHOPS

TRIMMING LOIN LAMB CHOPS

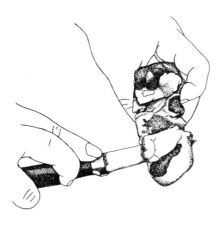

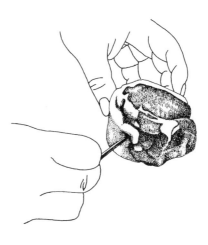

Above: With a small, sharp prep knife, remove all but a ⅛-inch-thick layer of fat from a loin lamb chop. **Right:** A flap of meat will remain. Toothpick the flap to the rest of the chop.

Lamb Chops with Red Wine Reduction Sauce

Mimi Santini Ritt thought that this was the kind of dish she could get only in a restaurant, so she was thrilled to discover that this rich sauce was easy to make at home. You may use any dry red wine, but if you can obtain a California Zinfandel, use it; it marries well with the lamb and its flavor is just fruity enough to complement the meat. If you have saved and frozen parsley stalks you can use them in the sauce. If you prefer to use loin chops, use 4 and broil them instead of sauteing. Serve this lamb with boiled potatoes and steamed asparagus.

8 rib lamb chops
2 tablespoons unsalted butter
1 small carrot, cut in ¼-inch dice
1 onion, finely chopped
1 celery stalk, cut in ¼-inch dice
⅓ cup diced fresh parsley stalks (optional)
2 cups strong homemade veal or chicken stock
1 cup dry red wine
3 tablespoons clarified butter (page 62)
1 tablespoon fresh thyme leaves (or 2 tablespoons coarsely
    chopped fresh rosemary leaves)

1. Heat butter in a heavy 2-quart saucepan. Add vegetables and parsley and saute over medium heat until the onions are clear but not browned. Add stock.
2. Meanwhile, bring the wine to a boil in a stainless steel 1-quart saucepan. Ignite, then flame for 3 minutes. Add the wine to the chicken stock and vegetables and reduce to 1½ cups.
3. Strain out the vegetables and discard (or freeze to add later to a homemade stock).
4. The sauce may be refrigerated for 2 days.
5. Cut any excess fat off the chops, leaving a thin layer of fat around the outside.
6. Heat the clarified butter in a heavy 12-inch stainless steel saute pan. Add lamb chops and cook until they are golden brown on one side.

Turn them over and cook until this side is golden brown and they have cooked to the required doneness.

7. Remove the chops from the pan, place them on a serving platter, and allow them to rest in a warm place.

8. Remove all but 3 tablespoons of fat from the pan. Pour the red wine reduction into the pan and reduce until it has a light syrupy consistency. Add the thyme and salt and freshly ground black pepper to taste.

9. Arrange the lamb chops on 4 warm dinner plates. Pour the sauce over them.

Servings: 4   Preparation: Easy
Time: Fairly time consuming; some advance preparation possible

Lamb Piquante

Even if you are not an anchovy lover you will still love this sauce. You really don't taste the anchovies, as they blend so well with the other ingredients. The resulting dish, as its name suggests, is wonderfully piquant.

4 loin lamb chops
2 to 3 tablespoons Garlic Paste (page 63)
3 anchovy fillets
1½ cups homemade chicken stock (or 1 cup canned low-salt chicken broth)
1 tablespoon vegetable oil
2 tablespoons fresh marjoram leaves, coarsely chopped, or 2 tablespoons shredded fresh basil
juice of 1 lemon

1. Trim the excess fat from the lamb chops, leaving just ⅛-inch fat.
2. Mash 2 tablespoons of the garlic paste with the anchovies until they form a fine paste.
3. Place the chicken stock in a 1-quart saucepan and reduce it to ¾ cup.
4. Preheat broiler and adjust the oven rack 6 inches from the heat.
5. Place the lamb chops on an oiled broiler pan. Brush them with the tablespoon of oil and broil on both sides to desired doneness.
6. Meanwhile, place the garlic and anchovy paste in a 10- to 12-inch heavy stainless steel saute pan. Cook on a very low heat for 2 minutes, being careful not to brown. Add the chicken stock and 1 tablespoon of lemon juice and reduce to ¾ cup on high heat, whisking occasionally. Add 1 tablespoon marjoram and simmer for 3 minutes. Add freshly ground black pepper to taste. (Add more lemon juice, marjoram, and garlic paste if you wish.)
7. Arrange the lamb chops on 4 warm dinner plates and pour the sauce over them.

Servings: 4   Preparation: Fairly easy
Time: Fairly time consuming

Veal

Veal, "young of cow.... It must be white with a slight greenish tinge. The best meat comes from animals age two and one half to three months, fed on milk and eggs," says *Larousse Gastronomique.* "After twelve weeks, veal becomes calf and is of no further culinary interest until it develops into beef," says Julia Child. Harold McGee in *On Food and Cooking* states, "The French praised veal as the chameleon of their cuisine." Veal has long been the prima donna of beef and by far the luxury meat.

At the beginning of my career, I was taught to pound veal cutlets (taken from the top of the sirloin, back of the rump, or face of the sirloin) into thin pieces that were then used for scaloppine. This process broke down the connective tissue and made the meat more tender. Although this process is recommended, I do caution that the veal should be pounded just before cooking or the meat will lose some of its juices, and the finished product will be dry. My preference is to use the more tender cuts (the loin), boned and then sliced ⅛ to ¼ of an inch thick and then gently flattened just before cooking. This requires no pounding, and the finished product is tender and moist. For even better results, do not overcook, as the veal should be slightly rare to medium rare in the center. With a veal roast (taken from the top of the sirloin, back of the rump, or face of the sirloin), often tied and precut by your butcher, you will find it works well with the addition of a little stock in the roasting pan. With a veal loin roast, whether bone in or not, the addition of stock is not necessary.

Veal à L'Orange

Veal à L'Orange is a great summer dish because the tomatoes and the orange zest give it a very nice light flavor. At this time of year you will have no difficulty in finding the vine-ripened tomatoes that are so necessary to the success of this dish.

1 3- to 5-pound veal roast, boned and tied
5 tablespoons unsalted butter
1 small onion, finely sliced
1 small carrot, finely sliced
1 cup homemade chicken stock
5 large or 10 small shallots, thinly sliced
3 medium vine-ripened tomatoes, peeled, seeded, and chopped
1 large orange
½ cup crème fraîche (or sour cream)
3 tablespoons finely snipped fresh chives

1. Preheat oven to 350 degrees.
2. Heat 3 tablespoons butter in a heavy 12-inch saute pan, add the veal, and saute until golden brown all over. Place the veal in a roasting pan.
3. Add the onion to the saute pan and saute until clear; do not brown. Add the carrot and saute for 3 minutes. Add the stock, bring to a boil, and simmer for 3 minutes. Put the stock and vegetables in the roasting pan.
4. Roast the veal in the preheated oven for 1 to 1½ hours. Halfway through cooking, turn over the veal and cover it with aluminum foil. With an instant thermometer check the roast for doneness; the internal temperature is 137–147 degrees for medium-rare and 155 degrees for well done.
5. Finely grate ½ teaspoon of orange zest and set aside. Remove the remaining rind and pith from the orange; cut the orange crosswise into 6 slices. Set aside.
6. Thirty minutes before the veal is done, heat the remaining 2 tablespoons of butter in a heavy stainless steel 12-inch saute pan. Add the shallots, and saute until clear, being careful not to brown. Add the tomatoes and orange zest, and cook until the tomatoes are thick.

7. Remove the veal from the oven when it is done, and keep warm. Pour the pan juices through a sieve into a large measuring cup. If you do not have ¾ cup juices, add chicken stock. (If you have more than ¾ cup, you can freeze the juices for a future use.) Skim off and discard the fat. Add the pan juices to the tomatoes and cook on high heat until the sauce is fairly thick.
8. Stir in the crème fraîche or sour cream and chives, and add salt and freshly ground black pepper to taste.
9. Slice the veal and serve onto 6 dinner plates. Spoon the sauce onto the servings and garnish with the orange slices.

Servings: 6   Preparation: Fairly easy
Time: Time consuming

Veal Florentine

The wonderful combination of spinach, peppercorns, and fennel produces a flavor that is rich but simple, and adds strength to veal without becoming overpowering.

> 1 3- to 5-pound veal roast, boned and tied
> 5 tablespoons unsalted butter
> 1 small onion, sliced
> 1 small carrot, sliced
> 1½ cups homemade chicken stock (or low-salt canned chicken
>   broth)
> 1 10-ounce package fresh spinach, washed and stems removed
> 1 medium bulb fennel
> 1 tablespoon cornstarch
> ½ cup water
> 1½ to 2 tablespoons green peppercorns, drained
> ¼ cup heavy cream

1. Preheat oven to 350 degrees.
2. Heat 3 tablespoons butter in a heavy 12-inch saute pan, add the veal, and saute until light golden brown all over. Place the veal in a roasting pan.
3. Add the onion to the saute pan and saute until clear; do not brown. Add the carrot and saute for 3 minutes. Add 1 cup stock, bring to a boil, and simmer for 3 minutes. Put the stock and vegetables into the roasting pan.
4. Roast the veal in the preheated oven for 1 to 1½ hours. Halfway through cooking, turn over the veal and cover it with aluminum foil. After about 1 hour of cooking, check the roast for doneness with an instant thermometer. The internal temperature will be 137–147 degrees for medium-rare and 155 degrees for well-done.
5. While the veal is cooking, coarsely shred the spinach. Remove and discard the outer layer of the fennel. Cut the fennel bulb in half through the core. Cut out the core and finely slice the bulb up to the light-green part of the stalk.
6. When the veal has cooked to your satisfaction, remove it from the oven, transfer to a serving platter, and keep warm. Pour the pan juices through

a sieve into a measuring cup, skim off the fat, and add enough stock to measure 1¼ cups. Place in a 1-quart saucepan.

7. Mix the cornstarch with ¼ cup cold water. Slowly pour the cornstarch mixture into the saucepan. Place the pan on the heat and bring to a boil, stirring all the time. Add the 1½ tablespoons of green peppercorns and cream and gently simmer. Add salt and more green peppercorns to taste.

8. Meanwhile, heat the remaining 2 tablespoons butter in a 12-inch saute pan, add the fennel and ¼ cup water, and gently saute until lightly cooked, about 3 minutes. Turn up the heat, add the spinach, and cook, tossing all the time, until the spinach is cooked and all the water has evaporated. Add salt and freshly ground black pepper to taste.

9. Thinly slice the veal and serve it onto 6 dinner plates. Spoon a little of the peppercorn sauce on top and serve the rest of the sauce separately. Garnish the veal with the spinach-fennel mixture.

Servings: 6   Preparation: Fairly easy
Time: Time consuming

Stuffed Veal Noisette

Stuffed veal makes the perfect dinner-party dish, as the stuffing can be prepared well in advance and the roast can be cooking even after your guests have arrived. The stuffing will be less than perfect, though, if you do not use freshly cracked walnuts or pecans!

> *1 4- to 5-pound boneless veal roast*
> *5 tablespoons unsalted butter*
> *5 large or 10 small shallots, thinly sliced*
> *¾ cup freshly cracked walnuts or pecans*
> *½ cup dry currants*
> *⅓ cup loosely packed fresh parsley leaves, finely chopped*
> *2 tablespoons balsamic vinegar*
> *¾ cup homemade chicken stock (or low-salt canned chicken broth)*
> *2 teaspoons cornstarch*
> *¼ cup cold water*

1. Heat 4 tablespoons butter in a 10-inch saute pan, add the shallots, and saute until clear, being careful not to brown. Place in a bowl. Finely chop the nuts by hand or in a food processor. Add to the shallots along with the currants and parsley and add salt and freshly ground black pepper to taste.
2. This stuffing can be refrigerated for 24 hours.
3. Preheat oven to 375 degrees.
4. Place the stuffing in the cavity of the veal and tie up the roast. Spread the remaining tablespoon of butter on the veal and sprinkle freshly ground black pepper over the outside.
5. Put the veal in a 9 x 12-inch roasting pan, place it in the preheated oven and roast for 1 to 1½ hours. To test for doneness, insert an instant thermometer into the thickest part. Wait for 30 to 60 seconds to get a reading. The temperature should read 137–147 degrees if the veal is to be served lightly pink inside, which I think is the optimal presentation for this dish.

6. Remove the pan from the oven and pour the pan juices into a 1-quart stainless steel saucepan. Place the veal in a warm place in the kitchen.
7. Add the vinegar and stock to the veal juices and bring to a boil. Skim off any excess fat.
8. Whisk the cornstarch with the cold water, remove the saucepan from the heat, and slowly whisk in the cornstarch mixture. Return to the heat and bring to a boil, stirring all the time. Add salt and freshly ground black pepper to taste.
9. To serve, slice the veal and arrange slices on dinner plates. Serve the sauce separately. (There will not be very much sauce.)

Servings: 6   Preparation: Easy
Time: Time consuming; some advance preparation possible

Veal Chops Rosemary

This is a delicate combination of flavors that blend superbly.

4 8-ounce kidney loin veal chops, trimmed
¼ cup olive oil
1 medium onion, thinly sliced
1 tablespoon fresh rosemary leaves (or 1 teaspoon dried
*   rosemary)*
2 vine-ripened tomatoes, peeled, seeded, and sliced
¾ cup grated Gruyère or Emmenthal cheese

1. Heat 3 tablespoons oil in a 10-inch stainless steel saute pan, add the onion, and saute over medium heat until clear. If you are using dried rosemary, add it at this time.
2. Add the tomatoes and toss over high heat until all the liquid has evaporated and the mixture is thick. Be careful the sauce does not scorch. Add the fresh rosemary and salt and freshly ground black pepper to taste. Keep warm. (Or, if you wish, refrigerate the sauce for 24 hours; reheat before serving.)
3. Just before serving, preheat broiler.
4. Brush the veal chops with the remaining oil and sprinkle with freshly ground black pepper. Place them on a broiler pan and broil about 6 inches from the broiler until light golden brown. Turn the chops over and continue to broil until this side is light golden brown. The chops should be light pink in the center. To check for doneness, remove one chop and insert a small prep knife into the thickest part of the chop.
5. Cover each chop with the grated cheese, return to broiler, and melt the cheese.
6. Divide the warm tomato mixture between four plates. Place the chops on top of the mixture and serve immediately.

Servings: 4   Preparation: Easy
Time: Fairly time consuming; some advance preparation possible

Veal Basilic

How wonderful to find an easy saute dish that has such a light, aromatic flavor. The use of strong homemade chicken stock or consomme is highly recommended for the sauce. If you cannot find veal scallopini, purchase ¼-inch-thick slices of veal that have not been pounded. The best cut to use is a whole boneless veal loin that you slice yourself, but this is more expensive.

1½ pounds veal scallopini
¾ cup strong homemade chicken stock or consomme
¼ cup dry white wine
6 tablespoons unsalted butter
¼ cup loosely packed fresh basil leaves, finely shredded
4 large, fresh basil leaves for garnish

1. Place the chicken stock and wine in a 1-quart stainless steel saucepan and reduce over high heat to ½ cup.
2. If the veal is more than ¼-inch thick, gently pound.
3. Heat 4 tablespoons butter in a 12-inch saute pan. Add half the veal, and saute on medium to high heat until light golden brown on one side. Turn over and continue to saute until cooked through. This will take about 3 minutes. Be careful not to overcook or the veal will be dry. Remove from the pan and keep warm. Repeat the procedure with the remaining veal.
4. Pour the wine and stock mixture into the pan and reduce on high heat until it has a light syrupy consistency. Whisk in the remaining butter (1 tablespoon at a time) and shredded basil and cook for 1 minute. Add any juices that have accumulated from the cooked veal and continue to reduce a minute more. Add salt and freshly ground black pepper to taste.
5. Arrange the veal on warm dinner plates, spoon the sauce on top, and garnish with the basil leaves.

Servings: 4   **Preparation: Easy**
Time: Quick

Veal Clancy

The beauty of this dish lies in its simple, clean sauce. If fresh thyme is not available, fresh parsley should be substituted, as dry thyme tends to give this dish a slightly astringent flavor. If you cannot find veal scallopini, purchase ¼-inch-thick slices of veal that have not been pounded, or cut slices from a whole boneless veal loin. This veal dish is great served with Pureed Carrots and Tomatoes (page 426) and Sauteed Green Vegetables (page 439).

1½ pounds veal scallopini
½ cup Vermouth Madeira Sauce (page 30)
¼ pound Shiitake mushrooms (or Roman or cultivated)
6 tablespoons unsalted butter
1 teaspoon fresh thyme leaves (optional)
4 thyme sprigs for garnish (optional)

1. Reduce sauce to ⅓ cup over high heat.
2. If the veal is more than ¼-inch thick, gently pound.
3. Clean the mushrooms and trim off the coarse stalks. Slice caps ⅛-inch thick.
4. Heat 4 tablespoons butter in a heavy 12-inch saute pan. Add half the veal and saute on a medium to high heat until light golden brown on one side. Turn over and continue to saute until cooked through. This will take about 3 minutes. Be careful not to overcook or the veal will be dry. Remove from the pan and keep warm. Repeat the procedure with the remaining veal.
5. Melt the remaining 2 tablespoons butter in the pan. Add the mushrooms and saute over medium heat until soft, being careful to cook through without letting them brown.
6. Add the reduced sauce and thyme to the pan. Reduce over a high heat until it has a light syrupy consistency. Add any juices that have accumulated from the cooked veal and continue to reduce a minute more. Add salt and freshly ground black pepper to taste.
7. Arrange the veal on 4 warm dinner plates and spoon the sauce on top. Garnish with the thyme sprigs.

Servings: 4   **Preparation: Easy**
Time: Quick

Beef

After growing up in England, training in several European countries, and working in South Africa, coming to America was gastronomically quite a change for me. I had spent the early years of my life learning to adjust to the unavailability of certain foods. For example, beef was expensive in England, so I did not purchase it often. Suddenly I was in a country where many foods were available in large quantities and varieties. That was when I discovered that beef was the largest factor in the American diet.

I clearly remember my venture out to discover the Great American Steak. A friend took me to dinner and I ordered steak. When it arrived, I sat looking at it in total astonishment. Lying on a plate in front of me was the largest porterhouse I had ever seen in my life. I had no idea how I would eat a steak so large, yet not to eat it all would make my friend think I was wasting food. Although the meat was wonderful, to this day I will never forget the size of that steak nor the shock I felt when it arrived. It was truly a new experience, and one I would use later in planning menus for my restaurant.

Today, I am as accustomed to meats as any American. Although my preference is still seafood, I can appreciate a good steak every now and then and have found that the imagination can turn a piece of beef into a meal as wonderful as any seafood dish. Most of the recipes in this section use tenderloin, which will lead people to call this section extravagant. Although tenderloin is less flavorful than some cuts of beef, it is light in texture, tender, and moist. I find it extremely suitable for the smaller portions of beef I prefer to serve.

If you buy a whole unstripped 6- to 8-pound tenderloin from the butcher or supermarket, and do the stripping and tying yourself (see drawings on page 352 and 353), you will save some money. This also will allow you to cut the portions to your required sizes.

For the steak recipes, the following steaks may be used in place of tenderloin: small sirloin, Delmonico, and loin strip steaks.

PREPARATION OF

TENDERLOIN

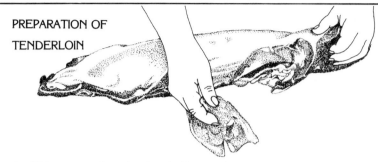

1. With a very sharp boning knife, starting at the top (on the right in this illustration, and this is the wider part of the tenderloin), begin to remove the fat and side muscles from the tenderloin, being careful not to cut into the flesh. The side muscles are 1 to 2 inches in diameter and look like flaps. The muscle that runs from the narrow, tenderloin tip end almost three-quarters of the way along the tenderloin should be taken off because it contains a lot of gristle. Another muscle starts about this point and runs up to the thickest point of the tenderloin. With a sharp knife remove the fat around this muscle, being careful to keep the muscle attached.

2. You also should remove the collagen and elastin. The collagen is a shiny membranous material. The elastin is a thicker, shinier, silver membrane. Together they are commonly referred to as "silver skin" or gristle in many cookbooks.

3. To remove the elastin and collagen, insert your knife just under them and work the knife along in a gentle sawing motion, as you remove 1-inch-wide strips.

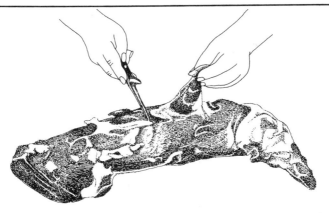

4. Turn the tenderloin over and remove the fatty parts with a sharp boning knife.

5. After you have removed the tenderloin tip about 4 to 5 inches from the tip (and saved it for another purpose), begin tying the tenderloin, using a natural fiber string. Bring the string around the meat and tie a knot, leaving one long end of string.

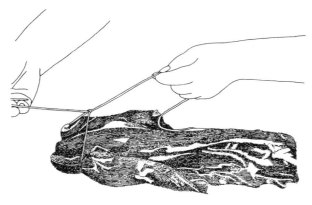

6. Continue to tie the string around the tenderloin, but you do not need to knot it. At the end, turn the meat over, and bring the string up under all the crosswise ties. Tie it to the string at the first knot.

Eva's Tenderloin of Beef

Served either hot or cold, this is an ideal dish for a dinner party because most of the preparation should be done a day ahead of time. When it is served hot, it is great with Grilled Polenta (page 442) or fresh pasta with chives. If you serve it cold, serve it with pasta salad.

> *1 tenderloin, 5 to 7 pounds, stripped (page 352)*
> *3 cups red wine*
> *3 tablespoons vegetable oil*
> *10 large shallots, very finely sliced*
> *½ bay leaf*
> *2 cups homemade veal stock or chicken-beef consomme*
> *1 tablespoon red wine vinegar or balsamic vinegar*
> *1½ tablespoons fresh rosemary, coarsely chopped (or 2*
> *   teaspoons dried rosemary)*

1. Bring the red wine to a boil in a 2-quart stainless steel saucepan, ignite, and allow to flame for 3 minutes.
2. Heat 2 tablespoons oil in another stainless steel saucepan. Add shallots and saute until soft. Add bay leaf, wine, stock, and vinegar, and gently simmer for 30 minutes. Cool the marinade.
3. Tie the tenderloin, as described on page 353. Place the meat in a Pyrex, china, or enamel pan, and pour marinade over tenderloin. Leave it in the refrigerator for 24 hours.
4. Remove the beef from the refrigerator 1 hour before cooking. Oil a roasting pan. Preheat broiler. Adjust an oven rack 6 inches from the heat.
5. Remove the tenderloin from the marinade; reserve the marinade. Place the meat in the roasting pan and brush it with the remaining tablespoon of oil.
6. Broil the tenderloin on both sides until light golden brown. Lower the oven temperature to 375 degrees and roast for 30 to 40 minutes. Check for doneness with an instant thermometer; the internal thermometer will read 127 degrees for rare or 135 degrees for medium-rare.

7. While tenderloin is roasting, reduce marinade by 30 percent in a stainless steel pan over high heat. Add the fresh rosemary. Add salt and freshly ground black pepper to taste.
8. If you are serving the meat hot, let it rest at least 10 minutes before carving. Slice the meat, arrange it on a serving platter, and pour the hot sauce on top.
9. If you are serving the meat cold, cool the meat and the sauce. Then put the whole tenderloin in the sauce and refrigerate for at least 3 hours before carving.

Servings: 8 to 10   Preparation: Fairly easy
Time: Time consuming; advance preparation necessary

Carne Asado

I love the flavor that prosciutto gives the beef in this recipe. Try serving it with Black-Eyed Peas and Mushrooms (page 431), White Bean Tomato Stew (page 418), or Black Bean Stew garnished with Avocado (page 419).

1 5- to 6-pound tenderloin
2 ounces prosciutto, sliced ⅛-inch thick
3 medium garlic cloves, crushed
¼ cup olive oil
¼ cup fresh lemon juice
¼ cup fresh lime juice
2 teaspoons Tabasco
½ cup strong homemade beef stock or consomme

1. Strip tenderloin and remove tenderloin tip. (See drawings on page 352.)
2. With a small sharp knife cut on the diagonal 12 incisions ¼-inch wide by 2 inches deep along the top of the tenderloin.
3. Cut prosciutto into 2-inch-long julienne strips and insert one strip into each tenderloin incision. Tie the beef (see drawings on page 353).
4. Mix the garlic with the oil, lemon juice, lime juice, and Tabasco. Pour over the beef and marinate for 24 hours in the refrigerator.
5. Remove beef from refrigerator 1 hour before cooking. Preheat broiler.
6. Remove beef from marinade and place it in an oiled roasting pan. Broil tenderloin about 6 inches from the broiler until it is light golden brown on both sides. Pour the marinade over the beef and roast at 350 degrees for 30 to 40 minutes until the internal temperature reads 130 degrees for rare and 135–140 degrees for medium.
7. When the beef is cooked let it rest at least 10 minutes before carving.
8. Pour the pan juices into a 1-quart saucepan and skim off fat. Add the stock and reduce by 50 percent. Add salt and freshly ground black pepper to taste.
9. Carve the tenderloin and serve the sauce separately.

Servings: 8   **Preparation: Fairly easy**
Time: Time consuming; advance preparation necessary

Tenderloin with Blue Cheese

Here is an unusual combination of strong flavors that will enhance the flavor of beef. Its strength will surprise as well as delight you. I prefer the wonderful taste of Roquefort because of its strength and smoothness, but Saga Blue or Pipo Crème cheese may be substituted. Instead of sauteing the steaks, you may broil or grill them.

4 6- to 7-ounce tenderloin steaks
2 ounces Roquefort cheese (or Saga Blue or Pipo Crème)
¼ cup sour cream
2 tablespoons unsalted butter
1 cup Red Pepper Puree (page 19)
2 tablespoons vegetable oil

1. Finely crumble the Roquefort, whisk in the sour cream and continue to whisk until well blended. Refrigerate.
2. Forty minutes before cooking, remove the steaks from the refrigerator and bring up to room temperature. Twenty minutes before serving, bring the Roquefort mixture up to room temperature.
3. Heat the Red Pepper Puree and 2 tablespoons of unsalted butter in a small saucepan, stirring occasionally to keep the sauce from scorching.
4. Heat the 2 tablespoons of oil in a heavy 12-inch saute pan. Add the steaks and saute on medium heat until the steaks are medium brown, being careful not to move the steaks until they are brown, as you might tear the meat. Turn over and saute until cooked to required doneness.
5. Spoon the sauce onto 4 warm dinner plates. Place the steaks on the sauce and spoon the Roquefort mixture on top. Serve immediately.

Servings: 4   Preparation: Easy
Time: Fairly time consuming; some advance preparation possible

Tenderloin Provençal

The addition of orange zest to this dish gives it a slightly sweet flavor. If you have prepared all the ingredients ahead of time, you can put this dish together very quickly at the last minute.

1 pound tenderloin tips, cut into 2-inch julienne strips
2 tablespoons olive oil
3 shallots, sliced
2 medium vine-ripened tomatoes, peeled, seeded, and chopped
1 tablespoon fresh thyme leaves
1 teaspoon finely grated orange rind (zest)
⅓ cup loosely packed fresh parsley sprigs, finely chopped

1. Remove any fat or gristle with a knife. Cut the beef into julienne strips, ¼ inch wide and 2 inches long. If the beef is quite cold, it is easier to cut.
2. Heat the oil in a heavy 12-inch saute pan. Add the meat and toss over high heat until they are light brown. Be careful not to overcook the meat because it should be rare in the middle. Remove the meat with a slotted spoon and put to one side.
3. Add the shallots to the pan and saute on high heat until clear, being careful not to brown.
4. Add the tomatoes, thyme, and orange rind, and cook on high heat, stirring all the time until the sauce is thick.
5. Add the meat and parsley to the pan and stir over medium heat to cook the beef to your desired doneness. Add salt and freshly ground black pepper to taste. Serve.

Servings: 4   **Preparation: Easy**
Time: Quick

Beef Tenderloin Athens Style

This tenderloin dish is a wonderful creation from Megan Tabor. The combination of the strong flavors of pancetta and chèvre is really successful and delicious. I prefer to use a fairly strong chèvre in the sauce, but you should use the variety of your tastes. I recommend you do not serve this dish with anything that is very pronounced in flavor; steamed green vegetables are a nice accompaniment.

> *4 6-ounce tenderloin steaks*
> *3 ounces chèvre cheese (Montrachet or Bucheron)*
> *1 ounce pancetta, finely diced*
> *1 tablespoon vegetable oil*
> *1 medium red onion, finely chopped*
> *½ cup strong homemade chicken consomme or stock (or*
> *   canned low-salt beef broth)*

1. Remove the steaks from the refrigerator 30 minutes before cooking. Slightly flatten the steaks. Peel the rind off the cheese; crumble cheese into very small pieces.
2. Heat the oil in a heavy 12-inch saute pan. Add the pancetta and saute until a light golden brown.
3. Add the onion and saute on medium-high heat, tossing all the time, until the onion is soft; be careful not to brown. Remove from the pan with a slotted spoon, put on a serving platter, and keep warm.
4. There should be 2 tablespoons fat left in the pan; if not, add a little more vegetable oil. Add the steaks and cook on medium heat until medium brown on both sides and cooked to the required doneness. To check for doneness, insert a small knife into the thickest part of the meat.
5. Remove the steaks from the pan and place them on the onion mixture. Keep warm.
6. Wipe out the pan, add the stock and reduce on high heat until it has evaporated to ⅓ cup. Keep scraping down the sides of the pan with a plastic spatula so the stock does not scorch.
7. Remove the pan from the heat and whisk in the chèvre. Put the pan back on the heat and continue to whisk on medium heat until the mixture is smooth and has a medium-thick consistency. Add salt and freshly ground black pepper to taste.
8. Pour the sauce over the beef and serve immediately.

Servings: 4   **Preparation: Easy**   **Time: Fairly time consuming**

Beef Peponata

I love the combination of the wine, the pine-scented juniper berries, and the red pepper with the beef in this dish. I enjoyed preparing it for Francie and Jeffrey Jowel—yes, from *Alice, Let's Eat.*

1¼ pounds tenderloin tips or flank steak
1 medium, sweet red pepper
½ cup homemade beef stock or consomme
¼ cup dry white wine
2 tablespoons vegetable oil
1 medium onion, very thinly sliced
1 teaspoon juniper berries, finely chopped
¼ cup loosely packed fresh parsley sprigs, finely chopped
fresh parsley sprigs for garnish

1. Remove any fat or gristle with a knife. Cut the beef into julienne strips, ¼-inch wide and 2 inches long. If the beef is cold, it is easier to cut.
2. Place pepper under a preheated broiler and broil until dark brown on all sides. Put into very cold water for 5 minutes, then peel. Remove core and seeds. Cut into thin julienne strips.
3. Heat the stock and white wine in a small saucepan over medium heat and reduce to ½ cup.
4. The beef, the pepper, and the stock may be refrigerated up to 8 hours.
5. Thirty minutes before cooking, remove the beef and pepper from the refrigerator.
6. Heat the oil in a 12-inch saute pan, add the beef, and toss over high heat until light brown but slightly rare in the center. Remove from the pan with a slotted spoon and put to one side.
7. Add the onion to the pan and saute over medium heat until clear, but not brown. Add the red pepper, stock and wine mixture, juniper berries, and parsley, and cook until almost all the liquid has evaporated. Add the beef and reheat for 2 minutes. Add salt and freshly ground black pepper to taste.
8. Place on a serving platter and garnish with parsley sprigs.

Servings: 4   Preparation: Easy
Time: Quick; some advance preparation possible

German-Style Beef

My German-Style Beef is quick and easy to prepare and much lighter and more flavorful than classic Sauerbraten. It is excellent served on egg noodles that have been tossed with chopped fresh parsley; boiled potatoes or boiled cabbage are also good with it.

> 1¼ pounds tenderloin tips
> ½ cup dry red wine
> 1¼ cups homemade beef, veal or chicken stock (or canned low-salt chicken broth)
> ¼ bay leaf
> ½ teaspoon finely chopped juniper berries
> 2 tablespoons vegetable oil
> 1 cup very finely sliced onion
> 1 to 2 tablespoons red wine vinegar
> 1 to 2 tablespoons unsalted butter, soft

1. Cut the tenderloin into ¼-inch-wide and ½-inch-long strips. Remove all but a small part of the fat.
2. Bring the red wine to a boil in a stainless steel saucepan and ignite. Allow to flame for 3 minutes, then add the stock, bay leaf, and juniper berries. Reduce over high heat to ¾ cup.
3. You may refrigerate the beef and the sauce for 6 hours, if you wish.
4. Thirty minutes before cooking the beef, remove it from the refrigerator, and bring it to room temperature.
5. Heat the oil in a heavy 12-inch saute pan, add the beef, and toss over high heat until light golden brown and still rare in the middle. Remove with a slotted spoon and put to one side.
6. Add the onion to the pan and saute over high heat until clear, stirring all the time.
7. Add the red wine sauce and 1 tablespoon vinegar, and reduce over high heat for 3 to 5 minutes until the sauce lightly coats a spoon. Add the beef and any juices that have accumulated from them. Continue to reduce the sauce over high heat for 1 to 2 minutes.
8. Add salt, freshly ground black pepper, and more vinegar to taste.

Servings: 4   **Preparation: Easy**
Time: Fairly time consuming; some advance preparation possible

Tenderloin of Beef Moutarde

The combination of mustard and watercress gives this dish a sharp, piquant flavor. Crème fraîche is really lovely in the sauce, but since it is not always available, sour cream can be substituted.

4 6-ounce tenderloin steaks
3 scallions
2 tablespoons clarified butter (page 62)
2 tablespoons unsalted butter
½ cup strong homemade beef stock or consomme
1 to 2 tablespoons Dijon mustard
6 tablespoons sour cream or crème fraîche
½ cup loosely packed fresh watercress leaves, chopped
⅓ cup loosely packed fresh parsley sprigs, finely chopped

1. Remove and discard the coarse outside layer from the scallions. Cut the scallions into thin slices halfway up the green part.
2. Remove the steaks from the refrigerator 30 minutes before cooking. Heat the clarified butter in a 12-inch saute pan until it is hot. Add the steaks and saute over medium heat until medium brown, being careful not to move the steaks until they have browned, as you might tear the meat. Turn over and saute the other side until medium brown. When the steaks have cooked to required doneness, remove them from the pan and keep them warm.
3. Add the 2 tablespoons unsalted butter to the pan. Add the scallions and saute over medium heat for 1 minute. Add stock and reduce to a light syrupy consistency.
4. Add 1 tablespoon mustard and sour cream or crème fraîche; reduce until the sauce is thick enough to coat a spoon. Taste; add more mustard if you wish. Add watercress and parsley and cook for 30 seconds. Add salt and freshly ground black pepper to taste.
5. Arrange the steaks on 4 large dinner plates and spoon the sauce on top.

Servings: 4   **Preparation: Easy**
Time: Quick

Provençal Beef Stew

The varied combination of ingredients in this stew gives a very richly flavored casserole that's delicious on a cold winter night. I like to serve it with rice or pasta and a tossed green salad. It is ideal to make a day or two ahead of time. My preference is to use chuck for this dish, as it gives a moister casserole meat; however, other beef or lamb stew cuts may be used.

> 2 pounds chuck beef stew meat
> 1 large sweet green pepper
> 2 bacon slices (or 2 ounces salt pork)
> 1 tablespoon vegetable oil
> 1 large onion, thinly sliced
> 3 medium garlic cloves, finely chopped
> 1 cup dry red wine
> 3 medium tomatoes, peeled, seeded, and chopped
> 2 teaspoons dried thyme
> 1½ teaspoons finely grated orange rind (zest)
> 1 cup strong homemade beef stock
> ¼ pound mushrooms, sliced ¼-inch thick
> 2 tablespoons tomato paste
> ¼ cup pitted olives

1. Place the green pepper under a preheated broiler and broil until dark brown all over. Leave in very cold water for 5 minutes, peel, remove the core and seeds, and cut into ⅛-inch slices. Set aside.
2. Remove any excess fat from the beef. Cut beef into 1-inch cubes.
3. Slice the bacon into 1-inch pieces. If you are using salt pork, remove the rind and discard it, then dice the pork into ⅛-inch pieces.
4. Heat the oil in a heavy 12-inch saute pan, add the bacon or salt pork, and saute until light golden brown. If using salt pork, discard all but 3 tablespoons of fat. Add the onions and garlic and saute until clera, being careful not to brown.
5. Bring the red wine to a boil in a 1-quart saucepan, ignite, and allow to flame for 3 minutes.
6. Preheat oven to 250 degrees.

7. Place the beef, onion mixture, red wine, tomatoes, thyme, orange rind, and beef stock in a 3- to 4-quart ovenproof casserole. Stir, cover, and cook at 250 degrees for 2 to 2½ hours until the meat is almost tender.
8. Add the mushrooms, tomato paste, olives, and green pepper to the stew, re-cover, and continue to cook for an additional 30 minutes. Then add salt and freshly ground black pepper to taste. Skim off any excess fat.
9. If you are preparing the stew ahead of time, cool, then refrigerate for up to 2 days. One and one half hours before serving, bring the casserole up to room temperature, then reheat at 300 degrees for 30 to 40 minutes, or on top of the stove on low heat.

Servings: 6   Preparation: Easy
Time: Time consuming; advance preparation possible

Pork

I remember dinners at home in England when we were served pork. It was rich and moist, and my father claimed it was because the pigs were slop-fed. My introduction to pork in the United States led me to believe that grain-fed pigs of this country were a little drier than their European counterpart. Then I met a friend from Iowa, the largest producer of pork in the world, and I began to think it over. I decided that pork was just as different in cuts as it was in breeding. It was not always the pork that was different, but also the way it was prepared.

To retain flavor and natural juices of the meat, I prefer to roast pork on the bone. I also favor the cut of meat known as pork tenderloin. It generally comes with a whole loin, but can, on occasion, be purchased separately. You will find the tenderloin just under the loin, usually surrounded by fat. Once the fat is removed from the outside of the tenderloin, you have a lovely, lean, and tender piece of meat. This cut is only large enough to serve 1 to 1½ persons, so you will need to buy several tenderloins for a dinner party. They may be sauteed until light golden brown, then roasted in the oven, sliced, and served with a sauce, such as I do in Pork Tenderloins with Artichoke Sauce (page 366).

The wonderful thing about pork is that it can take very strongly flavored sauces and robust garnishes. All the pork recipes in this section have an intensity of flavor and texture. I hope you will agree with me that they are delicious and distinctive.

Pork Tenderloins with Artichoke Sauce

Try to use fresh artichokes in this rich and satisfying dish. The sauce also can be served with a roast loin of pork or a roast of chicken.

>   3 pork tenderloins (weighing 8 to 12 ounces each)
>   3 tablespoons unsalted butter
>   2 large artichoke bottoms, cooked (page 85) or 4 frozen
>   artichoke hearts
>   1 cup homemade chicken stock (or low-salt canned chicken
>   broth)
>   1 to 2 tablespoons Dijon mustard
>   ¼ cup heavy cream

1. Trim all but ⅛-inch of fat from the pork tenderloins. Be careful to trim all the sinews. (Refer to the drawings for tenderloin of beef on page 352, although trimming a pork tenderloin is much simpler.)
2. Preheat oven to 400 degrees.
3. Reduce stock to ½ cup over high heat.
4. Heat 1 tablespoon butter in a heavy 12-inch saute pan. Place pork tenderloins, fat side down, in the pan. Saute on medium heat until light golden brown on both sides.
5. Lightly butter a roasting pan. Place tenderloins in pan and roast in the preheated oven for 30 to 35 minutes until cooked. To check for doneness, insert an instant thermometer into the thickest part of the meat. It should read 155 to 160 degrees. Remove from the oven and rest for 10 minutes.
6. While the meat is roasting, cut the artichoke bottoms in half and then into ¼-inch slices.
7. Heat the remaining 2 tablespoons butter in a large saute pan. Add artichokes and saute on low heat for 1 minute. Add chicken stock and mustard and reduce, stirring, until it has a light syrupy consistency. Slowly pour in the cream, stirring all the time. Turn up the heat and reduce until the sauce is thick enough to coat a spoon. Add salt, freshly ground black pepper, and more mustard to taste.
8. Slice the pork and arrange on 4 warm dinner plates. Spoon the sauce on top.

Servings: 4   Preparation: Fairly easy
Time: Fairly time consuming

Pork Loin Moldavienne

This is a very strong sauce, which I love, but you may want to adjust the horseradish to your taste. This dish is great served with Cabbage with Parsley and Caraway (page 420) and boiled potatoes.

1 4- to 5-pound pork loin
3 tablespoons Dijon mustard
1 cup homemade strong chicken stock (or canned low-salt chicken broth)
1 to 2 tablespoons white horseradish
1 tablespoon cornstarch
¼ cup cold water

1. Trim the excess fat from the outside of the pork, leaving a thin layer so as to keep the roast moist. Brush the pork with 2 tablespoons mustard.
2. Preheat oven to 350 degrees.
3. Place the pork loin, fat side up, in a roasting pan and place in the preheated oven. Roast for 1½ to 2 hours or until the internal temperature reads 155–160 degrees. To test for this, remove the pork from the oven and insert an instant thermometer into the thickest part of the meat. Be certain the thermometer does not touch the bone or a very fatty part of the roast, or you will get an incorrect reading. Leave the thermometer in at least 1 minute to get a reading.
4. When the pork is almost cooked, bring the chicken stock to a boil in a 1-quart saucepan. Whisk in the remaining 1 tablespoon mustard and 1 to 2 tablespoons horseradish to taste. Remove from the heat.
5. Mix the cornstarch with the cold water. Slowly whisk ¼ cup of the hot sauce into the cornstarch mixture, then return the sauce to the pan. Bring it to a boil, whisking all the time. Put to one side.
6. When the pork is cooked, remove from the oven and rest for at least 10 minutes before carving.
7. If there are any pan juices, pour them into a small bowl. Skim off and discard the fat, then add the juices to the sauce.
8. To serve, carve the pork and arrange on warm dinner plates. Spoon the sauce on top.

Servings: 6   Preparation: Easy
Time: Time consuming

Creole Roast Pork

The wonderfully spicy flavor of this dish comes from the strong spice mixture that coats the pork. It is good served hot or at room temperature. I like to serve it with Black Bean Stew (page 419) or White Bean Tomato Stew (page 418), Sauteed Green Vegetables (page 439), and Corn Bread (page 151).

1 4- to 5-pound pork loin
2 teaspoons fennel seed
1 teaspoon whole black peppercorns
2 teaspoons dried thyme
1 teaspoon salt
¼ teaspoon cayenne pepper
1 teaspoon dried basil
2 teaspoons Hungarian paprika

1. Trim the fat, leaving just ⅛-inch fat covering the roast.
2. Place the fennel seed and black pepper in a very dry blender and blend until fine. Add the thyme, salt, cayenne, basil, and paprika, and blend for 30 seconds until fairly fine, but not a powder. Press the spice mix all over the pork.
3. Preheat oven to 375 degrees.
4. Place the pork in a roasting pan and roast for 1½ to 2 hours until the internal temperature reads 155–160 degrees. To test for this, insert an instant thermometer into the thickest part of the meat, making sure the thermometer does not touch the bone or a very fatty part of the roast, or you will get an incorrect reading. Leave the thermometer in at least one minute.
5. Remove the pork from the oven when cooked and rest in a warm part of the kitchen at least 10 minutes before carving, as it will retain more juices.

Servings: 6   Preparation: Easy
Time: Time consuming

Pork Vallee Dauge

Juniper berries have a sweet and aromatic flavor and the scent of pine. The sauce is rich in flavor, and with the addition of cream (which is optional) even richer. As this dish can be entirely made in advance, it is a great company meal. Boiled parsleyed new potatoes work well with it.

4 8-ounce loin pork chops
3 tablespoons unbleached all-purpose flour
1 tablespoon unsalted butter
1 onion, finely diced
1 celery stalk, finely diced
1 tart apple, peeled, cored, and in 1/8-inch dice
3/4 cup dry white wine
3/4 cup strong homemade chicken stock or consomme (or
     canned low-salt chicken broth)
1 teaspoon finely chopped juniper berries
1/2 cup heavy cream (optional)
1 apple, sliced, for garnish

1. Preheat oven to 275 degrees.
2. Trim all but 1/8-inch of fat from each chop.
3. Place the flour on a plate, and add salt and freshly ground black pepper to taste. Lightly flour the pork.
4. Heat butter in a heavy 12-inch saute pan, add pork chops, and saute until they are light golden brown on both sides. Transfer the pork chops to an ovenproof casserole dish, which is also safe to use on a stove burner. Reserve 2 tablespoon fat in the saute pan, discard the rest.
5. Add onion and celery to the pan and saute until clear, but be careful not to brown. Add the diced apple, wine, stock, and juniper berries, and simmer for 5 minutes.
6. Pour the sauce over the pork chops, cover, place in the preheated oven, and cook for 1½ to 2 hours, until the chops are tender.
7. Remove the chops from pan and reduce the pan juices until they are very thick. Cool a little, then very slowly stir in the cream, being careful not to boil or the sauce will curdle. Continue to reduce to a fairly thick consistency. (If you omit the cream in this recipe, reduce the sauce to 1 cup.) Pour the sauce over the pork.

8. This dish can be made 24 hours ahead of serving time and refrigerated. For reheating, remove from the refrigerator 1 hour before reheating; reheat, covered, in a 350-degree oven for 30 to 40 minutes.
9. Just before serving, garnish the pork with the apple slices.

Servings: 4   Preparation: Easy
Time: Time consuming; advance preparation possible

Sweetbreads

They are mentioned in every famous cookbook and are served in the finest restaurants throughout the world. Escoffier calls them "one of the finest delicacies provided by the butcher," and *Larousse Gastronomique* says they are "considered to be the most delicate products of butchery." Prepared carefully and cooked creatively, sweetbreads are not only delicious but a wonderful addition to any menu.

Pale in appearance, sweetbreads are the thymus glands from the neck and heart of young animals, primarily calves and lambs. The most common and generally of the best quality are veal sweetbreads. Although they are available frozen, fresh are much more preferable and tender. They should be free of any odor when purchased fresh.

To achieve the best texture, sweetbreads should be peeled prior to cooking. You can do this 6 hours ahead of time, so this is not the enormous amount of work it may seem. In England we used to simmer sweetbreads gently in a stock, peel them, then cook them. Now I prefer to peel them raw, as I find that the superb texture I get makes it worth the extra effort. To peel sweetbreads, place them in a bowl of cold water and refrigerate for 30 minutes. Then, taking one piece at a time out of the water, peel off as much of the outer tissue as you can. Do not be concerned if the sweetbreads break up during this process.

Since sweetbreads have a soft texture, it is a good idea to garnish the plate with a crisp pastry round or brioche-toast triangles to give an interesting contrast of texture.

Sweetbreads Fenouil

I love this combination of fennel, fresh tomatoes, and garlic butter. It gives a much lighter sauce than many of the classic executions for sweetbreads. This dish is good served with steamed green vegetables.

1½ pounds fresh veal sweetbreads
1 small fennel bulb
2 small vine-ripened tomatoes, peeled and seeded
3 tablespoons unsalted butter
1 medium garlic clove, finely chopped
½ cup homemade chicken stock (or canned low-salt chicken broth)
4 tablespoons all-purpose unbleached flour
3 tablespoons clarified butter (page 62)

1. Place the sweetbreads in a bowl, cover with cold water, and refrigerate for 30 minutes. Soaking the sweetbreads makes them easier to peel; but I have found that if they are left in over 30 minutes, they are quite difficult to peel.
2. Meanwhile, remove and discard the coarse outside layer from the fennel. Cut the bulb in half, cut out the core, and discard. Finely dice the fennel.
3. Cut the tomato into thin julienne strips. Heat 2 tablespoons unsalted butter in a 1-quart saucepan, add the garlic, and gently cook over medium heat, being very careful not to brown. Add the tomatoes and stock and cook on medium heat until reduced by 30 percent. Put to one side.
4. Take the sweetbreads out of the water one by one and peel off as much of the outside tissue (collagen) as possible. The sweetbreads might break up in the process; however, their texture will be much better the more diligent one is with this step.
5. The above steps may be done 6 hours ahead of serving time; refrigerate the fennel, the tomato sauce, and the sweetbreads.
6. Just before serving, drain off any liquid under the sweetbreads and pat them dry. Mix a little salt and freshly ground black pepper with the flour and very lightly dust the sweetbreads.

7. Heat the clarified butter in a heavy 12-inch saute pan. Add the sweetbreads, and saute without moving them (as they turn brown they will come away from the pan more easily and will not tear) until light golden brown on one side. Turn them over and saute until golden brown on the other side and cooked through. Remove from the pan and keep warm.
8. Add the remaining tablespoon of butter and the diced fennel to the pan and saute on medium heat until lightly cooked and still slightly crunchy. Add the tomato sauce and cook on high heat until it has a fairly thick consistency. Add salt and freshly ground black pepper to taste.
9. Spoon the sauce on four dinner plates and arrange the sweetbreads on top. Serve immediately.

Servings: 4   Preparation: Fairly difficult
Time: Time consuming; advance preparation possible

Sweetbreads Nora

The tomato gives this cream sauce a lighter-than-usual consistency, and the dash of cayenne pepper adds spiciness. Adjust the cayenne to your taste.

1½ pounds fresh veal sweetbreads
⅓ cup heavy cream
½ cup homemade chicken stock or consomme
5 tablespoons unsalted butter
3 tablespoons unbleached all-purpose flour
3 small vine-ripened tomatoes, peeled, seeded, and finely diced
¼ teaspoon cayenne pepper
fresh parsley sprigs for garnish

1. Place the sweetbreads in a bowl, cover with cold water, and refrigerate for 30 minutes. Soaking the sweetbreads makes them easier to peel; but I have found that if they are left in over 30 minutes, they are quite difficult to peel.
2. Take the sweetbreads out of the water one by one and peel off as much of the outside tissue (collagen) as possible. The sweetbreads might break up in the process; however, their texture will be much better the more diligent one is with this step.
3. Place the cream and stock in a 1-quart saucepan. Over a high heat reduce to ⅓ cup, stirring all the time.
4. You may refrigerate the sweetbreads and the cream-stock reduction for 6 hours.
5. Just before serving, drain any liquid collected from the sweetbreads and pat them dry. Mix a little salt and freshly ground black pepper with the flour and very lightly dust the sweetbreads.
6. Heat 3 tablespoons butter in a heavy 12-inch saute pan, add the sweetbreads, and saute without moving them until they are light golden brown on one side. Turn them over and saute until golden brown on the other side and cooked through. Remove from the pan and keep warm.

7. Wipe out the pan and heat the remaining 2 tablespoons of butter. Add the diced tomatoes and cayenne pepper and reduce over high heat until thick. Add the cream-stock reduction and continue to reduce until fairly thick. Add salt and freshly ground black pepper to taste.
8. Spoon the sauce onto 4 warm dinner plates. Arrange the sweetbreads on the sauce. Garnish with the parsley and serve.

Servings: 4   Preparation: Fairly difficult
Time: Time consuming; some advance preparation possible

Sweetbreads Champignons

This rich and delicious entree was created by me for Allan Ross. The Vermouth Madeira Sauce used in the dish can be made ahead of time and frozen. If you want you can use wild mushrooms, such as Chanterelles or Tromp de Morts.

> *1½ pounds fresh veal sweetbreads*
> *¼ pound cultivated or wild mushrooms, cleaned*
> *6 tablespoons unsalted butter*
> *3 tablespoons unbleached all purpose flour*
> *½ cup Vermouth Madeira Sauce (page 30)*
> *¼ cup heavy cream*

1. Place the sweetbreads in a bowl, cover with cold water, and refrigerate for 30 minutes. Soaking the sweetbreads makes them easier to peel; but I have found that if they are left in over 30 minutes, they are quite difficult to peel.
2. Take the sweetbreads out of the water one by one and peel off as much of the outside tissue (collagen) as possible. The sweetbreads might break up in the process; however, their texture will be much better the more diligent one is with this step.

3. Cut the mushroom stalks even with the caps and slice ⅛-inch thick. If using wild mushrooms, discard the stems.
4. The sweetbreads and mushrooms may be refrigerated for 6 hours.
5. Just before serving, drain any liquid collected from the sweetbreads and pat them dry. Add a little salt and freshly ground black pepper to the flour and very lightly dust the sweetbreads.
6. Heat 3 tablespoons butter in a heavy 12-inch saute pan, add the sweetbreads, and saute without moving them until they are light golden brown on one side. Turn them over and saute until golden brown on the other side and cooked through. Remove from the pan and keep warm.
7. Wipe out the pan and heat the 3 remaining tablespoons of butter. Add the mushrooms and saute on high heat, tossing all the time, until they are light golden brown.
8. Add the Vermouth Madeira Sauce and reduce on high heat until it has a light syrupy consistency. Add the cream and continue to reduce until it is thick enough to coat a spoon. Add salt and freshly ground black pepper to taste.
9. Arrange the sweetbreads on four dinner plates and spoon the sauce on top.

Servings: 4   Preparation: Fairly difficult
Time: Time consuming; some advance preparation possible

Vegetarian Entrees &

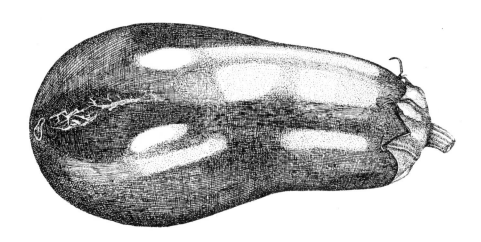

Supper Dishes

Vegetarian Entrees and Supper Dishes

In the sixteen years that I have owned a restaurant, I have always offered a choice of vegetarian and meatless entrees on the menu. This variety has not only proved successful with the ever-increasing number of vegetarians in the area, but also has proved to be popular with people who are looking for new and interesting foods.

Therefore, I am including here a variety of my most popular vegetarian recipes, and a few recipes containing a small amount of meat that fall into the "supper dish" category. These nutritious recipes can be served for lunch or dinner or as an interesting appetizer. They not only will fulfill your expectations of what a meal should be, but also offer a nutritionally well-balanced dish.

Stuffed Mushrooms Provençal

It is not advisable to serve this dish as a cocktail hors d'oeuvre. The stuffing is softer than most but the wonderful combination of flavors makes these mushrooms a great vegetarian entree for 4 or a fine accompaniment to a plain roast meat dish for 6 people. Choose only the largest mushrooms to stuff.

24 large mushrooms
5 tablespoons olive oil
3 medium vine-ripened tomatoes, peeled, seeded, and chopped
1 small onion, very finely diced
2 medium garlic cloves, finely diced or crushed
1 tablespoon fresh thyme leaves (or 1 teaspoon dried thyme leaves)
¼ cup dry unflavored bread crumbs
unsalted butter
1 cup freshly grated Emmenthal or Gruyère cheese
fresh parsley sprigs for garnish

1. Brush or wipe the mushrooms clean. Remove the stalks from the caps and finely dice the stalks.
2. Heat 2 tablespoons oil in a 10-inch saute pan and add the tomatoes. On medium heat reduce the tomatoes until they have a very thick consistency, scraping down the sides and stirring occasionally so that the mixture does not scorch. Pour the mixture into a bowl and cool.
3. Clean the pan and heat 3 tablespoons oil in it. Add the onion and garlic, and, if you are using dried thyme, add it at this point. Saute over medium heat until the onions clear, being careful not to brown. Add the mushroom stalks and saute until they are cooked and all the liquid has evaporated. Cool the mixture.
4. Mix the tomato mixture with the mushroom mixture, bread crumbs, and, if you are using fresh thyme, add it at this point. Add salt and freshly ground black pepper to taste.
5. Lightly butter the inside and outside of each mushroom cap before filling them with the stuffing. Place on a buttered sheet pan. Cover each mushroom cap with the cheese.
6. Refrigerate up to 8 hours, if you wish.
7. Preheat oven to 375 degrees.
8. Bake the mushrooms for 15 to 20 minutes. Serve garnished with parsley sprigs.

Servings: 4 to 6   Preparation: Easy
Time: Fairly time consuming: advance preparation possible

Stuffed Zucchini Noisette

Created by Jeffrey Starr, this recipe is a good way to serve zucchini when it is plentiful during the summer. It makes a nice light summer meal or a vegetable side dish. The wonderful crunchy texture of the stuffing makes it a great stuffing for large mushroom caps (not to be served as an hors d'oeuvre, however). You may substitute mozzarella or cheddar cheese.

> *4 small zucchini*
> *½ cup blanched almonds*
> *3 tablespoons vegetable oil*
> *1 small onion, finely chopped*
> *1 small carrot, coarsely grated*
> *1 celery stalk, finely diced*
> *⅓ cup loosely packed fresh parsley sprigs, finely chopped*
> *3 ounces chèvre (Montrachet or an American chèvre)*

1. Place the almonds on a sheet pan and bake in a preheated 400-degree oven for 7 to 10 minutes or until they are a light golden brown. Be careful that they do not burn. Cool.
2. Cut the zucchini in half lengthwise; scoop out the seeds and pulp, leaving a ¼-inch-thick shell. Discard the pulp.
3. Have a bowl of ice water ready. Bring 2 quarts water to a boil in a 4-quart saucepan. Add 1 teaspoon salt and zucchini shells and boil for 2 minutes. Remove from the boiling water with a slotted spoon and place in the ice water until cool. Drain and pat dry. Set aside.
4. Heat the oil in a 12-inch saute pan, add the onion, and saute over medium heat until clear, being careful not to brown. Add the carrot and celery and saute until just cooked. Place in a bowl.
5. Coarsely chop the almonds and add to the vegetables. Cool.
6. Remove and discard the rind from the chèvre. Break chèvre into small pieces. Add the parsley and the chèvre to the vegetables. Add salt and freshly ground black pepper to taste.
7. The recipe can be prepared up to this point 24 hours ahead of serving. Refrigerate the zucchini shells and stuffing.
8. Just before serving, preheat oven to 375 degrees.
9. Fill each zucchini shell with the stuffing and place on an oiled baking sheet. Bake for 20 minutes and serve immediately.

Servings: 4   Preparation: Easy
Time: Fairly time consuming; some advance preparation possible

Corn Terrine

This rich terrine is ideal served hot, warm, or chilled. It is delightful served as a supper dish on a fresh Tomato Coulis with fresh, very young, blanched okra.

2 cups cooked fresh corn kernels (about 5 ears)
4 whole eggs
2 egg yolks
4 ounces mozzarella, finely grated
1½ cups heavy cream
Tomato Coulis (page 16)

1. Preheat oven to 325 degrees.
2. Butter a Pyrex mold that is 8 inches long, 4 inches wide, and 2⅓ inches deep; line the bottom with wax paper.
3. Boil ears of corn about 3 minutes. Drain well and cut off the corn to measure 2 cups. Puree corn in food processor until medium-fine.
4. Place eggs and egg yolks in a bowl; whisk for 1 minute. Whisk in mozzarella, cream, and corn until well blended. Add salt and freshly ground black pepper to taste. Pour into mold.
5. Place the mold in a roasting pan with enough hot water to come up to two-thirds of the mold sides. Bake the terrine, uncovered, at 325 degrees for 1 hour and 45 minutes to 2½ hours, until the center is firm. Be careful not to overcook, as the terrine will become rubbery.
6. Remove the terrine from the water bath.
7. If terrine is to be served hot or warm, let it rest 10 minutes before turning it out of the pan. If terrine is to be served cold, let it cool in mold and then refrigerate up to 2 days before turning out. To turn out, run a metal spatula around the outside edges. Place a plate on top and turn over. Serve, sliced, on the tomato coulis.

Servings: 6 to 8   Preparation: Easy
Time: Fairly time consuming; advance preparation possible

Curried Eggplant

If you like the flavor of curry, Curried Eggplant makes a wonderful vegetarian Indian meal, served with Rice and Potato Pilaf (page 436) and Cucumber Raita (page 179).

> *2 medium eggplants (about 5 to 6 inches long)*
> *½ cup vegetable oil*
> *2 medium leeks*
> *1 medium onion, thinly sliced*
> *1 medium garlic clove, finely chopped*
> *2 teaspoons to 1 tablespoon homemade curry powder (see page*
> *64) or Madras curry powder*
> *¼ pound mushrooms, sliced ⅛-inch thick*
> *1 cup peas, frozen (or fresh if young)*
> *⅓ cup whole blanched almonds, coarsely chopped*

1. Cut the eggplants in half lengthwise through the stem end. Score by running a small sharp prep knife all around the edge. Then cut crisscrosses through the flesh, being careful not to puncture the skin. (See diagrams on page 70.) Lightly sprinkle with salt and let stand 1½ hours.
2. Meanwhile, remove the coarse outside layer from the leeks. Thinly slice up to the medium-green part. Place slices in a bowl of cold water for 30 minutes, then drain, rinse, drain well, and pat dry.
3. Preheat oven to 400 degrees.
4. Rinse the eggplants under cold water for 1 minute, lightly squeeze to release the water, and pat dry.
5. Brush a heavy baking sheet with oil. Place the eggplant halves on it, skin side down, and brush the eggplant flesh lavishly with oil. Cook in the preheated oven for 10 minutes. Turn over, flesh side down, and bake for 10 to 15 minutes until soft. Remove from the oven and cool.
6. Heat 2 tablespoons oil in a heavy 10-inch saute pan, add the onion, and toss over medium heat until clear, being careful not to brown. Add the leeks, garlic, and curry powder and toss until the leeks are cooked. Pour into a bowl.

7. Heat 3 tablespoons oil in a 12-inch saute pan, add the mushrooms and toss over medium heat until light golden brown and all liquid has evaporated. Add to the onion-leek mixture.

8. Scoop the flesh out of the eggplant, being careful to leave a ⅛ or ¼-inch shell intact. Set aside. Place the eggplant pulp in a sieve to drain for 5 minutes, then coarsely chop and add to the mushroom-onion mixture with salt and freshly ground black pepper to taste.

9. This part of the recipe may be done 2 days ahead of time. Refrigerate the stuffing and eggplant shells.

10. Preheat oven to 400 degrees.

11. Bring 1 quart of water to boil in a 2-quart saucepan. Add the peas and boil until tender. Drain, run under cold water, and pat dry. Add to the stuffing.

12. Place the eggplant shells on an oiled heavy sheet pan and fill them with the stuffing. Sprinkle with the almonds and bake for 20 minutes. Place on 4 dinner plates and serve.

Servings: 4   Preparation: Easy
Time: Time consuming; some advance preparation possible

Vegetarian Moussaka

Be sure to leave the skins of the eggplants intact so that you can stuff them successfully. For a dramatic presentation, as we do in the restaurant, serve the eggplants skin side up on plates to show off the beautiful, shiny black surface, then spoon the sauce down the center.

> 2 medium eggplants (about 5 or 6 inches long)
> ½ cup vegetable oil
> 2 medium onions, thinly sliced
> 1 medium garlic clove, finely chopped
> ½ pound mushrooms, sliced ⅛-inch thick
> ½ cup feta cheese, crumbled
> 1 small egg
> 1 tablespoon fresh thyme leaves (or 1 teaspoon dried thyme leaves)
> 1 cup Tomato Sauce (page 14)

1. Cut the eggplants in half lengthwise through the stem end. Score by running a small sharp prep knife all around the edge. Cut crisscrosses through the flesh, being careful not to puncture the skin. (See diagram on page 70.) Lightly sprinkle with salt and let stand 1½ hours.
2. Preheat oven to 400 degrees.
3. Rinse the eggplants under cold water for 1 minute, lightly squeeze to release the water, and pat dry.
4. Oil a heavy baking sheet and place the eggplant, skin side down, on it. Brush the flesh with oil. Bake for 10 minutes. Turn over, flesh side down, and bake for 10 to 15 minutes until soft. Remove from the oven and cool.
5. Heat 1 tablespoon oil in a 10-inch saute pan, add the onions and garlic, and saute until clear. Pour into a bowl.
6. Heat 3 tablespoons oil in a 12-inch saute pan, add the mushrooms, and toss over medium heat until light golden brown. Remove from the pan with a slotted spoon and mix with the onions.

7. Scoop the flesh out of the eggplant, being careful to leave a ⅛- or ¼-inch shell intact. Set aside. Place the eggplant pulp in a sieve and leave to drain for 5 minutes, then coarsely chop and add to the mushroom-onion mixture.
8. This part of the recipe may be prepared 2 days ahead of time. Refrigerate the stuffing and eggplant shells.
9. Preheat oven to 400 degrees.
10. Mix the feta, egg, and thyme into the stuffing and add salt and freshly ground pepper to taste. Place the eggplants, skin side down, on an oiled heavy baking sheet. Fill with the stuffing and bake at 400 degrees for 25 minutes.
11. Heat the tomato sauce while the eggplant is baking.
12. To serve, remove the eggplants from the baking sheet and flip over onto individual serving plates so they are skin side up. Spoon the sauce on top.

Servings: 4   **Preparation: Easy**
Time: Time consuming; some advance preparation necessary

Mushroom-Pancetta Frittata

A frittata is similar to an omelet, though the eggs are not moved in the pan, giving you a slightly denser egg dish. Ham may be substituted for the pancetta or bacon. In this case, do not cook the ham, and use 4 tablespoons butter for cooking the onions and mushrooms.

7 large eggs
2 tablespoons unsalted butter
2 ounces pancetta or bacon, finely diced
4 large shallots, thinly sliced
¼ pound mushrooms, sliced ¼-inch thick
2 tablespoons water
¼ cup loosely packed fresh parsley sprigs, coarsely chopped
slices of tomato for garnish

1. Heat the butter in a heavy ovenproof 12-inch saute pan. Add the pancetta or bacon and saute until light golden brown. Add shallots and saute until clear. Remove from the pan with a slotted spoon.
2. Add the mushrooms to the pan and toss over medium heat until light golden brown. Remove with a slotted spoon and combine with the pancetta and shallots. Add salt and freshly ground black pepper to taste.
3. Check that you have 3 tablespoons fat in the pan. If not, add a little more butter.
4. Whisk the eggs with the water, a pinch of salt, and freshly ground black pepper; add the parsley and whisk until the eggs are emulsified.
5. Preheat broiler.
6. Heat the 3 tablespoons of fat in the pan. Add the eggs and cook on medium heat until the underside is light golden brown (not more than 3 to 5 minutes). Remove the pan from the heat. Spread the mushroom mixture over the eggs and place the pan about 6 inches away from the broiler; broil until light golden brown and the eggs are set on top.
7. Cut the frittata into 6 wedges and place on serving plates, garnished with sliced tomatoes.

Servings: 6   **Preparation: Easy**
Time: Quick

Zucchini Frittata

This lovely, light vegetable frittata is great to make when you have an abundance of garden zucchini and vine-ripened tomatoes.

7 large eggs
4 tablespoons unsalted butter
1 small onion, peeled and thinly sliced
1 small zucchini
2 tablespoons shredded fresh basil leaves
2 tablespoons water
¼ cup freshly grated Parmesan cheese
slices of vine-ripened tomatoes for garnish

1. Coarsely grate the zucchini.
2. Heat 2 tablespoons butter in a heavy ovenproof 12-inch saute pan, add the onion, and saute over medium-high heat until clear. Add the zucchini and toss over high heat for 2 minutes, being careful not to brown. Remove from the pan. Add the basil and salt and freshly ground black pepper to taste.
3. Place the eggs in a bowl, add the water and a little salt and freshly ground black pepper, and whisk until the eggs are well emulsified.
4. Preheat a broiler.
5. Heat the remaining 2 tablespoons butter into the same 12-inch pan, add the eggs, and cook on medium heat until the underside of the eggs is light golden brown (about 3 to 5 minutes). Remove from the heat and spread the zucchini-onion mixture over the eggs. Place the pan about 6 inches from the broiler; broil until light golden brown and the eggs are set on top. Sprinkle with the cheese and broil for 1 more minute.
6. Cut the frittata into 6 wedges and place on serving plates with sliced tomatoes. Serve immediately.

Servings: 6　　**Preparation: Easy**
Time: Quick

Parmesan Crêpes with Broccoli Filling

When making something as simple and delightful as a crêpe, I cannot help but look beyond just a bit to make it even more wonderful. This recipe and the following crêpe recipes have that extra imaginative touch that makes them much more exciting to prepare and to eat.

CRÊPES:
3 large eggs
1¼ cups cold water
½ teaspoon salt
¼ teaspoon freshly ground black pepper
¾ cup all-purpose unbleached flour
½ cup finely grated fresh Parmesan cheese
4 tablespoons butter

FILLING:
1 small bunch broccoli (2 medium stalks) ½ cup blanched
     almonds
1 cup ricotta cheese

SAUCE:
6 tablespoons unsalted butter
6 ounces mushrooms, sliced ⅛-inch thick
2 tablespoons fresh lemon juice

1. Place the eggs, water, salt, and pepper in a blender and blend for 1 minute. Add the flour and blend until the flour is well incorporated into the egg. Pour into a bowl and whisk in the cheese. This batter should not be allowed to rest as is traditional with crêpe batters; proceed with making the crêpes.
2. For making the crêpes, heat 2 teaspoons butter in an 8-inch sloping-sided iron pan, a heavy Teflon pan (use only 1 teaspoon of butter in a Teflon pan), or a heavy stainless steel-lined aluminum pan. When the butter bubbles pour in just under ¼ cup of the batter. Roll the pan so

its whole bottom surface is covered. Cook on medium heat until the bottom of the crêpe is golden brown. Flip or turn it over with a round-ended metal spatula. Cook until the other side is golden brown. Set cooked crêpe on a plate. If the crêpe seems to be too thick, add a little water to the batter to thin its consistency. If the crêpes stick to the pan, you should use more than 2 teaspoons butter for cooking them; this will be true of any Parmesan crêpes. Continue to cook the other crêpes until you have used all the batter. Stack the crêpes one on top of the other, and cool.

3. For the filling, peel the broccoli stems and cut off the flowerettes. Dice the stems into ¼-inch pieces and divide flowerettes into ¼-inch pieces. Bring 2 quarts of water to a boil in a 4-quart stainless steel saucepan, add the broccoli, and cook until just tender. Drain and run under cold water until cool. Drain and pat dry.

4. In a preheated 400-degree oven, bake the almonds on a baking sheet for 7 to 10 minutes until golden brown. Cool, then coarsely chop.

5. Place the ricotta, broccoli, and almonds in a bowl and mix well. Add salt and freshly ground black pepper to taste.

6. The filling and the crêpes may be refrigerated up to 24 hours. I do not recommend freezing the crêpes.

7. Place ¼ cup of the filling on each crêpe and roll up. Butter a 9- by 13-inch ovenproof casserole that is 2- to 3-inches deep, and place the filled crêpes in it. (These may be held for a few hours before baking.)

8. Preheat oven to 400 degrees. Bake the crêpes for 20 minutes. Ten minutes before the crêpes are finished cooking, heat 6 tablespoons butter in a 12-inch saute pan. Add the mushrooms and toss over high heat until light golden brown. Add the lemon juice and salt and freshly ground black pepper to taste; cook for 1 minute.

9. Remove the crêpes from the oven, cover with the mushroom sauce, and serve.

Servings: 4 to 5   Preparation: Fairly difficult
Time: Time consuming; advance preparation possible

Parmesan Crêpes
with Mushroom Filling

If you are able to find at least 2 ounces wild mushrooms—Porcini, Romans, or Tromp de Morts—you will find that they add a wonderful earthy flavor to this dish. (Use up to 4 ounces of Porcini or Tromp de Morts, and up to ½ pound of Romans.) I recommend you use fresh buffalo milk mozzarella if possible, because it is very mild and light in flavor.

CRÊPES:
3 large eggs
1¼ cups cold water
½ teaspoon salt
¼ teaspoon freshly ground black pepper
¾ cup all-purpose unbleached flour
½ cup finely grated fresh Parmesan cheese
4 tablespoons unsalted butter

FILLING:
1 pound mushrooms, sliced ⅛-inch thick
6 tablespoons unsalted butter
¾ cup coarsely grated mozzarella cheese

SAUCE:
¼ cup loosely packed fresh parsley sprigs, finely chopped
6 small vine-ripened tomatoes, peeled, seeded (juice reserved)
3 tablespoons Garlic Butter (page 54)
¼ cup loosely packed fresh basil leaves, finely shredded
8 fresh basil leaves for garnish

1. Place the eggs, water, salt, and pepper in a blender and blend for 1 minute. Add the flour and blend until the flour is well incorporated into the egg. Pour into a bowl and whisk in the cheese. This batter should not be allowed to rest; proceed with making the crêpes.
2. For making the crêpes, heat 2 teaspoons butter in an 8-inch sloping-sided iron pan, a heavy Teflon pan (use only 1 teaspoon of butter in a Teflon pan), or a heavy stainless steel-lined aluminum pan. When the butter bubbles pour in just under ¼ cup of the batter. Roll the pan so

its whole bottom surface is covered. Cook on medium heat until the bottom of the crêpe is golden brown. Flip or turn it over with a round-ended metal spatula. Cook until the other side is golden brown. (If crêpe seems too thick, add a little water to the batter.) Set cooked crêpe on a plate, add a little more butter to the pan, and cook another crêpe. Repeat until you have used all the batter. Stack crêpes one on top of the other, and cool.

3. For the filling, heat 3 tablespoons butter in a 12-inch saute pan. Add half the mushrooms and toss over medium heat until they are light golden brown. Pour into a bowl. Repeat this procedure with the remaining mushrooms. Some liquid might come out of the mushrooms as they cook or as they cool; if so, drain the mushrooms. Cool the mushrooms, then process them in the food processor until they are a coarse puree. Return them to the bowl and add the cheese and parsley, and salt and freshly ground black pepper to taste.

4. The crêpes and the filling may be refrigerated up to 24 hours. Do not freeze the crêpes.

5. Place ¼ cup of the filling on each crêpe and roll up. Butter 9x13x2-inch deep ovenproof casserole dish and place all the filled crêpes in the dish. (These may be held for a few hours before baking.)

6. Preheat oven to 400 degrees. Bake the crêpes for 20 minutes. While the crêpes are baking, heat the garlic butter in a 10- or 12-inch saute pan, add the tomatoes and tomato juice, and stir over high heat for 3 to 5 minutes. Add the shredded basil and salt and freshly ground black pepper to taste.

7. Remove the crêpes from the oven, cover with the sauce, and garnish with the basil leaves before serving.

Servings: 4 to 5   Preparation: Fairly difficult
Time: Time consuming; some advance preparation possible

Thyme Crêpes Florentine

The late Barbara Young and I put this recipe together while I was cooking in South Africa. We used to serve it as an appetizer, but it also makes a great supper dish. The golden raisins are a nice addition when you want a sweeter variation.

CRÊPES:
3 large eggs
1¼ cup cold water
½ teaspoon salt
¼ teaspoon freshly ground black pepper
1 cup all-purpose unbleached flour
1 teaspoon dried thyme leaves
4 tablespoons unsalted butter

FILLING:
1½ cup cooked, drained, and well squeezed fresh spinach
½ cup pine nuts
¼ cup loosely packed fresh mint leaves, coarsely chopped
½ cup golden raisins (optional)

SAUCE:
½ pound mushrooms, sliced ¼-inch thick
6 tablespoons unsalted butter
¼ cup fresh lemon juice

1. Place the eggs, water, salt, and pepper in the blender and blend for 1 minute. Add the flour and blend until the flour is well incorporated into the egg. Add the thyme and blend for 30 seconds. Rest the batter in the refrigerator for at least 1 hour, or up to 8 hours, before making the crêpes. You will notice that the batter will thicken as it stands, so you may need to add a little cold water to thin its consistency. Or you may notice that the first crêpe you cook seems too thick, so you should add a little cold water to the batter.

2. To make the crêpes, heat 2 teaspoons butter in an 8-inch sloping-sided iron pan, a heavy Teflon pan (use only 1 teaspoon of butter in a Teflon

pan), or a heavy stainless steel-lined aluminum pan. When the butter bubbles pour in just under ¼ cup of the batter. Roll the pan so the whole bottom surface is covered. Cook on medium heat until the bottom of the crêpe is golden brown. Flip or turn it over with a round-ended metal spatula. Cook until the other side is golden brown. Set cooked crêpe on a plate, add a little more butter to the pan, and cook another crêpe. Repeat until you have used all the batter. Stack crêpes one on top of the other, and cool.

3. For the filling, finely chop the spinach. Place in a bowl with the pine nuts, mint, and raisins if you are using them. Add salt and freshly ground black pepper to taste.

4. The filling and the crêpes may be refrigerated up to 24 hours. I do not recommend freezing the crêpes.

5. Preheat oven to 400 degrees. Place ¼ cup of the filling on each crêpe and roll up. (The filled crêpes may be held a few hours before baking.) Butter a 9x13x2-inch ovenproof casserole dish and place the filled crêpes in the dish and bake for 20 minutes.

6. Ten minutes before the crêpes are finished cooking, heat 6 table-spoons butter in a 12-inch saute pan, add the mushrooms, and toss over high heat until light golden brown. Add the lemon juice and salt and freshly ground black pepper to taste and cook for 1 minute.

7. Remove the crêpes from the oven, cover with the sauce, and serve.

Servings: 4 as an entree, 8 as an appetizer   **Preparation: Fairly difficult**
Time: Time consuming; some advance preparation possible

Almond Crêpes
with Summer Squash Filling

If you like the flavor of almonds you will love these unusual crêpes. Because the almonds are blanched, their flavor is not as strong as that of the hazelnuts in the hazelnut crêpes. You will need a drop of almond extract to accentuate the nut flavor, but be careful not to overdo it or the flavor will be overpowering. I use a variation of these crêpes for a delicious dessert—Autumn Almond Crêpes on page 487. The squash filling will go well with the mushroom or hazelnut crêpes.

CRÊPES:
3 large eggs
1 1/4 cups cold water
1/2 teaspoon salt
1/4 teaspoon freshly ground black pepper
3/4 cup all-purpose unbleached flour
1/2 cup finely ground blanched almonds
1 drop almond extract
4 tablespoons unsalted butter

FILLING:
2 small summer squash
2 tablespoons unsalted butter
3 large shallots, thinly sliced
1 tablespoon coarsely chopped fresh savory or basil leaves
1/4 cup heavy cream
2 vine-ripened tomatoes, sliced, for garnish

1. Place the eggs, water, salt, and pepper in the blender and blend for 1 minute. Add the flour and blend until it is well incorporated into the egg. Add the almonds and extract and blend for 30 seconds. Rest the batter in the refrigerator at least 1 hour, or up to 8 hours, before making the crêpes. If the batter thickens too much, as it stands, add a little cold

water to thin its consistency. Or, if you notice that the first crêpe you cook seems too thick, add a little water to the batter before cooking any more.

2. Just before making the crêpes, make the filling. Cut the summer squash in half lengthwise, scoop out the seeds, and thinly slice. Heat the 2 tablespoons butter in a 10-inch saute pan, add the shallots, and saute until clear, being careful not to brown. Add the summer squash and saute until it is *al dente.* Add the chopped savory or basil and cream and reduce on high heat for 1 minute. Add salt and freshly ground black pepper to taste. Keep warm.

3. To make the crêpes, heat 2 teaspoons butter in an 8-inch sloping-sided iron pan, a heavy Teflon pan (use only 1 teaspoon of butter in a Teflon pan), or a heavy stainless steel-lined aluminum pan. When the butter bubbles pour in just under ¼ cup of the batter. Roll the pan so the whole bottom surface is covered. Cook on medium heat until the underside of the crêpe is golden brown. Flip or turn it over with a round-ended metal spatula. Cook until the other side is golden brown.

4. Slide half the crêpe onto a serving plate. Top with one-sixth of the squash filling, and flip the rest of the crêpe over the filling. Keep warm as you make the other crêpes. You will need to work quickly.

5. Garnish each plate with tomato and serve immediately.

Servings: 6   Preparation: Fairly easy
Time: Fairly time consuming; some advance preparation possible

Spinach Crêpes

Spinach crêpes make a superb lunch or supper dish. They are good made with Gruyère or Emmenthal cheese, or you may substitute chèvre, cheddar, or your favorite cooking cheese. They also would be nice filled with sauteed mushrooms. These crêpes are thicker than my other crêpes.

CRÊPES:
3 large eggs
3/4 cup cold water
1/2 teaspoon salt
1/4 teaspoon freshly ground pepper
3/4 cup all-purpose unbleached flour
3/4 cup cooked and drained spinach
4 tablespoons unsalted butter.

FILLING:
1 cup coarsely grated Gruyère or Emmenthal cheese
2 medium tomatoes, peeled, seeded, and sliced (preferably vine-ripened)
1 small bunch watercress

1. Place the eggs, water, salt, and pepper in the blender and blend for 1 minute. Add the flour and blend until the flour is well incorporated into the egg. Add the spinach and continue to blend for 1 to 2 minutes, until the spinach is a semicoarse puree. Do not overpuree. Rest the batter in the refrigerator at least 1 hour, or up to 8 hours, before making the crêpes.
2. Remove the coarse stalks from the watercress.
3. Heat 2 teaspoons butter in an 8-inch sloping-sided iron pan, a heavy Teflon pan (use only 1 teaspoon of butter in a Teflon pan), or a heavy stainless steel-lined aluminum pan. When the butter bubbles pour in 1/3 cup of the batter. Roll the pan so the whole bottom surface is covered. Cook on medium heat until the bottom of the crêpe is golden brown and the top is set. At this point it will turn dark green. Flip or turn it over with a round-ended metal spatula.

4. As soon as you turn over the crêpe, sprinkle the center with one-sixth of the cheese. Let the cheese melt, then place one-sixth of the tomato slices in the center and cook the crêpe until the underside is light golden brown.
5. Slide half of the crêpe onto a plate, put one-sixth of the watercress on the crêpe, then flip over the rest of the crêpe. Keep warm and continue to cook the rest of the crêpes. Serve them as soon as you have finished cooking.

Servings: 6   Preparation: Fairly difficult
Time: Fairly time consuming; some advance preparation possible

Hazelnut Asparagus Crêpes

The freshness of the hazelnuts is pivotal to the good taste of this wonderful crêpe. They provide the most gorgeous nutty flavor to the crêpe, and the asparagus filling is very simple and good.

CRÊPES:
1 cup hazelnuts
3 large eggs
1 cup cold water
½ teaspoon salt
¼ teaspoon freshly ground black pepper
½ cup all-purpose unbleached flour
4 tablespoons unsalted butter

FILLING:
1½ pounds peeled fresh asparagus
1 cup crème fraîche or sour cream, room temperature

1. Preheat oven to 400 degrees. Place the hazelnuts on a heavy sheet pan and place in the oven for 7 to 10 minutes until the skins start to crack off and the nuts are a medium brown. Watch them carefully, as they can easily burn. Remove from the oven, cool a little, and rub the skins off. Cool completely and grind until fairly fine in a food processor.
2. Place the eggs, water, salt, and pepper in the blender and blend for 1 minute. Add the flour and blend until the flour is well incorporated into the egg. Add the hazelnuts and blend for 30 seconds. Let the batter rest in the refrigerator at least 1 hour, or up to 4 hours, before making the crêpes.
3. Just before making the crêpes, bring 2 quarts water to a boil in a 4-quart stainless steel saucepan. Add the asparagus and cook for 3 to 5 minutes. Drain and keep warm.
4. To make the crêpes, heat 2 teaspoons butter in an 8-inch sloping-sided iron pan, a heavy Teflon pan (use only 1 teaspoon of butter in a Teflon pan), or a heavy stainless steel-lined aluminum pan. When the butter bubbles pour in just under ¼ cup of the batter. Roll the pan so the

whole bottom surface is covered. Cook on medium heat until the underside of the crêpe is golden brown. Flip or turn it over with a round-ended metal spatula. Continue to cook until the other side is golden brown.

5. Slide half the crêpe onto a serving plate. Place 4 to 6 asparagus in the crêpe, fold over the rest of the crêpe, and keep warm. Cook the rest of the crêpes, working quickly.

6. Garnish crêpes with the crème fraîche or sour cream and serve.

Servings: 6   Preparation: Fairly difficult
Time: Time consuming; some advance preparation possible

Mushroom Crêpes

This crêpe makes excellent use of leftover mushroom stems, but it is equally good made with whole mushrooms. It has a very nice flavor.

CRÊPES:
3 large eggs
¾ cup cold water
½ teaspoon salt
¼ teaspoon freshly ground black pepper
1 cup all-purpose unbleached flour
2 cups well-drained poached mushrooms (page 171)
4 tablespoons unsalted butter

FILLING:
4 medium leeks
1 10-ounce package fresh spinach, washed and dried
4 tablespoons unsalted butter
1 cup grated Emmenthal or Gruyère cheese

1. Place the eggs, water, salt, and pepper in the blender and blend for 1 minute. Add the flour and blend until the flour is well incorporated into the egg. Add the mushrooms and continue to blend for 30 seconds to 1 minute until they are a semi-coarse puree. Rest batter in the refrigerator at least 1 hour, or up to 8 hours, before making the crêpes.
2. For the filling, remove and discard the coarse outside layer of the leeks. Thinly slice the leeks up to the medium-green part. Place slices in cold water for 30 minutes, drain, rinse, drain well, and pat dry.
3. Remove the coarse stalks from the spinach and coarsely shred.
4. Just before making the crêpes, heat 4 tablespoons butter in a 12-inch saute pan, add the leeks, and saute until clear, being careful not to brown. Add the spinach and toss over high heat until it is cooked and the liquid has evaporated. Keep warm.
5. To make crêpes, heat 2 teaspoons butter in an 8-inch sloping-sided iron pan, a heavy Teflon pan (use only 1 teaspoon of butter in a Teflon pan), or a heavy stainless steel-lined aluminum pan. When the butter bubbles pour in ¼ cup of the batter. Roll the pan, so the whole bottom

surface is covered. Cook on medium heat until the underside of the crêpe is light golden brown. Flip or turn it over with a round-ended metal spatula.

6. When you have turned over the crêpe, cover the center with one-sixth of the cheese and continue to cook until the underside is light golden brown. Slide half of the crêpe onto a serving plate, spoon on one-sixth of the spinach mixture, and flip over the other half of the crêpe. Keep the plate warm and continue with the next crêpe, working quickly. Serve the crêpes as soon as you have cooked them all.

Servings: 6   Preparation: Fairly difficult
Time: Time consuming; some advance preparation possible

Pasta

For many years pasta was something you bought at the grocery store and served with meatballs or cheese. It was perceived as something consumed in large quantities by Italians, and by and large it meant macaroni or spaghetti. Today, it is not only readily available in a number of specialty stores across the country, fresh and in all shapes and sizes, but is also easily made in one's own kitchen. Although a bit time consuming to make, I feel there is nothing better than homemade pasta. It can be rolled with a rolling pin or made in a small chrome pasta machine. After you have made it several times it will become as easy as making bread. Be forewarned, however, that you might have problems if you make it on a humid day.

I learned to make pasta with milk, rather than the traditional oil or water, in a cooking class in Milan, Italy.

3 large eggs
2 tablespoons milk
2½ cups all-purpose unbleached flour

1. Place the eggs and milk in a bowl and whisk until the eggs are well emulsified.
2. Place 2 cups flour on a Formica or stainless steel countertop, making a well in the center. With your fingertips, work the flour into the eggs, and continue to work it in until you have a stiff dough. If the dough is soft, work in more flour. The dough should be very stiff. Knead the dough until very smooth and pliable. If the dough gets too soft or sticky, work in a little more flour. Continue to knead the dough until smooth. This will take 5 to 7 minutes.
3. Wrap the dough in plastic wrap and store in a cool place (not the refrigerator) for 1 hour.
4. Divide the dough in half. Rewrap one half in plastic wrap. Lightly flour the dough and roll through the widest setting of the pasta machine. Lightly flour the dough again, fold in thirds, and repeat the roll. Fold the dough in half and roll through the medium-wide setting, lightly dust with flour, fold in thirds, and repeat this rolling procedure twice.
5. Cut the dough in half, fold it in half, and roll through the narrowest setting of the machine.

6. Place dry cotton cloths on several sheet pans.
7. For cannelloni wrappers, cut pasta into 4½x5½-inch rectangles. Place them on the sheet pans leaving a little space between each one. For fettucine or angel hair pasta, use the cutter on the machine; spread the cut pasta loosely over the pans.
8. Use the pasta now or let it dry 1 to 2 hours. Then place it in a container and refrigerate up to 3 days or freeze. If you are storing pasta, it is very important to make sure it is not sticky, or it will clump together.

Servings: 12 to 15 cannelloni wrappers or 5 to 6 servings fettucine
Preparation: Fairly easy
Time: Fairly time consuming; advance preparation possible

Fettucine Cavolfiore

Perhaps cauliflower is not your favorite vegetable. It is truly delicious in this recipe. Be careful not to overcook it when blanching, as you want to get its full crunchy texture in this dish. You may prefer to buy fresh fettucine rather than make your own (see recipe on page 402).

1 pound fresh thin fettucine
½ cup blanched almonds
1 small cauliflower
¼ cup olive oil
1 small onion, finely diced
1 carrot, coarsely grated
4 tablespoons unsalted butter
⅓ cup freshly grated Parmesan cheese
½ cup loosely packed fresh parsley sprigs, finely chopped

1. In a preheated 400-degree oven, bake the almonds on a sheet pan for 7 to 10 minutes or until they are a light golden brown. Be careful they do not burn. Cool, then coarsely chop.
2. Cut the cauliflower in half and remove the core, then cut the cauliflower into very small flowerettes with about a ½-inch stem. Discard the rest of the stems.
3. Bring 2 quarts water to a boil in a 4-quart saucepan, add 1 teaspoon salt and the flowerettes, and cook until they are still slightly crisp in the center. Drain and run under cold water until cool. Drain and pat dry.
4. Bring 3 quarts water to a boil in a 4-quart saucepan and add 1 tablespoon olive oil.
5. While the water is coming to a boil, heat the remaining olive oil in a 12-inch saute pan, and add the onion. Gently saute on medium heat until it is clear, but be careful not to brown. Add the carrot and toss for 2 minutes. Add the cauliflower and almonds and gently saute on low heat for 4 to 5 minutes, being careful not to brown.
6. While the vegetables are sauteing, add the fettucine to the boiling water and boil until tender but *al dente* (4 to 7 minutes). Drain well.
7. Place the butter in a bowl, add the fettucine, Parmesan, and ground black pepper to taste. Toss until well mixed. Put on a serving platter.
8. Combine the cauliflower mixture with the parsley and salt and freshly ground black pepper to taste. Spoon on top of the fettucine, and serve.

Servings: 6   **Preparation: Easy**   **Time: Fairly time consuming**

Fettucine Trote

Peter Pastan is one of the finest chefs that I have ever encountered. His recipes are a revelation, and this rich-tasting dish is one that he passed along to me. I suggest serving it with a salad of watercress, cucumber, croutons, and Creamy Herb Dressing (page 169).

1 pound fresh thin fettucine
2 6- to 8-ounce smoked trout
1 tablespoon vegetable oil
2 tablespoons unsalted butter
½ to ¾ cup light cream
2 teaspoons green peppercorns, drained (optional)

1. Remove the skin from the trout carefully, remove each fillet from the centerbone, and then remove all the bones. It is all right if the fish breaks up during this process, but try to have some 1-inch pieces.
2. Just before serving, bring 3 quarts water to a boil in a 4-quart saucepan, and add the vegetable oil. Boil the fettucine until tender but *al dente,* about 4 to 7 minutes. Drain.
3. While the fettucine is boiling, place the butter, ½ cup cream, and peppercorns in a 12-inch saute pan and bring to a boil. Add the pieces of trout and reheat. Then add the fettucine and gently stir over medium heat for 1 to 2 minutes. If necessary add a little more cream to thin the sauce. Add salt to taste.
4. Place on dinner plates or in a serving bowl, and serve.

Servings: 6   Preparation: Easy
Time: Fairly time consuming

Fettucine Moules

My good friend Mel Pell from the Great Eastern Mussel Farm inspired this recipe. If possible try to obtain farmed mussels because they are plumper, cleaner, and sweeter than shore mussels, but any mussels will suffice.

1 pound fresh thin fettucine
3 pounds mussels in their shells
2 cups mussel poaching liquid (page 12)
3 medium leeks
1 tablespoon olive oil
4 tablespoons unsalted butter
½ cup light cream
¼ cup loosely packed fresh dill sprigs, coarsely chopped

1. Remove and discard the coarse outside layer from the leeks. Thinly slice leeks up to the medium-green part. Place in a bowl of cold water and let soak for 30 minutes. Drain, rinse, drain well, and pat dry.
2. Check that the mussels are still alive by lightly tapping any opened ones on a hard surface. Discard those that do not close. Remove beards from mussels and scrub the shells under running water. (See page 12.)
3. Boil the mussel poaching liquid in a 4-quart stainless steel saucepan. Add half the mussels and simmer gently until cooked, about 5 minutes. Mussels should open about ½-inch. Remove with a slotted spoon and allow to cool. Repeat procedure with remaining mussels. Discard any that remain closed. Freeze the poaching liquid for a future use.
4. Remove all but 6 mussels from the shells.
5. This part of the recipe may be done 8 hours ahead of serving time; refrigerate leeks and mussels.
6. Just before serving, bring 3 quarts water to a boil in a 4-quart saucepan and add the olive oil. Bring the mussels up to room temperature.
7. Add the fettucine and boil until tender but *al dente*, about 4 to 7 minutes. Drain well.

8. While the fettucine is cooking, heat the butter in a 12-inch saute pan, add the leeks, and toss over medium heat until cooked; be careful not to brown. Add the cream and dill, bring to a boil, and turn down to a gentle simmer. Add the mussels and reheat, then add the fettucine and salt and freshly ground black pepper to taste. Toss gently until well mixed. Add more cream if the fettucine seems dry. Pour onto a serving platter and garnish with the 6 mussels in their shells.

Servings: 6　　　**Preparation: Fairly easy**
Time: Time consuming; some advance preparation possible

Cannelloni Bergamo

The mild flavor of this pasta dish is best achieved by the use of Italian parsley; if it is not available, curly parsley will suffice.

> *12 fresh pasta wrappers (page 402)*
> *2 medium leeks*
> *4 tablespoons unsalted butter*
> *2 small carrots, coarsely grated*
> *3 tablespoons vegetable oil*
> *1 teaspoon salt*
> *1 pound ricotta cheese*
> *1/3 cup freshly grated Parmesan cheese*
> *1 large egg*
> *1/3 cup loosely packed fresh Italian parsley sprigs, chopped*
> *1/3 cup loosely packed fresh basil leaves, finely shredded*
> *2 cups Tomato Fennel Sauce (page 15)*
> *1/3 cup toasted pine nuts for garnish (optional)*

1. Remove the coarse outside layer from the leeks. Thinly slice leeks up to the medium-green part. Leave in a bowl of cold water for 30 minutes. Drain, rinse, drain well, and pat dry.
2. Heat the butter in a heavy 10-inch saute pan. Add the leeks and toss over high heat until soft and all the liquid has evaporated, being careful not to brown. Add the carrots and toss over medium heat for 3 minutes, being careful that the vegetables do not brown. Pour into a bowl and cool.
3. While the leeks and carrots are cooking, bring 3 quarts of water to a boil in a 4-quart saucepan. Add 1 tablespoon oil and 1 teaspoon salt, then add the wrappers and boil 3 to 5 minutes until just tender. Drain and run under cold water, separate each wrapper, and pat dry.
4. Combine the ricotta, Parmesan, egg, parsley, and basil with the vegetables, mix well. Add salt and freshly ground black pepper to taste.
5. Place ¼ cup of stuffing on each wrapper and roll up.
6. Brush the remaining 2 tablespoons oil on a 9- by 13-inch ovenproof baking dish that is 2 to 3 inches deep. Place the cannelloni, seam side down, in the dish.
7. Refrigerate the cannelloni, covered, up to 24 hours if you wish.
8. Bring the cannelloni up to room temperature and preheat oven to 400 degrees.
9. Pour the Tomato Fennel Sauce over the cannelloni, place in the oven, and bake for 30 to 40 minutes until cooked through. The cannelloni will puff up a little when cooked. Serve garnished with the toasted pine nuts.

Servings: 6   Preparation: Easy
Time: Time consuming; advance preparation possible

Triple Cheese Cannelloni

Gorgonzola Dolce is an Italian blue cheese with a strong flavor; it really works to perfection in this cannelloni. I have served this dish to people who weren't sure if they liked Gorgonzola; they loved it! If you are unable to find a mild Gorgonzola, you may use chèvre or Pipo Crème blue cheese.

12 fresh pasta wrappers (page 402)
3 tablespoons vegetable oil
1 teaspoon salt
4 ounces mild Gorgonzola cheese
1 pound ricotta cheese
1/3 cup freshly grated Parmesan cheese
1/2 cup loosely packed fresh Italian parsley sprigs, finely chopped
2 cups Pureed Vegetable Sauce (page 18) or Tomato Sauce
    (page 14)
fresh Italian parsley sprigs for garnish

1. Brush 1 to 2 tablespoons oil on an ovenproof casserole that is approximately 9x13 and 2 to 3 inches deep.
2. Bring 3 quarts water to a boil in a 4-quart saucepan. Add 1 tablespoon oil and 1 teaspoon salt, then add the wrappers and boil 3 to 5 minutes until just tender. Drain and run under cold water, then separate each wrapper and pat dry.
3. Crumble the Gorgonzola into a bowl and add the ricotta, Parmesan, and parsley. Mix well. Divide the mixture into 12 portions. Place one portion on a wrapper and roll up. Lay the pasta in the ovenproof casserole, seam side down.
4. Refrigerate the cannelloni, covered, up to 24 hours if you wish.
5. An hour before serving, remove the casserole from the refrigerator and bring up to room temperature. Preheat oven to 400 degrees.
6. Pour the sauce over the pasta and bake, uncovered, for 30 to 40 minutes until cooked through. The cannelloni will puff up a little when it is done. Serve garnished with the parsley sprigs.

Servings: 6   Preparation: Fairly difficult
Time: Time consuming; advance preparation possible

Cannelloni Pesto

This flavorful vegetarian supper dish takes full advantage of the wide-spread popularity of pesto. If you have some frozen pesto it will work well here.

> *12 fresh pasta wrappers (page 402)*
> *2 medium leeks*
> *4 tablespoons unsalted butter*
> *1 small carrot, coarsely grated*
> *3 tablespoons vegetable oil*
> *1 teaspoon salt*
> *1 pound ricotta cheese*
> *1 large egg*
> *1 cup Pesto (page 27)*
> *Pureed Vegetable Sauce (page 18)*
> *fresh basil leaves for garnish*

1. Remove the coarse outside layer from the leeks. Thinly slice leeks up to the medium-green part. Leave in a bowl of cold water for 30 minutes. Drain, rinse, drain well, and pat dry.
2. Heat the butter in a heavy 10-inch saute pan, add the leeks and toss over high heat until soft and all the liquid has evaporated, being careful not to brown. Add the carrots and toss over medium heat for 3 minutes, being careful that they do not brown. Pour into a bowl and cool.
3. While the leeks and carrots are cooking, bring 3 quarts of water to a boil in a 4-quart saucepan. Add 1 tablespoon oil and 1 teaspoon salt, then add the wrappers and boil for 3 to 5 minutes until just tender. Drain, run under cold water, separate each wrapper, and pat dry.
4. Combine the ricotta, egg, and pesto with the cooled vegetables. Add salt and freshly ground black pepper to taste. Divide this filling into 12 parts; place one part on a wrapper and roll up. Fill all 12 wrappers.
5. Brush the remaining 2 tablespoons oil on a 9x13-inch baking dish that is 2 to 3 inches deep. Place the cannelloni, seam side down, in the dish.
6. Refrigerate the cannelloni, covered, up to 24 hours if you wish.
7. Bring the cannelloni up to room temperature and preheat oven to 400 degrees.
8. Pour the Pureed Vegetable Sauce over the cannelloni, place in the oven, and bake for 30 to 40 minutes until cooked through.
9. Serve garnished with basil leaves.

Servings: 6   Preparation: Fairly difficult
Time: Time consuming; advance preparation possible

Cannelloni Veronese

The wonderful flavor of fine prosciutto gives this dish its richness. Serve it with a mushroom watercress salad tossed with a creamy vinaigrette.

12 fresh pasta wrappers (page 402)
3 tablespoons vegetable oil
1 pound ricotta cheese
1/3 cup freshly grated Parmesan cheese
1/3 cup loosely packed fresh basil leaves, finely shredded
1/3 cup loosely packed fresh parsley leaves, finely chopped
1 large egg
12 thin slices of prosciutto
2 cups Tomato Fennel Sauce (page 15)
fresh basil leaves or Italian parsley sprigs for garnish

1. Bring 3 quarts water to a boil in a 4-quart saucepan. Add 1 tablespoon oil and 1 teaspoon salt, then add the wrappers and boil for 3 to 5 minutes until just tender. Drain, run under cold water, separate each wrapper, and pat dry.
2. Mix the ricotta, Parmesan, basil, parsley, and egg in a bowl until well combined. Add salt and freshly ground black pepper to taste.
3. Lay one slice of prosciutto on each wrapper, then 3 to 4 tablespoons of the cheese mixture. Roll up.
4. Brush 1 to 2 tablespoons oil on a 9x13-inch baking dish that is 2 to 3 inches deep. Lay the cannelloni, seam side down, in the dish.
5. You may refrigerate the cannelloni, covered, for 24 hours, if you wish.
6. Remove cannelloni from refrigerator and bring up to room temperature for 60 minutes. Preheat oven to 400 degrees.
7. Pour the sauce over the cannelloni and bake for 30 to 40 minutes until cooked through. Garnish with basil leaves or Italian parsley sprigs.

Servings: 6   Preparation: Fairly difficult
Time: Time consuming; advance preparation possible

Cannelloni Vitello

I was served this cannelloni many years ago in a small Italian restaurant in Kenya. It was such a surprise and delight that I later created the recipe from my memories of it. The fennel flavor comes through in this dish, but you may substitute rosemary if you do not like fennel.

12 fresh pasta wrappers (page 402)
2 leeks
2 teaspoons fennel seed
4 tablespoons olive oil
1 medium onion, finely diced
1 medium carrot, coarsely grated
2 tablespoons dried basil
1 pound ground veal
¼ cup white wine
⅓ cup loosely packed Italian or curly parsley sprigs, chopped
*   medium-fine*
3 tablespoons vegetable oil
Parmesan Sauce (page 32)
fresh Italian parsley leaves for garnish

1. Remove the coarse outside layer from the leeks. Thinly slice leeks up to the medium-green part. Leave the slices in a bowl of cold water for 30 minutes. Drain, rinse, drain well, and pat dry.
2. Blend fennel seeds in a dry blender until coarsely ground, or you may crush them on a board with a knife.
3. Heat the olive oil in a heavy 12-inch saute pan, add the onion and toss over medium heat until clear. Add the leeks and saute for 3 minutes, being careful not to brown. Add the carrot, basil, and coarsely ground fennel seed; saute for 2 minutes. Add the veal and saute until it is cooked. Add white wine and reduce until almost all the liquid has evaporated. Place in a bowl and cool. Add the parsley and salt and freshly ground black pepper to taste.

4. Bring 3 quarts water to boil in a 4-quart saucepan. Add 1 tablespoon vegetable oil and 1 teaspoon salt, then add the wrappers and boil for 3 to 5 minutes until just tender. Drain and run under cold water, then separate each wrapper and pat dry.
5. Divide the stuffing into 12 parts; place one part on a wrapper and roll up.
6. With the remaining 2 tablespoons vegetable oil, oil a 9x13-inch baking dish that is 2 to 3 inches deep. Place the cannelloni, seam side down, in the casserole.
7. The cannelloni may be refrigerated, covered, for 24 hours if you wish.
8. Remove cannelloni from the refrigerator 60 minutes before cooking. Preheat oven to 400 degrees.
9. Pour the Parmesan Sauce over the cannelloni and bake for 30 to 40 minutes until cooked through. Serve garnished with Italian parsley leaves.

Servings: 6   Preparation: Fairly difficult
Time: Time consuming; advance preparation possible

Vegetables

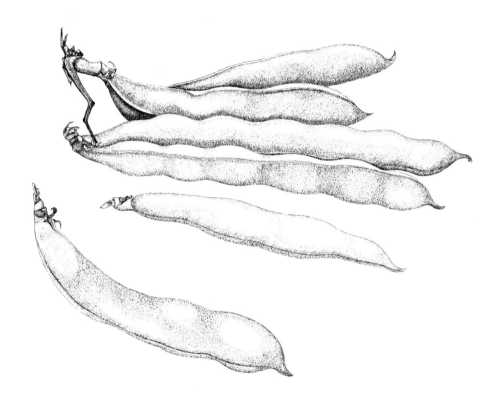

Vegetables

It has long been said that the English enjoy a wonderful growing climate for garden vegetables, but they have been known to overcook them. In 1956 Constance Spry wrote in *The Constance Spry Cookery Book:*

> Perhaps for the young, for whom this book is intended, when grown up, great changes will have taken place in English kitchens, and cooking may have become an accredited art with all its component materials given proper and informed consideration. In the meantime, it is not like that, and the general English public resignedly accepts badly cooked vegetables and is reluctant concerning new introductions, so perhaps I may be allowed to follow at least one line of thought for a moment.
>
> Vegetables, for the most part, are in some degree edible before being cooked, a characteristic which does not distinguish all other foods. Although I know that children like to scrape out uncooked cake mixture from a mixing bowl, most of us could not contemplate testing uncooked fish, meat, or poultry, or even raw egg, and yet we eat raw peas, nibble a bit of juicy cabbage stalk, and eat grated raw root vegetables with pleasure. This may sound irrelevant, but is it? In the cooking of vegetables to make them more digestible, special care must be taken to avoid destroying their intrinsic fresh and delicate flavour.

To further establish the importance of not overcooking vegetables, Henderson, in the *House Keeper's Instructor* (1809), begins his chapter by saying (in old English, which I have translated):

> [Vegetables] should always be brought crisp to the table, which will be affected by being careful not to boil them too much. Such are general observations necessary to be attended to in dressing of vegetables and roots.

So I offer the following advice and recipes with the experience of the English and the lessons I have learned in America.

When purchasing fresh vegetables, there are several criteria to keep in mind. Look for vegetables that are bright in color and crisp or firm in texture. They should be young enough to be tender, but mature enough to be full flavored and ripe. They should be unwilted and free from decay, bruises, and skin punctures. Vegetables that contain an excessive visible amount of sand or soil are a poor purchase. The price of fresh vegetables fluctuates widely with the supply; the weekly market news in the newspaper will be your best source of information as to availability and price. Buy only what you need, because vegetables are so perishable.

How should one choose the vegetables to accompany a dish, and what are the guidelines that one should follow? I think it is extremely important to balance the richness of the vegetable dish with that of the entree. If the entree calls for cream, you should not serve a vegetable requiring a lot of butter or cream. The flavor of a vegetable and the color of the vegetable should also balance. To give you an example. Pureed turnips are not good with delicate dishes, and steamed carrots are not great served with dishes that involve red tomato sauce. The strength of the turnips will overpower the delicacy of the entree and the carrots will not stand up to the flavor of the tomato sauce. They will also conflict with the color.

In the case of this book, where many of the entrees are rich or involve very definite flavors, I look at the richness of the whole meal, the color, and the intensity of the flavors. I think it is appetizing to balance such recipes with steamed, crisp green vegetables. It is important to ensure that your vegetables are seasonal and young; the seasonal availability of vegetables will influence both quality and price. Therefore, for many of my rich and flavorful entrees, I suggest serving lightly steamed asparagus, green beans, broccoli, or peas. They are not only appealing to the eye, but also are a fine complement to the meal. I do not recommend adding an acid (vinegar or lemon juice) to a green vegetable because it will change the color to an unappetizing brownish-green. Also, I feel that it distracts from the true flavor of some vegetables. I like to savor the flavor of steamed asparagus, for example, and feel that acid takes away from the wonderful taste. If you wish, you can garnish the vegetable with a wedge of lemon or lime, which can be squeezed on to your taste.

Other entrees in this book are perfect with many of the vegetable recipes included in this chapter. You also will find that many of these vegetables will beautifully enhance a plain meat, poultry, or seafood entree.

White Bean Tomato Stew

Let's bring dried beans back into our diet. This casserole is easy to make and wonderful to serve as an alternative to potatoes or rice. It is good with a spicy main dish such as Creole Roast Pork (page 368) or simple dishes like a roast chicken.

½ pound white navy beans, well washed
¼ cup olive oil
1 onion, finely diced
4 medium tomatoes, peeled, seeded, and diced (juice reserved)
1 small bay leaf
4 to 6 cups water (or canned low-salt chicken broth)
⅓ cup loosely packed fresh parsley sprigs, finely chopped

1. Pick over the beans carefully to check for any stones.
2. Soak the beans in cold water for 2 hours. Drain.
3. Heat the oil in a 3-quart saucepan, add the onion, and saute until clear. Add the beans, tomatoes, tomato juice, bay leaf, and water or chicken broth. Gently simmer for 1½ to 2 hours until the beans are tender. If the liquid evaporates and the bean mixture gets really thick, add a little more water.
4. The stew may be refrigerated for 2 to 3 days.
5. Just before serving, reheat, and add salt and freshly ground black pepper to taste. Add the parsley and cook for 2 to 3 minutes. Remove the bay leaf just before serving.

Servings: 8   Preparation: Easy
Time: Time consuming; advance preparation possible

Black Bean Stew

Try this richly flavored, very satisfying stew with Carne Asado (page 356), Creole Roast Pork (page 368), or a grilled swordfish. I like to garnish the stew with avocado or crème fraîche.

1 pound dried black beans
2 tablespoons vegetable oil
2 slices pancetta, thinly sliced (or 2 ounces salt pork)
1 large onion, finely diced
2 teaspoons dried crushed red hot pepper
5 medium tomatoes, peeled, seeded, and chopped (juice reserved)
1 bay leaf

1. Pick over the beans carefully to check for any stones. Soak the beans in cold water for 1 hour. Drain.
2. Very finely dice the pancetta. If you are using salt pork, remove and discard the rind. Heat the oil in a heavy 3-quart saucepan, add the pancetta or salt pork, and saute until light golden brown.
3. Add the onion and hot pepper and saute over medium heat until the onion is clear.
4. Add the tomatoes, tomato juice, bay leaf, black beans, and enough water to come 1 inch above the beans. Gently simmer for 1½ to 2 hours, stirring occasionally to keep the stew from scorching on the bottom of the pan. If the stew becomes too thick as it is cooking, add more water.
5. When the beans are very tender, add salt to taste.
6. The stew may be refrigerated for 2 days. Cool it completely before storing it in the refrigerator.
7. Before serving, reheat stew in a heavy saucepan, covered, on a low to medium heat. If the mixture is too thick, add a little water.

Servings: 8 to 10   Preparation: Easy
Time: Time consuming; advance preparation possible

Cabbage with
Parsley and Caraway

This vegetable dish is great served with chicken, game, or pork.

1 small cabbage
1 teaspoon caraway seeds
4 tablespoons unsalted butter
½ cup loosely packed fresh parsley sprigs, chopped
2 hard-boiled eggs, finely chopped (optional)

1. Remove the coarse outside leaves from the cabbage. Cut the cabbage into quarters through the core. Remove core and discard. Very finely slice or shred the cabbage.
2. Bring 2 quarts salted water to a boil in a 4-quart saucepan. Add the cabbage and bring to a boil. Boil for 3 to 5 minutes until the cabbage is still slightly crisp. Drain into a colander and immediately run under cold water until cool. Drain well, then pat dry.
3. The cabbage may be cooked a day before serving and refrigerated.
4. Just before serving, heat the butter with the caraway seeds in a 12-inch saute pan. Add the cabbage and saute over high heat until heated through (about 3 to 5 minutes). Be careful it does not brown. Add the parsley and chopped egg, and salt and freshly ground black pepper to taste. Serve immediately.

Servings: 6   Preparation: Easy
Time: Fairly time consuming; some advance preparation possible

Cabbage With Prosciutto

Although this dish includes pork (prosciutto), I find it works quite well with pork dishes. It is also great with beef.

1 small cabbage
1¼-inch slice of prosciutto
2 tablespoons unsalted butter
2 tablespons vegetable oil
½ cup loosely packed fresh parsley sprigs, chopped

1. Remove the coarse outside leaves from the cabbage. Cut the cabbage into quarters through the core. Very finely slice or shred the sections, discarding the core.
2. Bring 2 quarts of water to a boil in a 4-quart saucepan. Add the cabbage and bring up to a boil. Boil for 3 to 5 minutes; the cabbage should still be slightly crisp in texture. Drain into a colander and immediately run under cold water until cool. Leave in the colander for at least 30 minutes until well drained.
3. Dice the prosciutto into ¼-inch pieces.
4. The recipe may be made up to this point a day in advance. Refrigerate the cabbage and prosciutto.
5. Just before serving, heat the butter and oil in a large saute pan. Add the prosciutto and cook on a very low heat for 2 minutes. Turn up the heat to high and add the cabbage. Toss the cabbage until heated through. Be careful it does not brown. This will take about 5 minutes. Add the parsley and freshly ground black pepper to taste.

Servings: 6   Preparation: Easy
Time: Quick; some advance preparation possible

Braised Red Cabbage

This dish is a tasty and colorful accompaniment for pork and game entrees.

1 small red cabbage
¼ cup vegetable oil
1 medium onion, thinly sliced
1 medium carrot, thinly sliced
3 to 4 tablespoons red wine vinegar
1 tart apple, peeled and diced
¼ cup water
1 teaspoon sugar

1. Remove and discard the coarse outside leaves from the cabbage. Cut it into quarters, remove the core, and very thinly slice.
2. Heat the oil in a 4-quart saucepan, add onion and carrot, and saute over medium heat for 3 minutes.
3. Add cabbage, 3 tablespoons vinegar, apple, ¼ cup of water, and the sugar. Braise, uncovered, over medium heat for 30 to 40 minutes, until the cabbage is very well cooked, but not brown. Stir the cabbage occasionally as it cooks. If the liquid evaporates while cooking, add a little more water to keep the cabbage from scorching.
4. When the cabbage is tender, if there is a lot of liquid in the pan, turn up the heat under the pan and stir constantly until the liquid has evaporated.
5. Add salt, freshly ground black pepper, and more vinegar to taste.
6. This can be refrigerated for 2 days, if you wish. Reheat, covered, in a 350-degree oven for 40 minutes.

Servings: 6   Preparation: Easy
Time: Fairly time consuming; advance preparation possible

Carrot Ginger Puree

The ginger provides a wonderful flavor in this carrot puree. It is ideal served with roast chicken and lamb dishes, especially Lamb Chops Diane (page 336).

1½ pounds peeled carrots, coarsely grated
1 tablespoon peeled and grated ginger
6 tablespoons unsalted butter
¼ cup water

1. Heat the butter, water, and ginger in a heavy 2-quart saucepan. Add the carrots, cover, and gently simmer, covered, for 10 minutes. Stir; if the pan is dry, add another ¼ cup water. Continue to gently simmer, covered, for 30 minutes, stirring occasionally to be certain that the mixture does not scorch.
2. Puree in the food processor until smooth.
3. This may be refrigerated up to 3 days or frozen.
4. Gently reheat the puree in a heavy saucepan, stirring occasionally. Add salt and freshly ground black pepper to taste.

Servings: 4 to 6   Preparation: Easy
Time: Fairly time consuming; advance preparation possible

Carrots Noisette

This recipe presents a very different combination of flavors. It is wonderful served with roast chicken or lamb.

1 pound carrots
4 tablespoons unsalted butter
2 tablespoons water
2 to 3 tablespoons dry sherry
½ cup freshly cracked walnuts

1. Slice the carrots ⅛-inch thick on the diagonal, then cut the slices ⅛-inch thick into matchstick-shaped (julienne) pieces.
2. Just before serving, heat the butter in a heavy 12-inch saute pan. Add the 2 tablespoons water and the carrots, and toss over medium heat for 3 to 4 minutes until the carrots are almost tender. If the carrots start to brown, add a little more water.
3. Turn up the heat, add the sherry and walnuts, and toss the carrots until the liquid has evaporated. Add salt and freshly ground black pepper to taste. Serve immediately.

Servings: 6   **Preparation: Easy**
Time: Quick

Glazed Carrots Swedish Style

These carrots are wonderful served with roast lamb, beef tenderloin, or pork.

1 pound carrots
4 tablespoons unsalted butter
2 tablespoons fresh lemon juice
¼ cup loosely packed fresh dill sprigs, finely chopped

1. Slice the carrots ⅛-inch thick on the diagonal. Then cut the slices into ⅛-inch-thick matchstick-shaped (julienne) pieces, or you may very thinly slice them on the diagonal.
2. Heat the butter in a 12-inch saute pan and add the lemon juice and the carrots. Over medium heat, toss the carrots 4 to 5 minutes until almost tender. If the carrots start to brown, add 2 to 3 tablespoons water and continue to cook a few more minutes to required doneness.
3. Add the dill, and then add salt and freshly ground black pepper to taste, and serve immediately.

Servings: 6   **Preparation: Easy**
Time: Quick

Pureed Carrots and Tomatoes

I love the slightly tart flavor that the tomatoes give to this recipe. It is very good with many entrees; try it with my Veal Clancy (page 350). It is an ideal way to use up ripe—even slightly overripe—vine-ripened tomatoes in the summer, because it can be frozen.

1 pound carrots
4 medium vine-ripened or hothouse tomatoes, peeled, seeded, and chopped (juice reserved)
6 tablespoons unsalted butter
1 tablespoon dried tarragon (or ¼ cup loosely packed fresh tarragon leaves, coarsely chopped)

1. Grate the carrots on a medium-size grater.
2. Heat the butter in a 2-quart stainless steel saucepan. Add the carrots, tomatoes, and tomato juice. If you are using dried tarragon, add it at this point. Cook over medium heat for 20 to 30 minutes, stirring occasionally to make sure the mixture does not scorch on the bottom of the pan. Cook until the mixture is thick and almost all the liquid has evaporated.
3. Puree the mixture in a food processor or blender until very smooth. If you are using fresh tarragon, add it at this point and puree for 30 seconds. Add salt and freshly ground black pepper to taste.
4. Refrigerate up to 2 days, if desired, or freeze. Before serving, reheat in a saucepan, or pipe into tart shells and reheat.

Servings: 6 to 8   Preparation: Easy
Time: Fairly time consuming; may be frozen

Cauliflower With Ginger

The addition of lemon and ginger gives this dish a really clean taste. The hot pepper should be adjusted to the level of spiciness that you desire. This vegetable dish goes well with roast beef or lamb.

1 small head of cauliflower
6 tablespoons unsalted butter
1 slightly heaping tablespoon peeled and very thinly sliced fresh
   ginger
3 tablespoons fresh lemon juice
½ teaspoon dried crushed red hot pepper

1. Cut the cauliflower in half and cut out the core. Cut the cauliflower into small flowerettes, leaving ¼- to ½-inch stalks.
2. Bring 2 quarts water to a boil in a 4-quart saucepan. Add 1 teaspoon salt and the cauliflower, and gently boil until almost tender. (The cauliflower should still be crisp on the inside.) Drain and run under cold water until cool.
3. The cauliflower can be refrigerated for 24 hours, if you wish.
4. Just before serving, heat the butter, ginger, lemon juice, and hot pepper in a 3-quart saucepan on low heat. Gently simmer for 2 minutes, stirring occasionally.
5. Add the cauliflower and gently simmer, uncovered, for 2 to 3 minutes, stirring occasionally. Turn up the heat and cook on high heat until almost all the liquid has evaporated, being careful not to brown. Add salt and freshly ground black pepper to taste and serve immediately.

Servings: 6   Preparation: Easy
Time: Quick; some advance preparation possible

Celery Root Puree

If you are not familiar with celery root, I encourage you to try this recipe. Light and creamy in texture, it has a nice, mild celery flavor. Served in individual tart shells, or by itself, Celery Root Puree goes well with pork or beef.

2 medium celery roots (1 to 1½ pounds)
6 tablespoons unsalted butter
¼ cup loosely packed fresh parsley sprigs, finely chopped

1. Peel the celery roots; cut them into ½-inch slices.
2. Bring 2 quarts of water to a boil in a 4-quart saucepan. Add the sliced celery roots and 1 teaspoon salt, and gently boil for 20 to 30 minutes until tender. Be careful not to overcook, or they will lose some flavor. Drain and let stand in a colander for 10 minutes.
3. While still warm, place the celery root in the food processor with the butter, and puree until smooth.
4. If the mixture is not thick, return it to the pan, and reduce over medium heat until thick, stirring all the time.
5. Add the parsley and salt and freshly ground black pepper to taste.
6. The puree can be refrigerated for 3 days, reheat it before serving.

Servings: 6   **Preparation: Easy**
Time: Fairly time consuming; advance preparation possible

Sauteed Cucumbers and Peas

Salting the cucumbers will change their texture; although they appear soft, they actually are crunchier to taste. This is a wonderful vegetable dish for poultry, such as Chicken Maurice (see page 292) or fish. If you serve it with fish in a cream sauce, use the unsalted butter in the recipe; if you serve it with grilled fish, use the olive oil.

1 medium English cucumber
2 tablespoons olive oil or unsalted butter
1 cup fresh young peas (or frozen peas)
2 tablespoons chopped fresh mint

1. Peel the cucumber. Cut in half lengthwise and thinly slice. Place layers of cucumber slices in a colander and lightly salt between each layer. Let stand for 1 hour. Then rinse under running cold water for 3 minutes. Drain very well and pat dry.
2. Blanch the peas in boiling water until *al dente,* drain, and then run under cold water until cool.
3. The cucumbers and peas may be refrigerated up to 8 hours.
4. Just before serving, heat the oil or butter in a 12-inch saute pan and add the cucumbers and peas. Toss over high heat until heated through. Add the chopped mint, and salt and freshly ground black pepper to taste.

Servings: 4   Preparation: Easy
Time: Fairly time consuming; advance preparation possible

Broiled Eggplant

Broiled Eggplant should be served hot or at room temperature. It goes wonderfully with barbecued lamb and may be grilled along with the lamb.

2 medium eggplants, unpeeled
½ cup olive oil
1 lemon or fresh Italian parsley sprigs for garnish

1. Slice the eggplants ½-inch thick.
2. Place a layer of eggplant in a colander, lightly sprinkle with salt, cover with more eggplants, lightly salt, and continue until all the eggplant is used up. Leave in the colander for 2 hours, then rinse under cold water and pat dry.
3. Preheat broiler. Dip the eggplant in the oil. Place the eggplant on a broiler pan 4 inches away from the flame and broil until golden brown on one side. Turn and broil until golden brown on the other side.
4. Place the eggplant on a serving dish and spoon over any remaining oil. Garnish with lemon wedges or parsley.

Servings: 6   Preparation: Easy
Time: Time consuming

Black-Eyed Peas with Mushrooms

This vegetable dish is superb with a spicy beef or chicken dish.

2 10-ounce packages frozen black-eyed peas, thawed (or 2½
    cups fresh)
½ pound mushrooms
4 tablespoons unsalted butter
2 small garlic cloves, finely diced or crushed
1 cup light cream

1. Slice the mushrooms ¼-inch thick.
2. Heat the butter in a heavy 12-inch saute pan. Add the garlic, and gently saute on low heat being careful not to brown. Add the mushrooms and toss over medium heat until just cooked.
3. Add the black-eyed peas and cream, cover, and gently simmer for 20 to 25 minutes, stirring occasionally. If the mixture becomes too thick, add a little water.
4. Add salt and freshly ground black pepper to taste and serve immediately.

Servings: 6 to 8   **Preparation: Easy**
Time: Quick

Chick Peas with Spinach

If you are unfamiliar with chick peas, I suggest you try this delicious vegetable dish. It is a great way to use chick peas, giving you an interesting recipe that is wonderful served with grilled or barbecued lamb.

> 2 16- to 18-ounce cans chick peas, drained
> 1 10-ounce package fresh spinach
> ⅓ cup olive oil
> 3 small garlic cloves, crushed
> ½ cup loosely packed fresh parsley leaves, coarsely chopped

1. Wash the spinach and drain well. Remove and discard the coarse stalks. Coarsely shred the spinach leaves.
2. Heat the olive oil in a heavy 12-inch saute pan. Add the garlic and cook on low heat for 1 minute, being careful not to brown. Add the spinach, chick peas, and parsley and toss over high heat for 5 minutes, stirring constantly. Add salt and freshly ground black pepper to taste. Serve immediately.

Servings: 8   **Preparation: Easy**
Time: Quick

Red Russet Potatoes with Chèvre

This combination of chèvre and potatoes is delicious, and made even more special by the use of fresh thyme or chives. For an especially attractive presentation, you can pipe the potato mixture into the potato skins, but it is acceptable to spoon in the mixture. If you use very small potatoes you can use this as an hors d'oeuvre.

> *2 pounds medium-sized red russet potatoes (12 to 16 potatoes),*
> *well scrubbed*
> *½ cup milk*
> *2 tablespoons unsalted butter*
> *6 ounces Montrachet chèvre with no ash, crumbled*
> *1 tablespoon fresh thyme leaves, finely chopped, or 2*
> *tablespoons finely snipped chives*

1. Place the potatoes in a 2- to 3-quart saucepan, cover with cold water, and bring them to a boil. Lower the heat and gently boil the potatoes for 15 to 20 minutes until they are just tender, being very careful not to overcook them.
2. Drain the potatoes. Cut them in half lengthwise so they will lie flat without tipping over. While potatoes are still warm, scoop out the inside using a melon baller or teaspoon, leaving approximately a ⅛-inch rim of potato in the skin. Don't try to remove all the potato, or the skin will fall apart. Set the skins aside.
3. Put the potato in a food mill, potato ricer, or press through a sieve; this step will get rid of any lumps. Do not use a food processor as it will give the potato a very pasty mixture.
4. Place the milk and butter in a heavy saucepan with the sieved potatoes and chèvre. Cover and simmer on low heat for 5 minutes, stirring occasionally to make sure the mixture does not scorch on the bottom of the pan. Add thyme or chives and salt and freshly ground black pepper to taste. Cool to room temperature; it is easier to pipe the potato mixture when it is warm rather than hot.
5. Pipe the potato mixture into the potato skins, using a wide pipe, or spoon the potato into the skins.
6. The potatoes may be refrigerated for 24 hours.
7. Before serving, preheat oven to 350 degrees. Bake potatoes on a buttered sheet pan for 15 to 20 minutes until hot.

Servings: 8   Preparation: Fairly easy
Time: Fairly time consuming; advance preparation possible

Potatoes with Mushrooms

This is a lovely, rich potato dish, which is wonderful served with roast beef or lamb. My preference is to keep the skins on the potatoes. The capers add a nice piquancy to the potatoes.

2 pounds red russet or new potatoes, well scrubbed
½ pound mushrooms, coarsely chopped
6 tablespoons unsalted butter
1 medium onion, very finely diced
1 cup light cream
2 tablespoons capers (optional)
⅓ cup loosely packed fresh parsley sprigs, finely chopped

1. Place the potatoes in a 2- to 3-quart saucepan, cover with cold water, and bring them to a boil. Lower the heat and gently boil the pototoes for 15 to 20 minutes until they are just tender, being very careful not to overcook them.
2. Drain the potatoes and run under cold water for 3 minutes. Let them drain until cool.
3. Heat the butter in a heavy 12-inch saute pan, add the onion, and saute for 2 to 3 minutes until clear, being careful not to brown. Add the mushrooms and toss over high heat until light golden brown.
4. Add the cream and gently simmer for 5 minutes.
5. Meanwhile, with a very sharp knife, cut the potatoes in half lengthwise. Slice them ¼-inch thick.
6. Add the potatoes to the pan and gently simmer for 5 minutes. Turn up the heat and reduce, stirring occasionally, until the sauce is fairly thick.
7. Add the capers, parsley, and salt and freshly ground black pepper to taste. Simmer for 1 minute.
8. This dish can be refrigerated for one day, if you wish. Reheat, covered, in a 350-degree oven. Should the mixture be too thick, stir in a little milk.

Servings: 8   Preparation: Easy
Time: Fairly time consuming; advance preparation possible

Potatoes with Basil

This potato side dish really enhances a spicy fish or meat dish. My preference is to leave the potato skins on; however, you should use a sharp knife for slicing the potatoes or the skins will start to come off.

1½ pounds red russet or new potatoes, well scrubbed
4 tablespoons vegetable oil
1 medium onion, thinly sliced
1 to 2 tablespoons white wine basil or tarragon vinegar
¼ cup loosely packed fresh basil leaves, shredded

1. Place the potatoes in a 2- to 3-quart saucepan, cover with cold water, and bring to a boil. Lower the heat and gently boil the potatoes for 15 to 20 minutes until they are just tender, being very careful not to overcook them.
2. Drain and run under cold water for 3 minutes, then leave to drain until cool. Cut the potatoes in half lengthwise and slice ¼-inch thick.
3. The potatoes can be refrigerated for 2 days.
4. Just before serving, heat the oil in a heavy 12-inch saute pan. Add the onion and toss over medium heat until clear; do not brown.
5. Add the potatoes and 1 tablespoon vinegar and gently toss over high heat for 4 to 5 minutes. Add the basil and salt, freshly ground black pepper, and more vinegar to taste. Serve immediately.

Servings: 4 to 6　　**Preparation: Easy**
Time: Quick

Rice and Potato Pilaf

This unusual combination of two starches is magnificent in this absolutely wonderful side dish. Try it with meat or poultry casseroles. You should adjust the amount of hot pepper to your taste.

¾ cup converted raw rice
2 medium potatoes, peeled
2 medium onions, finely diced
8 tablespoons unsalted butter
1 jalapeño pepper, finely diced (or 1 teaspoon dried crushed red
*   hot pepper)*
½ cup loosely packed fresh parsley sprigs, finely chopped
⅓ cup loosely packed fresh mint leaves, coarsely chopped

1. Place rice in a saucepan and cover with 4 cups cold water. Bring to a boil, stir, and then simmer until rice is just cooked, being careful not to overcook. Drain, then run cold water over the rice. Drain well.
2. Cut the potatoes into a ¼-inch dice. Place them in cold water until you are ready to cook.
3. Heat butter in a heavy 12-inch saute pan. Add the onions and saute until clear, being careful not to brown. Add pepper and saute for 1 minute. Add potatoes, cover, and saute on gentle heat until potatoes are tender. Stir occasionally to make sure the mixture does not stick to the pan or brown.
4. When potatoes are cooked, add rice and parsley and stir until heated through. If the mixture sticks to the pan, add a little water. Just before serving, add the mint and salt and freshly ground black pepper to taste.

Servings: 8   Preparation: Easy
Time: Fairly time consuming

Creamed Spinach

My Creamed Spinach is a fine accompaniment for Chicken Lundi (page 305) and especially good with a simple grilled fish or chicken.

1 10-ounce package fresh spinach
3 tablespoons unsalted butter
1 small onion, finely chopped
2 teaspoons cake flour
½ cup light cream
pinch of freshly grated nutmeg

1. Wash well and drain the spinach. Remove the coarse stalks.
2. Bring 2 quarts of water to a boil in a 4-quart saucepan. Add 1 teaspoon salt and the spinach and boil for 1 minute.
3. Drain the spinach immediately and run it under cold water until it is cool. Let it drain at least 30 minutes and then squeeze well until all the excess water is removed (or it is quite dry).
4. The spinach may be refrigerated up to 24 hours.
5. Just before serving, heat the butter in a 2- to 3-quart saucepan. Add the onion and gently saute over medium heat until it is clear, being careful not to brown.
6. Remove the pan from the heat and stir in the flour. Return it to the heat and cook for 30 seconds, stirring all the time. Remove from the heat and add the cream all at once. Return it to the heat and bring to a boil, stirring all the time. Lower the heat and gently simmer for 3 minutes.
7. Add the spinach, nutmeg, and salt and freshly ground black pepper to taste, and reheat.

Servings: 4   Preparation: Easy
Time: Fairly time consuming; advance preparation necessary

Summer Squash with Tarragon

If you are trying to stay away from oil and butter, this vegetable dish is ideal.

2 small summer squash
2 teaspoons dried tarragon or 1½ tablespoon fresh tarragon
   leaves

1. Wash the squash. Cut it in half lengthwise, scoop out the seeds, and thinly slice.
2. Place squash and tarragon in a steamer and gently steam until cooked, about 5 to 7 minutes. Add salt and freshly ground black pepper to taste. Serve immediately.

Servings: 4   **Preparation: Easy**
Time: Quick

Sauteed Green Vegetables

This is a light dish, with a wonderful combination of flavors. It is delicious with fish.

1 medium leek
2 small zucchini
1 10-ounce package fresh spinach
1 cup frozen, thawed, or young fresh peas
4 tablespoons unsalted butter

1. Remove and discard the coarse outside layers from the leeks. Thinly slice the leek up to the medium-green part. Soak in cold water for 30 minutes. Drain, rinse, drain well, and pat dry.
2. Cut the zucchini in half lengthwise. With a tomato shark or teaspoon, scoop out the seeds, and cut into thin slices.
3. Wash the spinach and drain well. Remove and discard the stalks. Coarsely shred the leaves.
4. Just before serving, heat the butter in a heavy 12-inch saute pan. Add the leeks and saute until soft; be careful not to brown. Add the zucchini and peas. On medium heat, toss for 3 to 5 minutes until the zucchini is *al dente.* If the pan becomes dry, add 2 tablespoons water. Add the spinach and toss on high heat, about 2 minutes, until cooked. Be careful not to overcook or the mixture will become watery. Add salt and freshly ground black pepper to taste. Serve immediately.

Servings: 6   **Preparation: Easy**
Time: Quick

Crunchy Zucchini

This method of preparation gives the zucchini a crunchy texture. It can be served chilled as a garnish for a seafood or chicken salad, or very lightly sauteed in butter or olive oil and served as a vegetable dish. It is not good the next day, however, as it turns bitter as it stands.

3 small zucchini, unpeeled

1. Scrub zucchini well. Cut them into ⅛-inch-thick slices. Place a layer of slices in a colander and lightly sprinkle with salt. Repeat this procedure until all the slices are used up.
2. Let them stand one hour. Rinse under cold water for 3 minutes, and then drain for at least 30 minutes. Pat dry.
3. It may be chilled up to 6 hours. Serve as a salad, or toss over medium heat in olive oil or butter and serve hot.

Servings: 6 to 8   Preparation: Easy
Time: Quick; advance preparation necessary

Butternut Squash Puree

The addition of the brandy or cognac turns the squash into a elegant dish. It is ideal for a holiday dinner. When peeling the squash, be careful to constantly wash your hands, as a film develops that you will find very hard to remove.

2 pounds butternut squash
6 tablespoons unsalted butter
3 tablespoons brandy or cognac

1. Peel the butternut squash, cut in half lengthwise, and scoop out the seeds. Cut the butternut into 2-inch pieces.
2. Bring 2 quarts of water to a boil in a 4-quart saucepan. Add the butternut and 1 teaspoon salt and simmer until tender, about 15 to 20 minutes. Be careful not to overcook or the butternut will lose some flavor.
3. Drain the butternut and leave it to drain 10 minutes. Then, while it is still warm, place it in a food processor with the butter and cognac and puree until smooth.
4. If the mixture is not thick, return to the pan and reduce over medium heat, stirring all the time.
5. Add salt and freshly ground black pepper to taste.
6. This mixture can be refrigerated up to 3 days or frozen.
7. Reheat it in a heavy saucepan, or in a 350-degree oven, covered, for 40 minutes.

Serves: 6   Preparation: Easy
Time: Fairly time consuming; may be frozen

Polenta

Admittedly, polenta should not be included in this chapter because it is not a vegetable, but I use it as many people use potatoes. In the restaurant I often serve broiled polenta as a side dish to roasted meat, poultry, or game birds. I also like broiled polenta as an entree, on a bed of fresh spinach or served with a tomato or tomato-meat sauce. As an entree, this recipe will serve 4 to 6.

2 cups yellow cornmeal
4 cups milk
1 small onion, sliced
1 small carrot, sliced
1 small bay leaf
1½ cup cold water
¾ cup freshly grated Parmesan cheese
2 tablespoons unsalted butter.

1. Place the milk, onion, carrot, and bay leaf in a 2- to 3-quart saucepan. Gently simmer for 40 minutes.
2. While this simmers, mix the cornmeal with the cold water and let it stand.
3. Butter a 9- by 9-inch pan.
4. Strain the vegetables out of the milk and discard. Pour the milk over the cornmeal mixture. Return the mixture to the saucepan and cook on medium heat. Whisk the mixture all the time until it is very stiff, approximately 5 to 7 minutes. Remove from the heat and whisk in the Parmesan and 2 tablespoons butter, and add salt and freshly ground black pepper to taste.
5. Pour the mixture into the sheet pan, cool, and then refrigerate for at least 2 hours, or up to 24 hours.
6. Preheat broiler.
7. Just before serving, cut the polenta into 1½- to 2-inch rounds with a cookie cutter and place on a buttered sheet pan. Broil 4 to 6 inches from the broiler until brown and heated through. Serve immediately.

Servings: 8   Preparation: Easy
Time: Fairly time consuming; some advance preparation necessary

Mushrooms Delon

This subtle Japanese mushroom—introduced only recently in this country—claims its own clean, simple distinction. As a side dish it is ideal with fish or meat dishes. It is also delicious as an appetizer.

½ pound Shiitake mushrooms, cleaned
4 medium vine-ripened tomatoes, peeled and seeded
4 tablespoons Garlic Butter, soft (page 54)
½ cup loosely packed fresh Italian parsley, coarsely chopped
6 sprigs fresh parsley for garnish

1. Remove and discard the stems from the mushrooms. Slice mushrooms ¼-inch thick. Cut the tomatoes into thin julienne strips.
2. Cover the bottom of a heavy shallow metal casserole dish with half the garlic butter. Arrange mushrooms on butter, then dot with remaining butter.
3. Refrigerate up to 4 hours.
4. Just before serving, preheat a broiler.
5. Place mushrooms under broiler and broil until they start to turn a very light golden brown. Remove from broiler and stir in tomatoes and chopped parsley. Continue to broil until the top of the mushrooms and tomatoes starts to turn a very light golden brown. Remove. Stir mixture so vegetables underneath come to the top. Broil until they start to turn a very light golden brown.
6. Remove from broiler. Add salt and freshly ground black pepper to taste. Serve immediately, garnished with parsley sprigs.

Servings: 4 to 6   Preparation: Easy
Time: Quick; some advance preparation possible

Desserts

Desserts

Desserts have held the fascination of more people than any other area of cooking. From the time you are a child and taste your first bite of ice cream, you are sold on the idea that nothing tastes as great as desserts. Every cookbook has a chapter about them and many cookbooks deal solely with them.

I have attempted to present recipes that not only continue that fascination, but also stretch the imagination beyond the normal. I have included a selection of chocolate desserts that are rich and heavy, but far from the common. There is a lighter side in the fruit desserts and a chilling delight in the ice creams.

You will find some of these desserts easy to make—a simple last-minute addition to any meal—and others will take more time and energy. I hope that they will all prove to be as pleasing to you as they are to me, regardless of the time involved in preparation.

Before starting, however, there are some important facts you need to know.

1. These dessert recipes call for large eggs, but if you have only medium or small eggs and don't want to run to the store, simply use one extra egg. Read about the importance of freshness of eggs, the beating of eggs, and separating eggs in Appendix I.

2. Use only the type of flour called for in the recipes. All-purpose unbleached flour is higher in gluten (protein) than the bleached variety, and slightly granular in texture. It is excellent for dusting cake tins and sheet pans, but too coarse to be used alone in a génoise or sponge cake. Cake flour, which I also use throughout this book, is low in gluten, but has a softer silkiness that will give your cakes a feathery texture. As low-in-gluten flour will not give a cake texture, I prefer to mix the two—unbleached and cake flour—together in some recipes, as I do in Lemon Génoise (page 466).

3. Many of my desserts call for superfine sugar, not granulated sugar. When beating yolks with sugar or when beating sugar into egg whites, I have found that superfine sugar gives the best results because it blends into the yolks or whites more easily. When superfine sugar is not available, put ½ cup granulated sugar into a blender and pulverize it for 30 seconds, being careful not to overblend as this will turn it to a powder. Work with small batches of sugar at a time.

4. My preference for semisweet chocolate is Surfine Lindt from Switzerland. It melts down to a glossy, smooth mixture, and in the seven years that I have used this product, the chocolate has never seized as it melts. Baker's semisweet chocolate also works well in the following recipes. For unsweetened chocolate, use Baker's. For white chocolate, I prefer Tobler.

5. Ideally, a microwave oven is best for melting chocolate, but I must admit, I do not own one, at home or in the restaurant. As a second choice, I suggest melting chocolate in a bowl over simmering water. Choose a heavy stainless steel or Pyrex bowl that will fit inside a pan, with the edge of the bowl being held by the outside of the pan. Make sure the water does not touch the bowl and is kept at a gentle simmer. Cover the bowl and allow most of the chocolate to melt. Remove the lid and gently stir with a plastic spatula. Do not agitate or whisk as you will risk seizing (stiffening) the chocolate. (During the melting process be careful no water from the steam drops into the chocolate as it will cause the chocolate to seize.) Once the chocolate has completely melted let it cool at room temperature. Do not refrigerate; this will cause the chocolate to stiffen around the edges. You should also avoid drafts. This process can be time-consuming and many times tedious. Just remember that good things come to those who wait and what can be better than those favorite chocolate desserts.

6. Read about utensils and pans for baking in Appendix II.

Apricot-Almond Souffle Torte

This is a perfectly lovely dessert. It has a fairly light texture and the pureed apricots give it a tart and rich flavor. It is wonderful finished with a Chocolate Glaze (see page 454) or served with Basic Crème (see page 505), or both. It is fairly easy to prepare and may be made a day in advance of serving. This cake does fall in the center when cooked.

> 1 cup very finely ground blanched almonds
> 1 cup whole dried apricots
> 1/4 cup granulated sugar
> 1/2 cup water
> 6 large eggs, separated
> 1 cup superfine sugar

1. Butter a 10-inch springform cake pan. Line the bottom with wax paper and butter it lightly. Dust the pan with sugar, then with all-purpose flour; knock out excess.
2. Place the granulated sugar in a heavy 2-quart saucepan with the apricots and water. Gently simmer, stirring occasionally, until the apricots are soft, approximately 30 minutes. While cooking the apricots, the liquid in the pan should reduce, so the mixture is thick; be careful it does not scorch.
3. While the apricots are still hot, puree them in a food processor until very smooth. Cool.
4. Beat the egg yolks and 1/2 cup superfine sugar with an electric mixer until light in color and thick. Stir in the cooled apricot puree.
5. Preheat oven to 325 degrees.
6. With an electric mixer, beat the egg whites until stiff; gradually add the remaining superfine sugar. Continue to beat until stiff and glossy.
7. Fold one-third of the egg whites into the egg yolk mixture until well incorporated. Gently fold in the remaining egg whites and almonds until well mixed, being careful not to overmix or the cake will lose its volume.

8. Pour the mixture into the prepared cake pan. Place the pan on the center shelf of the oven and bake at 325 degrees for 25 minutes. Lower the heat to 300 degrees and bake for 50 to 60 minutes until the torte is slightly firm to the touch in the center. Remove the pan from the oven and cool. Leave the torte in the pan at room temperature up to 24 hours. The center will fall a little as it cools.
9. Before serving, remove the torte from the pan and place it on a serving platter. Trim the edges. Lightly dust with confectioners' sugar or glaze with Chocolate Glaze. Serve.

Servings: 10 to 12   **Preparation: Fairly easy**
Time: Time consuming; advance preparation possible

Almond Torte

This simple, rich, and moist torte will keep for 3 to 4 days at room temperature. It is a very buttery torte; you may reduce the butter to 6 tablespoons if you wish. Try serving the torte with Blueberry Sauce (page 504), Strawberry Sauce (page 505), or Raspberry Sauce (page 503) and whipped cream. Delicious!

>   2 cups whole blanched almonds
>   1 teaspoon baking powder
>   8 tablespoons unsalted butter, soft
>   ½ teaspoon almond extract
>   1¼ cups superfine sugar
>   7 large eggs, separated

1. Butter a 10-inch springform cake pan. Line the bottom with wax paper and butter it. Dust the pan first with sugar, then with all-purpose flour; knock out the excess.
2. Place the almonds in a food processor with the baking powder and process until very fine.
3. Preheat oven to 325 degrees. Place the butter in a mixer bowl with almond extract and beat on medium speed until soft and light. Gradually pour in ½ cup sugar and beat on high speed until very light and fluffy, about 5 minutes. Turn off mixer. Remove the bowl and scrape the sides and bottom with a plastic spatula to make sure all the butter and sugar is incorporated.
4. Return the bowl to the mixer. On a high speed add the egg yolks one at a time, being certain that one yolk is completely incorporated into the mixture before you add another yolk. Continue to beat until very light and fluffy. The mixture should be a pale yellow color.
5. Put this butter mixture in a large mixing bowl. Wash out mixer bowl and beaters and dry well. Place the egg whites in the mixer bowl and beat on a high speed until fairly stiff. Slowly add the remaining ¾ cup sugar and continue to beat until stiff.
6. Gently fold a third of the ground nuts and a third of the egg whites into the butter mixture until well incorporated. Gently fold in the remaining egg whites and the almonds until well incorporated, being careful not to overfold or the egg whites will lose their volume.

7. Pour the mixture into the cake pan. Bake at 325 degrees for 45 to 55 minutes, or until the cake slightly pulls away from the sides of the pan.
8. Remove the cake from the oven and cool for 30 minutes in the cake pan, then remove from the pan and cool on a cake rack. Store at room temperature until ready to serve.

Servings: 10 to 12   Preparation: Fairly easy
Time: Time consuming; advance preparation

Chocolate Souffle Torte

Some years ago I visited Le Français, an elegant restaurant in Wheeling, Illinois, a suburb of Chicago. While experiencing one of the most enjoyable meals I have ever had, I discovered a Torte Souffle au Chocolate, later defined in Maida Heatter's *Chocolate Cook Book*. It was not until I visited Icarus, a small restaurant in Boston's south end, that I again discovered this torte and found its presentation to be equally delightful. Since that time, I have adapted my own recipe for Chocolate Souffle Torte. I hope you will find this recipe as enchanting as those experiences were for me.

4 ounces unsweetened chocolate, finely chopped
6 ounces semisweet chocolate, finely chopped
11 tablespoons unsalted butter, room temperature
7 large eggs, separated
¾ cup superfine sugar
Chocolate Glaze (page 454)
Whipped cream for garnish

1. Butter a 10-inch springform cake pan. Line the bottom with wax paper and butter it. Dust pan with sugar and then with all-purpose flour; knock out the excess.
2. Place the chocolate and butter in a heavy bowl that will fit over a saucepan, making a double broiler. Pour about 3 inches of water into the saucepan, making sure that the water will not touch the bowl. Bring the water to a simmering point, place the bowl over the water, and cover with a lid. Over the gently simmering water, melt the chocolate and butter, stirring occasionally. When they have melted, remove the bowl from the heat and gently stir until smooth. Set aside and cool to room temperature.
3. Preheat oven to 300 degrees. Adjust a rack to the lower third of the oven.
4. Beat the egg yolks with ¼ cup of sugar until light in color. Gently stir in the chocolate and butter mixture.

5. Beat the egg whites until fairly stiff, then add ½ cup of sugar and beat until stiff. Fold one-third of the egg whites into the mixture until well incorporated, then gently fold in the rest of the whites, being careful not to overmix, or the cake will lose volume.
6. Pour into the cake pan. Bake at 300 degrees for 30 minutes, then turn down the heat to 200 degrees and bake for 1 hour.
7. Remove the torte from the oven. Cool. Do not be concerned if the center of the cake falls as it cools.
8. Refrigerate the cake, covered, up to 2 days, if you wish. A few hours before serving, remove it from the refrigerator. Take it out of the pan and set it, right side up, on a serving platter. Pour the Chocolate Glaze into the dip in the center of the cake. Spread the glaze evenly across the top of the cake. Refrigerate up to one hour before serving.

Servings: 10 to 12   Preparation: Fairly easy
Time: Fairly time consuming; advance preparation possible

Glaze for Chocolate Cake

The key to making this simple and delicious glaze is to use a really fine European semisweet chocolate; my preference is Lindt Surfine. The recipe makes enough to lavishly glaze the top of a cake, but not the sides. It can easily be doubled if you decide to glaze the sides. Any leftover glaze can be stored in the refrigerator in a sealed container for up to 2 weeks. To reuse, melt over gently simmering water.

> *3½ ounces semisweet Swiss chocolate, finely chopped*
> *⅓ cup heavy cream*

1. Combine ingredients in a heavy bowl. Place over gently simmering water, covered, and occasionally stir until melted and smooth. Remove bowl from pan and slightly cool.
2. With a dry pastry brush, carefully remove all crumbs and particles from the surface of the cake so they will not interfere with the glaze. Pour the glaze on the center of the cake and spread evenly over the top.
3. A glazed cake should only be refrigerated a few hours; any longer, and the glaze will lose its gloss. Remove the cake from the refrigerator 1 hour before serving.

Yield: ¾ cup **Preparation: Easy**
Time: Quick

Italian Chocolate-Orange Torte

Do not be put off by the length of this recipe; it is much easier than it may appear. The torte is truly delicious. The addition of the orange syrup makes it very moist and the grated chocolate gives it a wonderful texture. The torte is better if made 6 hours before serving. The cake is also wonderful filled with Chocolate Ganache (page 465) and whipped cream if you don't want to use the orange syrup and candied oranges.

CAKE:
4 ounces unsweetened chocolate, very finely grated
3 tablespoons unsweetened cocoa
1 teaspoon baking powder
¾ cup cake flour
6 large eggs, separated
2 tablespoons water
1 cup superfine sugar
1 teaspoon vanilla extract

SYRUP:
2 large oranges
¾ cup granulated sugar
¾ cup water
1 cup heavy cream
confectioners' sugar

1. Butter a 10-inch cake pan, then line the bottom with wax paper. Butter the wax paper, then lightly dust it with sugar and then with all-purpose flour. Knock out the excess.
2. Sift the baking powder, cake flour, and cocoa together.
3. With an electric mixer, beat the egg yolks in a large bowl with the 2 tablespoons water until foamy. Gradually beat in half the superfine sugar and the vanilla. Continue to beat until light and creamy, approximately 3 minutes. Mix in the grated chocolate.

4. Preheat oven to 350 degrees. Adjust oven rack slightly above the middle of the oven.

5. With an electric mixer, beat the egg whites until fairly stiff, slowly pour in the remaining ½ cup superfine sugar, and continue to beat until stiff and glossy.

6. Place half the egg whites on top of the egg yolk mixture. Resift half of the dry ingredients over egg whites and gently fold them and the egg whites into the egg yolks. Using a plastic spatula, fold until all the ingredients are well incorporated. Repeat with the remaining egg whites and the remaining dry ingredients. Be careful not to overfold or the mixture will lose its volume.

7. Pour the batter into the cake pan, place it on the oven rack. Bake for 25 to 35 minutes until the center of the cake is slightly firm to the touch and the cake has just started to pull away from the edges of the pan.

8. Leave the cake in the pan for 10 minutes before turning out. To turn out, run a rounded-end metal spatula around the edge of the pan and turn onto a cooling rack and remove the wax paper.

9. While the cake is cooking place the ¾ cup granulated sugar and ¾ cup water in a 2- to 3-quart stainless steel pan. Over medium heat, gently stir until all the sugar has dissolved. Boil for 3 minutes, then turn off the heat.

10. Peel the oranges. Cut them in half lengthwise, then cut into ⅛-inch slices across. Remove the seeds and discard the ends of the oranges. Add the orange slices to the syrup and simmer for 40 minutes over low to medium heat, being careful that the syrup does not caramelize. Strain the syrup and reserve. If the syrup is very thick, add a little hot water. Cool the candied orange slices, then finely chop.

11. Three to 4 hours before serving, cut the cake into 3 layers and whip the cream until stiff.

12. Place the bottom cake layer on a serving platter and brush with the orange syrup. Cover with half the whipped cream and half the chopped, candied oranges. Place the center layer on top, and repeat this procedure with the remaining syrup, cream, and oranges. Place the last layer on top. Refrigerate torte about 6 hours.

13. Just before serving, dust with confectioners' sugar.

Servings: 10 to 12   Preparation: Fairly difficult
Time: Time consuming; advance preparation necessary

Rhoda's Almond-Chocolate Torte

I love chocolate desserts that are slightly bitter, as I feel this bitterness intensifies the chocolate flavor. This torte recipe will give you that wonderful flavor. If you prefer a sweeter cake, however, use a semisweet Swiss chocolate.

> 6 ounces unsweetened chocolate
> ¼ cup clarified butter (page 62)
> 1 cup finely ground blanched almonds
> 8 large eggs, separated
> 1 cup superfine sugar
> 2 teaspoons vanilla extract
> Chocolate Glaze (page 454)

1. Butter a 10-inch springform cake pan. Line the bottom of the pan with wax paper, and butter it. Dust pan lightly with sugar and then with all-purpose flour; knock out excess.
2. Place the chocolate and clarified butter in a heavy bowl that will fit over a saucepan, making a double boiler. Pour about 3 inches of water into the saucepan, making sure that the water will not touch the bowl. Bring the water to a simmering point, place the bowl over the water, and cover with a lid. Over the gently simmering water, melt the chocolate, stirring occasionally. When it has melted, remove it from the heat and gently stir in the almonds. Set aside and cool just until the mixture is warm.
3. Using an electric mixer, beat the yolks with ½ cup sugar and the vanilla, until very thick and light in color, about 5 minutes.
4. Preheat the oven to 350 degrees.
5. Beat the egg whites until they are fairly stiff. While still beating, gradually add the rest of the sugar, and continue to beat until the whites are very stiff and glossy, about 2 minutes.
6. Fold the chocolate mixture into the yolk mixture. Fold one-third of the egg whites into the mixture until well incorporated. Then gently fold in the remaining egg whites.

7. Gently pour mixture into the prepared pan, and bake in the oven until slightly firm to the touch, approximately 30 to 40 minutes. The cake should be slightly undercooked in the center.
8. Cool the cake in the pan, then refrigerate up to 2 days.
9. Several hours before serving, run a metal spatula around the edges of the pan and turn the cake out, right side up, onto a serving plate. Pour the glaze into the dip in the center of the cake and spread it across the top of the cake until even and smooth. Refrigerate until one hour before serving time, then hold at room temperature.

Servings: 10 to 12   Preparation: Fairly easy
Time: Fairly time consuming; advance preparation possible

White Chocolate Almond Torte

This very rich, dense, and moist cake can be highlighted by a garnish of fresh peaches, strawberries, or raspberries and whipped cream. It also can be served on a pool of Raspberry Sauce (page 503), Strawberry Sauce (page 505), or Blueberry Sauce (page 504). It takes a while longer than most cakes to cook, so be absolutely certain it is completely cooked before you remove it from the oven. It will fall in the center when it is cooked.

> *6 ounces white chocolate, finely chopped*
> *1 cup superfine sugar*
> *8 large eggs, separated*
> *1 drop almond extract*
> *2 cups whole blanched almonds, very finely ground*
> *½ cup heavy cream, room temperature*
> *whipped cream and fresh fruit for garnish*

1. Butter a 10-inch springform pan. Line the bottom with wax paper and butter it. Lightly dust pan with sugar and then with all-purpose flour; knock out the excess.
2. Place the chocolate in a heavy bowl that will fit over a saucepan, making a double boiler. Pour about 3 inches of water into the pan; be certain that the water will not touch the bowl. Bring the water to a simmering point, place the bowl over the water, and cover with a lid. Over gently simmering water, slowly melt the chocolate, stirring occasionally. Then remove the bowl from the pan and cool until the mixture is warm.
3. Using an electric mixer, beat half the sugar with the egg yolks and almond extract until light in color.
4. Mix the nuts into the cooled chocolate. Slowly stir in heavy cream to lighten the mixture, then fold the mixture into the yolks.
5. Preheat oven to 325 degrees. Adjust the rack to the lower third of the oven.
6. Beat the egg whites until fairly stiff. Gradually add the remaining sugar and beat until the whites are stiff and glossy. Fold half the egg whites into the egg yolk mixture until well incorporated, then gently fold in the remaining egg whites. Do not overfold or the mixture will lose its volume.

7. Pour the mixture into the prepared cake pan. Bake in the lower third of the preheated oven for 1 hour, until the cake is dark golden brown. Remove the cake from the oven and cool. It may be held at room temperature up to 24 hours. (If the kitchen is very hot, refrigerate the cake.)
8. Before serving, turn the cake out onto a serving platter and decorate with whipped cream and fresh fruit.

Servings: 10 to 12   Preparation: Easy
Time: Time consuming; advance preparation possible

LEMON SEMOLINA TORTE

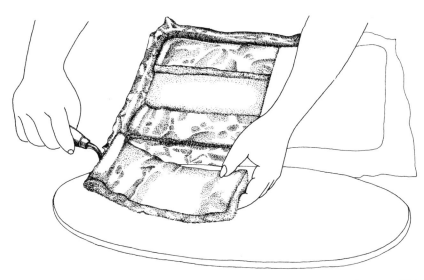

1. Slice the cake into thirds lengthwise. Then slice each third in half across. With a wide metal spatula, remove the cake from the pan and put one-sixth of it on a long serving platter.

2. Lay the next piece on the platter, end to end with the first piece. Spread with whipped cream and berries. Top with the next layer, working with one-sixth of the cake at a time.

Lemon Semolina Torte

The next time you want to impress your guests, make this very attractive torte. It is served on an oval or rectangular platter that is at least 17 inches long. It is moist, with a wonderful texture, thanks to the use of Semolina, which can be found in Italian food markets. (If you can't find it, finely blend yellow cornmeal in a blender in two batches.) The flavor is very nice and lemony. I use unsweetened whipped cream in the filling because I find it more refreshing than sweetened, but if you prefer a sweet taste, add a little sugar to the whipped cream. Be sure to refer to the drawings on page 461 as you put this torte together.

> rind (zest) of 1 lemon, finely grated
> 1/2 cup fresh lemon juice
> 1/2 cup + 1 tablespoon fine Semolina (or finely blended
>   cornmeal)
> 6 tablespoons ground blanched almonds
> 6 large eggs, separated
> 1 1/2 cups superfine sugar
> 2 cups heavy cream, stiffly whipped
> 1 1/2 pints fresh raspberries or blueberries

1. Butter or oil a 13- by 17-inch sheet pan. Line it with tin foil, bringing the foil 1/2 inch above the rim of the pan. Preheat oven to 350 degrees.
2. Place the Semolina, ground almonds, and lemon juice in a bowl and stir until well mixed. Put to one side for a maximum of ten minutes.
3. Place the egg yolks in a large bowl. Add 1/2 cup sugar and the lemon zest and beat until light in color. Mix the Semolina mixture into the egg yolk mixture and stir until the Semolina is well incorporated.
4. Beat the egg whites until fairly stiff. Slowly pour in the remaining sugar and continue to beat until stiff and glossy. Be careful not to overbeat the egg whites or they will become runny. Fold one-third of the egg whites into the egg yolk mixture until well incorporated. Fold the remaining egg whites into the mixture. Be careful not to overmix or the cake will be heavy.
5. Pour the mixture into the sheet pan, spread evenly with a metal spatula, and bake at 350 degrees for 15 to 20 minutes until light golden brown.

Remove from the oven and cool. It may be held at room temperature for 6 to 8 hours.

6. A few hours before serving, slice the cake into thirds lengthwise. Then slice each third in half across. (This step facilitates removing the slices from the pan without breaking them. The whipped cream will hide the seams.)

7. Lay the two pieces that make up the first third on a long oval or rectangular platter with their cut ends touching. Spread with one-third of the whipped cream and berries. Lay the next layer down on top of the whipped cream and spread with one-third of the whipped cream and berries. Position the top layer. Pipe on the remaining whipped cream and garnish with the remaining berries. This may be refrigerated up to 6 hours before serving.

Servings: 12   Preparation: Fairly difficult
Time: Time consuming; advance preparation possible

Almond Roulade

This light roulade is wonderful with the fresh fruit and whipped cream filling described below. In the wintertime, when fresh fruit is not so readily available, try filling it with Chocolate Ganache (see page 465).

2 cups finely ground blanched almonds
1 teaspoon baking powder
9 eggs, separated
¾ cup superfine sugar
½ teaspoon almond extract

FILLING:
1 cup stiffly whipped cream
*1 cup diced peaches, sliced strawberries, fresh raspberries, or
     chopped candied oranges (page 456)*

1. Preheat oven to 350 degrees. Butter or oil a 17-inch by 13-inch heavy sheet pan. Line it with parchment or wax paper. Butter the paper, dust with sugar and flour, and knock out the excess.

2. Mix the almonds with the baking powder. With an electric mixer, beat the egg yolks with ¼ cup of sugar and the extract until light in color. Fold the almonds into the egg yolk mixture.

3. Beat the egg whites with the electric mixer until fairly stiff; add the remaining sugar and beat until stiff and glossy. Fold one-third of the egg whites into the almond and egg yolk mixture until well incorporated. Fold in the remaining egg whites. Be careful not to overmix or the mixture will lose its volume.

4. Pour the mixture into the sheet pan. Using a long metal spatula, spread evenly; do not overwork. Bake at 350 degrees for 20 minutes, then check. The top should be slightly firm; it may take another 5 to 10 minutes.

5. Have a clean cotton cloth ready on a countertop. Sprinkle it with confectioners' sugar. Take the roulade from the oven and turn it upside down onto the cloth. Remove the paper and gently and loosely roll the roulade up with the cloth into just three folds. Leave it rolled for 2 hours, but no longer than 4 hours, before filling.

6. Gently mix the whipped cream and fruit together. Unroll the cake. Spread with the fruit mixture and roll up. Chill in the refrigerator no more than 6 hours. Dust the top with confectioners' sugar before serving.

7. If you use Chocolate Ganache for filling, the roulade may be refrigerated up to 8 hours.

Servings: 12   Preparation: Fairly difficult
Time: Time consuming; advance preparation necessary

Chocolate Ganache

This Chocolate Ganache is a very light version of a chocolate butter cream, which still has a really good, full chocolate flavor. It is a wonderful filling for cakes and roulades. It also is nice piped around the edge of Hazelnut Meringues (page 488). This recipe can easily be doubled, if you wish.

1½ ounces unsweetened chocolate, finely chopped
3½ ounces semisweet Swiss chocolate, finely chopped
1¼ cups light cream
3 egg yolks
2 tablespoons sugar
5 tablespoons unsalted butter, very soft, but not melted

1. Place the chocolate in a bowl.
2. Scald the light cream in a 1-quart heavy saucepan.
3. Beat the sugar with the egg yolks until light in color.
4. Pour the cream over the egg yolks, constantly whisking, then return the mixture to the saucepan.
5. Whisk the egg yolks and cream over medium heat until the foam starts to disappear and the custard starts to thicken. (It should lightly coat the back of a spoon.) Be careful not to boil or the custard will curdle.
6. Pour immediately over the chocolate, whisking all the time. Whisk until the chocolate is well emulsified into the custard.
7. Cool the custard down to room temperature and then slowly whisk in the butter a tablespoon at a time. Whisk until all the butter is well mixed in.
8. Refrigerate at least 8 hours, or up to 48 hours, before using.

Yield: 1¾ cups   **Preparation: Fairly easy**
Time: Fairly time consuming; advance preparation necessary

Lemon Génoise

This is not an easy dessert to make, but it is delicious, lemony, and very light in texture. It is the base for Gâteau Tierney (page 468), or can be filled with whipped cream and fresh berries or peaches. Besides loving its taste, I am including it here to show you an alternate technique to preparing a génoise. In a classic génoise recipe, you should hand-whisk the batter in a bowl over gently simmering water. This génoise is made with an electric mixer. It is crucial to the success of this recipe that you follow my instructions precisely. You may still fail, but I urge you to keep trying. I have seen cooks fail on their first attempt, and then go on to a complete success. You may substitute orange zest or 1 teaspoon vanilla extract for the lemon zest.

> 7 whole large eggs, in the shell
> ¼ cup cake flour
> ¾ cup all-purpose unbleached flour
> 1 cup superfine sugar
> 2 teaspoons grated lemon rind (zest)
> ⅓ cup clarified butter, melted but not hot (room temperature)

1. Butter a 10-inch cake pan. Line the bottom with wax paper and butter it. Sprinkle the pan with superfine sugar, and then with all-purpose flour; knock out the excess. Preheat oven to 375 degrees.
2. Sift the cake flour and all-purpose flour together.
3. Check that the eggs are very fresh, as this will give a thicker consistency to the mixture. (See Appendix I.) Place the whole eggs in the shells in a bowl of hot water (130 degrees) for 10 minutes.
4. Remove the eggs and dry with a paper towel. Then crack the eggs into a mixer bowl.
5. With an electric mixer set on high speed, beat the eggs until foamy (approximately 3 minutes). Then add the sugar and lemon rind and beat until very thick, approximately 10 minutes. It is extremely important that you beat the mixture the full 10 minutes; even if the mixture seems very thick after 5 minutes, do not stop beating. After 10 minutes the mixture should have a thick mousselike consistency.
6. Turn down the mixer to a low speed (3 to 5) and add the flour. Beat for exactly 30 seconds, then slowly pour in the clarified butter. Turn up the

speed and count exactly 5 seconds. (One of the keys to the success of this recipe is that you do not overmix the batter at this point.)

7. Immediately remove the bowl from the mixer and gently fold over the batter with a plastic spatula for exactly 30 seconds to ensure you have no pockets of flour and that the butter is well incorporated into the mixture. (If the batter is runny at this point, unfortunately it has been overmixed and the cake will be too dense.)

8. Pour the batter into the prepared cake pan and bake at 350 degrees for 45 minutes, until the cake starts to pull away from the edges of the pan. Remove from the oven, cool for 10 minutes in the pan, then turn out onto a platter.

9. Leave at room temperature at least 6 hours before slicing with a serrated knife into 2 or 3 layers. Use in the Gâteau Tierney recipe, or fill with whipped cream and fruit and refrigerate 1 to 2 hours.

Servings: 10 to 12   Preparation: Difficult
Time: Time consuming; advance preparation possible

Gâteau Tierney

Once you have mastered Lemon Génoise, make this delicious plum cake. It is wonderful to serve in the summer when plums are ripe and plentiful, or you can freeze the plum filling and make the cake in the winter.

Lemon Génoise (page 466)
1 pound ripe, fresh Santa Rosa plums, unpeeled, pitted, and
   finely sliced
½ cup sugar
1 cup water
1½ cups heavy cream
2 tablespoons confectioners' sugar
thin lemon slices for garnish

1. Place the sugar and water in a 2-quart stainless steel saucepan, bring to a boil, and boil for 3 minutes. Add the plums and boil over medium heat until the mixture has become fairly thick; stir occasionally to make sure it does not scorch on the bottom.
2. Cool the plum mixture. This mixture can be made a couple of days ahead of time or can even be frozen. Bring the mixture back to room temperature before finishing the cake.
3. A couple of hours before serving, beat the cream until stiff. Carefully slice the Lemon Génoise into 3 layers with a serrated knife.
4. Place the bottom layer on a serving plate, cover with half the plum mixture, then spread with half the whipped cream. Cover with the middle cake layer and spread with the remaining plum mixture and the whipped cream. Cover with the top cake layer and store in the refrigerator.
5. Thirty minutes before serving, remove cake from the refrigerator.
6. Just before serving, dust with the confectioners' sugar and decorate with thin lemon slices.

Servings: 12   Preparation: Difficult
Time: Time consuming; advance preparation possible

Pfahl's Chocolate Delight

Gary Pfahl and I combined our efforts to create this rich and dense cake. The chocolate flavor is highlighted by the prunes.

> ½ cup pitted dried prunes
> 6 ounces semisweet chocolate, finely chopped
> 3 ounces unsweetened chocolate, finely chopped
> ⅓ cup cognac
> 10 tablespoons soft unsalted butter, but not melted
> 4 large eggs, separated
> 1 cup superfine sugar
> ¼ cup Coffee Essence (page 477)
> Chocolate Glaze (page 454)
> whipped cream for garnish

1. Place prunes in cognac, cover, and let them soak for 2 to 3 hours. Then puree prunes in a food processor until very smooth

2. Preheat oven to 350 degrees. Butter a 10-inch springform cake pan. Line the bottom with wax paper and butter it. Sprinkle pan with sugar and then with all-purpose flour. Knock out the excess.

3. Place the chocolate in a heavy bowl that will fit over a saucepan, making a double boiler. Pour about 3 inches of water into the saucepan, making sure that the water will not touch the bowl. Bring the water to a simmering point, place the bowl over the water, and cover with a lid. Over gently simmering water, slowly melt the chocolate, stirring occasionally. Then remove the bowl from the pan, slowly stir in the butter, and cool until mixture is warm.

4. With an electric mixer, beat the egg yolks in a large bowl while gradually adding ½ cup sugar. Beat on high speed until light in color. Stir in prune-cognac puree, the coffee, and the melted chocolate.

5. Beat egg whites until fairly stiff. Add the remaining ½ cup sugar and continue beating until stiff. Fold one-third of the whites into the batter, then gently fold in the remaining whites, being careful not to overmix as the cake will lose its volume.

6. Pour the mixture into the buttered cake pan and place on the middle shelf in the preheated oven. Bake for 40 to 45 minutes. When the cake is done, the center of the cake still should be slightly soft. Remove the cake from the oven and let it cool in the pan.

7. The cake can be refrigerated up to 3 days before serving.
8. Two to three hours before serving, remove the cake from the refrigerator, remove it from the pan, and place it on a serving platter. Spread with Chocolate Glaze. Refrigerate until one hour before serving, then hold at room temperature. Serve the cake with a bowl of whipped cream.

Servings: 10 to 12   Preparation: Fairly easy
Time: Time consuming; advance preparation necessary

Greek Orange-Almond Cake

This lovely citrus-flavored cake is especially wonderful served the day after you make it. Store it at room temperature. Garnish it with fresh, sliced oranges, or fresh strawberries and whipped cream. If you prefer a very moist cake, decrease the bread crumbs to ½ cup.

6 large eggs, separated
⅔ cup dried bread crumbs
⅓ cup fresh orange juice
⅓ cup fresh lemon juice
1¼ cups finely ground blanched almonds
2 teaspoons finely grated orange rind (zest)
¾ cup superfine sugar
confectioners' sugar
whipped cream for garnish
orange slices or fresh strawberries for garnish

1. Butter a 10-inch springform cake pan. Line the bottom with wax paper and butter it. Lightly sprinkle the pan with sugar and then with all-purpose flour; knock out the excess.
2. Mix the orange juice, lemon juice, and bread crumbs. Let stand for 10 minutes, then mix in the almonds and orange rind.

3. With an electric mixer, beat the egg yolks with half the sugar until light in color. Mix in the bread crumb mixture.
4. Preheat oven to 350 degrees.
5. Beat the egg whites with an electric mixer until fairly stiff. Beat in the remaining sugar and then beat until stiff and glossy.
6. Gently fold one-third of the egg whites into the egg yolk mixture, then gently fold in the remaining egg whites. Fold until the egg whites are well incorporated, but be careful not to overfold or the cake will lose its volume.
7. Pour the mixture into the cake pan. Bake at 350 degrees for 30 minutes, then reduce the heat to 300 degrees and bake for 25 more minutes. The center of the cake should be just slightly soft, not runny. If the cake overcooks, it will be dry.
8. Remove the cake from the oven and cool in the pan at room temperature for 1 day.
9. Just before serving, remove the cake from the pan and place it on a serving platter. Dust with confectioners' sugar and garnish with whipped cream and fresh fruit.

Servings: 12   Preparation: Fairly easy
Time: Time consuming; advance preparation necessary

Maple Pecan Gâteau

Using maple syrup in place of sugar gives this cake an intriguing texture and a delightful taste. Note that you will need to beat the egg whites more than usual. The nuts for this recipe need to be a fine-ground consistency. However, be careful not to overwork them in the food processor or they will become oily and start to stick together.

> *2 cups finely ground pecans*
> *¾ cup pure maple syrup*
> *¾ cup sifted cake flour*
> *2 teaspoons baking powder*
> *6 large eggs, separated*
> *1 teaspoon vanilla extract*
> *¾ cup melted unsalted butter, cooled to room temperature*
> *Apple Pear Compote for garnish (page 497)*
> *vanilla ice cream for garnish*

1. Butter a 3-quart tube or Bundt pan, dust with sugar, and then dust with all-purpose flour. Tap out the excess.
2. Mix the nuts, flour, and baking powder in a bowl.
3. Preheat oven to 350 degrees.
4. In a separate bowl, beat the egg yolks with half the maple syrup and the vanilla until well mixed. Add butter gradually, continuing to beat until well incorporated into the mixture.
5. Beat the egg whites until fairly stiff. While still beating, slowly pour in the remaining maple syrup; continue to beat until very stiff. (This will take longer than if you were using sugar.)
6. Gently fold a third of the egg whites and a third of the nut mixture into the egg yolks. When well incorporated, gently fold in another third of each mixture. When well incorporated, fold in the final third.
7. Pour the mixture into the tube pan and bake at 350 degrees for 45 minutes to 1 hour, until the cake slightly pulls away from the edge of the pan.
8. Remove from the oven and cool for 5 minutes in the pan, then turn out onto a cake rack and serve within 6 hours.
9. Serve with Apple Pear Compote and vanilla ice cream.

Servings: 12   Preparation: Fairly easy
Time: Time consuming; advance preparation possible

Caribbean Gâteau

There is a delightful combination of textures in this gâteau; the moist cake contrasts beautifully with the crunch of the nuts and the chewiness of the pineapple.

3/4 cup hazelnuts
8 large eggs, separated
1 cup superfine sugar
1 teaspoon finely grated orange rind (zest)
1/2 cup soft white bread crumbs
1 cup unsweetened grated coconut
fresh pineapple slices for garnish
whipped cream for garnish

1. Butter a 10-inch springform cake pan. Line the bottom with wax paper and butter it. Sprinkle pan with sugar and then with all-purpose flour; knock out the excess
2. Preheat oven to 375 degrees.
3. Place the hazelnuts on a baking sheet and roast for 7 to 10 minutes. Watch carefully, as the nuts can burn easily. Remove, cool, and then rub the nuts in a sieve until almost all the skins are rubbed off. Grind the nuts in a food processor to a fine grind.
4. Place the egg yolks in a large bowl, add half the sugar, and beat with an electric mixer until light in color. Add the orange rind and bread crumbs.
5. With an electric mixer, beat the egg whites until fairly stiff. Slowly add the remaining sugar and beat until stiff and glossy.
6. Gently fold one-third of the beaten whites into the egg yolk mixture, then fold in the coconut and hazelnuts. Fold in the remaining egg whites until well incorporated, being careful not to overfold or the mixture will lose its volume. Pour batter into prepared pan.
7. Bake cake in the preheated 375-degree oven for 35 to 40 minutes or until the center of the cake is firm but not hard. Remove from the oven. Cool in the cake pan.
8. This cake may be made a day in advance and stored at room temperature in the cake pan.
9. Serve with whipped cream and pineapple slices.

Servings: 10 to 12   Preparation: Easy
Time: Fairly time consuming; advance preparation possible

Hazelnut Gâteau

The honey gives this gâteau an absolutely wonderful flavor. It is great served with fresh raspberries or strawberries and whipped cream. Check that the nuts are not rancid.

> *10 ounces hazelnuts*
> *1 teaspoon baking powder*
> *¼ teaspoon baking soda*
> *2 tablespoons all-purpose unbleached flour*
> *½ cup honey*
> *7 large eggs, separated*
> *½ cup superfine sugar*
> *fresh raspberries or strawberries and whipped cream for garnish*

1. Butter a 10-inch springform cake pan. Line the bottom with wax paper or parchment and butter it. Sprinkle pan with sugar and then with all-purpose flour; knock out the excess.
2. In a preheated 400-degree oven, roast the hazelnuts on a large sheet pan for 7 to 10 minutes until the skins crack. Watch carefully, as the nuts can burn easily. Remove, cool, and then rub nuts in a coarse sieve until almost all the skins are rubbed off.
3. Place the hazelnuts, baking powder, baking soda, and flour in the food processor and grind until fairly fine.
4. Place the honey and egg yolks in a bowl and beat until light in color with an electric mixer.
5. Lower oven temperature to 325 degrees. Position oven rack in the lower third of the oven.
6. Beat the egg whites with electric mixer until fairly stiff, add the sugar, and continue to beat until stiff.
7. Gently fold one-third of the egg whites and half the nut mixture into the egg yolks. Add another third of the whites and the rest of the nuts and fold. Fold in the remaining egg whites.
8. Pour the batter into the prepared cake pan. Bake for 70 to 80 minutes until golden brown and fairly firm in the center. The outside rim of the top of the cake will be a little carmelized. Remove the cake from the oven and cool in the pan. The center will fall as it cools.
9. This cake may be made a day in advance of serving and held at room temperature in the cake pan. Just before serving, place it on a serving platter. Garnish with the whipped cream and berries.

Servings: 10 to 12   Preparation: Fairly easy
Time: Fairly time consuming; advance preparation possible

Chocolate Divine

Serve this extremely rich dessert semifrozen. Make it extra special by filling with raspberries or fresh pitted and halved sweet cherries. If using hazelnuts, roast them to remove the skins. (See Hazelnut Gâteau, page 474.)

7 ounces semisweet chocolate, preferably Swiss chocolate
2 ounces unsweetened chocolate
2 cups heavy cream
4 egg yolks
¼ cup superfine sugar
1 cup whole blanched almonds or hazelnuts, ground fairly fine
4 tablespoons unsalted butter, soft, but not melted
1 pint fresh raspberries
fresh raspberries and whipped cream for garnish

1. Finely chop or grate the chocolate and place in a large mixing bowl.
2. Lightly oil a 10-inch cake pan. Line the pan with plastic wrap. (The adhesion of plastic wrap to an oiled mold will give the mousse an even surface and will make the mousse easier to remove from the mold.)
3. Scald the heavy cream over medium heat in a heavy 1-quart saucepan.
4. Beat the egg yolks and sugar until light in color. Pour the scalded cream over the eggs, whisking all the time, and return to saucepan. Cook over medium heat, stirring constantly, until thick enough to coat the spoon. Be very careful not to boil the custard, or it will curdle.
5. Pour the custard immediately over the shaved chocolate and stir until blended. Stir in the nuts. Allow to cool until room temperature.
6. Whisk in the butter a little at a time until well emulsified. Allow to cool.
7. Pour half the mixture into cake pan. Cover with the pint of raspberries and cover with the rest of the mixture. Cover the pan with plastic wrap and freeze for 3 to 4 days.
8. Place dessert in refrigerator 1 hour before serving. Just before serving, turn out onto a serving platter and remove the plastic wrap. Decorate with raspberries and whipped cream.

Servings: 12 to 16   Preparation: Fairly difficult
Time: Time consuming; advance preparation necessary

Chocolate Orange Mousse

This dense, zesty mousse is at its best when served semifrozen with fresh strawberries or a raspberry sauce. For an entirely different taste, substitute Coffee Essence for the orange liqueur.

6 ounces semisweet chocolate (Swiss chocolate preferred)
3 ounces unsweetened chocolate
1 cup heavy cream
7 large egg yolks
½ cup superfine sugar
½ cup orange liqueur or ½ cup Coffee Essence (page 477)
6 tablespoons unsalted butter
2 egg whites

1. Very finely chop or grate the chocolate. Place in a large bowl.
2. Whip the cream stiff and refrigerate.
3. Beat egg yolks and sugar in a heavy bowl until light in color. Stir in the orange liqueur.
4. Place the egg yolk bowl over a saucepan of gently simmering water, making a double boiler. (Be certain that the water does not touch the bowl.) Whisk to a thick mousselike consistency. During this procedure, scrape down the sides occasionally with a plastic spatula to ensure that the mixture does not overcook on the sides of the bowl. Be careful not to overcook or overheat the mixture as it may curdle. Remove the bowl from the pan.
5. Immediately add chocolate and very gently stir until it is well mixed and melted. Then whisk in the butter a little at a time, whisking until it has melted. Cool the mixture by placing the bowl over a bowl of ice water, and slowly stir. Cool to room temperature, being careful it does not get too cold or the chocolate will harden.
6. Beat the egg whites until stiff. Gently fold whipped cream and egg whites into the chocolate mixture until well incorporated. Be careful not to overmix or the mixture will lose its volume. (If the kitchen is hot, place the bowl of chocolate mixture over a bowl of ice water as you fold in the whites and cream, being careful that the chocolate does not harden. If it does, remove the bowl from the ice water immediately.)

7. Pour into dessert glasses, filling them half full, or into a serving bowl. Place in the freezer for 30 minutes, then in the refrigerator until serving. The mousse can be refrigerated up to 24 hours.

Servings: 7 to 8   **Preparation: Fairly difficult**
Time: Time consuming; advance preparation necessary

Coffee Essence

This richly flavored liquid will not only give you a wonderful flavoring to use in dessert making, but also is great to use for ice coffee. (Place 2 to 4 tablespoons coffee essence in a glass, add ½ cup of cold water, and then ice cubes.) As you will note, the coffee is never heated; this gives the essence a strong, but never bitter, flavor. (When you boil or reduce coffee, bitter oils are drawn out of the coffee giving it a bitter flavor.) Coffee essence may be frozen in small batches and used as needed. It is important that you use freshly ground coffee; if you do not have a coffee grinder, have the store grind it and make the essence within one day. If you do have a coffee grinder, grind the beans just before preparing the essence.

¼ pound strong coffee beans (preferably espresso or dark roast)
2 cups water
1 4-cup canning jar with lid

1. Grind the coffee beans very fine. Place the coffee in a jar and add 2 cups cold water. Shake well.
2. Let stand for 2 hours, then shake the jar well. Refrigerate for 10 to 12 hours.
3. Place a filter paper or a fine cloth in a sieve and pour the mixture through it.
4. Pour the liquid into an airtight container (this will keep in the refrigerator up to 2 weeks) or freeze in small amounts.

Yield: ¾ to 1 cup   **Preparation: Easy**
Time: Time consuming; may be frozen

Peruvian Cream

This rich dessert brings together the flavor of chocolate, coffee, and caramel. The texture is between that of a custard and a mousse. Should you not have made caramel before, beware that the pan and the caramel get extremely hot. Also, when you add the hot coffee essence, it will splatter, so do not lean over the pan or allow children to be near the stove.

2 ounces unsweetened chocolate
4 ounces semisweet chocolate (preferably Swiss chocolate)
½ cup Coffee Essence (page 477)
½ cup superfine sugar
1 pint light cream
4 egg yolks
1 cup heavy cream, whipped, for garnish
cinnamon sugar for garnish

1. Very finely chop the chocolate and place in a bowl. Heat the coffee essence and put to one side.
2. Heat a heavy 10-inch saute pan. Sprinkle in the sugar and allow it to dissolve over medium heat, gently twisting the pan from side to side so the sugar dissolves evenly. (Do not stir it with a spoon as the caramel tends to stick to the spoon.) Continue to cook the caramel until it turns a dark golden brown.
3. Remove the pan from the heat and add the hot coffee essence immediately. Hold your head away from the pan, watching out for splatters of hot liquid. Return the pan to low heat, gently stir the mixture until all the caramel has dissolved, then boil until it has a light syrupy consistency. Put the pan to one side.
4. Heat the light cream to the scalding point in a 1-quart heavy saucepan.
5. Beat the egg yolks for 2 minutes, then slowly pour in the cream, whisking all the time. Return the mixture to the pan and over a low to medium heat, whisk the cream until it starts to thicken (it should coat the back of the spoon). Be careful not to boil, as the custard may curdle. Pour immediately over the chocolate and gently whisk until the chocolate is thoroughly incorporated into the custard.

6. If the caramel-coffee mixture has thickened (hardened), add a couple of tablespoons water and dissolve over a low heat. Slowly whisk the caramel-coffee mixture into the chocolate mixture.
7. Pour into a serving dish or 6 to 8 dessert glasses. Place in the refrigerator for 1 hour, then cover with plastic wrap.
8. This dessert should be refrigerated 4 hours, or up to 2 days.
9. Just before serving, pipe with whipped cream and sprinkle with a dash of cinnamon sugar.

Servings: 6 to 8   Preparation: Fairly difficult
Time: Time consuming; advance preparation necessary

ROLLING OUT PÂTE BRISÉE

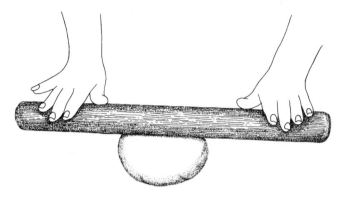

1. After chilling the dough, shape it into a round and roll out. Move the rolling pin back and forth in front of you, not from side to side.

2. After every three rolls, turn the pastry to one side and roll again.

3. Lift the pastry onto the rolling pin so it will not break as you gently ease it into the pie pan.

Pâte Brisée

This pastry, also known as Shortcrust Pastry, is rich and crisp and buttery. It is suitable for fruit tarts, pumpkin or squash pie, or quiches. It can be made in the food processor or by hand (see Variation). Be certain that you do not overwork the butter and flour mixture or the cooked pastry will be quite hard in texture, rather than flaky. The cooler the surface for rolling out the dough, the better; I suggest a marble slab or a metal or Formica countertop. If you are rolling out the dough on a hot summer's day, ice down the surface, then dry it well before rolling out. I prefer tin pie plates to glass or aluminum ones. The tin seems to give a really nice and crisp crust. Do not use a pie pan with a removable bottom.

1¼ cups all-purpose unbleached flour
6 tablespoons cold unsalted butter
¼ to ⅓ cup cold water

1. Place the butter in the food processor. Cut the butter into small pieces and add the flour. Turn on the machine and process for 7 to 8 on/off turns, approximately 30 seconds. Check the consistency; the butter should be in pieces about 1/16-inch in diameter.
2. Pour the mixture into a bowl and very quickly and lightly mix the water into the dough, using your hands, and being careful that the water is evenly distributed through the dough. The dough should be soft, not wet.
3. Shape the dough into a flat round. Wrap it in plastic wrap and store in a cool place or refrigerator for 30 minutes before rolling out. If the dough is stored in the refrigerator, it might become hard. If this is the case, leave it at room temperature at least 10 minutes before rolling out.
4. To roll out, lightly flour the countertop and rolling pin. Roll lightly 2 or 3 strokes in front of you, and then turn the dough to one side. Continue to roll out, turning the dough after 2 or 3 strokes, lightly flouring the board between each turn, until the dough is the thickness you like and the shape of the pie tin. Fit the dough into the pie tin.
5. Let the dough rest in the refrigerator for 30 to 60 minutes.
6. Preheat oven to 400 degrees. Line the pie crust with wax paper, weight the paper, and bake the crust on the top rack of the oven for 7 to 8

minutes. Remove the weight and paper. (See Baking Blind in Appendix I.)

7. If the pie crust is to be entirely baked empty, prick it all over and bake about 20 more minutes, or until it is golden brown. If the pie crust is to be cooked with a filling, bake it about 5 minutes empty and then follow baking instructions for the pie or quiche.
8. The baked pie crust can be held up to 8 hours at room temperature.

Variation: To make the pastry by hand, you will need to use the same amount of flour, 8 tablespoons of cold unsalted butter, and 3 tablespoons of cold water. Cut the butter into the flour using a pastry blender or two knives, until all the pieces are about $1/16$-inch in diameter or smaller. Dribble in the water, cutting it into the pastry until the pastry begins to come together and the mixture is soft, but not wet. Add more water if necessary. Gather the pastry into a ball. If it is too soft to roll out, chill until firmer; otherwise it can be rolled out immediately as described above, beginning at step 4.

Yield: 1 10- or 12-inch pie shell   Preparation: Fairly easy
Time: Fairly time consuming; advance preparation possible

Plum Almond Tart

This is a rather difficult dessert that you will find well worth mastering. It should be assembled and baked only 1 hour before serving. Adjust the granulated sugar to compensate for the tartness of the plums.

PASTRY:
1 cup all-purpose unbleached flour
6 tablespoons cold unsalted butter
½ cup coarsely ground blanched almonds
2 to 4 tablespoons cold water

FILLING:
3 pounds medium-ripe plums
½ cup cold water
¾ cup granulated sugar
3 egg whites
½ cup superfine sugar
½ cup very finely ground blanched almonds

1. To make the pastry, place the butter and flour in a bowl and lightly rub in the butter. Add almonds and sprinkle in 2 tablespoons cold water. Work the water into the flour, adding a little more water as necessary, until the dough comes together in one piece. The dough should be soft, but not wet. Wrap in plastic wrap and leave in a cool place for 30 minutes.
2. To roll out, lightly flour your counter and rolling pin. Roll lightly 2 or 3 strokes in front of you, and then turn the dough. Continue to roll out, turning the dough a little after 2 to 3 strokes, lightly flouring the board between each turn until the dough is the size of your tart pan. Fit the dough into a 10-inch pie tin and refrigerate.
3. Make the filling. Bring the water and the granulated sugar to a boil in a stainless steel or enamel saute pan. Turn off heat.
4. Slice the plums in half. Remove the pits and slice plums ½-inch thick. Turn the heat on under the syrup. Add half the plums and poach them for 3 minutes in the uncovered pan. Be careful not to overcook. Remove with a slotted spoon and set aside.

5. Reduce the syrup over medium high heat until it has a medium syrupy consistency. Add the remaining plums and cook until the plums have broken up. Continue to cook until the plums are a thick puree, stirring occasionally to keep them from scorching. Cool the puree.
6. The pastry shell, the poached plums, and the plum puree may be refrigerated up to 6 hours.
7. Preheat oven to 375 degrees. Line the pie shell with wax paper, weight the paper (see Baking Blind in Appendix I) and bake at 375 degrees for 10 minutes. Remove the paper and bake for another 5 minutes until light golden brown around the edges. Then remove the pie shell from the oven. Pour the plum puree into the pie shell and arrange poached plums on top.
8. Beat the egg whites until fairly stiff. Beat in the superfine sugar and continue to beat until glossy and stiff. Fold in the finely ground almonds gently, being careful not to overmix or the mixture will become runny. Spread the meringue over the plums.
9. Bake for 20 minutes until light golden brown. Cool the tart at room temperature and serve it within 1 hour.

Yield: 1 10-inch tart, serving 8   Preparation: Fairly difficult
Time: Time consuming; some advance preparation possible

Hazelnut Pumpkin Pie

The hazelnut crust gives this pie an added special flavor. Served with cognac-flavored whipped cream, it makes a great presentation at Thanksgiving.

PASTRY:
Pâte Brisée (page 482)

FILLING:
½ cup coarsely chopped hazelnuts
3 large eggs
½ teaspoon cinnamon
½ teaspoon ground ginger
¼ teaspoon ground cloves
¼ teaspoon ground allspice
½ to 1 cup pure maple syrup
2 cups thick pureed pumpkin (or hubbard squash)
¾ cup heavy cream

1. In a preheated 375-degree oven, cook hazelnuts for 7 to 10 minutes. Watch carefully that they do not burn. Cool, then rub in a coarse sieve until almost all the skins come off.
2. Chop the nuts in a food processor to a medium to fine consistency, being careful that you do not overprocess them. Add the hazelnuts to the Pâte Brisée recipe before adding the water. Roll out the pastry as described for Plum Almond Tart (page 484). Line a 10-inch pie tin, and rest in the refrigerator for 30 to 60 minutes.
3. Make the filling. Place the eggs in a bowl and whisk with the spices and ½ cup maple syrup, then whisk in the pumpkin or squash and heavy cream. Add more maple syrup to taste.
4. Both the pie crust and filling may be made the day before serving and stored in the refrigerator.
5. Preheat oven to 375 degrees.
6. Line the pie crust with wax paper, weight the paper, and bake the pie for 10 minutes. Remove the paper and bake for 5 more minutes until light golden brown on the edges. (Read about baking blind in Appendix I.)
7. Add the filling and bake for 30 to 40 minutes until the filling is set. Remove from the oven. Serve the pie at room temperature.

Yield: 1 10-inch pie, serving 10   Preparation: Fairly easy
Time: Fairly time consuming; advance preparation possible

Autumn Almond Crêpes

This is a fun crêpe dessert to serve in the fall when pears are available. It is especially good served with whipped cream flavored with cognac. Tart apples are a lovely substitute.

CRÊPES:
3 large eggs
1 cup cold water
3 tablespoons superfine sugar
¾ cup all-purpose unbleached flour
½ cup finely ground blanched almonds
1 drop almond extract
4 tablespoons unsalted butter

FILLING:
2 large medium-ripe pears
3 tablespoons unsalted butter
4 tablespoons sugar
Garnish: whipped cream flavored with cognac

1. Blend the eggs, water, and sugar in the blender for 1 minute. Add the flour and blend until it is well incorporated into the egg. Add the almonds and extract and blend for 30 seconds. Rest the batter in the refrigerator at least 1 hour, or up to 8 hours, before making the crêpes.
2. Just before making the crêpes, peel the pears. Cut them in quarters and remove the cores. Cut them in ¼-inch lengthwise slices, then slice across into ¼-inch cubes.
3. Heat the 3 tablespoons butter in a heavy 12-inch saute pan. Add the pears and sugar, and saute over a medium to high heat, tossing the whole time until the pears begin to caramelize. Be careful not to overcook or the pears will become mushy. You want them to retain some crispness. Set pan aside in a warm place.
4. To make the crêpes, heat 2 teaspoons butter in an 8-inch sloping-sided iron pan, a heavy Teflon pan (use only 1 teaspoon of butter in a Teflon pan), or a heavy stainless steel-lined aluminum pan. When the butter bubbles, pour in ¼ cup of the batter. Roll the pan so the whole bottom surface is covered. Cook on medium heat until the underside of the crêpe is golden brown. Flip or turn it over with a round-ended metal spatula. Cook until the other side is golden brown.

5. Slide half the crêpe onto a dessert plate. Top with one-sixth of the pear filling, and flip the rest of the crêpe over the filling. Keep warm as you make the other crêpes. You will need to work quickly.
6. Garnish filled crêpes with whipped cream and serve.

Servings: 6   **Preparation: Fairly easy**
Time: Fairly time consuming; some advance preparation possible

Hazelnut Meringues

These crisp and flavorful nut meringues make a very light dessert. They may be held for 5 days before serving. It is not advisable to make them on a rainy humid day, as they tend to turn soggy. These may be served with fresh fruits or Chocolate Ganache (see page 465).

1 1/4 cup hazelnuts
1 tablespoon cornstarch
3/4 cup superfine sugar
6 egg whites
Strawberries, blueberries, or raspberries
whipped cream

1. Bake the hazelnuts in a preheated 400-degree oven for 5 to 7 minutes until the skins begin to crack and the nuts are lightly brown. Do not overcook or the nuts will burn. While warm, rub the nuts in a coarse sieve until almost all the skins are removed; however, a little skin left on is fine. Cool.
2. Reduce the oven temperature to 300 degrees. Butter and flour two heavy cookie sheets. Mark 3-inch rounds on the sheets.
3. Place the hazelnuts, cornstarch, and 1/4 cup sugar in a food processor and grind until fine. Do not overprocess or the nuts will become oily.
4. Beat the egg whites until fairly stiff, then beat in the remaining 1/2 cup sugar until the whites are very stiff and glossy. Remove from the mixter and gently fold in the nut mixture with a plastic spatula, being careful

not to overfold or the mixture will lose its volume. Pipe or spread the mixture on the marked rounds on the cookie sheets.

5. Bake in the preheated 300-degree oven for 25 to 30 minutes. Loosen the meringues from the baking sheet with a sharp metal spatula, then return them to a 150-degree oven for 1 hour until they have dried out. (If you have any trouble loosening the meringues from the baking sheet, return them to the oven for 5 minutes and then try again.)

6. Place meringues on a cooling rack for 30 minutes, then store in an airtight container until ready to use. They may be made 5 days ahead of time. If they lose their crispness, dry in a 250-degree oven for 15 minutes.

7. To serve, place a meringue on a dessert plate, pipe flavored whipped cream around the outside, and fill the center with fresh fruit. Or pipe Chocolate Ganache (see page 465) around the outside.

Yield: 10 to 12 meringues   **Preparation: Fairly difficult**
Time: Time consuming; advance preparation possible

Shortbread Cookies

The addition of fine Semolina (available in Italian food markets) gives these cookies a wonderful texture. (Finely blended yellow cornmeal can be substituted for the Semolina, but Semolina is preferable.) They may be stored for 5 days in an airtight container at room temperature.

8 tablespoons unsalted butter, very soft but not melted
¼ cup superfine sugar
1 teaspoon finely grated lemon rind (or 1 teaspoon vanilla extract)
1 to 1½ cups all-purpose unbleached flour
¼ cup fine Semolina

1. Beat the butter until very soft and very smooth. Gradually beat in the sugar and add the lemon or vanilla and continue to beat until light and fluffy.
2. Add the Semolina and stir until smooth. Beat in enough flour to give a stiff, but still pliable dough.
3. Place the dough in aluminum foil, shape into a sausage, 1½ inches in diameter, and tightly roll up in the foil. Refrigerate for at least 1 hour or up to 24 hours.
4. Preheat the oven to 375 degrees. Remove the dough from the refrigerator 30 minutes before slicing. Butter a heavy baking sheet.
5. Slice the dough ⅛-inch thick. If the dough is difficult to slice or starts to break up, dip the knife into boiling water. Place cookies on the sheet pan, leaving a 1½-inch space between each one. Slightly flatten with your hand.
6. Bake for 10 to 15 minutes until light golden bown. Remove the cookies from the sheet pan with a spatula and immediately place on a cooling rack. When cool, store in an airtight container.

Yield: 25 to 30 cookies   **Preparation: Easy**
Time: Fairly time consuming; advance preparation possible

Coconut Caramel

Here is a fine variation on the classic crème caramel, which is fun to garnish with a selection of fresh fruits. Instead of using individual molds, you may use one 5- to 7-cup mold, but then you need to decrease the sugar for the caramel to ½ cup. It is extremely important to choose molds that are ovenproof; they should be warm and dry before you put in the caramel, or they may crack. Read about bain maries (water bath) in Appendix I .

> ¾ cup superfine sugar
> 2½ cups light cream
> 4 egg yolks
> 2 large eggs
> ½ cup unsweetened grated coconut
> ½ cup Coco Lopez
> fresh fruits for garnish

1. Heat a heavy 10- to 12-inch saute pan, add ¾ cup sugar, and dissolve over medium heat. During this process, occasionally tilt the pan from side to side so the sugar dissolves evenly. (Do not use a spoon, as the caramel will stick to it.) Once the sugar is dissolved, continue to cook, still tilting the pan occasionally, until the sugar is dark golden brown.
2. Immediately, using a metal spoon, pour the caramel into 6 to 8 6-ounce molds. Quickly twist each mold so the caramel comes halfway up the sides. Be extremely careful during the process as the caramel is very hot. Set molds to one side.
3. Scald the cream in a saucepan, then cool it down to 120 degees.
4. Preheat oven to 325 degrees.
5. Place the egg yolks, whole eggs, coconut, and Coco Lopez in a bowl and whisk until well mixed. Very slowly whisk in the cream and continue to whisk for 1 minute.
6. Pour the mixture into the molds, place the molds in a roasting pan, and add enough hot water to the pan to come three-fourths of the way up the sides of the molds.
7. Cook at 325 degrees for 1 to 1½ hours for individual molds and 1½ to 2 hours for a large mold until the custard is just set.
8. Remove the molds from the roasting pan and cool. Cover each one and refrigerate at least 2 hours or up to 48 hours.
9. To unmold, ease a small, rounded-end knife around the custard and turn it out on a dessert plate. Garnish with fresh fruits.

Servings: 6 to 8   Preparation: Fairly easy
Time: Time consuming; advance preparation necessary

Lime Caramel

The addition of lime gives this caramel a very pleasing tart flavor. Be careful not to overcook the custard, as it will shrink and the texture will be a little rubbery. If you do not have individual molds, use a 5- to 7-cup mold and decrease the sugar for the caramel to ½ cup.

> *1 cup + 2 tablespoons superfine sugar*
> *2½ cups light cream*
> *4 egg yolks*
> *3 whole eggs*
> *1 teaspoon finely grated lime rind (zest)*
> *⅓ cup fresh lime juice*
> *whipped cream, strawberries, and kiwi fruit for garnish*

1. Heat a heavy 10- to 12-inch saute pan, add ¾ cup sugar, and dissolve it over medium heat. During this process, tilt the pan from side to side occasionally so the sugar dissolves evenly. (Do not use a spoon, as the caramel tends to stick to the spoon.) Once the sugar is dissolved, continue to cook, still tilting the pan occasionally, until the sugar is dark golden brown.
2. Immediately, using a metal spoon, pour the caramel into 6 to 8 6-ounce molds. Quickly twist each mold so the caramel comes halfway up the sides. Be extremely careful during this process as the caramel is very hot. Set the molds to one side.
3. Scald the cream in a saucepan, then cool it down to 120 degrees.
4. Preheat oven to 325 degrees.
5. Place the egg yolks, whole eggs, lime rind, lime juice, and ⅓ cup sugar in a bowl and whisk until well mixed. Very slowly whisk in the cream and continue to whisk for 1 minute.
6. Pour the mixture into the molds, place the molds in a roasting pan, and add enough hot water to the pan to come three-fourths of the way up the sides of the molds.
7. Cook at 325 degrees for 1½ to 2 hours in a large mold until the custard is just set.
8. Remove the molds from the roasting pan and cool. Cover each one and refrigerate at least 2 hours or up to 48 hours.
9. To unmold, ease a small, rounded-end knife around the custard and turn it out on a dessert plate. Garnish with whipped cream, strawberries, and slices of kiwi fruit.

Servings: 6 to 8   **Preparation: Fairly easy**
Time: Time consuming; advance preparation necessary

Pears Chinoise

The sauce for this dish is clean, sweet, and hot from the ginger. If you are concerned that it may be too spicy, decrease the ginger to ½ tablespoon. Be careful that the pears are not too ripe.

6 medium-ripe Comice pears
3 cups water
¾ cup sugar
½ cup fresh lemon juice
1 tablespoon peeled and very finely sliced ginger
fresh mint sprigs for garnish
whipped cream

1. Place the water, sugar, and lemon juice in a 3-quart stainless steel saucepan. Dissolve the sugar over medium heat and then boil for 3 minutes. This is your poaching liquid.
2. Peel the pears, cut lengthwise, into quarters, and remove the cores.
3. Add the pears to the poaching liquid and gently simmer for 10 to 15 minutes until they are soft. Remove the pears with a slotted spoon and place in a serving bowl.
4. Add the sliced ginger to the pear syrup, reduce on high heat to ¾ cup and then cool.
5. Pour the liquid that has accumulated around the pears into the syrup and stir. Pour the cooled syrup over the pears and chill 1 to 2 hours, or up to 2 days.
6. Just before serving, garnish with the mint sprigs. Serve with the whipped cream.

Servings: 6   Preparation: Easy
Time: Fairly time consuming; advance preparation necessary

Pear Almond Pudding

This is a very simple dessert to prepare. It has a wonderful rich flavor and is lovely served warm with whipped cream.

4 medium-ripe Bartlett or Bosc pears
1 cup finely ground blanched almonds
12 tablespoons unsalted butter, room temperature
½ cup superfine sugar
4 egg yolks
4 tablespoons cake flour
⅛ teaspoon almond extract
whipped cream for garnish

1. Butter a 10-inch round, ovenproof serving dish with 1 tablespoon butter. (The dish should be 1½ inches high.)
2. Place the remaining butter in a bowl and beat with an electric beater until smooth. Slowly add the sugar and beat on a high speed until light in color. Add the egg yolks one at a time and beat until they are well incorporated.
3. Turn down the mixer to low speed, add the flour and almond extract, and beat for 1 minute. Stir in the ground almonds with a spoon or plastic spatula.
4. Peel pears. Cut them in quarters lengthwise and remove the core. Cut each quarter in half lengthwise.
5. Arrange the pears in the baking dish in a circle, tightly packed together. Then fill the center with more pears. Spread the almond mixture over the top.
6. This dessert can be prepared up to this point 1 hour before cooking and stored at room temperature.
7. Preheat oven to 400 degrees.
8. Place dish in the oven and bake for 35 to 45 minutes until light golden brown and the almond mixture is firm. Serve warm, topped with whipped cream.

Servings: 6   Preparation: Easy
Time: Fairly time consuming; advance preparation possible

Fruits Creole

This is a wonderful and very attractive winter fruit dessert.

½ cup dried apricots
1 small pineapple
2 oranges
1 pint strawberries, washed
1 cup water
½ cup sugar
⅓ cup fresh lemon juice
½ cup toasted slivered almonds
½ cup shredded toasted coconut (optional)

1. Place the water, sugar, and lemon juice in a 1-quart stainless steel saucepan. Bring to a boil, stirring occasionally, then boil for 5 minutes.
2. While the sugar syrup is cooking, thinly slice the apricots. Remove the syrup from the heat, put the apricots into the hot syrup, and pour into a large bowl.
3. Cut the top and outside skin off the pineapple. Cut pineapple in half lengthwise, then cut it into quarters lengthwise, and cut out the core. Slice into ¼-inch-thick slices. Add slices to the syrup.
4. Cut away the rind and pith from the orange. Cut in half lengthwise, then in quarters lengthwise, and slice. Add to the syrup.
5. Cut the tops off the strawberries, and if they are large, cut them in half. Add to the syrup.
6. Refrigerate the mixture at least 1 hour before serving. However, to maintain the best texture and freshness from the fruit, do not make more than 3 hours ahead of serving.
7. Just before serving, pour fruit into a serving bowl, and sprinkle the top with the almonds and coconut.

Servings: 8   **Preparation: Easy**
Time: Quick, advance preparation necessary

Two-Melon Compote

What could be nicer on a hot, sultry day than this cool and light dessert? Just be sure to use ripe melons.

1 small ripe honeydew
1 small ripe cantaloupe
⅓ cup sugar
⅓ cup water
2 thin slices of peeled ginger
¼ cup fresh lime juice
2 tablespoons fresh mint, coarsely chopped (optional)
1 lime, sliced thin, for garnish

1. Place the sugar, water, and ginger in a stainless steel pan over low heat. Stir occasionally until the sugar has dissolved, then gently simmer for 10 minutes.
2. Strain the liquid, cool, and add the lime juice.
3. Cut the melons in half, scoop out the seeds, and scoop out the melon with a large melon baller. Place the melon balls in a serving bowl, add the syrup, and refrigerate for 2 to 4 hours. After an hour or so of chilling, taste the syrup, add more sugar if you wish.
4. Just before serving, stir and add the mint leaves.
5. Thinly slice the lime and garnish the melon with the lime slices.

Servings: 8 to 10   Preparation: Easy
Time: Quick; advance preparation necessary

Apple Pear Compote

This fruit dish is delightful with my Maple Pecan Gâteau (page 472), Hazelnut Gâteau (page 474), or a warm gingerbread.

> 3 medium-ripe pears, peeled
> 3 tart apples, peeled
> ¾ cup water
> 2 tablespoons fresh lemon juice
> ½ cup sugar

1. Place the water, lemon juice, and sugar in a stainless steel pan. Bring to a boil, stirring occasionally, until all the sugar has dissolved, then gently simmer for 10 minutes.
2. Cut the pears and apples into quarters, remove the cores, and cut into 2-inch cubes. Add to the syrup and gently simmer for 15 to 20 minutes, stirring occasionally.
3. Remove from the heat and serve warm.
4. This may be cooked a couple of days ahead of serving and refrigerated. Reheat just before serving.

Servings: 6   **Preparation: Easy**
Time: Fairly time consuming; advance preparation possible

Peach and Blueberry Compote

This simple and light fruit is especially popular with children. It is important to choose ripe, not mealy, peaches.

4 ripe peaches
1 pint blueberries
¼ cup water
⅓ cup sugar
⅓ cup fresh lemon juice
fresh mint sprigs for garnish

1. Place the water, sugar, and lemon juice in a 1-quart stainless steel saucepan and slowly bring to a boil, stirring occasionally. Then gently simmer for 5 minutes. Remove from the heat and cool.
2. Bring 2 quarts water to a boil in a 4-quart saucepan. Place the peaches in the water for 15 seconds, and remove with a slotted spoon. Slip off the peach skins. Cut the peaches in half, remove the pits, and slice. Place in the cooled syrup.
3. Add the blueberries to the peaches and refrigerate for at least 1 hour, but no more than 3 hours, before serving.
4. Before serving, place compote in a serving bowl and garnish with the mint sprigs.

Servings: 6   Preparation: Easy
Time: Quick; advance preparation necessary

Raspberries Maurice

This recipe was given to me by Maurice Moore-Betty. It is a very easy dessert, perfect to make when raspberries are plentiful and ripe. For an interesting contrast in texture, serve it with a Shortbread Cookie (page 490) or a Hazelnut Meringue (page 488).

2 pints ripe strawberries
1 pint ripe raspberries
sugar to taste
1 cup heavy cream

1. Wash the strawberries and hull them. Refrigerate.
2. Puree the raspberries in a food processor until smooth. Add sugar to taste and puree for 30 seconds. Refrigerate for 30 minutes or up to 3 hours.
3. Just before serving, whip the cream until stiff; add sugar if desired.
4. Place the strawberries on 6 dessert plates. Spoon raspberry sauce over the strawberries, and pipe on the whipped cream. Serve with Shortbread Cookies or Hazelnut Meringues.

Servings: 6   Preparation: Easy
Time: Quick; advance preparation necessary

Fresh Figs with Ginger Crème

The combination of ripe fresh figs served on the chilled ginger crème is absolutely sublime.

6 ripe black or white figs, unpeeled
1¼ cups heavy cream
2 tablespoons peeled and ⅛-inch-thick sliced ginger
4 egg yolks
2 tablespoons sugar
2 tablespoons finely chopped crystallized ginger
6 fresh mint sprigs for garnish

1. Place the cream in a heavy 1-quart saucepan with the fresh ginger. On a low heat bring up to the scalding point. The cream might curdle; however, it emulsifies when the custard is made.
2. Meanwhile, beat the egg yolks and the sugar with an electric mixer until light in color.
3. Have a bowl of ice water ready. Find another bowl that will fit into the bowl of ice water, with its bottom touching the water.
4. Pour the cream slowly through a fine sieve onto the egg yolks, whisk and return to the saucepan. Whisk over medium heat until the custard starts to thicken. Be careful not to boil or the custard might curdle.
5. Pour the custard immediately into the bowl placed over the ice water, and whisk until the custard has cooled to warm. Stir in the crystallized ginger.
6. Refrigerate the custard 2 hours, or up to 24 hours.
7. One hour before serving, place 6 dessert plates in the freezer. Thirty minutes before serving, place the custard in the freezer.
8. Just before serving, cut the stem off each fig. Slice figs ¼-inch thick.
9. Spoon the custard onto each plate, arrange the fig slices on the custard, and garnish with a mint sprig.

Servings: 6   **Preparation: Easy**
Time: Time consuming; some advance preparation necessary

Figs, Cheese, and Honey

This simple yet elegant dessert is one I have eaten many times on the island of Ibizia. There it is always served with beautifully ripe figs, and local wild honey and cheese. The key to preparing this dessert is to choose a mild chèvre or a soft cheese of your preference and an aromatic wild honey. Flowering herbs are delightful as the garnish.

6 ounces mild chèvre cheese (or another soft cheese)
6 fresh figs, unpeeled
⅓ cup wild honey
6 fresh thyme sprigs or fresh basil leaves for garnish

1. Chill 6 dessert plates.
2. Just before serving, slice each fig into ¼-inch-thick slices and arrange on one side of the plates. Spoon the honey onto each plate. Divide the chèvre into 6 parts. Place on the other side of the plates.
3. Garnish each plate with a thyme sprig or basil leaf.

Servings: 6   **Preparation: Easy**
Time: Quick

Fresh Peaches Diane

You should use only perfectly ripe peaches to get the finest texture and flavor from this multifaceted dessert. Strawberry Sauce (page 505) or Raspberry Sauce (page 503) may be substituted for the Blueberry Sauce.

4 large ripe peaches
¾ cup shelled unsalted pistachio nuts
4 tablespoons confectioners' sugar
⅓ cup crème fraîche (or sour cream)
1 cup Blueberry Sauce (page 504)

1. Grind pistachios in a food processor until fairly fine. Mix with sugar and crème fraîche in a bowl and refrigerate 1 to 2 hours.
2. Just before serving, peel peaches by dipping them in boiling water for 10 seconds, then slip off the skins. Cut in half and remove pit. Fill each half with ⅛ of the pistachio mixture.
3. Arrange the peach halves on a platter, pistachio stuffing down, and pour the blueberry sauce on top.

Servings: 4   Preparation: Easy
Time: Fairly time consuming; some advance preparation possible

Raspberry Sauce

Here is an ideal sauce to make when raspberries are plentiful—even when they're somewhat overripe and mushy. You can make it quickly and freeze it for use during the winter. Try serving it with White Chocolate Almond Torte (page 459) or Hazelnut Gâteau (page 474).

1 pint raspberries
1 cup red wine
⅓ cup sugar
⅓ cup crème de Cassis (optional)

1. Place the red wine in a 1-quart stainless steel saucepan, bring it to a boil, and ignite. Allow to flame for 3 minutes. Remove from the heat and add the sugar. Return the pan to a low heat, and gently stir until all the sugar has dissolved. Then turn up the heat and boil for 10 minutes.
2. Add the raspberries and cassis and boil for another 10 minutes. Then press the mixture through a fine sieve. Chill.
3. This sauce may be made 3 days ahead of serving time and stored in the refrigerator, or frozen.

Yield: 1½ cups   Preparation: Easy
Time: Quick; may be frozen

Blueberry Sauce

The color of this sauce is stunning. It is an ideal way to use slightly mushy, overripe blueberries, as it can be made in large batches and frozen. It is excellent with fresh Peaches Diane (page 504), Almond Torte (page 450), or White Chocolate Almond Torte (page 459).

> *1 pint ripe blueberries*
> *1 cup red wine*
> *⅓ cup sugar*
> *⅛ teaspoon cinnamon*
> *1 teaspoon finely grated orange rind (zest)*

1. Place the red wine in a 1-quart stainless steel saucepan, bring it to a boil, and ignite. Allow it to flame for 3 minutes. Remove from the heat and add the sugar, cinnamon, and orange zest.
2. Return the saucepan to a low heat and gently stir until all the sugar has dissolved. Then turn up the heat and boil for 5 minutes. Add the blueberries and boil for 10 minutes. Press the mixture through a fine sieve. Chill.
3. This sauce may be refrigerated for up to 3 days, or frozen.

Yield: 1¼ to 1½ cups   **Preparation: Easy**
Time: Quick; may be frozen

Strawberry Sauce

This very quick and simple sauce is great served with White Chocolate Almond Torte (page 459) or Almond Torte (page 450).

> 1 cup fresh strawberries, hulled and sliced in half
> 2 tablespoons sugar
> 1 teaspoon grated orange rind (zest)

1. Place all the ingredients in a food processor or blender and process until a fine puree. Taste, and add more sugar if desired.
2. Refrigerate to chill, or to hold up to 24 hours. It will thicken as it chills, just whisk a little before serving.

Yield: 1 cup   Preparation: Easy
Time: Quick; advance preparation necessary

Basic Crème

These custards are great served with fresh fruits and desserts such as Apricot-Almond Souffle Torte (see page 448). It is quick to make; however, you must be careful not to let it curdle. Take it almost to the boiling point to ensure maximum thickening of the custard, but do not let it boil. (Read about curdling in Appendix I.) If you want a thinner custard, substitute light cream or milk for the heavy cream. Four flavor variations of the recipe are listed at the end.

> 1¼ cups heavy cream
> 4 egg yolks
> ⅓ cup sugar
> 1 teaspoon vanilla extract

1. Heat the cream in a heavy 1-quart saucepan until it reaches the scalding point.
2. Beat the egg yolks with the sugar until light in color.

3. Have a bowl of ice water ready plus another bowl that can fit into the bowl of ice water. The ice water should just touch the bottom of the top bowl.
4. Pour the cream slowly into the egg mixture. Then return the mixture to the heat and cook, whisking all the time, until the custard starts to thicken (it should coat the back of a spoon). The foam that is on the top of the custard should start to disappear at this point. Be very careful at this point; you want maximum thickness for the custard, but if it boils, the custard might curdle.
5. Pour the custard immediately into the top bowl over the bowl of ice water and stir until warm. (If you want a smoother consistency, strain the custard through a fine sieve.)
6. Pour the custard into a container or serving bowl and refrigerate at least 2 hours, or up to 2 days, before serving.

Kirsch Crème Variation: This crème is delicious with raspberry and cherry desserts. Omit the vanilla from the Basic Crème recipe. Add ¼ cup of a good-quality Kirsch after you have completed the custard.

Lemon Crème Variation: Lemon Crème is great served with raspberries, strawberries, blueberries, or sliced fresh peaches. Omit the vanilla from the Basic Crème. Add 1 teaspoon finely grated lemon rind (zest) to the cream before scalding. On completing the crème, stir in 2 tablespoons fresh lemon juice. Do not sieve crème upon completion.

Orange Crème Variation: Raspberries, strawberries, or sliced fresh peaches are delicious with Orange Crème. To make it, omit the vanilla from the Basic Crème recipe. Add 1 teaspoon finely grated orange rind (zest) to the cream before scalding. On completing the crème, stir in 1 to 2 table-spoons fresh lemon juice. Do not push crème through a sieve on completion.

Coffee Crème Variation: If you like coffee, serve Coffee Crème with Hazelnut Gâteau (page 474), Chocolate Souffle Torte (page 452), or a chocolate cake. To make it, omit the vanilla from the Basic Crème recipe. Upon completion, add ¼ cup Coffee Essence (page 477).

**Servings: 4 to 6   Preparation: Easy
Time: Quick; advance preparation possible**

Cognac-Currant Ice Cream

This is my mother's recipe for a dessert that she always served during the Christmas season.

2 cups light cream
2 cups milk
8 egg yolks
½ cup sugar
½ cup cognac
¼ cup currants

1. Place the currants in the cognac, cover, and let soak for at least 1 hour.
2. Scald the cream and milk in a heavy 3-quart saucepan. Meanwhile, beat the egg yolks and sugar until light in color.
3. Have a bowl of ice water ready and another bowl that fits into the bowl of ice water.
4. Pour the scalded milk slowly over the egg yolks, whisking all the time. Return the custard to the pan and whisk over medium heat until the custard starts to thicken. Be careful not to boil or the custard might curdle. Pour immediately into the bowl over the ice water and whisk until warm. Add the cognac and currants.
5. Chill the mixture until cold, or up to 24 hours if you wish.
6. Pour the mixture into an ice cream maker and freeze according to manufacturer's instructions. Meanwhile, place a container in a freezer to chill.
7. When the ice cream is frozen, spoon into the cool container immediately and store in the freezer no more than 2 hours. Thirty to 60 minutes before serving, remove from freezer and refrigerate to slightly soften.

Yield: 1½ quarts   Preparation: Fairly difficult
Time: Fairly time consuming; advance preparation necessary

Chocolate-Cognac Ice Cream

This is a lovely and rich chocolate ice cream.

2 cups light cream
2 cups milk
8 egg yolks
½ cup sugar
4 ounces semisweet chocolate (preferably Swiss chocolate),
    finely chopped
2 ounces unsweetened chocolate, finely chopped
¼ cup cognac (optional)

1. Scald the milk and cream in a heavy 3-quart saucepan. While the milk is scalding, place the egg yolks in a bowl, add the sugar, and beat until light in color.
2. Place the chocolate in a separate bowl.
3. Pour the scalded milk over the eggs, whisking all the time. Return the custard to the pan and whisk over medium heat until the custard starts to thicken. Be careful not to boil, or the custard might curdle.
4. Pour the custard immediately over the chocolate and gently whisk until all the chocolate is dissolved and the mixture is well emulsified. Add the cognac.
5. Chill the mixture until cold, or up to 24 hours if you wish.
6. Pour the mixture into an ice cream maker and freeze according to manufacturer's instructions. Meanwhile, place a container in a freezer to chill.
7. When the ice cream is frozen, spoon into the cool container immediately and store in the freezer no more than 2 hours. Thirty to 60 minutes before serving, remove it from the freezer and place in the refrigerator to slightly soften.

Yield: 1½ quarts   Preparation: Fairly difficult
Time: Fairly time consuming; advanced preparation necessary

Maple-Coffee Ice Cream

The extra effort of using coffee essence in this recipe gives the ice cream a wonderful flavor.

2 cups light cream
2 cups milk
9 egg yolks
¾ cup pure maple syrup
⅓ cup Coffee Essence (page 477)

1. Scald the milk and cream in a heavy 3-quart saucepan. While the milk is scalding, place the egg yolks in a bowl, add the syrup, and whisk until light in color.
2. Have a bowl of ice water ready and another bowl that fits into the bowl of ice water.
3. Pour the scalded milk over the egg yolks, whisking all the time. Return the custard to the pan and whisk over medium heat until the custard starts to thicken. Be careful not to boil or the custard might curdle.
4. Pour the custard immediately into the bowl over the ice water and whisk until it is just warm. Add the coffee essence.
5. Chill the mixture until cold, or up to 24 hours.
6. Pour mixture into an ice cream maker and freeze according to manufacturer's instructions. Meanwhile, place a container in the freezer to chill.
7. When the ice cream is frozen spoon into the cool container immediately, and store in the freezer no longer than 2 hours. Thirty to 60 minutes before serving, remove it from the freezer and place in the refrigerator to slightly soften.

Yield: 1½ quarts   Preparation: Fairly difficult
Time: Fairly time consuming; advance preparation necessary

Menus

Recipes preceded by an asterisk are not in this book.

Spring Menus

Simple Dinner Menu
Ceviche of Halibut
Cannelloni Veronese
Green Bean and Cucumber Salad
Black Pepper Bread
Fruits Creole

Elegant Dinner Menu
Crème D'Or
Chicken Terrine with Watercress and Cucumber
Sauteed Scallops with Pesto
*Steamed Asparagus
Hazelnut Meringues with Fresh Strawberries and Whipped Cream

Summer Menus

Simple Dinner Menu
Mint and Pea Soup
Barbecued Lamb
Tabouli
Greek Eggplant Salad
Walnut Cumin Bread
Fresh Peaches Diane

Elegant Dinner Menu
Chilled Avocado and Zucchini Soup
Shrimp Venetian Style with Boston Lettuce
Chicken Maurice
Sauteed Cucumbers and Peas
White Almond Chocolate Torte with Raspberry Sauce and Whipped Cream

Fall Menus

Simple Dinner Menu
Tomato, Mushroom, and Thyme Soup
Autumn Chicken Casserole
Cabbage with Parsley and Caraway
Warm Corn Bread
Pear Almond Pudding

Elegant Dinner Menu
Solferino Soup
Italian Seafood Salad
Veal Florentine
* Boiled Red Russet Potatoes with Fresh Herbs
Chocolate Souffle Torte with Whipped Cream

Winter Menus

Simple Dinner Menu
Crème Élysée
Watercress, Cucumber, and Mushroom Salad with Creamy Dill Dressing
Pork Vallee Dauge
* Steamed Broccoli
Greek Orange-Almond Cake

Elegant Dinner Menu
Spanish Fish Stew
Tossed Green Salad with Hazelnut Dressing
Carne Asado
Black Bean Stew Garnished with Avocado
* Zucchini with Parsley
Carribean Gâteau with Whipped Cream and Pineapple

Lunch Menus

Soup Piment
Fettucine Trote
Tomato, Avocado, and Watercress Salad
Two-Melon Compote

Asparagus Soup
Crabmeat Salad Dana with Vine-Ripened Tomatoes and Watercress
Lime Caramel

Dinner Menus

Potage Savoyarde
Chicken Lundi
Creamed Spinach
Glazed Carrots Swedish Style
Almond Roulade with Candied Oranges

Beef Milanese
Trout Piment
Sauteed Green Vegetables
Hazelnut Bread
Cognac-Currant Ice Cream with Shortbread Cookies

Cold Buffet

Italian Fish Salad
Chicken Almond Salad
Pasta Salad with Marinated Carrots
Green Bean Salad Garnished with Sliced Vine-Ripened Tomatoes
Onion Rosemary Bread
Apricot-Almond Souffle Torte

Late-Night Supper
Salmon Tart
Fagiolini Verdi con Proscuitto
Raspberries Maurice

Appendix I: Hints for the Kitchen

It has been my experience both in operating a kitchen and in teaching cooking classes that although styles change, the problems and questions remain basically the same. In this section I wish to bring to your attention the answers to those problems and questions that I have learned.

Alcohol in cooking: Flaming red wine is a practice I was taught in the beginning of my training and have used ever since. In flaming red wine, by removing the alcohol the intention is to remove the roughness of the wine and keep only the very best. Some chefs have said that this is not necessary, but having tried it both ways, I can say that this step produces a much more pleasant dish, particularly when the wine is added in the final reduction of a sauce.

It is a simple procedure to follow: Place the wine in a stainless steel pan (an aluminum pan should not be used, as the acid and minerals in the wine will react with this metal and give the wine a metallic taste) and bring it to a boil. Tilt the pan forward and ignite the wine with a long match. Allow the (still simmering) wine to flame for 2 to 3 minutes. Should the wine not ignite, do not be concerned; simply boil for 4 minutes, and this will dissipate the alcohol.

Do not flame white wine, as it will change the flavor of the wine, making it quite acidic. Do not boil such alcohol as cognac, whiskey, or kirsch. They need to be heated only slightly, to 130 degrees, then added to the other ingredients, and ignited. Never take these spirits in a bottle to the stove. When you are pouring from the bottle (especially if the bottle is warm), the flame could ignite the portion being poured, as well as the contents of the bottle, causing it to explode. Pour only the amount of alcohol required into a measuring cup, and pour it into the pan.

Do not pour alcohol into pans containing a large amount of hot butter or oil, as the fat might catch on fire.

Al dente: To prepare vegetables and pasta in such a way that they remain lightly crisp or firm. As soon as you have determined that a food is *al dente*, remove it from the stove and immediately drain. Run cold water over vegetables (a process called refreshing) to halt the cooking process and produce the desired effect.

Bain marie: Also defined as a water bath. When a gentle heat for cooking food is called for, put the dish of food in a container of water in the oven rather than directly on the oven rack. Using a bain marie allows the food to cook at a lower temperature so that the ingredients will not toughen or curdle. A bain marie is typically used in the preparation of mousselines, terrines, pâtés, and custards. Place the mold or dish of food in a deep roasting pan, then pour water heated to a temperature of 150 or 160 degrees into the pan to a level not more than three-fourths of the height of the mold or dish.

Although this method is the best way to cook delicate foods, it is still possible to overcook in a bain marie. Crème caramel often suffers this fate, becoming rubbery and releasing moisture that will float on the surface of the custard. To prevent overcooking, do not cook at a high temperature; and remove the dish from the bain marie as soon as it has reached the required temperature and/or it is set.

Baking blind: To prebake a pie shell with no filling. The reason is to make certain that the pastry will hold its shape in the pie pan. For this process, you should line the pastry shell with wax paper and weight the paper with purchased "pie weights" or raw converted rice. (The rice can be used time and time again.) Two important points: Do not overweight the pie shell or the bottom will become soggy; and halfway through cooking (when the top of the crust turns light golden brown) remove the weight and paper and finish baking. It is also important to refrigerate the pastry for one hour before baking. Do not add the wax paper and weights until you are ready to bake the pastry because the weights will get cold and affect the cooking of the pastry.

Baste: To spoon the pan juices or a marinade over roasts or broiled foods, using a large metal spoon. Basting helps keep the food moist and adds to the flavor.

Beat: To beat food items by applying a vigorous motion with a wooden spoon, whisk, electric mixer, or hand-held beater. Some examples are beating egg whites until they are stiff, or beating egg yolks until light in color.

Blanch: To cook foods for a short period of time in boiling water. This method is used for the following reasons:

1. When tomatoes and peaches are blanched, it facilitates the peeling process. The blanching takes from 10 to 30 seconds, depending on the ripeness of the fruit; the less ripe, the longer you need to blanch. Be careful not to leave the food in the water too long, as the food's surface will begin to cook and it will not retain its firm texture. For some recipes, onions, shallots, and garlic are blanched to make removing the skin easier; this is helpful when you have a large quantity to peel. In the case of garlic, it is necessary to separate the cloves from the bud before blanching. With any of these vegetables or fruits, immediately after blanching run the food under cold water (refresh) to halt the cooking process.
2. Vegetables to be used in a cold vegetable salad or as crudités may be

lightly blanched to remove their pungency and make them more digestible. This is especially true of broccoli and cauliflower. After blanching, green vegetables should be refreshed under cold water; this not only stops the cooking process but will also help them retain their brilliant green color. Vegetables that are going to be marinated, such as cauliflower, yams, or carrots, should be allowed to drain for 2 minutes and then be added to the marinade while still warm, so that the vegetables absorb the flavor of the marinade.

3. If you wish to saute green beans, cabbage, broccoli, or cauliflower, you will get a finer finished product if you preblanch. This will remove the strong flavor of the vegetable and ensure that it will cook evenly. With some vegetables, this may be done several hours before cooking. Blanching also removes strong flavors, such as salt in bacon or the astringent flavor in sliced onion.

4. Blanching is a required step in freezing vegetables. They should be blanched a designated period of time to inactivate the enzymes. It is important that the vegetables be refreshed with cold water immediately after blanching, drained well, and patted dry.

5. Blanching nuts, such as almonds and pistachios, loosens the skins, making them easier to peel. For the procedure, see page 533.

Blender uses: I prefer the blender for certain executions and offer the following reasons:

1. Pureeing in the blender gives soups, sauces, and chicken livers (for pâtés) a much smoother consistency.

2. One can obtain greater results (a thicker, silkier mixture) when using the blender to make mayonnaise.

3. It is perfect for grinding hard spices (a finer grind may be achieved): for example, black peppercorns, fennel seeds, cumin seeds, and coriander seeds. (Just be sure that the blender container is very dry before adding the spices.)

4. It gives a smooth consistency to a crêpe batter.

5. It is extremely helpful in turning a lumpy cooked sauce into a smooth sauce.

The following may be done in a blender; however, I find that a food processor gives better results.

1. Grinding nuts: Only small amounts should be done at a time, as the nuts will tend to stick to the bottom of the blender, producing an oily paste.

2. Making bread crumbs: These also require only small batches at a time and tend to be time consuming.

3. Chopping cooked spinach and fresh herbs: This is better in the food processor, as the blade gives a cleaner cut.

4. Thick mixtures such as vegetable purees: These may be done in the blender, but only in very small batches.

When you puree hot liquids in the blender, you should be very careful. I have found that the safest procedure is to turn on the blender while it is still empty. Then slowly pour in the hot mixture. This technique will prevent the forming of an air pocket that would cause the liquid to burst out of the top. This not only would create a mess but could also burn you.

Boil: Boiling is to cook foods either in water or other liquids, bringing them up to 212 degrees Fahrenheit, at which point they will boil. It should be mentioned that there are two degrees of boiling: gentle boiling, on a low heat, and rapid boiling, on high heat. I tend to boil foods without the lid on. I find, for example, that this method will help green vegetables retain their color and will get rid of some of the sulfur. Keep in mind that if vegetables are to be added to boiling water, they should be at room temperature. If they are cold, they will drastically decrease the water temperature, thus requiring additional time to reach a boil again.

Braise: A method of long and slow cooking of food in a liquid. Generally, this method is applied to fish, meat (such as pot roast), celery, and endive.

Broil: To cook by direct heat. Broiling is a fast method of cooking, ideal for fish and meat. They can be broiled to obtain a medium golden brown on the outside, while still being moist on the inside. I should mention that in the restautant I enjoy the use of a high-heat broiler with easily adjustable racks. For home use, this may be a problem, as some broilers do not give off a great deal of heat.

For obtaining the best results, these procedures should be followed:

1. It is important to preheat the broiler for 4 to 5 minutes to obtain the optimal heat.
2. My recommendation is not to broil food that is too thick. The maximum thickness of fish should be 1 inch; the maximum for meat should be 1½ to 2 inches. The reason is that by the time the inside is cooked to the required doneness, the outside might be overdone. If you wish to broil a 2- to 3-inch-thick piece of fish or steak, it may be broiled 4 to 6 inches away from the heat source until golden brown, and then baked in the oven until done.
3. It is important too to salt the steaks, chops, and fish (unless they are covered by a thin layer of fat), as the salt will tend to draw the juices out, making the finished product fairly dry.
4. Foods that are very fatty, such as lamb chops and pork chops, should be

trimmed, leaving a thin covering of fat so that the meat retains both moisture and flavor. When you broil very fatty foods, the fat melts and often splatters, making a mess of your oven and possibly catching fire.

5. Lean foods such as fish and meats should be lightly brushed with oil or butter to add a protective coating that will prevent the food from drying out.

6. The distance of food from the broiler should be determined by the thickness of the food. A thin fillet of sole should be placed close to the heat source, as the time required to cook it is so short. A ½-inch to 1-inch-thick steak should be placed farther away (4 to 6 inches). If it is placed too close, the outside will burn before the inside is cooked.

7. When your broiler is part of the oven, it is a good idea to leave the oven door ajar as you broil foods. When the door is closed, the food will both broil and bake at the same time.

Cheese purchase and storage: When I was growing up in England, my mother would take me to her cousin's cheese shop, the official cheese shop of the Royal Family. I would watch her carefully select the cheeses we enjoyed. At home, she stored them in a larder at 45 to 55 degrees. The cheese would often form a light crust on the outside (because we wrapped them in wax paper), but the flavor was wonderful. Letting the cheese return to room temperature after storing it at the colder temperature ensured the maximum flavor.

In the United States, I do not have the advantage of purchasing my cheeses from my mother's cousin, so I find I am much more particular. I am often disappointed by the precut and prewrapped (in plastic wrap) cheeses. Stores generally do not change the wrappings, and thus there is an unpleasant sour flavor to the cheese. Wherever possible, I try to purchase cheese cut to order, and, in many cases, stores will let you taste them before purchasing.

Once the cheese is brought home, you should change the wrapping every 2 to 3 days, which will prevent it from tasting sour. Allow the cheese to return to room temperature before serving it in order to ensure the maximum flavor.

Cornstarch: A thickening agent. When used in a sauce, it gives the sauce a translucent quality when it is brought to a boil. Cornstarch is generally mixed with cold water to soften before it is added to a hot liquid. (This is referred to as a slake or a slurry.) It is important that enough water be used (1 tablespoon of cornstarch to ⅓ cup of water). When this mixture is added to the hot liquid, it is advisable to first add a small amount of the hot liquid to the cornstarch mixture. Once this has been whisked in, return it to the pan of hot liquid and slowly add the cornstarch, continually whisking the mixture over a medium heat until thick. This method will prevent the mixture from lumping.

Arrowroot is another thickening agent. It is much more expensive than cornstarch, and a little more fragile. It should not be boiled for more than 3 minutes, as it will lose its thickening properties. However, it provides a little more translucency than cornstarch and adds a nice silky texture to sauces. It is often used to thicken fruit sauces.

Cream: As a verb, to soften foods. The term is usually applied to a butter and sugar mixture in baking, where softened butter is beaten with sugar until light and well incorporated.

Cream as a noun requires a more substantial explanation. Cream is labeled light, whipping cream (or medium), heavy, and extra heavy. The classification is based on the percentage of butterfat in the cream, but it may vary according to the dairy. Light cream is no less than 17 percent butterfat, whipping cream is no less than 30 percent, heavy cream is no less than 36 percent, and extra heavy cream is from 45 to 55 percent. The higher the percentage of butterfat under *ideal* conditions, the easier to whip the cream until stiff, and the less time it will take to reduce.

Because of light cream's low percentage of butterfat, it is not possible to whip it to a stiff consistency.

The percentage of butterfat in whipping cream makes it possible to beat it until stiff, but this will take longer to beat than heavy cream. During the beating process, the cream becomes aerated, making it ideal (because it is lighter than heavy cream) to serve as an accompaniment for rich chocolate desserts. Being lighter in consistency makes it a little fragile, and therefore it is not stable enough to fold into mousses and souffles. During the folding process, it tends to lose its volume more easily than heavy cream. Also, because of its lower percentage of butterfat, whipping cream will take longer to reduce in sauces, so it should be prereduced in order to save time. Should only whipping cream be available, it may be used for the sauces in this book; however, increase the amount required by ¼ cup and reduce it by 50 percent before adding it to a sauce. For reducing, pour the cream into a 1-quart heavy saucepan and reduce over a high heat, whisking or stirring all the time. If the cream is not agitated, it will boil over. This may be done up to two hours ahead and held at room temperature.

Because of heavy cream's higher percentage of butterfat, it will whip faster and be stiffer in quality than whipping cream. This makes it better for folding into a cold mousse or souffle, as well as ideal as a whipped cream accompaniment for desserts in which a richer cream is truly more satisfying. It also is ideal for cream reduction sauces, taking less time to reduce than whipping cream; but caution should be taken to continually scrape down the sides of the pan with a plastic spatula to ensure that the cream does not crust or scorch on the edges of the pan.

Extra-heavy cream, under ideal conditions, beats to a stiff consistency very quickly. It is wonderful served whipped with lighter desserts and is excellent used as a whipped cream filling in desserts as it stands up so well.

The colder the cream, the easier and faster it is to beat it to a stiff consistency. In whipping cream, the fast agitation of whipping introduces air into the cream, making it light, and the percentage of butterfat will give the cream a stiff consistency. The combination of cold cream and fast agitation is imperative. If your kitchen is hot, cool the cream by placing it in a bowl in the freezer for 30 minutes before beating. The size of the bowl used is important; cream will increase in volume when beaten, so the bowl should be able to accommodate it. However, if the bowl is too wide and large, the surface of the cream is exposed to too much warm air in a hot kitchen and therefore will take longer to beat. This could give the cream an unacceptable buttery consistency. (When cream is overbeaten, the mixture changes from a stiff aerated mixture to a slightly grainy mixture; in the case of heavy and extra heavy cream, the mixture will often be light yellow in color.)

When this happens to cream, you do not need to throw it out (though it won't be useful as whipped cream). Continue to beat, as during this process the butterfat will completely separate from the whey. Once this has taken place, pour the entire mixture into a fine sieve resting over a bowl, preferably in a cool place, and leave for 20 to 30 minutes to drain. Gently squeeze any remaining whey out of the butter and then use the butter for cooking.

To whip cream properly, just beat it until it is stiff. You can pick up the bowl and tip it over slightly to see if the cream tends to slide out. If it does, it is not whipped enough. Just whip some more and test again.

Crème fraîche: Crème fraîche is thickened, coagulated cream, made by the addition of 1 teaspoon buttermilk to 1 cup of whipping or heavy cream. The addition of buttermilk activates the cream's lactic acid; when the mixture is held at 60 to 85 degrees for 6 to 36 hours in a glass jar, the cream will coagulate or thicken, producing a very thick and very lightly sour mixture. Unlike sour cream (which is also thickened by the addition of lactic acid), crème frache may be boiled, as it will not curdle. It has a lovely, light, clean taste and is still rich.

Julia Child's *Mastering the Art of French Cooking* gives a very good recipe for crème fraîche that I once used in many of my recipes. Alas, since the dating of cream was introduced, I have had many failures, which I have attributed to the additional additives in the cream. I have also been given recipes to make crème fraîche with sour cream and heavy cream. Frankly, I do not like the texture or flavor. So I now purchase crème fraîche. In the Boston area, the commercially made crème fraîche by Vie de France and Vermont Farms are the most available. I have good results with them.

Crème fraîche has a very special place in cooking. It's wonderful with a bowl of fresh blueberries, raspberries, and the finest strawberries, lightly sprinkled with sugar. It is sublime served with fresh American caviar or salmon caviar for gravlax, smoked salmon, consomme served with caviar, and as an ingredient in meat or fish sauces.

Cucumbers: You will notice that when my recipes call for cucumbers, they specify English cucumbers. These are also called European, seedless, or burpless cucumbers. I prefer these cucumbers because they are rarely bitter, have fewer seeds, and are easily digested. They are more expensive.

Curdling: Not easily defined, as it varies according to the food mixture. A custard that has been thickened with egg yolks will curdle easily if it is boiled. As the mixture is heated (being whisked all the time), it will thicken. When the mixture is boiled, the yolk hardens, as in a hard-boiled egg. First the custard, at the bottom of the pan, will take on the appearance of a scrambled egg, then the tiny flecks of "hard-boiled" egg run through the custard. The custard is then a thin grainy consistency, which cannot be rectified, unlike a separated mayonnaise.

Soups and sauces that are high in acids (such as lemon, vinegar, tomatoes, and some vegetables) will curdle when cream is added and allowed to boil. They should not curdle if you are careful not to boil them. If the soup or sauce is flour-based, it is a little more stable, and curdling will be less likely.

Dredge: A process of coating foods with a small amount of flour just prior to cooking. Dredging adds a light protective coating to meats and fish. I suggest an all-purpose flour, preferably unbleached, which will leave a fine, not lumpy, coating on the food. The flour may be lightly seasoned with salt and pepper and should be applied just before cooking. Be sure that the meat or fish is completely dry before coating, as moisture will cause the flour to become lumpy.

Eggs: As with other ingredients, using fresh eggs will result in a finer product. Test for freshness by breaking an egg onto a plate. The yolk should be slightly higher than the white, and the white should be gelatinous with most of it clinging to the yolk. When you separate an egg that is not very fresh, the yolk tends to break more easily.

I suggest that when breaking the shell of an egg, you do it on the counter rather than on the side of the bowl. This will prevent getting any of the shell in the bowl, as breaking the shell on a sharp edge may push some shell into the egg.

Because eggs are a high-protein food, it is important to not separate them until you are ready to use them. When exposed to the air for any length of time (more than 30 minutes), the yolks will form a crust and will be difficult to emulsify with another ingredient. When you beat the egg yolks with sugar in baking, it is important to continue beating until they lighten in color (a little darker in color than sweet butter).

For twenty years I have watched many chefs and cooks approach the procedure of beating egg whites in various ways—they beat eggs to a soft peak, fairly stiff, or extremely stiff. I take the middle approach for the following reasons: I find that egg whites beaten just to soft peaks tend to lose their volume when they are folded into a cake or mousse mixture. If the egg whites are too stiff, they are very difficult to incorporate evenly into a mixture.

To ensure a fairly stiff consistency with egg whites, follow these simple suggestions:

1. Egg whites should be at room temperature for about 30 minutes, as they will give a better volume and will beat up faster.
2. The bowl and the beaters should be dry.
3. Be very careful that there are no particles of egg yolk in the whites. If any egg yolk is in the whites, it can be removed with the sharp edge of the eggshell.
4. The shape of the beaters can affect the volume of the egg whites, so it is therefore important to choose the right mixer. (See the information on mixers on page 548).
5. In cake recipes calling for beaten egg whites, I add 30 to 50 percent of the sugar to the egg whites and the rest of the sugar to the yolks. This will stabilize the egg white for folding into a stiff cake mixture. Be careful that the egg whites are fairly stiff and that they have turned glossy.

Emulsifying: Some terms in cookery are much easier to understand if you see them performed rather than if you read an explanation. Emulsifying (emulsification) is one such example. Therefore, I strongly suggest that once you have read this explanation of emulsifying, you go to your kitchen and prepare both a vinaigrette and a mayonnaise to see the process for yourself. This will help you in future preparations of recipes in which emulsification takes place.

Emulsification, as it applies to cookery, is the process of creating a "whole" substance by bringing ingredients together in a suspension that when simply mixed together will not stay together.

A vinaigrette is a good example of an impermanent emulsion. When the ingredients are whisked together, the oil and vinegar become one. If the dressing is allowed to stand for 5 to 10 minutes, the two ingredients will separate, with the oil rising to the top of the mixture.

Mayonnaise (see page 38) is a permanent emulsion. When all the ingredients are added in their proper proportions and the correct technique is used, the addition of whole egg or egg yolks (protein) will enable the mixture to become a "whole" substance that will stay together and does not separate. The addition of protein (the egg yolk), high agitation (whisking or mixing constantly), and the correct balance of acid (vinegar, lemon juice, etc.) in this case results in a permanent rather than impermanent emulsion.

Other examples of emulsifications include hollandaise, beurre blanc, and some pan-reduced sauces. The ingredients of a hollandaise sauce are similar to those of mayonnaise. However, in the case of hollandaise, the careful application of heat to the egg yolks aids in the thickening process. With too little heat the sauce will not thicken; with too much heat, the sauce will curdle.

Unlike a hollandaise or mayonnaise, a beurre blanc contains no eggs. My recipes for beurre blanc differ from the more traditional versions, as I add some fish or chicken stock to the base (see page 33). I find that this additional protein aids in the emulsification process and gives a slightly less acidic sauce as well. Care should be taken that the ingredients be in the proper proportions and that the correct technique is used in order to avoid separation.

Emulsification also takes place when butter is added to a pan-reduced sauce, such as in Salmon with Tarragon Sauce on page 241. It is important that the butter be soft and whisked in slowly over a medium heat. If brought to a boil, the sauce must be whisked constantly and not overboiled or it may separate. Too high a proportion of butter may also result in separation. If an acid such as tomato, wine, vinegar or lemon juice is in the sauce base, the sauce will be less likely to break.

Fats, oils, and butter: When I was growing up, lard and beef fat were used in cooking. They were used sparingly and not only enhanced the flavors of foods but also added to the thrift of the kitchen budget my mother planned. Today, there has been a great deal of publicity on the need to remove animal fats from the American diet in order to prevent heart disease and to aid in the control of one's weight. I suggest that if one has a well-balanced diet—one that includes lots of fresh vegetables, whole grains, fresh fish, fruits, and small portions of beef—then the occasional use of beef fat, lard, salt pork, pancetta, and non–sugar-cured smoked bacon will probably be fine. If it is used in excess, or in the case of certain medically restricted diets, there is proper cause for concern, and it should be avoided. But I must admit that I cannot imagine my mother baking her delightful Yorkshire pudding, always so crisp and light, without the use of beef fat. Taking a teaspoon of beef fat from the roast, she placed it in the muffin pan with the pudding (if you are making popovers, try the same) and created the difference between an ordinary and a wonderful meal. Occasionally she would add pancetta or salt pork to a bean casserole, cabbage, or a meat dish, and suddenly the dish was given a wonderful lift.

So, what is the difference between oils and fats, and why is it important? To quote Howard Hillman in *Kitchen Science,* "An oil is a fat. However, it is common practice to use the term 'fat' for those fats that are in a solid state while at room temperature. Those that are liquid at room temperature are called oils." He goes on to explain, "Fats from animals are solid, and, generally, fats from vegetables are liquid.... Chemically speaking, there is less difference between animal and vegetable fats than most people would suspect." The importance in the difference between the two comes in understanding their smoking points. But, before discussing this, I would first like to cover the different products available. Let us start with the most common of fats, butter.

It was during a vacation in Switzerland that I was first served unsalted butter. I found the taste a little insipid, but after a few days of breakfasting on crusty bread, wonderful fruit preserves, and sweet, creamy butter, I found that I *preferred* the flavor of butter without the addition of salt.

When the recipes in this book call for butter, I mean unsalted butter. This conforms with my policy of baking without salt, and is far easier to control salt levels in foods if the ingredients you are using do not already contain salt. However, you should be aware that unsalted butter is more perishable than the salted variety and has a tendency to pick up food odors when stored in the refrigerator longer than two weeks. Care should be taken to wrap it tightly before storing. Unsalted butter will, however, freeze better than salted, as the salt has a tendency to be drawn to the edges of the block of butter, resulting in an uneven distribution of salt throughout the butter.

There is no butter like fresh butter, whether it be salted or unsalted. Both will lose their lovely taste if stored too long and if stored more than a month or two run the risk of turning rancid. You should always check the date on butter before buying it to ensure maximum freshness.

Recently, I have noticed that some cheese and health food stores have adopted the European practice of buying fine butter from small dairies that use a higher quality cream. Although these products are wonderful, they should be purchased with caution. Specialty stores generally have a lower turnover than the larger chains, and thus there is a problem with freshness.

When cooking with butter, you should be careful not to heat it higher than 250 degrees. Above that temperature, the proteins in the butter will burn. If you prefer to saute with butter, I suggest you use clarified butter (see page 62), as it will tolerate higher temperatures.

Other solid fats include margarine and shortening. I do not use margarine because I personally do not like its taste. I feel that its flavor will especially affect sauces and cakes. I admit that this is strictly a matter of personal opinion. As for shortening, its makeup can be either animal or vegetable, or a combination of both. Pure vegetable shortening is made only of vegetable fats; shortening can be either animal or vegetable or a combination of both.

Because of the cautions mentioned before, saturated animal fats have been replaced by vegetable and nut oils. For the most part, these oils have been deodorized (the flavor has been removed), leaving a light, clean oil. They are bland for cooking, and the smoking point of these oils is high, making them particularly good for frying, as they can be heated to a temperature of 390 degrees Fahrenheit without burning. This allows the food to acquire a delicious crisp outside.

There also are nondeodorized oils (oils where the flavor is carefully preserved). Olive and sesame oils are two examples. From my childhood visit to Majorca and the Canary Islands, I began at an early age to develop a taste for the strong, sometimes sharp, locally made green olive oils. Some people will say that they are coarse, but frankly, I find them delicious. The finest olive oils come from Tuscany and Sicily, where the olives are "cold pressed": Virtually no heat is used in the extracting process, thus the wonderful and smooth flavor. Other oils are available in as large a variety as the range of quality—from almond and corn, to soybean and walnut, and many more in between. I suggest that you experiment, picking your favorites by trial and error. If you taste an olive oil that you like in a restaurant, ask the brand name. Italian pasta stores and specialty food stores are a good source for olive oils, and they are usually willing to help in your selection.

Olive oil, sesame oil, and walnut oil come in various strengths, from light, clear-colored oils that have less flavor to the darker oils that carry a wonderful strong flavor. This rich oil has a varying use, as in the walnut oils, which are wonderful with the strong flavors of greens such as raddichio, endive, watercress, and escarole.

Last, but by far not the least, are the oils of the Orient. In the mid—eighteenth century, Yuan Mei wrote *Shih-tan,* a comprehensive book on the food of China and prefaced the work with pages of warnings and cautions about those foods. "The search for ideal ingredients," he wrote, "meant that the credit for any fine banquet must be divided two ways, with 60 percent going to the man supervising the marketing." He continued, "The choice of the condiments was equally important: soys, oils, wines, and vinegars all have their own attributes and defects.... Thus for oils, one should choose the best grade of Su-chou." At that time, the traditional choice for oil was rapeseed. The seeds were crushed in the same manner as the olives, producing an oil. Today, the Chinese use peanuts, which are more readily available, or sesame seeds, which add a wonderful flavor to foods.

Now that we have discussed the different types of fats and oils, it is important to understand their smoking point. When sauteing, shallow-fat frying, or deep-fat frying, the smoking point is the temperature at which an oil or fat will begin to smoke, and if the temperature is not turned down, the fat or oil will burn. When frying or sauteing, the temperature of the oil or fat should reach between 350 and 385 degrees without smoking. Although clarified butter is excellent for sauteing, its smoking point is too low for deep-fat frying, as is the case with olive oil. Oils and solid vegetable fats vary from brand to brand as far as smoking points. This can go from 375 degrees for vegetable shortening to 510 degrees for safflower oil. I suggest using oils with a higher smoking point both for efficiency (a higher smoking point will prolong the life of the oil) and prevention of burning the food being fried. For example, vegetable oils such as corn oil or safflower oil are ideal. The smoking point is 425 to 510 degrees, which makes them perfect for frying chicken and fish (requiring a temperature of 350 degrees), and French fries (requiring a temperature of 390 degrees).

When you are shallow-fat frying and deep-fat frying, the fat used may be strained through a fine cloth or sieve after it is cooled, and used again. You should be aware that the smoking point will decrease with each use; and when it reaches a point below 400 degrees, it should be discarded. Another good sign of aged oil is color; once the oil has reached a semi–dark brown color, it is overused and will impart an unpleasant taste to the food. If you are frying foods that are breaded, the smoking point of the fat will decrease because of the particles of breading that break off and burn in the fat. This affects the smoking point, as well as the life of the fat.

Flour: I primarily use two kinds of flour in the recipes in this book, all-purpose unbleached flour and cake flour. I like all-purpose unbleached flour because it is higher in gluten (protein) than the bleached variety (bleached flour has been treated with chemicals) and has a more natural taste. It is slightly granular in texture. Cake flour is low in gluten and is softer and silkier in texture when cooked. It is excellent in desserts and in thickening soups and sauces. Cake flour needs to be sifted, as it will tend to lump, and it should be stored in an airtight container away from humid areas.

Fold: The process of gently combining some ingredients of your recipe (usually beaten egg whites or whipped cream) into other ingredients in such a way that the resulting mixture is very light. Using a metal spoon or plastic spatula, cut vertically through the mixture, turn, and come up, over and over again, so that the ingredients are evenly distributed throughout the mixture. Be careful not to overmix and to fold fairly quickly.

When folding egg whites into a thick mixture, it is advisable to fold in one-third of the whites more vigorously and then add the remaining two-thirds very gently to maintain the lightness. The first third softens the mixture and makes it easier to then fold in the remaining whites without letting the mixture lose any volume.

Food processor uses: I have found that the following culinary tasks work very well in the food processor:

1. Grinding nuts
2. Pureeing raw fish and meats for terrines and pâtés
3. Making compound butters
4. Chopping cooked spinach and coarsely chopping fresh herbs
5. Grating chocolate, cheese, and vegetables (using the grating blade)
6. Coarsely chopping tomatoes (using the cutting blade)
7. Pureeing thick vegetable mixtures (Not potatoes, as the blade rotates so fast you'll end up with gluey textured potatoes. Although very smooth, they are quite unappetizing).

When using the food processor for hot liquids, it is important to not fill the processor more than half full, or the mixture will come out where the lid fits on. In caring for your processor, make sure that you always clean it out well. Manufacturers generally supply an implement to clean the inside part of the blade that fits over the shaft. It is a very necessary tool, as some mixtures, such as fish terrines, can work up into the center of the blade as they are being processed. If this area is not well cleaned out, it could allow bacteria to form as well as affect the food when the processor is used again. If the machine does not come with a utensil to clean this area, use a cotton swab. I cannot stress enough the importance of this cleaning step.

Freezing foods: There are entire books written on how to freeze foods, so I am merely giving a few important hints here. Be sure that the freezer temperature remains at a constant 0 degrees Fahrenheit. Check the temperature with a refrigerator/freezer thermometer and adjust the setting to maintain a zero-degree reading. It is important to make sure that all products are cold before freezing; place containers of hot or warm stocks or soups in ice water, then when they are fairly cool place them in the refrigerator for four hours before freezing. If they are frozen before they have cooled, they may swell in the center and force the lid to come loose, thus allowing ice crystals to form in the food.

Foods that are not tightly wrapped are also subject to freezer burn. A freezer, in the process of maintaining the cool temperature, removes moisture from the surface area of the food; when the food is exposed to this cool air, it will become dehydrated, not causing spoilage but causing it to dry out. I strongly suggest that in organizing your freezer, you put all foods in containers or packages, putting a piece of masking tape across them and, with a non-water-soluble marker, writing the name of the item and the date you put it in the freezer. If your freezer is large enough, put all meat, fish, vegetables, stocks, and dessert items in their own area. It is also important to rotate your provisions—for example, if you add a package of ground beef and have an existing one in the freezer, put the older package in the front and the newer in behind it.

For freezing large batches of stews, stocks, and soups, package the product in small containers, which will facilitate faster and safer defrosting. When larger containers are allowed to defrost, the outer edge is often warm, becoming susceptible to bacteria, by the time the center is finally thawed. These bacteria may be harmful. If at all possible, I suggest that you defrost all frozen foods in the refrigerator. Although this requires much planning ahead, as in the case of larger items that require several days, it will cut down on the risk of bacteria. The best example of this is the large turkey: It takes hours to finally thaw the center, while the outer edges are more quickly thawed; and bacteria may grow in these areas.

If you like to buy foods in bulk and freeze them for future use, or if you freeze homegrown vegetables and fruits, be certain that you are aware how long different foods may be frozen. In my opinion, freezing affects the taste or consistency of cheese, cream, chocolate, coffee beans, nuts, smoked products, and salted butter, and I recommend that you do not freeze them at all.

Frying and sauteing: To maintain the best results in sauteing, shallow-fat frying, and deep-fat frying, I offer the following general hints:

1. It is important that you understand about the smoking points of different fats and oils. See pages 524–25.
2. It is important that the food being cooked is at room temperature. Cold food will lower the temperature in the pan; thus the food will absorb fat and the texture will not be crisp.
3. It is equally important that the pan not be overcrowded. This will also lower the temperature in the pan, preventing the food from frying properly.
4. Unless the foods are later to be baked, roasted, or used in a casserole, they should not be too thick as the outside will burn before the inside is cooked. In the case of stewing meats or pot roasts, they are browned first and then cooked in the oven.
5. After frying foods (French fries, fried chicken, breaded fish), drain them on paper towels, allowing the paper to absorb any excess oil.
6. Fried foods should be served immediately for the best result. The longer they are kept warm, the greater the risk of their losing their crispness.

Sauteing is cooking at a lower temperature than frying and with less fat or oil in the pan. Whole butter may be used, but only for items that require a temperature of 250 degrees or lower, as the butter will burn at a higher temperature. For sauteing at temperatures higher than 250 degrees, you should use either clarified butter (see recipe on page 62) or an oil with a high smoking point. Sauteing is ideal for cooking chicken breasts, escalopes of veal, thin beef steaks, and fish and shellfish (such as sole, trout, scallops, and shrimp). Mushrooms, eggplant, and onions may be sauteed until brown; however, green beans, cabbage, zucchini, and spinach should be tossed constantly over a medium heat, being careful not to brown them, which will give the vegetables an unpleasant acrid taste.

Shallow-fat frying is ideal for croutons, breaded chicken, or fish and fish cakes. It is best to use a vegetable oil with a high smoking point. Choose a heavy saute pan, at least 3 inches high, and fill it only one-third full with oil. Any more oil than this could cause the oil to overflow or reach a height too close to the lip of the pan once the food is added. If you do not have a frying thermometer, heat the oil, being careful to avoid smoking, until it is hot. Add a small piece of bread, which will sizzle and quickly turn a light shade of brown. This will tell you when the oil is at the desired temperature and you can begin frying your food. Fry until it is golden brown; if the food is thick you will need to turn it over to fry the other side. If the oil does not burn and there are not many particles of food or breadcrumbs in the oil, it may be strained through a fine sieve or a coffee filter and used again. (See page 525 for guidelines as to how long the oil may be re-used.)

For deep-fat frying, I strongly suggest that you purchase an electric deep-fat fryer. These are equipped with a thermostat, making it easier for you to regulate the temperature of the oil, and much safer than using a pan over a heat source. Be sure you fill it no more than half full, as once the food is added the oil could boil over and catch on fire. For the best results, heat the fat or oil to the desired temperature. With the exception of French fries, dumplings, and pastries, the food to be fried should be coated with bread crumbs or a batter for frying. This protects the food from drying out in the frying process and adds an additional crisp layer. It is especially important with deep-fat frying that you drain the food well after frying and serve it quickly to maintain the food's crispness. The oil may be re-used as long as it does not burn and you strain it through a sieve (see page 525).

Garbage odor prevention: For those who live in apartments or have no separate trash area, I hope this hint will be useful, especially during the hot and humid months. If you have washed out the milk cartons and cans but still have an objectionable odor coming from your garbage container, sprinkle the trash with distilled white vinegar. This will aid in dissipating the odor for several days and also help in controlling the growth of bacteria. In the case of outside storage, it will help to prevent infestation by small animals such as mice and rats.

Garlic: Garlic comes in two varieties, white and purple. The purple variety will have thin purple streaks running through the skins of the cloves. While living in Europe I was led to believe that the purple variety was milder than the white. But after working with both varieties in the United States, I have found that there is little difference.

Gelatin: A high-protein food that should be handled carefully. Too much gelatin will produce a hard, rubbery consistency, and too little will cause the mixture to not set properly. If gelatin is overcooked when added to a mixture, it will give the dish a rubbery texture when set.

To achieve the best results, first sponge the gelatin: Place in cold water, 1/4 cup per packet, in a small saucepan, sprinkling the gelatin evenly over the water to assure that all is absorbed. If the water is warm, the gelatin will not completely absorb it. Put this mixture aside to rest in a cool place for 10 to 15 minutes. This sponging process will allow the gelatin to soften, thus eliminating a need for cooking it over high heat.

After 15 minutes, dissolve the gelatin over a low heat, being careful not to boil. Once the gelatin has dissolved, it is important to be sure that the mixture you are adding to it is at room temperature. A cold mixture will force the gelatin to set immediately, thus leaving streaks of gelatin in the mixture, and thus will not set evenly. This often gives an unpleasant texture, and in the case of the cold mousses and souffles you will not be able to achieve the best volume.

On the other hand, if the recipe calls for combining a gelatin mixture with beaten egg whites and/or whipped cream, the gelatin mixture should be gently stirred over ice water to just before the point of setting as it begins to thicken before you gently fold in the cold whipped cream or beaten whites. It is important that the whipped cream and whites be cold, so that when you fold them into the gelatin mixture, they will start the setting of the gelatin and the mixture will maintain the maximum volume. Should the mixture start to set before the addition of the egg whites and/or cream, place the bowl over warm water to soften the gelatin. It is also helpful to chill the serving bowls or glasses in the freezer before filling them. If the kitchen is hot when you prepare a mousse or souffle, it is best to put the mousse or souffle in the freezer for 30 minutes before placing it in the refrigerator.

As a general rule of thumb, one packet of gelatin will set 2 cups of liquid. For a light consistency for a cold souffle or mousse, one packet of gelatin will set 3 to 4 cups of mixture, depending on the denseness of the base used.

Fresh pineapple, kiwi fruit, and alcohol will adversely affect the setting properties of gelatin. I have also discovered when using a high proportion of fresh asparagus in a cold souffle or mousse that the setting properties of gelatin are slightly decreased, so you may want to slightly increase the amount of gelatin.

Ginger: Ginger has many varieties of applications in cooking. My mother enjoyed serving ripe melon wedges lightly sprinkled with powdered ginger, and in English restaurants a small dish of ginger is often placed on the table as a condiment when melon was served. Taking this one step further, may I suggest studding ripe melon with fine slivers of fresh ginger for two hours before serving.

Ginger is available in a variety of forms: powdered, fresh, pickled, crystallized, or preserved in syrup. Fresh ginger is peppery (spicy) in taste but in its other forms takes on different flavors.

When I first started cooking, I used powdered ginger in a few savory and many dessert recipes. Now, I use fresh ginger more often, as it is easily attainable in Chinese stores, some supermarkets, and specialty food stores. Powdered ginger is spicier, slightly acrid, and pungent; I feel that it has a valuable place in spice cakes and squash or pumpkin pies. I suggest that you experiment by combining both freshly grated and dried ginger in recipes such as cookies and gingerbread, as it provides a delicious flavor.

If you are using fresh ginger in an infusion with milk or cream while scald-ing, I must caution you that it will curdle the milk or cream (see page 520). Although my next caution may be controversial, I feel that it is very necessary. When I use fresh ginger in a marinade for meat and leave the meat to marinate for a couple of hours, the proteins in the meat are denaturized (broken down) and the meat changes in texture. It acquires a soft, unpleasant texture, making it equally unpleasant to eat. Therefore, ginger should be added just before or while the food is cooking. I do use ginger in my Ginger Shrimp recipe (page 253), but the shrimp shells are left on, and I have not encountered any problem with this recipe.

In purchasing ginger make sure it is firm. Unfortunately, it may be fibrous, which is difficult to see on purchasing. Occasionally you might purchase ginger that is sprouting (light green points) from the knobs; if you have a shaded, humid, hot area in the garden, plant the ginger and it will grow. Fresh ginger may be kept at room temperature for a couple of weeks. It should be peeled before use, unless it is used in an infusion (and later strained out). If you grate it, the fiber will cling to the grater, making it easier to remove the fiber.

Pickled ginger can be found in Chinese and Japanese stores. Very fine slivers of ginger pickled in vinegar, sometimes with a little sugar or salt added, is a fine product to use in garnishes and salads.

Crystallized ginger is ginger crystallized in sugar. It is used for dessert cookery and for garnishes on desserts. It is wonderful dipped in bittersweet chocolate; it is sometimes commercially available in this form.

Ginger in syrup is stemmed ginger that has been preserved in a sugar syrup. Both the ginger and syrup are great used in dessert cookery and are wonderful used as garnish on desserts.

These are only a few of the many ways to use ginger. Let your imagination be your guide.

Grate: To cut food into medium, small, and fine pieces with a grater, although it now can also be done in a food processor. Most often grating applies to carrots, cheese, and chocolate.

Heat and high-protein foods: Fish, shellfish, and eggs are examples of high-protein foods that will become tough and rubbery when subjected to certain levels of high heat. Although there are many exceptions to this rule (sauteing, broiling, frying, and grilling are ideal for these foods), it is important to be aware of the problems and the care that is necessary in cooking these foods at high temperatures. Two examples of this are hard-boiled eggs and boiled lobster.

When an egg is boiled rapidly, it will become rubbery and have a tough tex-ture. If instead you gently simmer the egg, it will maintain a soft texture and will be more appealing to eat. Although simmmering is a longer process (approximately 20 to 30 minutes), the result will be far more satisfying. Similarly, plunging a live lobster into boiling water will cause the outer flesh to quickly contract, giving it a tough, rubbery texture. If you steam the lobster, or place it in gently simmering water, the longer process at a lower heat will produce a tender, more succulent product as well as decrease the amount of shrinkage.

If you keep the following points in mind when cooking high-protein foods, you will avoid the problems I have mentioned.

1. When sauteing, frying, broiling, and grilling, caution should be used to not overcook. These foods should be seared to a golden brown; overcooking will cause them to become tough, sinewy, and stringy, forming a hard, unpleasant crust on the outside before the inside has completed cooking.
2. Stews, pot roasts, and casseroles should be gently simmered. I find that this works well in the oven. Although a longer cooking time is necessary, the meat will be tender, and less shrinkage will occur. Start cooking in a 250-degree oven. If the mixture starts to boil, lower the temperature to 200 degrees.
3. When poaching fish, shellfish, eggs, and poultry, cook at a gentle simmer to ensure that the end product is tender and has a pleasing texture.

Herbs and spices: There have been thousands of words and hundreds of books written on herbs and spices, everything from their importance and value to the human diet, to how to grow them, and even how to decorate with them. To all of this, I can add only my preferences and feelings.

I have always felt that it is important to use fresh herbs in cooking. In many cases, dried herbs impart an astringent flavor to a dish, while fresh herbs have a milder, more refreshing, more appealing flavor. If you are skeptical, I encourage you to make the same recipe twice—once with fresh herbs and once with dried. I am certain that you will then appreciate the difference.

Until recently, few fresh herbs were available during the late fall and winter months; however, more specialty stores and supermarkets are now offering them. Although they are expensive for the small amount required, in these recipes I feel that it is really worthwhile to indulge. Should this not be possible, you may grow your own. If you do not have a garden, just a few of your favorites may be grown on a fire escape, and during the winter months by a sunny window.

When purchasing fresh herbs, make sure that the leaves are fresh and not wilted. Store them in a plastic bag that has a few small holes in it. A couple of hours before using the herbs, wash them under cold water, draining well. If you have a lettuce dryer, dry the herbs in it. Sprig the leaves and then dry them completely with a paper towel. It is extremely important to be sure that they are very dry before chopping, because if they are not, the herbs will lose their crispness. If basil or mint are not dry, the leaves will turn black as you chop them.

Should you have to substitute dried herbs for fresh, the best rule of thumb is to use 1 teaspoon of dried to 1 tablespoon of finely chopped fresh herbs.

(In this book I have from time to time strayed from this conversion, as in testing recipes, I adjusted the amount of dried herbs to give the most balanced flavor possible.) As a general rule, I do suggest that you do not substitute dried parsley, dill, or coriander, as the fresh will far outdistance the dried.

It is especially important that you do not store dried herbs in a bright or warm area, as they will lose some flavor and color. Care also should be taken with the storage of spices. Once a jar of a spice, such as paprika or curry powder, is opened, it should be tightly sealed between each use. Keep spices in a cool and dry place so that they do not lose any flavor or color, but keep in mind that this loss will automatically occur over time.

As you will notice, I use a freshly grated nutmeg in some of my recipes. I find that it has a softer and less acrid taste than preground nutmeg. For my own cooking I apply the same rule to cardamom, cumin, and coriander. I purchase them in seed form and grind them prior to use, finding that I get a much more satisfactory flavor.

Julienne: To julienne a food—generally a vegetable, such as carrots—is to cut it in thin strips varying from one to two inches in length. The strips resemble a matchstick. The width of the julienne strip is determined by the recipe: Fine julienne is cut a little thicker than paper thin; medium julienne is ⅛-inch thick; coarse julienne is ¼-inch thick.

Measuring and weighing out ingredients: In England, we used pound and ounce measurements. The scale became an intrinsic part of the kitchen. Studying in Paris, I was introduced to the metric system, again using a scale to determine amounts. When I arrived in the United States I had to work with cup measurements. Although this seems to be an easy form of measurement, I found it a bit confusing. Even now, when teaching students in my cooking classes, I find that there is still some confusion with the ounce measurement of a cup versus the weight measurement of a cup. I hope that the following explanation will give you a clearer understanding.

Two cups of water, when weighed on a scale, equal one pound, hence the ounce markings on a measuring cup. What makes this confusing is the fact that 2 cups of sugar or 2 cups of butter weigh one pound while 4 to 4½ cups flour or 2½ cups of raw rice also weigh one pound. It is important, therefore, when converting weight measurements from foreign cookbooks to cup measurements to use conversion tables.

Mustard: Mustard is available in many different forms. One can purchase mustard seeds, dry ground mustard, or prepared mustard. In this book I have used two kind of mustard: mustard seeds (see Chicken Lundi, page 305) and prepared mustard. Most of the recipes call for Dijon mustard (finely ground mustard mixed with vinegar, salt, white wine, and spices). There are many varieties of prepared mustard available—herb-flavored, green peppercorn–flavored, and so on. For many of the recipes in this book you may substitute a mustard that suits your taste.

Nuts: Many of the recipes in this book call for nuts. Once again I stress the importance of freshness so that the nuts provide the maximum flavor and are not rancid. I have found that the freshest nuts may often be obtained at health food stores. I recommend that you purchase walnuts in the shell and crack them yourself, but meticulous care should be taken to remove all the shells. Other nuts should be purchased shelled and whole. Those already chopped or slivered are often not fresh and are rather dry in texture when ground. If you purchase nuts in large quantities, be sure to store them in a cool, dry place such as a basement or the refrigerator. I do not recommend freezing nuts, as I feel that it changes the balance of the oils, giving them a grainy texture. If they are extremely fresh when purchased, they will last 2 to 3 months when stored in a cool place.

For recipes calling for cashews or peanuts, I prefer to use raw nuts and roast them, as I find the flavor to be far superior to that of preroasted nuts. The raw nuts can be found in health food stores.

Roasting of nuts is a step that makes the skins easier to remove (for example, hazelnuts) and adds flavor (as is the case with blanched almonds, pine nuts, raw peanuts, raw cashews, and hazelnuts). Place the nuts on a heavy baking sheet in an oven preheated to 375 or 400 degrees. Cook for 7 to 9 minutes, watching them carefully, as they will burn easily. If they slightly overcook, remove them from the pan immediately, as the sheet pan will retain the heat and continue to cook the nuts.

To remove the skins from the hazelnuts, let them cool, then rub between your fingers or in a coarse sieve until the skins come off. This is quite easy. I do not recommend purchasing blanched hazelnuts, as I have found that these often are not fresh and sometimes are even quite rancid. I do recommend, however, the purchase of blanched almonds. I have spent endless hours removing the skins of almonds and finally decided that the time involved was unreasonable. Once I discovered that I could buy fine-quality fresh blanched almonds, I never had to worry about skinning them again. Should you ever need to skin almonds because you can't find good blanched almonds, I suggest the following procedure: Place 1 cup almonds in a bowl and cover with plenty of boiling water. Soak for 3 to 5 minutes. Remove a small amount of almonds with a slotted spoon and peel immediately. Place the nuts on a cotton cloth or a paper towel to dry.

Nuts may be ground in a food processor. It is more effective than a blender for grinding nuts, as they will collect at the base of a blender and form an oily paste. If the nuts have been roasted, it is essential that they be cooled before grinding to prevent them from forming an oily paste. If almonds or pistachio nuts have been blanched (to remove their skins), dry well before grinding. For a coarse grind in a food processor, turn the pulsers on and off quickly, being careful to chop only small batches at a time in order to have more control over the size of the chop. For a medium-grind, be careful to not overgrind or you will give them a fine consistency. For a fine consistency, be careful to not overgrind to avoid turning the nuts into an oily paste.

You may also use a nut chopper (found in kitchen shops) to chop nuts, or chop them on a cutting board with a sharp chef's knife. In fact, for a coarse chop, you'll have more control using a knife.

Onions, dicing: I suggest that you do not slice or dice an onion in the food processor. When cut up in the food processor, the onions release some liquid during the process. When you saute the onions, they will boil in the liquid and acquire a slightly acidic flavor, rather than the sweet flavor normally achieved in sauteing. I suggest you dice onions as shown in the drawings on page 535.

Papillote: Cooking *en papillote* is to cook fish or meat with a compound butter or an herb mixture in a paper package so that the food cooks in its own juices and retains all its flavor. Parchment paper is the preferred wrapping. Wax paper melts and taints the food and is not as strong as parchment. If parchment is not available, aluminum foil may be used. However, the papillotes should be made only 2 hours before cooking, as opposed to a possible 6 hours for parchment wrapping. Be certain to seal the edges very tightly, so that none of the juices can leak out during cooking. (See drawings on page 228.)

Pare: To peel. The term is generally used in referring to trimming the rind (zest) from an orange, lemon, or lime.

Peeling vegetables: Sometimes vegetables need to be peeled because their skin is bitter (often true of cucumbers), coarse (broccoli stalks), unattractive (carrots), or indigestible (peppers).

In the case of broccoli, the flowerettes cook in 50 percent of the time it takes to cook the coarse stalks, creating an unappetizing product. The inner part of the stalk is so tender and sweet that by peeling it, you will produce a much better dish. (If the stalk is very wide, peel it and cut it in half lengthwise.) Peeling takes only a few minutes and is very easy. Using a vegetable peeler, start at the bottom of the stalk and peel upwards. (Refer to the diagram of peeling celery on page 536, which is the same technique.) The bottom of asparagus stalks often needs to be peeled to get rid of the fibrous and tough skin. Peel in the same manner. If you peel the fibrous layer from celery stalks, you will find them more enjoyable to eat.

The skin of raw or cooked sweet peppers is quite tough, therefore unpleasant, and sometimes indigestible. Peeling off the skin make the peppers more appealing. The method is very easy: Preheat the broiler. Place a broiler pan

1. Cut the onion in half through the root with a chef's knife, leaving the root on to hold the onion together. Then, slice the onion toward the root in ¼-inch-thick slices with a small, sharp prep knife.

2. Starting ¼-inch from the root end, slice down through the onion in ¼-inch-thick slices, using a small, sharp prep knife.

3. Holding the root end of the onion in your fingers, slice the onion using a sharp slicing knife or a chef's knife. If you want a different size dice, you may change the thickness of your slices in all these steps.

JULIENNE, SLICING, AND DICING

Carrots, and similar vegetables, can be cut up in a variety of ways. This drawing shows julienned carrots, diced carrots, and carrots sliced on the diagonal.

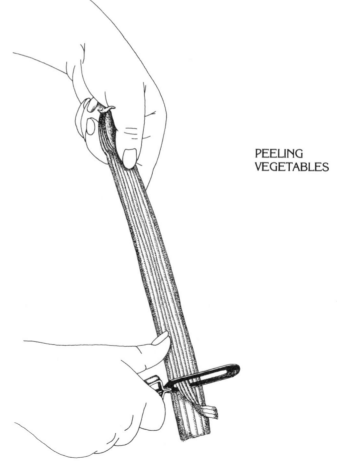

PEELING VEGETABLES

When you peel celery, broccoli, or asparagus, use a vegetable peeler. Start at the bottom and move upwards, exerting pressure with your thumb muscle.

with the peppers on it approximately 6 to 8 inches from the heat source. Broil the peppers until the skin turns dark brown, then turn the peppers to brown on another side. Continue to broil until the pepper skins are dark all over. Plunge into very cold water and leave for 5 minutes. Then peel, and remove the core, seeds, and fiber.

Some cooks suggest placing the broiled peppers in a brown paper bag, rather than in water. I find that this method overcooks them and gives them a much softer consistency.

Pepper for seasoning: Green, black, and white peppercorns are all berries of the *Pipernigrum* tree. Green peppercorns are pickled, immature berries. White peppercorns are fully mature berries, whereas black peppercorns are harvested slightly before full maturity is reached. Red chili peppers, on the other hand, are a vegetable produced by a species of capsicum.

Why do I always specify freshly ground black pepper (as opposed to preground pepper)? I came to appreciate freshly ground black pepper at my home in England, where my father always brought the pepper grinder to the table. We learned that when using the aromatic freshly ground pepper, we needed less salt or other seasoning. Like coffeebeans, if peppercorns are preground, they lose their aromatic qualities quite easily, leaving behind the spiciness without the scented flavor.

White pepper is spicier in taste than black and generally used in white sauces, mousselines, and mayonnaises because some people dislike the small black flecks that black pepper leaves in the mixture. Personally, I am not offended by these flecks and prefer the taste of black pepper.

Over the last ten years, green peppercorns have suddenly become readily available. Picked, packed, and pickled when underripe, they are soft in texture and mildly spicy, and they have a very scented flavor. If desired, they may easily be crushed with the back of a knife. Some people find the taste very pleasing, whereas others find the flavor offensive, so I strongly advise that you taste them before using them for the first time. If using the canned variety, after opening transfer the contents to a glass container and seal and store in the refrigerator.

The use of red chili peppers in cooking is popular in many countries with hot climates. Used correctly and carefully, they are a wonderful accent to many dishes. Red chili peppers are available in many forms. Cayenne pepper (often sold as "red pepper") is the finely ground powder made from a very hot type of chili pepper. Dried crushed red pepper is produced from red chili peppers that have been roasted, dried, and crushed. The spiciness will vary from one brand to another, depending on the variety of peppers used. Tabasco is a commercially bottled hot sauce made from hot red peppers. I prefer its fiery and slightly acidic flavor over other varieties of bottled hot sauces.

Different varieties of fresh red chili peppers are becoming increasingly available in local supermarkets and farmers' markets. If you like spicy foods, you will want to experiment with these peppers to find varieties you particularly like. As the varieties vary greatly in degree of hotness, taste a tiny bit before using so that you can properly adjust the level of spiciness in your recipe. Be aware, however, that working with hot peppers will leave a residue on your hands for hours afterwards, producing an unpleasant burning sensation. I suggest wearing surgical gloves, which will prevent the residue from clinging to your skin. It is also important to avoid rubbing your eyes while cooking, as the peppers will make them burn.

Poach: To cook food at 170 to 180 degrees, a temperature lower than simmering. The lower heat will give a finer texture to the food and is generally used for eggs and fish. (Read about poaching fish and shellfish on page 220.)

Puree: A mixture that is rendered smooth in a blender, food processor, food mill, or sieve. It may be a mixture of cooked food, such as a sauce or vegetables, or uncooked food, such as a base for a fish mousseline or strawberries for a sauce. The smoothness of a puree is determined by how long you have cooked the food, the equipment you use, and how long you puree it. Also read about pureeing in blenders on page 516 and in food processors on page 525.

Reduction: Reducing a liquid over medium to high heat to intensify the flavor and/or to thicken the consistency of a flourless sauce so that it coats the food. You will note that I often reduce a sauce until it has a light syrupy consistency, then I add cream and reduce until it is thick enough to coat the spoon. This thickness might be described as the consistency of cold heavy cream. The process of reduction produces a very rich sauce with a silky consistency. As long as you have started with a good stock or poaching liquid, you will find that the process of reduction creates a delightfully well-flavored sauce, without necessitating the use of lots of additional butter for flavor or flour for thickening.

Keep in mind that after you have removed the fish or meat from the cooking pan, you must keep it warm on a warm platter or dinner plates in a warm oven while you make the sauce, as the reduction step will take 3 to 5 minutes to complete. Should you be cooking dinner for from 6 or more people, I suggest that you reduce the stock ahead of time, as this will cut down the time necessary to reduce the sauce at the last minute. Finally, some juices might accumulate on the plate under the meat or fish. Pour these juices into the sauce and reduce a little more before pouring the sauce over the food.

Refresh: This is the technique of running cold water over foods to halt the cooking process. For blanched green vegetables, refreshing not only stops the cooking process but also ensures that they will retain their fresh green color. (If blanched and left warm, the vegetables would quickly discolor.)

Refrigerator use: Easily available and quite inexpensive, a refrigerator thermometer is not only an important addition to your kitchen but also is essential to regulating the temperatures of the foods inside your refrigerator. This becomes particularly important during the change of seasons. I suggest that you turn the temperature to a cooler setting during the humid months and monitor it during the rest of the year, with the optimal temperature being 37 to 45 degrees. I purchase a lot of fish, so I prefer a lower setting.

Opening and closing the refrigerator is probably the most frequent cause of loss of temperature. If you anticipate this happening with great frequency, as in the case of a large dinner party, or many people using the refrigerator, I suggest that you turn down the temperature to adjust for the loss that occurs when the door is opened often. This should be done gradually, as food will tend to freeze when exposed to a low temperature.

Hot foods should never go immediately into the refrigerator, as they directly affect the temperature, causing it to rise quickly. They also will affect the surrounding foods—and milk and cream, especially, are extremely perishable. Dense mixtures, such as dried bean or meat stews, cool on the outside long before they cool in the center, which can easily cause spoiling. To properly care for these foods, I suggest packing in small containers, being sure to allow enough space so that the cool air can circulate. Stand these containers in ice water to allow them to cool down completely at a faster rate. If you find that it is absolutely necessary to store these foods in a large container, place a metal spoon in the container and allow the handle to rise 2 to 3 inches above the mixture. This will allow the cold air to enter the center of the mixture by way of the spoon and aid in the cooling process.

Good refrigerator organization is a must. This avoids unnecessary time with the door open and will help cut down on unpleasant odors. Cut melons, cucumbers, onions, garlic, and cabbage can be the source of many of these odors and should be tightly wrapped. The odors can penetrate butter, cream, and milk, producing unpleasant flavors. Besides washing down the refrigerator with a mild soap or baking soda, leave a dish of baking soda in the refrigerator to absorb odors.

One final and important note: Along the outer edge of the refrigerator door is a rubber seal intended to seal the cold air inside the refrigerator. At least twice a year you should thoroughly clean this seal with warm water and mild soap, removing the food and dirt that has collected. This simple task will produce a tighter-fitting seal and in turn a more effective refrigerator, as well as help lower the utility bill.

Roux: A mixture of fat and flour used to thicken sauces and soups is called a roux. I prefer to use cake flour in a roux because it gives the soup or sauce a softer, silkier texture. A roux containing cake flour needs to be cooked only a couple of minutes, while a roux made with all-purpose flour takes longer (2 minutes for every tablespoon of fat to start the starch expanding). Follow these suggestions when working with a roux:

1. When you have added the flour to the fat, make sure the roux remains soft, almost runny. It is easier to incorporate the liquid if the roux is soft. Add a little more fat if necessary.
2. Cook the roux about 2 minutes on a very even medium heat, stirring all the time to make sure that it does not scorch.
3. To keep the mixture from becoming lumpy, cold liquids should be added to the roux all at once and hot liquids should be added gradually and away from the heat. Once the liquid is added and whisked for a minute, scrape the corners and the bottom of the pan with a plastic spatula to be certain that the roux is incorporated into the sauce. Bring the mixture to a boil on a medium heat, stirring all the time.
4. After the mixture has come to a boil, gently simmer for 5 to 10 minutes, whisking occasionally. This will ensure a soft and silky texture.

Salting of cabbage, cucumbers, and eggplant: Throughout this book, you will notice that cucumber, eggplant, and occasionally cabbage are placed in a colander and lightly salted between layers, and then left to stand for 1 to 2 hours. This method is not only used to remove the bitter flavors from the eggplant and cucumbers, but with cucumbers and cabbage, it changes the texture of the food. Although after this process, cucumber and cabbage are flabby in appearance, the texture of these foods drastically changes. They become quite crunchy. I do caution you to lightly salt the vegetable, and afterwards, rinse well under cold running water to remove all the salt. In the case of cabbage and cucumbers, drain them well; with eggplant, pat dry.

Scald: To heat milk or cream to a temperature just below the boiling point. Scalding is often used in recipes for custard to increase the temperature of the milk or cream, making it easier to blend with other ingredients and decreasing the amount of time needed to whisk the custard over heat to thicken.

Shallot: Shallots are similar to an onion in taste, with a more delicate flavor. If you cannot find shallots in your store, you may substitute onion, but it is not my preference to do this for beurre blanc sauces.

Shred: To some cooks, shredding refers to coarsely grating cheese. I use the term, for example, with fresh basil, where I put together the leaves and shred them across to resemble julienne strips; if chopped, they might become mushy and black. Cabbage may be shredded on the slicing side of a grater.

Simmer: To cook foods in water or a poaching liquid at 180 to 195 degrees. The way to tell when the water has reached the simmering point is to watch for the small bubbles that form in the pan. Ideally, if you have an instant thermometer, you can check the temperature. Simmering allows food to cook at a lower temperature than boiling, and in the case of lobsters, eggs, and fish, the lower temperature will not toughen the protein (see page 530).

Steam: To cook food in a moist heat. Food is placed on a perforated rack over gently boiling water and is cooked by the heat of the steam that rises from the surface. The following procedures should be observed:

1. The pan used for steaming should have a tight-fitting lid.
2. Water should be kept at a constant gentle boil.
3. During steaming, water will collect in the lid, so be careful when removing it that no water drips into the food. Also be careful to hold your head back when removing the lid, as there may be a thrust of steam that could scald your face and hands.

For steaming, I have used the small fan rivets that sit in a pan, and for even better results, the Chinese bamboo steamers. They have several layers that can be put on top of one another; however, I find one should not use more than three layers when using a domestic stove. Should you purchase a bamboo steamer, soak it in cold water to dissipate a slight odor that may prevail. It also should be soaked each time before using. They are ideal for steaming fish, chicken, vegetables, and, of course, many wonderful Chinese dishes. After use, the steamer should be cleaned with a solution of warm water and a little salt to kill the bacteria. Soak it and then lightly scrub with a vegetable brush. Rinse well. Each layer should be air-dried individually and then carefully stored in a dry place to prevent mildew.

Tomatoes: For most of my recipes I prefer to use vine-ripened tomatoes rather than those that are artificially ripened. The artificially ripened tomatoes are picked when green to reduce spoilage through shipping. They are then gassed with ethylene gas, which gives them a pinkish to red color. The flavor and the texture of these tomatoes are in no way as good as those of vine-ripened tomatoes, and the skins are often much tougher. I realize, however, that it is not always easy to buy vine-ripened tomatoes, as they are so seasonal; nonetheless, I urge you to take advantage of them when they are in season by making tomato sauces, soups, and so on, and then freezing them.

As an alternative to vine-ripened tomatoes, I purchase hydroponically grown tomatoes. They are grown in water in a hothouse and are quite lovely both in flavor and in texture. Hothouse tomatoes, ideally, are tomatoes that are grown and ripened in a hothouse. These, too, are preferable to artificially ripened tomatoes.

With any of the tomatoes that are not vine-ripened, I have had some success with improving their flavor and texture by placing them in a sunny window to ripen for 4 to 5 days before using them. You might ask why I do not use canned tomatoes in my recipes. Frankly, I do not like their flavor, but for soups and sauces you might find them to your taste.

As you will notice, all my recipes that call for tomatoes also call for peeling and seeding the tomatoes. I find that this is very important, as the skin is tough and adds an unpleasant texture to a dish. I remove the seeds because I do not like the texture they add.

For the peeling process bring to a boil enough water to completely submerge all the tomatoes needed. It is important not to overcook them in the water, as you will make the outer layer of tomato pulp become mushy. If you follow these guidelines, you will obtain the best results:

1. Very ripe tomatoes: Place in the boiling water for 10 seconds, then run under cold water for 1 minute.
2. Semi-ripe tomatoes: Place in the boiling water for 15 to 20 seconds, then run under cold water for 1 minute.
3. Tomatoes other than vine-ripened (after they have sat in a sunny window 4 to 5 days): Place in boiling water for 20 to 30 seconds, then run under cold water for 1 minute.

Once you have blanched and refreshed the tomatoes, remove the outer skin very carefully; it should slip right off. Then core the tomatoes with a tomato shark (see page 553), a sharp paring knife, or a melon baller. To seed a tomato, cut in half and gently squeeze. If the recipe calls for reserving the juice, put the seeds in a sieve to let the juice collect in a bowl.

Whip: A term generally used for beating cream until stiff. It is also used commercially for products such as whipped butter, meaning the butter has been aerated.

Whisk: To aerate food (such as egg whites) by using a wire whisk, moving the whisk through the mixture in a quick folding motion. The term is also used to incorporate an ingredient, such as butter, into a sauce. Whisking requires a good deal of physical energy. To cut down on this work, some people use a rotary hand-beater or an electric mixer. However, I have noticed that many fine chefs continue to use the hand-held whisk, as they feel the results are optimal.

Yeast: A "gas-producing metabolism of a particular kind of fungus" is Harold McGee's definition of yeast in *On Food and Cooking*. Yeast is the ingredient that makes bread dough rise.

There are two varieties of yeast: dry active yeast, granules of yeast in a paper package; and compressed yeast, yeast in a moist cake form. One major difference between them is that dry active yeast has a longer shelf life than compressed yeast. Compressed yeast also seems to have a milder taste. It should be purchased in a health food store and should be refrigerated at all times. I also prefer to store dry active yeast in the refrigerator. On purchasing yeast, first check the date on the package, assuring the freshest product.

When mixed with sugar or starch, the yeast will rapidly grow, producing the leavening power necessary to make bread dough rise. To start the process you simply add the yeast to warm water (approximately 90 to 100 degrees Fahrenheit) and then add sugar. Within 5 to 10 minutes the mixture will start to bubble, meaning that the fungus is alive. If it does not bubble, either the water was too hot and killed the fungus, the water and kitchen were too cool, or the yeast was already dead.

Zest: The finely pared or grated rind of oranges, lemons, and limes. It should not be confused with the pith, which is the white part beneath the rind. Zest adds a very aromatic flavor to dishes. Today this use is more readily acceptable in the United States. This flavoring is excellent when used in some seafood, poultry, and meat dishes.

There are three methods of obtaining these flavorings. Absolute caution should always be taken not to include any pith with the zest, as it is bitter.

1. Use a sharp vegetable peeler to remove a thin layer of the rind, and then finely chop or julienne it.
2. Use a fine sharp grater to remove the rind by grating.
3. Rub the rind with lump sugar to remove the oils. The sugar is then dissolved and used in a custard or syrup, adding a very aromatic flavor.

Appendix II: Kitchen Equipment

Throughout this book I have stressed the importance of choosing the highest quality of ingredients to make the recipes reach their fullest potential. I urge you now to read carefully about choosing kitchen equipment. In the sixteen years that I have been cooking in my own restaurant, I have found the following items to be essential. They not only simplify the process of cooking, but they also enhance the preparation and help produce the best results. (I am not mentioning every item required to stock a functional kitchen, such as measuring spoons, but rather items that can be confusing to select, as well as items that I find indispensable.) Although some of these pieces are not readily available without a little searching, I strongly urge you to take the extra time; look through kitchen specialty stores and even try restaurant supply houses. This will offer you the chance to become more familiar not only with prices and quality, but also with the different brands and makes. It will be an educational venture, but you may very well find it to be more fun than you think.

My preference for certain brands is not meant to suggest that you should discard your current equipment. They are the brands that work for me, and I hope that my recommendation will aid in your selection should you decide you need a replacement.

Blender

It may be thought that the food processor has replaced the blender. However, I believe that the ideal kitchen is not complete without both items. The blender is ideal for certain procedures (see blender tips on page 515). If possible, choose a blender with a glass top, rather than a plastic top, as the glass tends to outlast the plastic. Avoid models that have lots of buttons (whip, frappe, beat, etc.). A blender is for blending, pureeing, and grinding, all of which require three speeds: low, medium, high.

Cake Pans

I prefer heavy tinned steel cake pans because of their fine conduction of heat. (However, given the poor availability of these pans, we tested all the recipes in this book in heavy aluminum cake pans.) If you do choose aluminum, look for a heavy gauge, as it will not buckle in the oven as easily as lightweight aluminum and will conduct heat more evenly. I suggest that you buy cake pans 10 inches in diameter and 2 inches high, and a springform cake pan 10 inches in diameter and 3 inches high. The springform pan is useful for baking cakes that are not easily turned out of cake pans.

It is important that you do not scratch the metal of your cake pans, because a cake is more likely to stick to a scratched pan. If you need to ease a cake from the edges of a pan, use a round-ended metal spatula rather than a sharp knife, so the pan will not be scratched. Do not scrub a cake pan with a metal scouring pad. If some cooked cake remains in the pan after the cake is turned out, soak the pan in warm soapy water for 30 minutes, and the crumbs will be easily removed. Dry the pan well after washing so that it will not corrode.

Cooking Pans

Weight and thickness (gauge) and metal composition should be important factors in your decision of what pans to purchase. The weight of the metal is important, as it has a direct bearing on the pan's efficiency and the pan's ability to conduct the maximum heat from the burner. For example, if the pan has buckled, it will not conduct heat as well as it should and will require additional heat to reach the desired temperature. This can increase your utility bills. The ingredients in a buckled pan will not brown evenly when they are sauteed or fried and may scorch or burn in some areas. This will also happen with a pan that is too thin. If the wrong metal is used in the construction of the pan, it will not only conduct heat improperly, it can also be toxic. Therefore, to help in your selection, I have listed different types of pans and the reason for using or not using them.

All-Clad: These are the optimal cooking pans, in my opinion. Aluminum on the outside and lined with stainless steel, they are heavy gauge, will not buckle, and are a good conductor of heat. The stainless steel lining makes them nontoxic and means they will take heavy scouring. I have found that food tends not to stick in these pans; if you should burn the bottom, soak the pan for a couple of hours and the food will dislodge easily. Although these pans are expensive, I have used them in my restaurant and find them durable, sturdy, and pleasing to cook with.

Aluminum: If you choose aluminum, it is important to choose a heavy gauge to be certain that it will not buckle and will provide a more even conduction of heat than a thin pan. Aluminum pans can be quite toxic when cooking high-acid foods or shellfish, and they should not be used for boiling eggs, as the pan will turn black and can impart an unpleasant flavor in foods next cooked in that pan. The metal is slightly softer than stainless steel and should not be scoured with a metal scouring pad. If you scorch foods, soak the pan rather than risk scratching it by scrubbing.

Copper: Copper is the best conductor of heat. Two drawbacks with copper pans are that they are expensive and need to be polished frequently. Copper can be toxic if not lined with tin, chrome, or stainless steel. Before using an unlined copper pan, clean it with salt, lemon, or vinegar to prevent any unpleasant flavor and reduce the pan's toxicity.

Tin-lined copper pans are not very practical, as tin is a soft metal with a lower melting point than either stainless steel or chrome. The lining will wear easily, and if you should burn the pan, the lining could flake or melt, leaving particles of tin in the food. It is possible to have the pans retinned, but the process is expensive and very few companies offer this service. A chrome lining is nontoxic, but to date I have had no luck with these pans. The surface tends to scratch easily, causing food to stick and sometimes burn. Stainless steel–lined copper pans are nontoxic, and the lining does not wear out. They are great for cooking as well as for serving. The heavier pans offer the best results.

Enamel-lined: These are iron pans that have been lined on the inside and outside with enamel. They are heavy and are good conductors of heat (slow at the beginning of cooking). Although expensive, they are ideal if you like to cook and serve in the same pan. They are available in many attractive colors, sizes, and shapes. The one drawback to them is that if they are dropped or nicked, the enamel can chip off on the inside of the pan, increasing the risk of toxicity.

Iron: Heavy cast-iron pans are even conductors of heat. They should be seasoned for best results. This can be done by rubbing them lightly with vegetable oil. When you wash them, be sure to dry thoroughly to prevent them from rusting. High-acid food and shellfish should not be cooked in these pans as the iron can produce a toxic effect. These pans are excellent for omelets and crêpes.

Stainless steel: Stainless steel is not a great conductor of heat, which is why many stainless steel pans come with a copper-lined bottom. They are nontoxic with high-acid sauces, shellfish, and eggs. They can take a considerable amount of scouring without being scratched. They are extremely durable pans.

Pan sizes: Once you have chosen the type of cooking pan you prefer, consider what sizes you need. Although a great deal of money may be saved by buying saucepans in sets, I find that some sizes are not as useful as others; for example, two 4-quart pans might be more useful than a 3-quart and a 4-quart pan. Also, if you do not buy pans in sets, you can add gradually to your collection over a period of time after you have defined your needs.

Sizes of pans vary with brands. The following pan sizes are ones that work best for me. I recommend: one 1½-quart saucepan, one 2½- to 3-quart saucepan, two 4-quart saucepans, and one 5- to 6-quart saucepan. I also suggest a 4-gallon stockpot, which is ideal for making stocks, large batches of soups, stews, and casseroles for large parties. It should be a heavy gauge pan, and if you are going to use it for fish stocks and shellfish, it should be stainless steel–lined.

For saute pans I recommend an 8-inch pan for crêpes and omelets, and 10-inch and 12-inch pans for general sauteing. Although larger saute pans are available, the heat source on your stove might not reach the outer edge of the pan, and it is difficult to fit other pans on the stove at the same time.

Cutting Boards

It is not only important to choose a fine-quality board to make cutting and chopping an easy task, but it is also important to find a board that is easy to clean to prevent transferral of odors from one food to another and to prevent bacterial growth. I have listed three commonly used types of cutting boards. Whatever the type you use, do not buy one that is too small; choose a board 12 inches by 18 inches, giving you plenty of space for chopping.

White plastic: These boards are easy to clean and absorb few of the odors common in dealing with foods. They are the least porous, making them ideal for cutting fish, poultry, and meats as well as garlic and onions. These boards will last for more than ten years with heavy use. On the negative side, however, they are extremely hard and therefore will dull your knives very quickly. They also have a tendency to slide while you use them (placing a wet towel under them will prevent this). Being thin, they will warp when exposed to water or when not stored correctly. I suggest you consider only a ¼-inch to ½-inch thickness.

Rubber: I prefer these cutting boards. They are softer than the plastic and are better on the edge of your knives. They will last at least ten years if properly taken care of. On the minus side, they are slightly porous and will stain if used for chopping foods such as parsley, carrots, winter squash, or beets. If they are less than one inch in thickness, they will warp.

After cutting raw protein foods (especially chicken), clean these boards by lightly scrubbing them with a little salt. The salt will not only kill the bacteria but also will bleach the board. Then wash and dry well. If strong odors persist, use a combination of salt and lemon. If you do a lot of cooking, buy two boards: one for onions, garlic, poultry, and odor-bearing foods, and the other for fruits and breads only.

Wood: This surface is good for your knives, but not very sanitary for chopping fish, poultry, or meat. Being wood, they can form fine cracks where high-protein foods will penetrate, inviting problems with bacteria. Should you choose a wood cutting board, look for a hardwood board. When cleaning it, use the same procedure suggested for rubber cutting boards. I suggest two cutting boards: one for fruits and breads; the other for meats, poultry, fish, onions, and garlic.

As a final note, after cleaning all boards, stand them upright to air dry. This will prevent the growth of bacteria under the board.

Electric Mixer

If you are purchasing your first electric mixer or replacing your existing one, I recommend the 5-quart Kitchen Aid mixer. This is a fine mixer featuring an expertly designed whisk. It is possible to buy many helpful attachments, such as a sausage maker, meat grinder, and more. If you decide you want a hand-held electric mixer, I prefer the Braun or the Drupps mixers because of their whisk designs. These are well made and solid, and they last longer than most brands. Unfortunately, they also are more expensive than most mixers on the market.

Food Mill

A food mill is a very useful kitchen tool for pureeing foods. I prefer it to a blender for pureeing such foods as pea soup or spinach soup. It will separate the fine particles of the food from the coarse fiber, leaving the fiber in the food mill to be discarded. Certain brands come with three different sizes of blades, which are excellent for pureeing potatoes. For the best results, wind clockwise approximately six times, then turn counterclockwise once. This pulls the fiber of the food up and away from the blade so that it can be discarded, making it easier to push the remaining food through. When pureeing large batches of food, I suggest you clean the blade and remove the fibers several times during the puree process. This will make it easier to push the food through and assure that the fiber stays out of the finished product.

Food Processor

A food processor is ideal for certain procedures (see page 525). My absolute preference for a food processor is the Cuisinart. The blade on it has a fine serrated edge that is curved slightly upwards, giving it a sharper cutting edge. I have also found that this particular blade keeps a sharper edge than the other brands. The machine comes with slicing and grating attachments, and now some models come with a juicing attachment. The blades and bowls are easily replaced.

If space allows, I suggest that you keep your food processor on the countertop, rather than put it away, as there it is more accessible and will become an integral part of your cooking.

Food Storage Containers

My preference for food storage containers is the Cambro containers. They are a clear, hard plastic that is easy to clean (fats do not adhere to them). They can go in the dishwasher; because of their design they don't flip over during the washing cycle as other containers do. Because they are clear, you can easily determine their contents. The lids not only fit tightly but are also designed for easy stacking. They come in various sizes, and food can be frozen in them. Until recently they were available only from restaurant supply houses; now they are more readily available in kitchen specialty stores.

Grater

A grater is used for cutting foods (generally cheese, chocolate, and carrots) into fine, small, or medium pieces. The current graters on the market come in a variety of shapes and sizes. The three-cylinder rotary graters are ideal for grating hard cheeses, such as Parmesan. With the square and flat varieties, care should be taken not to cut your hand or nick your knuckles. Most graters available today are made of stainless steel; the old-fashioned ones are made of tin. The advantage of stainless steel is the absence of rust as well as the ability to resist stains. However, I do find that the tin graters keep a sharper edge.

Instant Thermometer

An instant thermometer is an essential part of my kitchen equipment. I use it for roasts as well as pâtés and terrines. It can also be used as a freezer thermometer; just leave it in the freezer for 5 minutes to get a reading. It has a temperature range of 0 to 212 degrees Fahrenheit and is very accurate. The thermometer is fairly expensive (about $10), but it will last many years. It can be found in specialty food stores and restaurant supply houses.

To use it, remove the food from the oven. Insert the thermometer into the food, avoiding areas of high fat or bone. If you look on the side of the thermometer, you will see a small indentation. This part should be immersed in the food to ensure an accurate reading. Leave it in for 30 to 60 seconds to obtain a reading. Do not leave the thermometer in the oven, as its plastic coating will melt.

Knives

I suggest that you have at least five varieties of knives in your kitchen to help expedite food preparation: prep, chef's, boning, slicing, and serrated. But first it is important to understand the metals that your knives are made of. As recently as eight years ago, I used carbon steel knives exclusively. I still have five of them and take very good care of them. I feel that soon they may become difficult to obtain. Stainless steel knives are more readily available. Carbon steel knives are much easier to sharpen with a steel or a stone. The drawback of carbon steel knives is the fact that they stain easily. When slicing lemons or other high-acid foods, the acid will turn the carbon steel a bluish-black color, and this will taint the food. This discoloration can be cleaned easily by rubbing the blade well with scouring powder and a damp cloth. Afterwards, be sure to dry the blade thoroughly. The drying is of the utmost importance, as the blades will rust badly if the moisture is not removed. It is also wise, if you live in an area with high humidity, to oil the blades lightly with vegetable oil if you are going away for any length of time. Because of these few problems with carbon steel knives, I keep a couple of stainless steel knives. They are more difficult to sharpen, but they do not stain and are stronger than the carbon steel.

The following are the types of knives I recommend for expediting your food preparation:

Prep knife: This knife is used for paring, peeling, and making pockets in meat and fish. I recommend a blade length of 3½ to 4 inches.

Boning knife: I recommend a 5- to 6-inch blade that is flexible rather than stiff. The flexibility makes the knife easier to work with and makes boning easier. Stiff-bladed knives are used in restaurants and butcher shops for boning large pieces of meat.

Slicing knife: I recommend a 6½- to 7-inch blade length and a 1-inch width across the base. This knife also should be flexible. I was first introduced to the knife by Jacques Pépin at a cooking demonstration he gave. Since then I have found this knife great for slicing vegetables, meats, and fish, and for carving small roasts.

Chef's knife: A knife with a 10-inch blade length. I use it for chopping and slicing; it's wonderful for chopping fresh herbs, onions, and garlic. If the knife seems large to you, try it for several weeks. I am sure that you will find it a pleasure to work with. You should have a 12x18-inch cutting board when you use this knife.

Slicing knife: A knife with a 10- to 12-inch blade length with a thin blade width. It is ideal for carving hams, roasts, and turkeys.

Serrated knife: A knife with a 8- to 10-inch blade length. It is ideal for slicing bread, citrus fruits, and tomatoes. Gourmet kitchen shops carry a large variety of these knives.

Beware of buying knives in knife sets, as they often include knives that are not necessary. You will have better luck if you purchase your knives from a reputable kitchen supply store, where you can select sizes that suit your needs. I will caution that good knives are expensive, and you may have to add to your collection slowly, but the expense will be offset by their durability and the ease they provide in food preparation.

Caring for knives: Sharp knives are much safer to use than blunt knives, as less pressure is required, making the knife less likely to slip. (Also, I recommend that when you slice foods, you curl your fingers under, almost as a claw, as you hold the food. If you hold your fingers out, you're likely to cut them.) To maintain a better edge on your knives, sharpen them each time you use them by running them gently on a steel. This takes only a couple of seconds. As I have already mentioned, carbon steel knives will sharpen easily, whereas stainless steel knives are more difficult. If you lose the edge on a stainless steel knife, very gently run the blade over the stone of a knife sharpener (often found on electric can openers) a couple of times, being careful not to apply too much pressure, as this wears down the blade over a period of time. Then finish sharpening on a steel.

In choosing a steel for sharpening your knives, I suggest one that is 12 inches long. This length will make it easier to wield the longer knives along the steel. For the best results, lightly rub the steel with a dry cloth after each use.

It is not a good idea to put knives in a dishwasher, not only because this will damage the tips, but also because the heat will affect the studs in the handle, causing contracting and expanding. This will damage the handles.

If you do not have a knife rack and need to store your knives in a drawer, put a cork on the tip of each knife. This will prevent the tips from being damaged or snapped off.

Loaf Pans

I like to use loaf pans for pâtés, terrines, and fish mousses. I prefer to use a Pyrex pan because I find the heat conduction a little more gentle than that provided by metal loaf pans. Pyrex is inexpensive and will not rust, nor does it have the toxic consequences of tin. I suggest a loaf pan 9 inches long by 5 inches wide by 3 inches deep.

Mushroom Brush

When purchasing mushrooms you will find that the amount of dirt on them will vary. It is important that you do not wash mushrooms unless they are going to be poached or are extremely dirty, because they will absorb the water. The easiest way to clean mushrooms is to buy a mushroom brush. All you need to do is just lightly brush the mushrooms to remove the dirt. The bristles are very soft, so the outside of the mushroom will not be marred as it is cleaned. This tool costs several dollars and is available in specialty kitchen shops.

Piping Bag

A necessary piece of equipment for decorating foods both in dessert and savory cookery. I use Delware nylon bags. I find they are easier to use and clean than the plastic-coated bags or canvas bags. The Delware bag comes in varying bag and nozzle sizes and is obtainable in large quantities from Victoria Works, Wilton Street, Denton, Manchester, England M34 3NB. They are also sold in kitchen stores in England. I also have found a French nylon bag available in the United States at kitchen shops. Both the Delware and French bag are fairly durable, should last a couple of years, and are fairly inexpensive.

Sometimes you will find that a piping bag will acquire an unpleasant odor. Should this happen, soak the bag for a few hours in a solution of water and baking soda, then hang to air-dry.

Rolling Pin

The American Ball Bearing Rolling pin (25 inches overall, roller length 15 inches, and 3¼ inches in diameter) is the ultimate. The ball bearing design makes it so smooth and easy to work with that its expense, which is more than some, and its awkward size for storing can be overlooked. As an alternative, I suggest the French rolling pin (17¾ inches long, and 2 inches in diameter). It has no handles, but it is easy to use. After a few uses, you will find that you have mastered the technique.

Sheet Pan

This is one item that I do suggest you purchase from a restaurant supply house. These houses sell a 17-inch by 13-inch heavy aluminum sheet pan that will not buckle in the oven and will last longer than most on the market. They are not very expensive, and I urge you to buy two, one for general cooking and one specifically for baking. You should not use these pans for broiling, as they will buckle under the broiler. Avoid scratching or marking the pans, which can easily happen if a metal scrubber is used in cleaning, or a knife or metal utensil is used in cutting on it. The more you scratch the surface of the pan, the more food will stick to the surface. Before purchasing this pan, you should measure your oven, as some ovens are not large enough to accommodate it.

Spatulas

Flexible metal: In making crêpes and omelets, spreading roulades, and removing cakes from pans, I have found these spatulas not only the best, but actually indispensable. In choosing a spatula I suggest the rounded edge, as the squared-off end tends to tear crêpes. A wooden handle with nickel, silver, or brass rivets is best. The spatula should have an overall length of 12 to 15 inches and a width of 1¼ inches. These are generally found in specialty kitchen shops or the kitchen departments of better department stores.

Plastic: While attending the Cordon Bleu I was taught to fold whipped egg whites and cream with a shallow metal spoon. However, in the last eight years I have used Rubber Maid white plastic spatulas. I use a 10-inch spatula for small portions (code #1901–12) and a larger 14-inch spatula (code #1905–4) for folding egg whites and larger portions, as efficiently and easily as the metal spoon. They also are very handy for general kitchen use, to keep ingredients from scorching when reducing sauces (by scraping down the sides of the pan with a spatula) or when scraping down the sides of bowls and the food processor and blender. Their handles do not come off, which is a problem with many other brands. I suggest that you buy two of each and use one set for baking only. They are not expensive and are readily available in restaurant supply stores and kitchen specialty shops. Once the edges wear down or become nicked, they can be reserved for general use. Their estimated life for home use is 2 to 3 years.

Tomato Shark

This is an inexpensive tool that is wonderful for coring tomatoes and hulling strawberries. It can be found in specialty kitchen shops or restaurant supply houses.

Whisks

Whisks come in various sizes and are both flexible and stiff. My preference is for flexible whisks. In the restaurant we use a variety of shapes for different purposes, but in the home I find that the 10-inch and 12-inch thin-wire stainless steel whisks are good for baking and general use. I also like the 9-inch stainless steel whisk with only eight wires. Look for whisks that have a fairly high amount of flexibility. You will find them in specialty kitchen shops.

Wooden Spoons

Because wood does not conduct heat, wooden spoons are ideal for stirring hot liquids for any length of time. They are nontoxic, so they are perfect for stirring acidic foods, such as tomato sauce.

Wooden spoons are made out of many different woods. As wood is porous, it will stain and absorb food flavors. It also may splinter. It is therefore important to choose spoons made of hardwoods; the most available is beech, although boxwood, cherry, and maple also are available. Because even these woods may absorb food flavors, I think that it is a good idea to have some for savory cooking and one for baking.

Wooden spoons come in varying sizes, both in the length of the spoon and the width and shape. My recommendation is to produce one small 8-inch-long spoon for stirring foods in small pans. Then you should also have a 12- or 14-inch-long spoon, plus an 18-inch long spoon for making large quantities of soups or sauces. They come with a bowl-like design or a flat design. (Flat ones are also called spatulas.) I prefer the flat wooden spoons because I find them easier to beat with and useful for scraping down the edges of bowls and pans.

After use, wash the spoon well, dry it thoroughly, and leave it out to air dry. I do not recommend putting it in the dishwasher, because the wood will contract and dry out during the drying cycle.

Appendix III: A Collection of Cookbooks

Like many chefs and cooks, I have an extensive and varied cookbook collection. Besides the 150 volumes that I use at the restaurant, I have another six shelves of cookbooks at home, and none have been overlooked. I felt it is important that I share with you at least some of the books I enjoy so much.

I strongly advise you to read *Kitchen Science* by Howard Hillman. This theory book is very easy to read and full of culinary information. It will aid you in your cooking, making it easier for you to approach the kitchen and avoid many disasters.

As you will note, many of the books listed are published in the United Kingdom. As I visit there each year, I am able to visit Foyles in London. Their cookbook selection is vast and marvelous. Much as in the United States, the British publish many exciting new cookbooks each year, and many are fortunately available in paperback.

You will also note that some books are out of print. I list these because I have purchased most of them from second-hand bookstores. Old cookbooks are generally very expensive, but books only twenty to thirty years old can often be purchased for a reasonable price.

One good source of second-hand and antique cookbooks is Janet Clark (Antiquarian Books, specializing in Gastronomy), 3 Woodside Cottages, Freshford, Bath BA3 6EJ, United Kingdom. She sends out a quarterly catalogue listing numerous cookbooks ranging in price and suited to a market of both cookbook collectors and those who love to cook.

Cookbooks are not only for recipes, but also for expanding one's knowledge. They are the trials, tribulations, and triumphs of all the cooks and chefs who ever wished to share their successes and failures with others. I offer this list of cookbooks in hopes that they will expand your horizons as they have mine.

Abehsera, Michel. *Zen Macrobiotic Cooking: Book of Oriental and Traditional Recipes.* New York: University Books, 1968.

Baily, Adrian. *The Cooking of the British Isles* (Foods of the World Series). Alexandria, VA: Time-Life Books, 1969.

Baily, Adrian, and Philip Dowell. *The Book of Ingredients.* Great Britain: Dorling Kindersley, 1984.

Beard, James. *James Beard's New Fish Cookery.* Boston: Little, Brown, 1976.

Beck, Simone. *Simca's Cuisine.* New York: Vintage Books, Random House, 1976.

Beck, Simone, with Michael James. *New Menus from Simca's Cuisine.* New York: Harcourt Brace Jovanovich, 1979.

Biachini, F., and F. Corbetta. *The Complete Book of Fruits and Vegetables.* New York: Crown, 1973.

Bickel, Walter. *Hering's Dictionary of Classical and Modern Cookery.* Boston: C.B.I. Publishing, 1980.

Bloch, Barbara. *If It Doesn't Pan Out: How to Cope with Cooking Disasters.* New York: Red Dembner Enterprises, 1981.

Bowen, Carol. *Hamlyn All Colour Book of Puddings and Desserts.* London: The Hamlyn Publishing Group, 1982.

Broadbent, Michael. *Michael Broadbent's Pocket Guide to Wine Tasting.* New York: Simon & Schuster, 1982.

Brown, Dale, and Time-Life Books Editors. *The Cooking of Scandinavia* (Foods of the World Series). Alexandria, VA: Time-Life Books, 1977.

Brunet, E., trans. *Le Repertoire de la Cuisine.* Woodbury, NY: Barron's Educational Series, 1976.

Casas, Penelope. *The Foods and Wines of Spain.* New York: Knopf, 1982.

Cassella, Delores. *A World of Baking.* Port Washington, NY: David White, 1978.

Child, Julia, Louisette Bertholle, and Simone Beck. *Mastering the Art of French Cooking, Volumes I and II.* New York: Knopf, 1961 and 1970.

Clayton, Bernard, Jr. *The Breads of France and How to Bake Them in Your Own Kitchen.* Indianapolis, IN: Bobbs-Merrill, 1978.

———. *The Complete Book of Pastry: Sweet and Savory.* New York: Simon & Schuster, 1981.

Conran, Caroline, ed. and adapter. *The Nouvelle Cuisine of Jean and Pierre Troisgros.* London: Papermac, MacMillan Publishers, 1983.

Cooper, Derek. *Wine with Food.* New York: Crescent Books, Crown, 1980.

Cummins, Richard Osborn. *The Rise of Urban America: The American and His Food.* New York: Arno Press and the New York Times, 1970.

Dali, Salvador. *Les Diners de Gala.* New York: Felicie, 1973.

David, Elizabeth. *Summer Cooking: A Penguin Handbook.* Great Britain: Penguin Handbooks, 1967.

———. *English Bread and Yeast Cookery.* Great Britain: Penguin Books, 1979.

———. *French Provincial Cooking.* Middlesex, England: Penguin Handbooks, 1973.

———. *Classics: Mediterranean Food, French Cooking and Summer Cooking.* New York: Knopf, 1980.

Davidson, Alan. *North Atlantic Seafood.* New York: Viking Press, 1980.

Escoffier, A. *Le Guide Culinaire.* New York: Mayflower Books, 1921.

———. *The Escoffier Cookbook: A Guide to the Fine Art of Cookery.* New York: Crown, 1967.

Garmey, Jane. *Great British Cooking: A Well-Kept Secret.* New York: Random House, 1981.

Geise, Judie. *Great Meals from the Northwest—A Seasonal Cookbook.* Los Angeles: J. P. Tarcher, 1978.

Goodman, Harriet Wilinsky, and Barbara Morse. *Just What the Doctor Ordered.* New York: Holt, Rinehart & Winston, 1982.

Greer, Anne Lindsay. *Cuisine of the American Southwest.* New York: Harper & Row, 1983.

Grigson, Jane. *The Mushroom Feast.* Great Britain: Penguin Books, 1978.

Guerard, Michel; Narcisse Chamberlain with Fanny Brennan, trans. *Michel Guerard's Cuisine Minceur.* New York: William Morrow, 1976.

Hazan, Marcella. *The Classic Italian Cookbook.* New York: Harper's Magazine Press, Harper & Row, 1973.

Hazelton, Nika. *The Unabridged Vegetable Cookbook.* New York: M. Evans, 1976.

Heatter, Maida. *Maida Heatter's Book of Great Desserts.* New York: Knopf, 1977.

———. *Maida Heatter's New Book of Great Desserts.* New York: Knopf, 1982.

———. *Maida Heatter's Book of Great Chocolate Desserts.* New York: Knopf, 1981.

Hemphill, Rosemary. *Herbs for All Seasons.* New York: Penguin Books, 1972.

Heseltine, Marjorie, and Ula M. Dow. *The Basic Cookbook.* Boston: Houghton Mifflin, 1967.

Hillman, Howard. *Kitchen Science: A Compendium of Essential Information for Every Cook.* Boston: Houghton Mifflin, 1981.

Hornblower, Malabar. *Do-Ahead Dining: Cooking for Company with Do-Ahead Menus and Recipes.* Chester, CT: The Globe Pequot Press, 1986.

Jacobs, Greta, and Jane Alexander. *The Bluefish Cookbook, third edition.* Chester, CT: The Globe Pequot Press, 1986.

Jaffrey, Madhur. *Madhur Jaffrey's Indian Cooking.* Woodbury, NY: Barron's Educational Series, 1981.

Kamman, Madeleine. *The Making of a Cook.* New York: Atheneum, 1971.

———. *In Madeleine's Kitchen.* New York: Atheneum, 1984.

Kavasch, Barrie. *Native Harvests: Recipes and Botanicals of the American Indian.* New York: Vintage Books, Random House, 1979.

Kennedy, Diana. *The Cuisines of Mexico.* New York: Harper & Row, 1972.

Kotschevar, Lendal H. *Quantity Food Purchasing, 2nd Edition.* New York: Wiley, 1975.

Lenotre, Gaston, with Philip and Mary Hyman. *Lenotre's Desserts and Pastries.* Woodbury, NY: Barron's Educational Series, 1977.

———. *Lenotre's Ice Creams and Candies.* Woodbury, NY: Barron's Educational Series, 1979.

Lockwood, Lu. *Truly Unusual Soups, second edition.* Chester, CT: The Globe Pequot Press, 1983.

Lucas, Dione, and Marion Gorman. *The Dione Lucas Book of French Cooking.* Boston: Little, Brown, 1973.

Maclean, Veronia. *Lady Maclean's Book of Sauces and Surprises.* Great Britain: William Collins, 1978.

McGee, Harold. *On Food and Cooking: The Science and Lore of the Kitchen.* New York: Scribner, 1984.

Montagne, Prosper. *New Larousse Gastronomique.* New York: Hamlyn, 1977.

Morton, W. Scott. *China, Its History and Culture.* New York: Lippincott and Crowell, 1980.

Murphy, Margaret Deeds. *The Boston Globe Cookbook, Revised Edition.* Chester, CT: The Globe Pequot Press, 1981.

Nicolas, Jean F. *The Complete Cookbook of American Fish and Shellfish.* Boston: C.B.I. Publishing, 1981.

Olney, Judith. *Judith Olney's Entertainments: A Cookbook to Delight the Mind and Senses.* Woodbury, NY: Barron's Educational Series, 1981.

Peck, Paula. *The Art of Fine Baking.* New York: Simon & Schuster, 1961.

Pépin, Jacques. *La Technique.* New York: Wallaby, Simon & Schuster, 1978.

Puck, Wolfgang. *Modern French Cooking for the American Kitchen.* Boston: Houghton Mifflin, 1981.

Root, Waverly. *The Food of France.* New York: Atheneum, 1958.

————. *The Food of Italy.* New York: Atheneum, 1971.

————. *Food.* New York: Simon & Schuster, 1980.

Root, Waverly, and Richard de Rochemont. *Eating in America—A History.* New York: Morrow, 1976.

Sahni, Julie. *Classic Indian Cooking.* New York: Morrow, 1980.

Schorr, Denise Khaitman. *My French Kitchen.* Chester, CT: The Globe Pequot Press, 1985.

Smith, Peter. *The Picayune's Creole Cook Book, 2nd Edition.* New York: Dover, 1971.

Spear, Ruth A. *Cooking Fish and Shellfish.* Garden City, NY: Doubleday, 1980.

Spinazzola, Anthony, and Jean-Jacques Paimblanc. *Seafood As We Like It.* Chester, CT: The Globe Pequot Press, 1985.

Spry, Constance, and Rosemary Hume. *The Constance Spry Cookery Book.* London: J. M. Dent, 1956.

Stobart, Tom. *Herbs, Slices and Flavourings.* Middlesex, England: Penguin Books, 1977.

Time-Life Books, editors of. *Fruits: The Good Cook, Techniques and Recipes.* Alexandria, VA: Time-Life Books, 1983.

————. *Variety Meats: The Good Cook, Techniques and Recipes.* Alexandria, VA: Time-Life Books, 1983.

Toulouse-Lautrec, Mapie the Comtess; Charlotte Turgeon, trans. *La Cuisine de France*. New York: Berkeley Windhover Books and Orion Press, 1964.

Trillin, Calvin. *Alice, Let's Eat*. New York: Random House, 1979.

Verge, Roger; Roberta Wolfe Smoler, trans. *Roger Verge's Cuisine of the South of France*. New York: Morrow, 1980.

Walters, Alice. *Chez Panisse Menu Cookbook*. New York: Random House, 1982.

Wechsburg, Joseph. *The Cooking of Vienna's Empire* (Foods of the World Series). Alexandria, VA: Time-Life Books, 1968.

Wile, Julius, ed. *Frank Schoonmaker's Encyclopedia of Wine*. New York: Hastings House, 1978.

Wolfert, Paula. *The Cooking of Southwest France*. Garden City, NY: Dial Press, Doubleday, 1983.

Worthington, Diane Rossen. *The Cuisine of California*. Boston: Houghton Mifflin, 1983.

Index